The Adams Papers

L. H. BUTTERFIELD, EDITOR IN CHIEF

SERIES I

DIARIES

*Diary and Autobiography
of John Adams*

Diary and Autobiography of John Adams

L. H. BUTTERFIELD, *EDITOR*

LEONARD C. FABER AND WENDELL D. GARRETT

ASSISTANT EDITORS

———————— ☆ ————————

Volume 4 · *Autobiography*
Parts Two and Three 1777–1780
Index

THE BELKNAP PRESS
OF HARVARD UNIVERSITY PRESS
CAMBRIDGE, MASSACHUSETTS

1962

Published September 1961

Second Printing, January 1962

Distributed in Great Britain by Oxford University Press · London

Funds for editing *The Adams Papers* have been provided by Time, Inc.,
on behalf of *Life*, to the Massachusetts Historical Society, under whose
supervision the editorial work is being done.

Library of Congress Catalog Card Number 60–5387 · Printed in the United States of America

Contents

Illustrations

vii

the Adams party in Spain, see a note under the Diary entry of 17 December 1779, vol. 2:412. (Courtesy of the Boston Public Library.)

5. JOHN ADAMS' FRENCH GUIDEBOOK   130

Titlepage of J. A. Piganiol de La Force, *Nouveau voyage de France; avec un itinéraire, et des cartes* . . . , nouvelle édition, Paris, 1780. John Adams purchased this book in Paris, 7 April 1780, and it remains among his books in the Boston Public Library. See his Personal Expenditures, February–July 1780, vol. 2:438. (Courtesy of the Boston Public Library.)

6. THE AMERICAN COMMISSIONERS AT WORK IN 1778: LETTER
   BEGUN BY JOHN ADAMS AND CORRECTED AND COMPLETED
   BY BENJAMIN FRANKLIN   131

Apparently the recipient's copy of a letter in the Presidents Collection in the William L. Clements Library showing a remarkable instance of cooperation between Adams and Franklin in their joint role as American representatives in France. Adams' retained version of the letter is printed in the present volume, p. 110–111. (Courtesy of the William L. Clements Library.)

7. HÔTEL DE VALENTINOIS, RESIDENCE OF THE AMERICAN COM-
   MISSIONERS AT PASSY   162

Anonymous *gouache* painting of the mansion owned by Donatien Le Ray de Chaumont in Passy. Benjamin Franklin occupied quarters on the grounds from 1777 to 1785; John Adams joined his entourage there in April 1778 in succession to Silas Deane. The Hôtel de Valentinois "had two wings, each terminated by a belvedere, ornamented with balustrades and supported by Tuscan columns. In the right wing was a drawing-room, ornamented with busts, and, at the side, near a little quincunx, a conservatory. By means of a flight of steps in the courtyard, Franklin could reach a garden consisting of four separate plots surrounding an octagonal piece of water, bordered by two fine alleys of linden-trees, which were trimmed after the Italian style. Various contiguous buildings led to a gallery, filled with pictures and busts, at the end of which was a small bedroom and a terrace where Franklin could sit and take in a wonderful view of the Seine and its shady banks, in the immediate foreground, and of the wooded slopes of Issy, Meudon, and St. Cloud in the distance" (Frederick Lees, "The Parisian Suburb of Passy," *Architectural Record*, 12:671–673 [December 1902]). See Adams' Diary entry of 9 April 1778 and note, vol. 2:297. (Courtesy of the Musée de Blérancourt, France.)

8. VERGENNES, FRENCH MINISTER OF FOREIGN AFFAIRS   162

Engraving of Charles Gravier, Comte de Vergennes (1717–1787), dated 1791, by the Amsterdam engraver, Reinier Vinkeles. (Courtesy of the Boston Athenæum.)

Folded map, 7¾″ × 9¾″, engraved by Thomas Kitchin, in William Bollan, *The Ancient Right of the English Nation to the American Fishery* . . . , London, 1764. The map admirably illustrates the recurrent and extensive discussions by John Adams of the problem of American rights in the Atlantic fisheries. See for example the Diary entries for 25–30 November 1782 and notes, vol. 3:72–85; and a passage in the present volume, p. 247. (Courtesy of the Massachusetts Historical Society.)

Adams copied this commission into his Autobiography, at p. 178–179 in the present volume. On his election by Congress as minister plenipotentiary to negotiate treaties of peace and commerce with Great Britain, see the note under the Diary entry of 13 November 1779, vol. 2:401. (From the original in the Adams Papers.)

This view of the Adams Mansion in Quincy, here shown in three mediums, was the work of Mrs. George Whitney of Roxbury in August 1828; the woodcut was printed in the *American Magazine*, 3:449 (September 1837). The accompanying article said of the engraving:

"We turn now to the vignette engraving. For our information on these matters we are indebted to the Honorable John Quincy Adams. He traces back the existence of this house only as far as the Revolution. Perhaps the registry of deeds would afford an earlier account. At that time it was owned by one Leonard Vassal Borland [actually his father, John Borland, who died in Boston in 1775]. He was a refugee; the estate was confiscated, and his family withdrew. The Honorable Judge Cranch, then a citizen of Quincy, was one of the commissioners for managing the confiscated estates; and while in his hands, Major General Joseph Palmer, of the Massachusetts militia, made the house his headquarters. Other individuals occupied the place till 1787, when a son of Mr. Borland [Leonard Vassall Borland] returned and recovered it. The regular forms of confiscation had not been complied with, and he sued out and took possession of it. He gave the deed, dated twenty-sixth September, 1787, by which it passed into the hands of John Adams. The estate comprised between eighty and ninety acres of land, and was sold for six hundred pounds lawful money. It was purchased by Dr. Tufts, of Weymouth, for John Adams, who was then in England. He returned in June, 1788, passed a few days with his family at Governor Hancock's, in Boston, came out to Quincy, and went into his house while still the workmen were repairing it. One old barn was standing, which was taken down by him. He erected the two stables, and an addition was made on the right end of the house in the year 1798. The house has been twice on fire — in the year 1804 or 1805, and in September, 1821, when it narrowly escaped entire destruction.

"The vane which is seen on the mound in front of the house was placed there by President Adams senior, a few years before his death. It had been on one of the old churches of the Congregational Society with which he worshipped until the church was struck by lightning; and from his love of the relics of antiquity he had it placed where he could see it from the window of his chamber. It is supposed that the house was built about the year 1730."

For further information on the purchase and occupancy of the "Old House," as it has long been called by the family, see vol. 1:72, 74–75; vol. 3:217. Having been occupied by five generations of Adamses, it was opened to the public by the Adams Memorial Society in 1927, and was presented to the nation by the family in 1946. It is now the Adams National Historic Site. (Courtesy of the Massachusetts Historical Society.)

VOLUME 4

Autobiography

PARTS TWO AND THREE

Autobiography of John Adams

Part Two: 1777-1778

TRAVELS, AND NEGOTIATIONS.[1]

Quincy December 1. 1806.

1777

When I asked Leave of Congress to make a Visit to my Constituents and my Family in November 1777, it was my intention to decline the next Election, and return to my practice at the Bar.[2] I had been four Years in Congress, left my Accounts in a very loose condition, my Debtors were failing, the paper Money was depreciating, I was daily loosing the fruits of seventeen Years industry, my family was living on my past Acquisitions which were very moderate, for no Man ever did so much Business for so little profit. My Children were growing up without my care in their Education: and all my ⟨pay⟩ imoluments as a Member of Congress for four Years, had not been sufficient to pay a labouring Man upon my farm. Some of my Friends, who had more compassion for me and my family than others, suggested to me what I knew very well before, that I was loosing a fortune every Year by my Absence. Young Gentlemen who had been Clerks in my Office and others whom I had left in that Character in other Offices were growing rich, for the Prize Causes, and other Controversies had made the profession of a Barrister more lucrative than it ever had been before. I thought therefore that four Years drudgery, and Sacrifice of every thing, were sufficient for my Share of Absence from home and that another might take my place. Upon my Arrival at my home in

---

[1] JA inserted this title at some point after he had filled up the first page of the MS with the opening passage of his autobiographical narrative as newly resumed. The next dozen sheets of the MS of Part Two have the title "Travels &c." or "Travels," with a date, at the head of each new four-page sheet; thereafter only dates, without captions, ap-pear. In the present text dates are given only at the head of entries.

[2] See JA's Diary entry of 15 Nov. 1777 and note 1 there. The thirteen-month gap (Oct. 1776 – Nov. 1777) between Parts One and Two of the Autobiography is very meagerly filled in by occasional Diary entries, but see especially the entry of 15 Sept. 1777 and note 1 there.

I

Braintree I soon found that my old Clients had not forgotten me and that new ones had heard enough of me to be ambitious of engaging me in Suits which were depending. I had applications from all quarters in the most important disputes. Among others Coll. Elisha Doane applied to me to go to Portsmouth in New Hampshire, upon the Case of a large Ship and Cargo which had been seized and was to be tried in the Court of Admiralty before Judge Brackett.[3] At the Tryal of the

[3] This was the initial stage of a case that became famous, not merely because it was in and out of the courts for almost eighteen years but because it raised complex and important issues respecting state, confederation, and federal jurisdiction in admiralty law and touched directly on the sensitive issue of state sovereignty—or so the aroused citizens and officials of the State of New Hampshire thought. As JA knew it, the case was that of Penhallow and Treadwell *v.* Brig *Lusanna* and Cargo. (By an understandable confusion the vessel's name was sometimes later written as *Susanna* or *Susannah*, and it is so found in modern references to the case. But the published notices of the original trial upon libel give it as "Lusannar," adding only a touch of New England dialect to its correct form; see Portsmouth *Freeman's Journal*, 15, 29 Nov. 1777.) The *Lusanna* was owned by the wealthy Cape Cod merchant Elisha Doane and had been recently captured in highly compromising circumstances, after voyages in 1775–1777 from Plymouth to London, from there to Gibraltar, and back to Halifax, by the New Hampshire privateer *McClary*. *Lusanna* was brought into Portsmouth, libeled by its captors, and its trial fixed for December in the New Hampshire Maritime Court (established under certain resolves of the Continental Congress, 25 Nov. 1775, in which JA had probably had a part; see entries in his Autobiography, 23, 25 Nov. 1775 vol. 3:346–349, above). This court was presided over by Joshua Brackett, who was both a physician and a judge. JA was engaged to defend *Lusanna's* owner by Shearjashub Bourne, son-in-law of Doane and the man who, as supercargo, had conducted the vessel's complicated operations during the past two years (Bourne to JA, 6 Dec. 1777, Adams Papers; this letter originally enclosed "a Brief of facts" which has not been found). It was Bourne's contention that the vessel's British papers merely enabled him to *masquerade* as British, whereas he was really loyal to the American cause while vending whale oil in England and carrying supplies to British garrisons. The parties to the case were persons of some eminence, and the trial attracted a great deal of attention; see JA to AA, 15 Dec. 1777 (Adams Papers; JA-AA, *Familiar Letters*, p. 325–326); Stiles, *Literary Diary*, 2:236–239, which contains a vivid record of JA's conversation during this visit to Portsmouth, together with references to the trial. JA presented his argument on 16 Dec., but the jury (for Congress' resolves recommending the establishment of local prize courts recommended jury trials therein) found for their neighbors the libelants. Thus ended JA's part in the *Lusanna* case, because he soon afterward left for Europe. But the Doane party appealed to the New Hampshire Superior Court, which sustained the lower court, and from there to the Court of Appeals established by the Continental Congress in 1780, which in 1783 upset the previous verdicts and found for the Doanes. Through John Sullivan the captors of the *Lusanna* now appealed directly to Congress, and Thomas Jefferson wrote a report for a special committee that upheld the New Hampshire captors and courts, on the ground that "neither Congress nor any persons deriving authority from them had jurisdiction in the said case." This report was long and fiercely contested in Congress and in the end not adopted. To skip several stages, the case finally came before the United States Supreme Court, which in 1795 found for representatives of JA's original client Doane, on the broad ground that when

Cause at Portsmouth and while I was speaking in it, Mr. Langdon came in from Phyladelphia and leaning over the Bar whispered to me, that Mr. Deane was recalled, and I was appointed to go to France. As I could scarcely believe the News to be true, and suspected Langdon [to] be sporting with me, it did not disconcert me. As I had never solicited such an Appointment, nor intimated to any one, the smallest inclination for it, the News was altogether unexpected. The only hint I ever had of such a design in Congress was this. After I had mounted my horse for my Journey home Mr. Gerry at Yorktown, came out of the House of Mr. Roberdeau where We lodged together, and said to me, between him and me, that I must go to France. That Mr. Deanes Conduct had been so intollerably bad, as to disgrace himself and his Country and that Congress had no other Way of retrieving the dishonour but by recalling him. I answered that as to recalling Mr. Deane Congress would do as they thought fit, but I entreated him that neither Mr. Gerry nor any one else would think of me for a Successor for I was altogether unqualified for it. Supposing it only a sudden thought of Mr. Gerry and that when he should consider it a moment he would relinquish it, I knew not that I recollected it, again, till Mr. Langdone brought it to remembrance. At Portsmouth Captain Landais was introduced to me, as then lately arrived from France, who gave me an Account of his Voyage with Bougainville round the World and other particulars of his Life. Upon my return to Braintree I found to my infinite Anxiety that Mr. Langdons intelligence was too well founded. Large Packetts from Congress, containing a new Commission to Franklin, Lee and me as Plenipotentiaries to the King of France, with our instructions and other papers, had been left at my

---

the states yield exclusive powers to the United States the federal power becomes supreme.

JA's own brief notes on the case in 1777 are among his legal papers (M/JA/6, Adams Papers, Microfilms, Reel No. 185). A bulky MS record of the case through 1783 is in DNA:RG 267, Revolutionary War Prize Cases (Microcopy No. 162, Case No. 30, designated in the pamphlet accompanying this microcopy as "Doane et al., Appellants, v. Treadwell and Penhallow, Libellants, and the Brig Susannah"). The captors' appeal to Congress and Jefferson's Report thereon, Jan. 1784, are printed in Jefferson, *Papers*, 6:447–455. The arguments of counsel and opinions of the justices in the U.S. Supreme Court are in Alexander

J. Dallas, *Reports of Cases . . .*, Phila., 1790–1807, 3:54–120. After the Supreme Court's decision had been rendered, an anonymous pamphlet was published that furnished facts concerning the history of the *Lusanna* and the long course of litigation over it that are not elsewhere in print, put the case of the aggrieved New Hampshire men, and denounced the high court's decision as a miscarriage of justice and an "indignity" to the independence of the State: [John Hale,] *Statement of the Cause of the McClary Owners, and Doane & Doane's Administrators . . .*, Portsmouth, 1795. See also Charles Warren, *The Supreme Court in United States History*, Boston, 1922, 1:122–123.

House, and waited my Arrival. A Letter from the President of Congress informed me of my Appointment, and that the Navy Board in Boston was ordered to fit the Frigate Boston, as soon as possible to carry me to France. It should have been observed before that, in announcing to me the Intelligence of my Appointment, Langdon neither expressed Congratulation nor regret: but I soon afterwards had evidence enough that he lamented Mr. Deanes recall, for he had already formed lucrative connections in France by Mr. Deanes recommendation, particularly with Mr. Le Ray de Chaumont who had shipped Merchandizes to him to sell upon Commission, an Account of which rendered to Chaumont by Langdon, was shewn to me by the former at Passy in 1779, in which allmost the whole Capital was sunk, really or pretendedly, by the depreciation of paper money.

When the Dispatches from Congress were read, the first question was whether I should accept the Commission or return it to Congress. The dangers of the Seas and the Sufferings of a Winter passage, although I had no experience of either, had little Weight with me. The British Men of War, were a more serious Consideration. The News of my Appointment, I had no doubt were known in Rhode Island, where a part of the British Navy and Army then lay, as soon as they were to me, and transmitted to England as soon as possible. I had every reason to expect, that Ships would be ordered to intercept the Boston from Rhode Island and from Hallifax, and that Intelligence would be secretly sent them, as accurately as possible of the time when she was to sail. For there always have been and still are Spies in America as well as in France, England and other Countries. The Consequence of a Capture would be a Lodging in New Gate. For the Spirit of Contempt as well as indignation and vindictive rage, with which the British Government had to that time conducted both the Controversy and the War forbade me to hope for the honor of an Appartment in the Tower as a State Prisoner. As their Act of Parliament would authorise them to try me in England for Treason, and proceed to execution too, I had no doubt they would go to the extent of their power, and practice upon me all the Cruelties of their punishment of Treason. My Family consisting of a dearly beloved Wife and four young Children, excited Sentiments of tenderness, which a Father and a Lover only can conceive, and which no language can express. And my Want of qualifications for the Office was by no means forgotten.

On the other hand my Country was in deep distress and in great danger. Her dearest Interest would be involved in the relations she might form with foreign nations. My own plan of these relations had been deliberately formed and fully communicated to Congress, nearly two Years before. The Confidence of my Country was committed to me, without my Solicitation. My Wife who had always encouraged and animated me, in all antecedent dangers and perplexities, did not fail me on this Occasion: But she discovered an inclination to bear me Company with all our Children. This proposal however, she was soon convinced, was too hazardous and imprudent.

It was an Opinion generally prevailing in Boston that the Fisheries were lost forever. Mr. Isaac Smith, who had been more largely concerned in the Cod Fishery than any Man excepting Mr. Hooper and Mr. Lee of Marblehead, had spoken to me on the Subject, and said that whatever should be the termination of the War he knew We should never be allowed to fish again upon the Banks. My Practice as a Barrister in the Counties of Essex, Plymouth and Barnstable had introduced me to more Knowledge both of the Cod and whale fisheries and of their importance both to the commerce and Naval Power of this Country than any other Man possessed, who would be sent abroad if I refused, and this consideration had no small Weight in producing my determination. After much Agitation of mind and a thousand reveries unnecessary to be detailed, I resolved to devote my family and my Life to the Cause, accepted the Appointment and made preparation for the Voyage. A longer time than I expected was required to fit and man the Frigate. The News of my Appointment was whispered about, and General Knox came up to dine with me, at Braintree. The design of his Visit was As I soon perceived to sound me in relation to General Washington. He asked me what my Opinion of him was. I answered with the Utmost Frankness, that I thought him a perfectly honest Man, with an amiable and excellent heart, and the most important Character at that time among Us, for he was the Center of our Union. He asked the question, he said, because, as I was going to Europe it was of importance that the Generals Character should be supported in other Countries. I replied that he might be perfectly at his ease on the Subject for he might depend upon it, that both from principle and Affection, public and private I should do my Utmost to support his Character at all times and in all places, unless something should happen very greatly to alter my Opinion of him, and this I have done from that time to this. I mention this incident, because that insolent Blasphemer of things sacred and transcendent Libeller of all that is good Tom Paine has more than once asserted in Print, the scandalous Lye, that I was one of a Faction in the fall of the Year 1777, against General Washington. It is indeed a disgrace to the moral Character and

5

the Understanding of this Age, that this worthless fellow should be believed in any thing. But Impudence and Malice will always find Admirers.[4]

1778

I was almost out of Patience, in Waiting for the Frigate till the Thirteenth day of February 1778, when Captain Samuel Tucker, Commander of the Frigate Boston, met me at the House of Norton Quincy Esquire, in Braintree, where We dined.[5]

After dinner I bid Adieu to my Friend and Unkle Quincy, sent my Baggage, and walked myself with Captain Tucker, Mr. Griffin a Midshipman, and my eldest Son, John Quincy Adams between ten and eleven years of Age, down to the Moon Head where lay the Bostons Barge.[6] In our Way We made an halt of a few minutes at the House of Mr. Seth Spear on Hoffs neck, where some Sailors belonging to our barge had been waiting for Us. The good Lady, who was an Adams, came out very civilly to invite Us in. We had no time to spare and excused ourselves. She was an amiable Woman, with very delicate health, much afflicted with hysterical complaints, often a little disarranged in her imagination. At this time she was somewhat flighty and accosted me in an alarming manner. "Mr. Adams you are going to embark under

[4] Preceding two sentences omitted by CFA in his text. (Attention is called in Part Two of the Autobiography only to the more significant textual omissions and alterations made by CFA in the only text of JA's Autobiography hitherto published.) The particular attacks by Paine that JA alludes to have not been identified, though Paine had often enough abused JA in print, most recently and perhaps most bitterly in a series of letters "To the Citizens of the United States" published in Washington and Philadelphia newspapers, 1802–1805; see Paine's *Complete Works*, ed. Philip S. Foner, N.Y., 1945, 2:915–917, 952–957.

[5] Here for the first time in composing the three fragmentary parts of his Autobiography JA consulted his Diary in order to refresh his memory. Having done so, he began to incorporate large portions of it into his narrative, sometimes copying his Diary entries fully and faithfully, sometimes paraphrasing or summarizing

them, sometimes greatly expanding them. The Autobiography thus becomes from this point on a text with commentary, so that in order to distinguish what is new in it from what JA took from his Diary one must read the two texts in tandem. Any attempt by the editors to point out systematically the additional matter, not to mention all the variations in language between the contemporary Diary record and the later narrative distilled through JA's memory, would result in a veritable forest of footnotes. The editors have therefore limited themselves to pointing out only representative instances of altered language. For the same purpose of economy in annotation, cross-references to identifying and explanatory notes in the Diary have also been furnished very selectively in the Autobiography.

[6] On the topographical details see JA's Diary entry of 13 Feb. 1778 and note 2 there.

6

very threatening Signs. The Heavens frown, the Clouds roll, the hollow Winds howl, The Waves of the Sea roar upon the Beech," and on she went in such a Strain that I seemed to be reading Ossian. I thought this prophecy of the Sybill, was not very cheering to one whose Acquaintance with the Sea, had been confined to a few Trips to Half Moon a guning and one to Cohasset rocks a fishing when he was a Boy [7] and a few Parties to Rainsfords Island and the Light House in Company with the Select Men of Boston after he was grown up: but I was not enough of a Roman to believe it an ill Omen. It was only a prelude to a Commedy, which I feared all my Voyages and Negotiations would prove to be. It amused me enough to be remembered and that was all. [8]

The Wind was high and the Sea, very rough, but by means of a quantity of Hay in the bottom of the boat, and good Watch Coats with which We were covered, We arrived on board the Boston, about five O Clock, tolerably warm and dry. I found in the Frigate Mr. Vernon a Son of Mr. Vernon of the Navy board, who had that year graduated at Colledge; a little Son of Mr. Deane of Weathersfield between Eleven and twelve years of Age; and a Mr. Nicholas Noel, a french Gentleman, Surgeon of the Ship, who seemed to be a well bred man. He shewed me a Book which I was very glad to see as the French Language was then one of my first Objects. The Title is "The Elements of the English Tongue, develloped in a new, easy and concise manner, in which the pronunciation is taught by an Assemblage of Letters, which form similar Sounds in french, by V. J. Peyton. I mention this because Peytons Grammar is little known, and I think will be very Usefull to any American who wishes to acquire that Language.

Feb. 14. 1778. A fine morning, the Wind at North West. At day break orders were given for the Ship to unmoor. My Lodging had been a Cott with a double Mattross, a good Bolster, my own Sheets and Blanketts enough. My little Son with me, We lay comfortably and slept well though there was a violent gale of Wind in the night.

---

[7] "Cohasset rocks," a few miles east of Braintree but beyond the Nantasket peninsula in Massachusetts Bay, remained a favorite fishing and shooting area throughout the 19th century. As an example of the continuity of family habits it is worth remarking that in 1880 two of JA's great-grandchildren, JQA2 and CFA2, who had as boys gone on fishing jaunts there with their father, bought shares in a private summer colony, the Glades Club, whose property helps form Cohasset harbor, and that in the 1960's *their* great-grandchildren still swim, fish, and sail off "Cohasset rocks." See Mary B. Hunnewell, *The Glades*, Boston, privately printed, 1914.

[8] The incident of the pause at the house on Hough's Neck was written by JA on a separate sheet of the MS and keyed to its proper place in the text by a dagger mark.

On the morning of Sunday the fifteenth of February, the last Anchor was weighed and We came under Sail before breakfast, with fine
Wind, a pleasant Sun but a sharp cold Air. Thus I supposed I had bid
farewell to my native Shore perhaps forever: but I was disappointed.
The Captain, either to take leave of his friends, or in hopes of obtaining more Sailors, steered a course that was unexpected and We arrived
and Anchored in the harbour of Marblehead about noon. Major Reed,
Captain Gatchell, Father in Law of Captain Tucker, came on board
and a Captain Stevens, who came to make me a present of a single
Pistoll. He made many Apologies for giving but one. He had no more.
He had lately presented Mr. Hancock with a beautiful pair and this
was all he had left. I understood they had been taken from the English
in one of the Prize Ships. The friends of our Officers, and others came
on board in great numbers, and gave us formidable Histories of the
Cruelties of the English Men of War and Privateers to the Prisoners
they had taken from Us, in firing grape Shots into our defenceless
American Merchant Ships after they had struck their Colours &c.
Though I regretted these Things I was not sorry to hear them, because
the more I heard of the dangers I had to encounter I thought, the
better my mind would be prepared to meet the worst that could happen.

On Monday February 16. 1778. We had for our mortification another Storm from the North East, and so thick a Snow that the Captain thought he could not go to Sea. Our Excursion to this place, was
unfortunate, because it was almost impossible to keep the Men on board.
Mothers, Wives, Sisters came and begged leave for their Sons, husbands and Brothers, to go on Shore for one hour &c. so that it was
very hard for the Commander to resist their importunity. I was anxious
because I thought We should not have another Wind so good as that
We had lost. Congress and the Navy Board would be surprized at these
delays, and yet there was no fault that I knew of. The Commander of
the Ship was active and vigilant, and did all in his Power, but he
wanted Men. He had very few Seamen: all was as yet chaos on board.
His Men were not disciplined: even the Marines were not. The Men
were not exercised to the Guns. They hardly knew the ropes. My Son
was treated very complaisantly by Dr. Noel, and by a Captain and Lt.
of Artillery who were with Us, all French Gentlemen. They were
very assiduous in teaching him French. Noel was a genteel Man and
had received somewhere a good Education. He had Scars on his for-
head and on his hands which he said were wounds received last War,
in the light horse Service. The Name of the Captain of Artillery, was

Parison, and that of the Lieutenant was Begard. Since my Embarkation, Master Jesse Deane delivered me a letter from his Unkle Barnabas Deane, dated the tenth of February recommending to my particular care and Attention, the Bearer the only Child of his Brother Silas Deane Esqr. then in France, making no doubt, as the letter adds, that I shall take the same care of a Child in his Situation, which I would wish to have done to a Child of my own, in the like circumstances, it is needless to mention his Youth and Helplessness, also how much he will be exposed to bad company, and to contract bad habits, without some friendly Monitor to caution, and keep him from associating with the common hands on board. About the same time another Letter was delivered to me from William Vernon Esqr., of the Continental Navy Board at Boston dated February the ninth in these Words "I presume it is unnecessary to say one Word, in order to impress your mind with the Anxiety a Parent is under, in the Education of a Son, more especially when not under his immediate inspection, and at three thousand miles distance. Your parental Affection fixes this principle. Therefore I have only to beg the favour of you, Sir, to place my Son, in such a Situation, and with such a Gentleman, as you would choose for one of yours, whom you would wish to accomplish for a Merchant. If such a house could be found, either at Bourdeaux or Nantes, of Protestant Principles, of general and extensive Business, I rather think one of these Cities the best; yet if it should be your Opinion, that some other place might be more Advantageous to place him at, or that he can be employed by any of the States Agents, with a good prospect of improving himself in such manner, that he may hereafter be usefull to Society, and in particular to these American States, my views are fully answered. I have only one Observation more to make, vizt. in respect to the Œconomy of this matter, which I am persuaded will engage your Attention, as the small fortune that remains with me, I would wish to appropriate for the Education of my Son, which I know must be husbanded, yet I cannot think of being rigidly parcimonious, nor must I be very lavish, lest my money should not hold out. I imagine a gratuity of one hundred pounds Sterling may be given to a Merchant of Eminence to take him for two or three Years, and perhaps his yearly board paid for. I shall be entirely satisfied in whatever may seem best for you to do and shall ever have a grateful remembrance of your unmerited favours, and sincerely hope in future to have it in my Power to make Compensation. I wish you health and the Utmost happiness and am with the greatest regards" &c.

Thus I found myself invested with the unexpected Trust of a kind of Guardianship of two promising young Gentlemen, besides my own Son, a benevolent Office which would have been peculiarly agreable to me, if I had not a prospect before me of too much Occupation in my own to be at leisure to discharge the duties of it, with that Attention which it might [require].[9] I was soon relieved from the principal care of it, however, for Mr. Vernon chose to remain at Bourdeaux, and Mr. Deane, by the Advice of Dr. Franklin, was put to Le Cœur's Pension at Passy with my Son J.Q.A. and his Grandson Benjamin Franklin Bache, since that time famous enough as the Editor and Proprietor of the Aurora.

On Tuesday the Seventeenth of February 1778 I set a Lesson to my Son in Chambauds French Grammar and asked the favour of Dr. Noel to shew him the precise critical pronunciation of all the french Words, Syllables and Letters, which the Dr. very politely undertook to do, and Mr. John proceeded to get his Lessons accordingly very much pleased.

The Weather was now fair and the Wind right, and We were again weighing Anchor in order to put to Sea, when Captain Diamond and Captain Inlaker came on board and breakfasted, two Prisoners, taken with Captain Manly in the Hancock Frigate, and lately escaped from Hallifax. Our Captain was an able Seaman, and I believed a brave, active and vigilant Officer, but he had no great Erudition. His Library consisted of Dyche's english Dictionary; Charlevoix's Paraguay, which since the British Conquest of Buenos Aires, I regret that I did not read at that time with more attention; the Rights of the Christian Church asserted against the Romish and other Priests who claim an independent power over it; the second Volume of Chubbs posthumous Works, 1. Volume of the History of Charles Horton Esqr. and the first and second Volumes of the delicate Embarrassments a Novell. More Science than this is required in a Naval Officer....[1] About Sunsett we sailed out of Marblehead harbour.

February 18. Wednesday. We had a fine Wind for twenty four hours; but the constant rolling and rocking of the Ship, made Us all Sick. Half the Sailors were so. My young Gentlemen Jesse and John were taken about twelve O Clock the last night and had been very Sick all day. I was seized with it in the afternoon. My Servant Joseph Stevens and the Captain's Will, were both very bad.

February 19. Thursday. 1778. Arose at four O Clock. The Wind and

[9] MS: "acquire."

[1] Suspension points in MS, as are all those found below in Part Two of the Autobiography (and not hereafter noted editorially). In this instance they indicate matter not copied by JA from the Diary, but this is by no means always the case.

Weather still fair. The Ship rolled less than the day before, and I neither felt nor heard any thing of Sea Sickness last night nor this morning. Monsieur Parison, one of General Du Coudrai's Captains of Artillery, dined with Us Yesterday, and behaved like [a] civil and sensible Man. We learned from him, that the roads from Nantes to Paris are very good; no mountains, no rocks, no Hills, all as smooth as the Ships deck, and a very fine Country: But that the roads from Bourdeaux to Paris are bad and mountainous.

The Mal de mer, seems to be the Effect of Agitation. The vapours and exhalations from the Sea; the Smoke of Seacoal, the Smell of stagnant, putrid Water, the Odour of the Ship where the Sailors sleep, or any other offensive Odour will increase the Qualminess, but of themselves, without the violent Agitation they will not produce it.

February 19. 1778. In the morning We discovered three Vessells a head of Us. They appeared to be large Ships, and Captain Tucker observing them with his Glasses, gave it as his Opinion that they were British Frigates and was preparing to give orders to avoid them. But a murmur arising among the Men which was countenanced by some of the petty Officers, if not by some of the three Lieutenants, who were eager for Prizes; "They would not run from an Enemy before they saw him; they would not fly from danger before they knew they were in it. They were only three fine rich English Merchantmen, or perhaps transports, and would make fat Prizes" &c. To humour his Men Captain Tucker gave orders to make all sail towards them. It was not long before We were near enough to see they were Frigates and count their Guns, to the full Satisfaction of every Man on board. No man had an Appetite for fighting three Frigates at once in our feeble State. Orders were given to put away, and our Officers had discovered that our Frigate sailed uncommonly fast near the Wind. This Course was therefore taken, and We soon lost Sight of two of the Ships, but the third chased Us the whole day. Sometimes she gained up[on] Us, and sometimes We gained in our distance from her.

February the 20th. Fryday. In the morning nothing to be seen: but soon after a Sail discovered a head: supposed to be the same Frigate. She pursued Us the whole day. When the night approached, the Wind died away and We were left rolling and pitching in a Calm, with our Guns all out, our Courses or Coursers, I know not which is the right Word, all drawn up and every Way prepared for battle, the Officers and Men appeared in good Spirits and Captain Tucker said his orders were to carry me to France and to take any Prizes that might fall in his Way; he thought it his duty therefore to avoid fighting especially with an unequal force if he could, but if he could not avoid an Engagement he would give them something that should make them remember him. I said and did all in my power to encourage the Officers and Men, to fight them to the last Extremity. My Motives were more urgent than theirs, for it will easily be believed that it would have been more eligible for me to be killed on board the Boston or sunk to the bottom in her, than to be taken Prisoner. I sat in the Cabin at the Windows in the Stern and saw the Ennemy gaining upon Us very fast, she appearing to have a Breeze of Wind, while We had none. Our Officers were of Opinion she had Oars out or some other machinery to accellerate her Course. Our Powder, Catridges and Balls were placed by the Guns and every thing ready to begin the Action. Although it was calm on the Surface of the Sea where we lay, the heavens had been gradually overspred with very thick black clouds and the Wind began to spring up, our Ship began to move, the night came on and it was soon dark. We lost Sight of our Enemy who did not appear to me to be very ardent to overtake Us. But the Wind increased to a Hurricane. The Ship laboured under the Weight of her Guns which were all out ready for Use, she shuddered and shivered like a Man in an Ague, she darted from Side to Side and pitched forward with such Velocity, that it was a very dangerous Operation to get the Guns into their places. If by any Accident or want of Skill or care, one of those heavy cannon had got loose, it would have rolled with the Vessel and infallibly have gone through the Side. All hands were called, and with much difficulty the Guns were all got in and secured. As it was impossible to sleep upon deck or in the Cabin one of the Lieutenants came to me and begged me to go down to his Birth below. But such was the Agitation of the Vessell that instead of sleeping it was with the Utmost difficulty that my little Son and I could hold ourselves in bed with both our hands, and bracing our selves against the boards, planks and timbers with our feet. In this Situation, all of a sudden, We heard a tremendous Report. Whether the British Frigate had overtaken Us, and fired upon Us, or whether our own Guns had been discharged We could not conjecture, but immediately an Officer came down to Us and told Us that the Ship had been struck with lightening and the Noise we had heard, was a Crash of Thunder: that four Men had been struck down by it upon deck, one of them wounded by a Scortch upon his Shoulder as large as a Crown. This Man languished and died in a few Weeks.[2] That the Mainmast was struck and it was feared, damaged, but to what degree could not yet be ascertained. In the midst of all this terror and con-

[2] He died in three days; see Diary entry of 21–23 Feb. 1778 and note there.

12

fusion, I heard a Cry that the Powder room was open. Cartridges, Powder horns, if not some small casks of Powder had been left rather carelessly in various parts of the Ship, near the Guns. If a Spark of the lightening had touched any of these, the Consequences might have been disagreable enough, but if it had reached the Powder room, it would have made an End of the Business. The Men were allarmed at the danger of the Powder room, and Sailors and Marines scampered away with their Lanthorns in such a hurry, that I apprehended more danger to the Powder room from their candles than from the Lightening, but instantly I heard the Voice of an Officer. "Be cool! No Confusion! come back with all your lanthorns. I will go with mine and secure the Powder room." I was as much pleased to perceive the immediate Obedience of the Men, as to hear the Voice of the Officer. He soon returned and proclaimed that he had secured the Powder room and all was Safe.

February 21. Saturday. 22. Sunday. and 23. Monday exhibited such Scænes as were new to me, except in the Histories of Voyages, and the descriptions of the Poets. We lost sight of our Ennemy it is true, but We found Ourselves in the Gulph Stream, in one of the most furious Storms, that ever Ship survived, the Wind North East, then North and then North West. It would be fruitless to attempt a description of what I saw, heard and felt, during these three days and nights. Every School Boy can turn to more than one description of a Storm in his Virgil, but no description in P[r]ose or Verse of a hurricane in the Gulph Stream, the Wind always crossing the rapid current in various Angles, has ever[3] yet been Attempted, as far as I know. To describe the Ocean, the Waves, the Winds, The Ship, her motions, rollings, pitches, Wringings and Agonies, The Sailors, their countenances, language and behaviour, is impossible. No man could stand upon his legs; nothing could be kept in its place; an universal Wreck of every thing in all parts of the Ship, Chests, casks, chairs, Bottles &c.; no place or person was dry. The Wind blowing against the current, not directly, but in various Angles, produced a tumbling Sea, vast mountains of Water above Us, and as deep caverns below Us, the mountains sometimes dashing against each other, and sometimes piling up on one another like Pelion on Ossa, and not unfrequently breaking on the Ship threatened to bury Us all at once in the deep. The Sails were all hauled down but a foresail under which We hoped to scudd, but a sudden Gust of Wind rent it in an instant from the bottom to the top, and We were left with bare poles entirely at the Mercy of Wind

[3] MS: "never."

13

and Water. The Noises were such that We could not hear each other speak at any distance. The Shrouds and every other rope in the Ship exposed to the Wind became a Cord of a very harsh musick. Their Vibrations produced a constant and an hideous howl, of itself enough to deafen Us, added to this the howl and Whistle of the Winds, and incessant roar of the Ocean all in boiling rage and fury, white as Snow with foam through the whole Extent of the horrison; and to compleat the whole, a Sound more allarming I found to our Officers than all the rest, a constant Cracking night and day, from a thousand places in all parts of the Ship, excited very serious Apprehensions of the Starting of the Butts.

Tuesday. 24. Wednesday 25. and Thursday 26 of February. 1778. Our Mainmast and Maintopmast had been hurt by the Lightening. On Tuesday We espyed a Sail and gave her chase. We gained upon her, and upon firing a Gun to leward and hoisting American Colours, she fired a friendly Gun and hoisted the French Colours of the Province of Normandy. She lay to, for Us, and we were coming about to speak to her, when the Wind sprung up fresh of a sudden, and carried away our Maintopmast. We lost the Opportunity which I greatly regretted of speak[ing] to our Friend the Norman, and were sufficiently employed for the remainder of the three days, in getting in a new Maintopmast, repairing the Sails and rigging, which were much damaged in the late Storm and in cleaning the Ship and putting her in order. From the thirty sixth to the thirty ninth degree are called the Squally Latitudes and We found them fully to answer their Character. It was reported among the Seamen that two Sailors who happened to be aloft, had no way to save themselves but by wrapping themselves in the Sail and going over with it. Whether it was true or not, and for what purpose it was propagated if it was not true, I know not: but the report itself was a sufficient illustration of a great Truth of which I have had abundant Experience both before and since that Event, that He who builds on Popularity is like a Sailor on a topmast whether drunk or sober, ready at the first blast to plunge into the briny deep.

I[t] had been my intention to keep an exact Journal of all that happened in this Voyage, and I should have been much pleased to have preserved all the Occurrences in the late Chases, and turbulent Weather: but I was constantly so wett, and every Place and thing was so wett, and every Table and Chair was so wrecked, that is was impossible to touch a Pen or Paper. There is one Anecdote humorous and instructive too, which I will record from my memory. We had on board about thirty french Gentlemen, of General Du Coudrays Corps of Engineers, whom Congress had sent back to France at the Expence of the United States, because they could not ratify the absurd and unauthorised Contract which Mr. Deane had made with them, and among those was a Captain Parison, who has been repeatedly mentioned before. In the course of our three days chase, I had often heard this Gentleman when any danger, or difficulty occurred, exclaim among his Fellow Passengers, Patience! Pondicherry! By means of our Interpreter Dr. Noel, I enquired of him what he meant, by these Words, and he very civilly told me that in the last War between France and England, (the War of 1755. to 1763) he had been in the East Indies in the Garrison of Pondicherry, when that place was besieged by the English, and was finally taken Prisoner, and during his Siege and Captivity had been exposed to every danger, distress and hardship that human nature could endure. Since he had escaped from them all, when he found himself in any perplexity he had only to recollect his former misfortunes and every thing appeared to him a trifle in comparison with them. The Story was circulated among the Men and became generally understood. On one of the nights of our Hurricane, the French Officers and Men had got together in the Cabin under the Stern, and covering themselves in Blanketts as well as they could, endeavoured to get a little Sleep, when an enormous Sea broke upon the Stern, stove in the dead lights, and washed the Frenchmen forward as far as they could go. The first Voice that was heard was Patience! Pondicherry! thundered out by Captain Parison, as loud as he could cry, half drowned as he was in the Water, and it had such an Effect upon his Countrymen, as soon as they got their breath, as to revive their national Gaiety and they all broke out into a loud laugh, which, in spight of all that was dismal and terrible in the Scæne, sett us all a laughing. It was the Opinion of our Officers, and of Captain McIntosh, whom We took Prisoner soon afterwards, that We shipped from that Wave two hundred Tons of Water.

It was a vast Satisfaction to me to recollect, that I had been perfectly calm and collected during the whole of the late Chases and Tempests. I found by the Opinion of all the People on board, as well as that of the Captain and all the Officers that We had been in great danger, and of this I had all along been very certain by my own Observation, but I thought myself in the Way of my duty, and I did not for one moment repent of my Voyage. I often regretted however that I had brought my Son with me. I was not so clear that it had been my duty to expose him as well as myself: but I had been led to it, by his Inclination and by the Advice of all his Friends. The Childs Behaviour gave me a Satisfaction, that I cannot express. Fully sensible of our Danger, he was constantly endeavouring to bear up under it with a manly courage and patience, very attentive to me, and his thoughts always running in a serious Strain. In this he was not singular, for I found that Seamen have their religion as well as Landsmen, and that Sailors, as Corporal Trim said of Soldiers, have sometimes more pressing motives to Prayer than the Clergy. I believe there was not a Soul on board, who was wholly thoughtless of a Divinity. I more than once heard our Captain, who was no Fanatic, on stepping into his Cott, towards morning, offering up his Prayers to his God, when he had no Suspicion that any one heard him, and in a very low but audible Voice, devoutly imploring the Protection of Heaven for the Ship, and the preservation of himself, his officers, Passengers and Men.

I had made many Observations in the late bad Weather, some of which I should not have thought it prudent to put in Writing if I could have kept a regular Journal. A few of them however may be recalled in this place. 1. I had seen the inexpressible Inconvenience, of having so small a Space between the Decks as there was in the Boston. As the main deck was almost constantly under Water, the Sea rolling in and out of the Ports and Scuppers, We were obliged to keep the Hatchways down. The Air consequently became so hot and foul in the 'Tween Decks, as they call it, that for my own part I could not breath or live there; yet the Water would pour down, whenever an Hatchway was opened, so that all was afloat. 2. The Boston was over-metaled. The Number of her Guns, and the Weight of their metal, was too great for her tonnage. She had five twelve Pounders, and nine-teen nines. We were obliged to sail, day and night, during a Chace, with the Guns out, in order to be ready for Battle, and this exposed Us to certain Inconvenience, and very great danger. They made the Ship labour and roll, to such a degree as to oblige Us to keep the Chain pumps as well as the hand pumps almost constantly going: besides, they wring and twist the Ship, in such a manner as to endanger the Starting of a Butt, and still more to endanger the Masts and Rigging. 3. The Ship was furnished with no Pistols. She ought to have had a variety and a large Number of these Or at least a Number of Setts for the Officers, because, there is nothing but the dread of a Pistol, will keep many of the Men to their quarters, in time of Action. 4. The Frigate was not furnished with good Glasses, which appeared to me of very great consequence. Our Ships ought to [be] supplied with the best glasses that Art affords: the expence would be saved a thousand Ways. 5. There was I found, on board the Navy, the same general

Inattention to Œconomy, that there was in the Army. 6. There was the same general relaxation of order and discipline. 7. There was the same inattention to the Sweetness of the Ship, and the Persons and Health of the Sailors, as there was at land of the Neatness of the Camp, and the health and cleanliness of the Soldiers. 8. The practice of profane cursing and Swearing, so silly as well as detestable prevailed in a most abominable degree. It was indulged and connived at in the Men, and practised too, by Officers, in such a manner that there was no kind of Check, or discouragement to it. This may be thought trivial, by some, but to me it appeared that order of every kind would be lax, as long as this scurvy Vice was so wholly unrestrained.

In this place it will not be impertinent to take notice of an absurd and pernicious report which was propagated in this Country during my Absence, I know not by whom nor for what End. Certainly it could be with no good design. It was that I had been convinced by my own Observation that in critical times at Sea, the Sailors could not be stimulated to sufficient Activity and Exertion, unless the Officers terrified them by these vulgar Oaths and Execrations. The Rumour was wholly without foundation. On the contrary I have often observed, that a dry Sarcasm, or an Arch Irony, has excited the Ambition, Energy, Agility and Ingenuity of a Seaman more effectually, than any Oath I ever heard. If such vile Language ever has any effect upon the Men, it is only in the mouths of such Officers as are in the habit of speaking to them only in such a Style. They may possibly not think such an officer in earnest, when he does not Use his common Dialect. But this is more the fault of the Officer than of the Man. If he would mend his manners the man would soon understand him and reform his own. This report is however only a revival of a very ancient one. I have heard the same Story and the same insinuations of Dr. Sewall when I was very young, and of Dr. Cooper, when he sailed with Captain Hollowell in the Province Ship: and have no doubt they were as falsely imputed to them as they were to me.

This Morning Captain Tucker made me a present of Charlevoix's History of Paraguay and Dr. Noel put into my hand a Manual of Geography, containing a description of all the Countries of the World. These manuals come out annually, and are to be had in any of the great Towns in France.

February 27. Fryday. 1778. A calm. As soft and warm as Summer. A Species of black Fish, which were called Beneaters, appeared about the Ship.

One source of the disorders in our Ship was a great irregularity in

17

the meals. There ought to have been a well digested System, for eating, drinking and sleeping. At six all hands should have been called up. At Eight they should all breakfast. At one they should dine, and at Eight they should sup. It should have been penal for the Cook to fail of having his Victuals punctually, ready. This would have been much for the Health, comfort and Spirits of the Men, and would have greatly promoted the Business of the Ship. I was constantly giving hints to the Captain concerning Order, Œconomy and regularity. He seemed to be sensible of the necessity of them, and exerted himself to introduce them. He cleared out the 'Tween decks, ordered up the Hammocks to be aired, and ordered up the Sick, such at least as could bear it, upon Deck for sweet Air. That Ship would have bred the Plague or the Goal fever, if there had not been great exertions after the Storm to wash, sweep, Air, and purify Cloaths, Cotts, Cabins, Hammocks, and all other things, places, and Persons. In the Morning I very seriously advised the Captain to reform his Cockpit. I said to him "if you intend to have any reputation for Œconomy, Discipline or any thing that is good, look into that Scæne." He went down, accordingly and ordered up every body from that Sink of Devastation, Putrefaction and Ruin. He ordered up the Hammocks and every thing else that could be removed, and that required to be aired and cleansed.

The Captain brought in a Curiosity, which he had drawn up, over the Side in a Buckett of Water, and which the Sailors call a Portuguese Man of War. We saw many of them sailing by the Ship. They had some Appearances of Life and Sensibility. They spread a curious Sail and are wafted along very briskly. They have something like Strings or twisted and knotted Cords, hanging down in the Water, which are said to be caustic and in some degree poisonous to human Flesh, or perhaps it may be electricity, which gives a shock upon the touch of them. The Hulk is like blue glass. This was a very small one in comparison of many We saw around Us. I pierced it, with the sha[r]p point of a Pennknife and found it empty. The Air came out and the Thing shrunk almost to nothing. Ten Years afterwards in the Ship Lucretia Captain Callahan, I had a number of large ones brought on board, in the same Gulph Stream and found in them shell fishes growing of various Species, vizt. Cockles, Muscles, Scollops and large Clams.

February 28. Saturday. 1778. The last night and this day We enjoyed a fine easy breeze, the Ship had no motions but directly forward. I slept as quietly and as soundly as in my own bed at home.... Some of the Gentlemen had given me some West India Nutts, and not knowing the caustic quality in the outward Shell I had broken them with my hands, and probably carelessly rubbed my face or my Eyes afterwards, and I found myself poisoned. My Eyes swelled and were enflamed to an alarming degree. Dr. Noel gave me a Phial of Balsamum Fioraventi which abated the inflammation and gave me some relief. It is very much compounded, very subtle and penetrating. Pour a few drops into your hand, rub it over the palm and fingers, then hold the inside of your hand before the Eyes, and the Steam which evaporates enters the Eyes and works them clear. The Balsam derives its name from the Italian Inventor of it. For two or three years afterwards, at the return of the Season, a similar inflammation in my Eyes and Swelling about them, returned with it, a fact the Solution of which as beyond the reach of my Skill, I leave to the Physicians.

The Ship was now in very good order, cleared and cleaned between Decks, on the main Deck, in the Cabin, and on the Quarter Deck: the Masts, Yards, Sails and rigging were all well repaired.

The Captain sent written orders to the Steward, to make weekly returns to him, of the State of provisions, and to be very frugal in the Use and management of them and particularly of Candles, as nearly one half of the Ships Store of Candles appeared to have been expended.

This was Saturday night a fortnight and one day since I took leave of my family. What Scænes had I beheld in those fifteen days! What anxiety had my Friends on Shore suffered on my Account! during the North East Storm, which they must probably have felt at Land! But these Reflections were too tender to be indulged, especially as they could do no good to my friends or me. I diverted my mind from them by enquiring what was this Gulph Stream? What was the course of it? From what Point and to what Object did it flow? How broad it was? How far distant from the Continent? What were the longitudes and Latitudes of it? But I found but little satisfactory Information, till some years afterwards, I saw Governor Pownalls Treatise upon this Subject.[4]

March 1. 1778. Sunday. It was discovered that our Mainmast was sprung in two Places; one beneath the Maindeck, where, if the Mast had wholly failed in the late Storm it must have torn up the Main deck, and the Ship must have foundered. This was one among many instances in which it had already appeared that our Safety had not depended on ourselves. We had a fine Wind all day and night. The Ship was quiet and still; no disturbance, little noise; but the Velocity

[4] Thomas Pownall, *Hydraulic and Nautical Observations on the Currents in the Atlantic Ocean . . .* , London, 1787.

of our Motion was so great as to cause some Seasickness. My desire and Advice was to carry less Sail especially of nights, and at all times when We should not be in chace.

March 2. Monday. 1778. A fine Wind still and a pleasant morning. The Colour of the Water which was green, not blue as it had been for many days past, the appearance of large flocks of Gulls, and various other birds convinced many of the Gentlemen, that We were not far from the grand Bank of Newfoundland. The Captain however thought it thirty five Leagues to the North West of Us. Our Mast was the day before repaired with two large fishes, as they call them, that is to say large Oaken Planks cutt for the purpose, and put on. The Mast seems now to be firm. The Sailors were however very superstitious; they said the Ship had been so unfortunate, that they believed some Woman was on board. Women they said were the unluckyest Creatures in the World at Sea.

This Evening the Wind was very fresh and the Ship sailed at a great rate. I hoped We were out of the reach of the Gulph Stream and of British Cruisers, two Objects and Evils to which I had a strong Aversion. But my Exultation was too hasty. Other Storms and other Cruisers awaited Us, not much less formidable than those We had escaped.

March 3. Tuesday. 1778. Our Wind had continued brisk and fresh all the last night and this morning. Our Course was about North East. Showers fell in the night and in the morning. The Flocks of Gulls still pursued Us. This morning Captain Parison breakfasted with Us. Our Captain was in high Spirits and very gay, chattering in French, Spanish, Portuguese, German, Dutch, Latin [5] and Greek and boasting that he could speak some Words in every Language. He told Us, besides that he had ordered two more Fishes upon the Mainmast to cover the flaws above Deck. This Mast was very large and strong, and thought to be one of the best Sticks that our Country aforded: but it had been very roughly handled by the Lightening and the Storm, and dangerously injured.

The Captain, Lieutenants, Master, Mates, and Midshipmen, were now making their calculations to discover their Longitude, but I conjectured they would be very wild.

The Life I lead was a dull Scæne to me—No Business, no Pleasure, No Reading, no Study. Our little World was all wet and damp. There was nothing I could eat or drink, without nauseating. We had no Spirits for Conversation, nor any thing about which to converse. We

---

[5] The Latin is an addition to the list in the Diary entry of this date, and an improbable one.

saw nothing but Sky, Clouds and Sea, and then Seas, Clouds and Skies. I had often heard of Learning a Language, as English or French for example, on a Passage: but I believed very little of any thing was ever learned at Sea. There must be more health and better Accommodations. My young Friend Mr. Vernon had never had the least qualm of Sea Sickness since We came on board. I advised him to begin the Study of the French Tongue, methodically by reading the Grammar through. He began it accordingly.

March 4. Wednesday. 1778. The Weather was fair, but We had an adverse Wind from the North East, which obliged us to go to the Southward of the South East, which was out of our Course. Our general intention was to make for Nantes, one of the most commercial Cities of France, which I was very anxious to see, not only on Account of its Wealth and Antiquity, and the Connection of its Merchants with those of Bilbao, but also as the Scæne of the Edict of Nantes proclaimed by Henry the fourth in 1598 so much to the honour and Interest of Humanity, and revoked by Louis the 14th. in 1685 so much to its disgrace and Injury.

March 5. Thursday 1778. This morning We had the pleasantest prospect We had yet seen. An easy breeze from the Southward, gave Us an Opportunity of keeping our true course. With a soft, clear, warm Air, a fair Sun and no Sea, We had a great number of Sails spread, and went at the rate of nine Knots; yet the Ship had no perceptible motion and made no noise. My little Son was very proud of his Knowledge of all the Sails, and the Captain put him upon learning the Mariners Compass. I was ardently wishing that We might make Prize of an English Vessell, lately from London, with all the Newspapers and Magazines on board, that We might obtain the latest Intelligence and discover the plan of Operations for the ensuing Campaign in America. I was impatient to arrive in some Port or other, whether in France or Spain, that I might make Inquiries concerning the designs of the Enemy, what Force they meant to send to America; where they were to procure Men; what was the State of the British nation; what the State of Parties; what the State of Finances and of Stocks; what Supplies of Cloathing, Arms, Ammunition &c. were gone to America during the past Winter; The State of American Credit in France; what remittances had been made from America in Tobacco, Rice, Indigo or any other Articles; The State of Europe, particularly of France and Spain; what were the real designs of those Courts; what the condition of their Finances; what the State of their Armies, and especially of their fleets; what number of Ships they had, fitted for Sea; what their names, number of Men and Guns, Weight of Metal &c.; where they lay; the probability or improbability of a War, and the causes and reasons for and against each Supposition. I wanted to be employed in collecting and transmitting to Congress all the Information I could find upon these and all other points, which it might be Usefull for them to know, but the time was not yet come.

We were now supposed to be nearly in the Latitude of Cape Finisterre so that We had only to sail an Easterly course. Every one knows that this Cape and City of the same name, are the most westerly part not only of the Kingdom of Gallicia and of Spain but of all Europe, and therefore was called by the Ancients, who knew no other country, The End of the World.

We enjoyed, through the whole of this day, the clearest Horrison, the softest Weather, the smoothest Sea, and the best Wind, which We had ever found since We came on board. All Sails were spread and We went, ten Knots upon an Avarage the whole day.

March 6. Fryday. 1778. The Wind had continued in the same point all night; about South, and We had gone nine Knots upon an Avarage. This was great favour.

Many Years before I had accidentally purchased an Edition of Molieres Commedies in ten or twelve Volumes, with an English translation on the page opposite to the French. I had never made any Use of the French part untill I found myself destined to go to France. From that time I had compared the French and English together as well as I could, and now I had an Opportunity to apply myself, to the Study of the Language, which I did very closely as often as Winds and Seas and British Men of War would permit. But these Halcyon days were soon at an End.

We passed to the Northward of the Western Islands and were now supposed to be as near them as We should be at any time.

March 7. Saturday. 1778. The same prosperous Wind and the same beautifull Weather continued. We proceeded on our course about two hundred miles in twenty four hours. We had passed all the dangers of the American Coast; those of the Bay of Biscay and those of the Coast of France, and as it happened those of the English Channel remained to be encountered.

Yesterday the Ship had been all in an Uproar, with laughter. The Boatswains Mate asked one of the Officers if they might have a little Sport. The Answer was Yes. Jere accordingly, with the Old Sailors, proposed to build a Galley, and all the green hands to the Number of twenty or thirty were taken in, and suffered themselves to be tied together by their Legs. When, all on a sudden, Jere, and his knowing ones, were found, handing bucketts of Water over the Sides, and pouring them upon the poor Dupes till they were wet to the Skin. The Behaviour of the Gullies, their passions, Speeches and countenances, were diverting enough. So much for Jere's fun. This frolick I suppose, according to the Sailors reasoning was to conjure up a Prize.

This morning the Captain ordered all hands upon Deck, and took an Account of the Number of Souls on board, who amounted to one hundred and seventy two. Then the Articles of War were read to them. Then he ordered all hands upon the Forecastle, and then upon the Quarter Deck, to determine by Experiments whether any difference was made in the Sailing of the Ship, by the Weight of the Men when forward, or Aft. Then all hands were ordered to their Quarters to exercise them at the Guns. Mr. Barron gave the Words of command and they spent an hour at their exercise in which they appeared to be tolerably expert. After this a dance was ordered by the Captain upon the main Deck, and all hands, Negroes, Boys and Men were obliged to join in it.... When this was over the Old Sailors sett on foot another game, which they called The Miller. I will not spend time to describe this odd Scæne: but it ended in a very wild Vagary, in which all the Men were powdered over with flour, and wet again to the Skin. Whether these whimsical Diversions are indulged in order to compell the Men to wash themselves, shift their Cloaths and wash away Vermin, or whether it is to awaken the Spirits of the Men which are very apt to sink in a long Voyage, I know not: but there is not in them the least Appearance of Elegance, very little Wit, and a humour of the coarsest kind. It is not superiour to the dances of Indians.

March 8. Sunday. 1778. The same Wind and Weather continued and We went at the rate of seven and a half and Eight Knots.

Mr. Barrons our first Lieutenant, appeared to be an excellent Officer, very Attentive and diligent in his Duty; thoughtfull for the Safety of the Ship, and considerate about Order, Œconomy and regularity among the officers and Men. He had great experience at Sea. Had used the Trade to London, Lisbon, the West Indies, the Southern States, and I am sorry to add Africa.[6]

This morning the Captain ordered all hands upon the Quarter Deck to Prayers. Mr. William Cooper, the Captains Clerk, had prepared a composition of his own, a very decent and comprehensive Prayer, which he pronounced in a grave and proper manner. The

---

[6] The Diary passage of this date which JA was copying reads: "the Trade to London, Lisbon, Affrica, West Indies, Southern States &c."

Officers and Men all attended, in clean Cloaths and behaved very soberly. The Weather was cloudy the whole of this day. Towards night it became rainy and windy, and the Ship rolled a little in the old fashion. We were about two thousand miles from Boston.

The Hurricane in the Gulph Stream surpassed all Powers of description. Neither Milton in Verse, nor Gibbon in prose could have given any adequate Idea of it, but the present and subsequent turbulent Weather, as I was a Student in French turned my Attention to Boileaus description of a Tempest. As the Book happened to be at hand I amused myself with it and became very familiar with it. As it was the first morsel of french Verse, except Molières, which I ever attempted to Understand, it may be inserted here.

> Comme l'on voit les flots, soûlevez par l'orage,
> Fondre sur un Vaisseau, qui s'oppose a leur rage,
> Le Vent avec fureur, dans les voiles frêmit;
> La Mer blanchit d'ecume, et l'air au loin gémit;
> Le Matelot troublè, que son Art abandonne,
> Croit voir dans chaque flot, la mort qui l'environne.

March 9. 1778. Monday. Last night the Wind shifted to the North West, and blew fresh. It was then fairer for Us than before. The Weather was fair and We proceeded on our Voyage at a great rate. Some of our Officers thought We should reach our Port, by thursday night: others by Saturday night: But these made no Account of Cruisers and Chace's, nor any allowance for the variability of the Winds. From this time however till Saturday, We were in great Confusion and hurry.

Tuesday March 10. 1778. We espied a Sail and gave her chace. We soon came up with her, but as we had borne directly down upon her, she had not seen our Broadside and knew not our force. She was a Letter of Mark, with fourteen Guns, Eight nines and Six Sixes. She suddenly turned and fired a broadside into Us, but did Us no other damage, than by cutting some of our rigging, piercing some of our Sails, and sending one of her Shot through our Mizzen Yard. I happened to be standing in the gang Way between the Quarter Deck and the Main Deck, and in the direction from the Ship to the Yard, so that the Balls flew directly over my head. We upon this Salutation, turned our broadside towards her. As soon as she saw this she struck her colours. Our Sailors were all in a rage to sink her for daring to fire. But Captain Tucker very promptly and prudently ordered his Officers not to fire, for he wanted the Egg, without breaking the Shell. I suspected however that the Captain of the Prize knew our force better than he pretended, and that he discharged his Broadside, that he might have it to say that he had not surrendered his Ship, without firing a Gun.

The Prize was the Ship Martha, Captain McIntosh from London to New York, loaded with a Cargo of great Value. The Captain told me that seventy thousand Guineas had been insured upon her at Lloyds and that she was worth Eighty thousand. The Behaviour of the Captain was that of a Gentleman, and he bore his misfortune with fortitude but his Mate cryed like a Child in despair. The Sailors seemed to me to felicitate themselves that it was not a British Man of War, and that they were not impressed. There were two Gentlemen on board as Passengers. Mr. R. Gault was One, and Mr. Wallace of New York the other. There were two young Jews, on board. That and the next day were spent in dispatching the Prize, under the command of the third Lieutenant, Mr. Wells[7] to Boston.

We soon fell in chace of another Vessell, and overtaking her, found her to be a French Snow, from Bourdeaux to Miquelon. We then saw another Vessell, chaced and came up with her. She proved to be a French Brig from Marseilles to Nantes. This last cost Us very dear.... Mr. Barrons our first Lieutenant, attempting to fire a Gun as a Signal to the Brigg, the Cannon burst, and tore in pieces the right leg of this worthy officer so that the Surgeon was obliged to amputate it, a little below the Knee.

I was present at this afflicting Scæne, and, together with Captain Tucker, held Mr. Barron in our Arms, while the Doctor put on the Turnequett and cutt off the Limb. Mr. Barron bore it with fortitude, but thought he should die, and his principal concern seemed to be for his family.

I could not but think the fall of this officer, a great loss to the ⟨Public⟩ United States. His Prudence, moderation, Attention and Zeal were qualities much wanted in our Infant Navy. He was by Birth a Virginian.

He said he had a Mother, a Wife and Children who were dependant on him and in indigent Circumstances, and intreated me to take care of his Family. I promised him, that as soon as I could write to America I would recommend his Family to the Care of the Public as well as of Individuals. I recollect to have done something of this: but the Scenes of distraction in which I was soon involved, I fear, prevented me from

---

[7] JA's copying error for "Welch." On this and other incidents recorded in the present entry, see the Diary entry of 14 March 1778 and notes there.

doing so much as I ought to have done, and I feel it, to this hour to be one of the omissions which I ought to regret.

March 19. Thursday. Captain McIntosh assured Us that by his Reckoning when he was taken he was in the English Channel, and We had been beating about in it for some time. For the last five days We had been tossed in another Gale: I had been scarcely able to stand or sit, without holding fast with both my hands, upon some lashed Table, or Gun, or the Side, or beams of the Ship or some other fixed Object, such was the Agitation and perpetual motion of the Vessel by violent Gales and a heavy Sea. In the course of [the] last five days We had seen a great Number of Vessells two of which if not four were supposed to be large British Men of War, for they chased Us a long time and drove Us in various directions all out of our Course. The Wind had been much against Us, but this morning it veered and We steered, at least our head lay by the Compass South East. We consoled Ourselves as well as We could by reflecting, that possibly We had been favoured by the last Gale as We had been by the first. By the last We had escaped Cruisers, as We did by the first, which I own I considered as an Escape, because although We all agreed, Officers, Passengers and Men, in the necessity of Fighting the Frigate in the Gulph Stream, yet I had reasons enough to be apprehensive of the Consequences of an Engagement perhaps with a superiour force, probably with a superiour number of Men and certainly with greater Experience in the Officers and stricter discipline among the Men.

Possibly this violent Gale from the South East, had driven all the Cruisers from the Coast of Spain, and the southerly part of the Bay of Biscay, and by this means have opened a clear passage for Us to Bourdeaux. This was possible and so was the contrary. Heaven alone knew.

March 20 Fryday. 1778. Yesterday afternoon the Weather cleared up and the Wind came about very fair. We had a great run, last night. This Morning espyed a Sail under our leward Bow, chased and soon came up with her, a Snow from Amsterdam to Demarara and Essequibo.

I made Inquiry to day of our Prisoner, Captain McIntosh, concerning the Trinity House. He says it is the richest corporation in the Kingdom. That the Earl of Sandwich is an elder Brother of it. That any Master of a Vessell may be made a younger Brother of it, if he will. That there are many thousands of younger Brothers. That this house gives permission to every Vessell to take out, or take in ballast, and that a few pence, six pence perhaps a Ton are paid them for such Licence. That they have the care of all Lighthouses &c.

I had omitted to keep a regular and particular Journal, even when the Weather might have permitted it, from an Apprehension that these Papers might possibly fall into hands of an Ennemy as there might be no Opportunity of destroying them. My publick Papers were always prepared to be sunk in the Sea, at the moment when the preservation of the Ship should be no longer practicable.

We had now so fine a Wind that a few days We thought, would determine whether We were to meet any capital disaster, or arrive safe in port.

March 21. Saturday 1778. Five Weeks had elapsed Yesterday, since my Embarkation. We went East South East.

March 27. Fryday. On Wednesday Evening Mr. Barrons died, and Yesterday was committed to the Deep, from the Quarter Deck. He was laid in a Chest made for the purpose by the Carpenter; about a Dozen twelve pound Shot were put in with him and then nailed up. The Fragment of the Gun which destroyed him, was lashed on the Chest, and the whole launched overboard, through one of the Ports, in presence of all the Ships company after the funeral Service had been read by Mr. Cooper.

In the course of the last Week, We had some of the worst Winds, We had ever felt.

On monday last We made the Land on the coast of Spain.

On Tuesday We ran into the Bay of Saint Anthonio. Four or five Boats with fifteen or sixteen men in each, came to Us, out of one of which We took a Pilot.

At Sight of the Country of Spain, which I viewed as distinctly and particularly as the Glasses we had in our possession, would permit, I had a great Curiosity to go on Shore. Though the mountains at a distance were covered with Snow, there was a fine Verdure near the Sea. I saw one convent but We could not come in Sight of the Town. The moment We were about turning the point of the Rock, to enter the harbour, a Sail appeared. She might be an English Merchantman, and We must put out, to see who she was. As prizes were not my particular Objects, I had not enthusiasm enough to see any probability of a prize and felt much disappointed, but said nothing. After She was ascertained to be a Spanish Brigg, We found it impracticable upon repeated Efforts to get into the harbour. In the night a sudden Wind caught Us at Anchor, from the North West, obliged Us to weigh, make all the

Sail We could and put to Sea. We steered our course for Bourdeaux. Yesterday was almost a calm, the little Wind there was directly against Us. This morning the Wind was a little better. We were supposed to be within thirty Leagues of Bourdeaux River.

March 28. Saturday. 1778. Last night and this morning We were in the thoroughfare of all the Ships from Bourdeaux. A great number of them were always in Sight. By Observation to day our Latitude was forty six degrees three minutes north, about seven minutes South of the middle of the Isle of Rea. We were therefore about twenty leagues from the Tower of Cordovan. We had no Wind, but a very disagreable Suel [Swell], and nothing could be more tedious to me than this idle Life. I had not yet learned the French Word, Ennui, but I felt enough of it.

Last Evening We had two little Incidents, which were very unpleasant. One was, the French Barber, attempting very roughly to go below, contrary to orders, the Centinell, after repeatedly announcing his orders, and giving warning of the consequences to no effect, cutt off his Toe with a Cutlace. The French People on board, as was very natural, at first were allarmed and expressed much resentment, but finding on Inquiry, that the fellow had been wholly deserved[8] all he had suffered and the Centinell had done no more than his duty they all very honourably acquiesced.

The other disagreable incident was this. Our English Prisoners, though in general they behaved very well, were sometimes out of humour, and had made some invidious remarks upon our Officers and Men and their awkward Conduct of the Ship, and especially on the Evening of Saint Patricks day, when many of them declared they would get drunk, and I suppose had been as good as their Words, were overheard to wish to meet a British Man of War and hinted that We could not stand an Engagement of half an hour with a british Vessell of half our force &c. &c. &c. On this day one of these Prisoners a little more elevated than Usual, grew out of temper and was very passionate and abusive to Mr. Vernon, and afterwards to Captain Palmes of the Marines, but a little prudent language used to both parties composed their humours and the difficulty subsided.

Captain McIntosh was of North Britain, and had been twenty Years before a Lieutenant of a Man of War. He was very open and decided against America, in her contest, and his Passions were so engaged that they easily inkindled.

---

[8] Thus in MS. JA probably meant to write: "had been wholly in the wrong and deserved," &c.

Mr. Gault was an Irish Gentleman, and as decided against America, at least in her Claim of Independence as the other.

Mr. Wallace was more reserved, cautious, silent and secret. Jealousies arose among the Men, that the Prisoners were plotting with some of our profligate People. But I believed the Suspicion was not well grounded; at least that there was not much danger to be apprehended from any such Intrigues.

All day Yesterday, and all the forenoon of this day We had been looking out for Land, with no light Apprehensions on our Approach to the dangerous and unexperienced Coast of France, where a sandy Shore generally extends a great Way into the Sea, and very shoal Water is often at a great distance from Land. The Country also is very flatt and low so that a Vessell gets into very shallow Water before the Land is discerned. About four O Clock, We cryed France! France! We saw the Isles of Rhee and Oleron, between which two, is the Entrance into the Harbour of Rochelle, which is about half way between Nantes and Bourdeaux. The land was extreamly level and low, scarcely visible. We saw a Tower. The Water was but twenty or thirty fathoms deep. The Bottom all Sand: in all respects the reverse of the Spanish Coast on the other Side of the Bay of Biscay. In the Afternoon We had an entire calm and Mr. Goss played upon his Violin and the Sailors danced, which seemed to have a happy effect on their Spirits and put them all in good humour. Numbers of small Birds from the Shore, came along to day, some of which alighted on our Rigging, Yards &c. One of them a little Lark We caught. These Birds venture from the Shore till they loose sight of it, and then they fly till they are so fatigued, that the instant they alight upon a Ship, they drop to sleep.

March 29. Sunday. 1778. Becalmed all the last night. This morning a vast number of Sails were in Sight. Saint Martins and Oleron were visible, at least the Towers and Windmills, but the Land was very low and level. A Pilot boat, with two Sails and four Men, came on board of Us, and the Pilot instantly undertook to carry Us to Bourdeaux. He said the Ship might go quite up to the City, if she drew twenty feet of Water. We were soon sailing very agreably towards our Port. The Pilot said War was declaired last Wednesday, and that the Pavillions were hoisted Yesterday at every Fort and Lighthouse. This News, I did not believe, but it signified something, which I did not Understand nor the Pilot neither.

There was a civil Frenchman on board, whose name I had never asked till this day. His Name was Quillau, Fourier des Logis de Monseigneur Le Compte D'Artois. He was not of Du Coudrays Corps. I know not whether my Conjecture was well founded [but] [9] I then suspected that the Court of Versailles had sent some of their domestic and confidential Servants to America to reconnoitre the Country and that they might not receive all their Information from the Representations [1] of their Ministers.

The French Gentlemen on board could scarcely understand our new Pilot. They said he spoke Gascoine, the Dialect of Bourdeaux, which they said was not good French.

This day six Weeks We had sailed from Nantaskett Road. How many dangers, distresses, and hairbreadth escapes had We seen. There was one however which has been omitted. One Evening when We were approaching the French Coast, I was sitting in the Cabin, when Captain McIntosh our Prisoner came down to me and addressed me, with great solemnity "Mr. Adams this ship will be captured by my Countrymen, in less than half an hour. Two large British Men of War are bearing directly down upon Us, and are just by, you will hear from them I warrant you in six minutes. Let me take the Liberty to say to you that I feel for you more than any one else. I have always liked you since I came on board, and have always ascribed to you chiefly the good treatment I have received as well as my People; and you may depend upon it, all the good Service I can render you with my Countrymen shall be done with pleasure." I saw by his Countenance, Gestures, Air, Language and every Thing that he believed what he said, that he most heartily rejoiced in his own prospect of deliverance and that he heartily pitied me.... I smiled however at his Offers of kind Offices to me, knowing full Well that his Prayers and tears would be as unavailing as my own if he should be generous and I weak enough to employ them, with British Officers, Ministers, Judges or King, in the then Circumstances of Things and Temper of the Britons. I made him a bow expressive of my Sense of his politeness, but said nothing. Determined to see my danger before I would be intimidated at it, I took my hat and marched up to the Quarter Deck. I had before heard an uncommon trampling upon Deck and perceived Signs of some Alarm and confusion, but when upon Deck I saw the two ships indeed. They both appeared larger than our Frigate and were already within Musquet Shot of Us. The Air was clear and the Moon very bright. We could see every thing even the Men on board. We all expected every moment to be hailed, and possibly saluted with a broadside. But the two ships passed by Us without speaking a Word, and I stood upon Deck till they had got so far off as to remove all Apprehensions of dan-

[9] MS: "by."   [1] Possibly "Representatives."

ger from them. Whether they were English or French, or Spanish or Dutch, or whether they were two American Frigates which had been about that time in France We never knew. We had no inclination to inquire about their business or destination, and were very happy that they discovered so little curiosity about ours.[2]

Every Ship at Sea is a kind of Prison, and the poor Inhabitants are obliged to have recourse to songs, cards, dances and Stories to amuse them, and wear away the tedious hours. We had many Stories told but I remember very few. In some of the dull hours of calm upon the coast of France, some of the Officers or Passengers told a Story of Garrick. He had a relation convicted of a Capital Offence. He obtained Leave to wait upon his Majesty to beg a pardon. The King asked what was the Crime. He has only taken a Cup too much, may it please your Majesty. Is that all said the King? Then let him be pardoned.

One of Captain Tuckers Stories too diverted the Frenchmen as well as the Englishmen and Americans. A Frenchman in London Advertised an infallible Remedy against fleas. The Women as well as Men flocked to the place to purchase the Powder. But after many had bought it and paid for it, one only of the Women, asked for directions to Use it. Madam said the Frenchman, you must catch the Flea, and squeese him between your thumb and finger, till he gape, then put a little dust of this powder in his mouth, and he never will bite you again. But said the Lady when I have him between my fingers why may I not throw him in the fire or press him to death? Ah, Madam, said the Frenchman, dat will do just as well den. I should not perhaps have remembered this story, if the same had not been told me afterwards by Mr. Dumas at the Hague, who declared he had been present and seen and heard the same Sale and Dialogue between a German Mountebank and a Dutch Woman at the Hague.

We had been becalmed all day in Sight of Oleron. The Village of Saint Dennis was in Sight, and many Windmills and Sand Hills all

[2] This incident, somewhat improbable in itself and only vaguely alluded to in JA's Diary (see entry of 19 March 1778), is confirmed in both the *Boston's* Log (MH:Tucker Papers) and Capt. Tucker's "Abstract of a Journal Kept . . . on board the Contl. Frigate Boston" (Adams Papers, Microfilms, Reel No. 342). Both mention it under date of 15 March, five days after McIntosh's ship, the *Martha,* was taken. The account in the "Journal" is fuller than that in the Log and gives details not found elsewhere:

"Sunday 15th. Fresh Gales; at 8 PM saw two Ship[s] on my starboard Bow, standing to the Westward. I Cross'd them about 1/2 a Mile under their Lee, discovering them to be British Ships one a two decker, the other a Frigate, I then bore away from them by order, of the Hon. Jno. Adams. One of the gentl[eme]n passangers Informd me, they were boarded the Day before I took them by three Man of War Boats, that their were Six two Deckers, and a Frigate in Company. At 9 AM Lost Sight of them."

31

along the Shore: and Multitudes of Vessells in Sight, French, Spanish and Dutch Merchantmen and English Smugglers.

I felt a strong curiosity to visit this Island of Oleron, so famous in Antiquity for its Sea Laws.

March 30. Monday. 1778. This Morning the Officer came down and told the Captain that a lofty Ship was in Sight and had fired two heavy Guns. All hands were called up: but the lofty Ship appeared to be an heavy loaded Snow. The Weather was Cloudy, but there was no Wind. All very still excepting a small Suel. The Tower of Cordovan or as our Sailors called it The Bourdeaux lighthouse, was in Sight over our larbord Bow. The Officers were now employed in clearing the Ship and removing all warlike Appearances.

This day had been fortunate and happy.... Our Pilot had brought Us safely into the River of Garonne, and We had run up with Wind and Tide as far as Pouliac, when We anchored for the night and took in another Pilot.

This forenoon a Fisherman came along Side of Us, with Hakes, Skates and Gennetts. We bought some of them and had a high regale.

The River was very beautiful: on both sides of it, the plantations were pleasant. On the South Side especially We saw Horses, Oxen, Cows and great flocks of Sheep, grazing. The Husbandmen ploughing and Women half a dozen in a drove with their hoes. The Churches, Convents, Gentlemens Seats, and the Villages appeared to me, simple Inhabitant of the American Wilderness, very magnificent.

The River seldom swells with Freshes, for the rural Improvements and even the Fishermens Houses, are brought quite down to the Waters Edge. The Water in the River is to all Appearance very foul, being saturated and stained with red or purple Earth, washed into it I suppose from the banks on each Side of it. The Tide setts in at the rate of five Knotts. The Wind was directly fair, and We outsailed every Thing in going up the River. The Lands on each Side of Us and the Vessells in the River seemed to fly away from Us.

The Buildings public and private were of Stone: and a great number of pleasant Groves, appeared between the principal Seats and best plantations. The Vessells at Anchor and sailing in the River were very numerous. The Pleasure resulting to a Novice, from the Sight of Land, Houses, Cattle, after Three tremendous Storms and three equally tremendous Chases, one in the Gulph Stream, one in the English Channell and one in the Bay of Biscay, if it was ever experienced before I hope it never will be again, delicious as it was, by any human Being.

It gave me a pleasing kind of Melancholly Reverie, to see this Country and to look at a Part of Europe, as a few Weeks before[3] I had never expected to see this great Theatre of Arts, Sciences, Commerce and War.

March 31. Tuesday. 1778. Lying in the River, near Pouliac; a twenty four Gun Ship close by Us, under French Colours bound to Dominique. A dark misty morning. I was anxious to enquire, who was Agent for the United States of America at Bourdeaux, at Blaye &c., who were the principal Merchants on this River, concerned in the American Trade? What Vessells French or American had sailed, or were about sailing for America? What their Cargoes and for what Ports? Whether on Account of the United States, of any particular State, or of private Merchants French or American? But I could get no satisfactory Intelligence on any of these Subjects.

This Morning the Captain and a Passenger came on board The Boston from The Julie, a large Ship bound to Saint Domingo, to make Us a Visit. They invited Us on board to dine. Captain Palmes, Jesse Deane, John Quincy Adams and myself, went, and found a very pretty Ship, an elegant Cabin and every Accommodation. The white Stone plates were laid, a clean Napkin in each and a Cut of very fine Bread. The Cloth, Plates, Servants, all things were as neat as in any Gentlemans House. The first Dish was a French Soup. I had heard of Soup Meagre, which in America as well as in England had been Words of Contempt: but I thought if this was Soup meagre, it was a very respectable thing. Then a dish of boiled Beef, as I called it, having never heard the Word Bouillie. Then the Lights of a Calf dressed one Way and the Liver another. Then roasted Mutton. Then fricasseed Mutton. A good Sallad and something very like Asparagus, but not it. The Bread which had been baked on board was very fine. We had then Prunes, Almonds and the most delicious Raisins I ever saw; Dutch Cheese, then a Dish of Coffee, then a little glass of French Liqueur. Wine and Water and excellent Claret with our dinner. All these Appearances and provisions were luxuries to which We had been Strangers for many Weeks. None of our Hosts who entertained Us so hospitably understood English: None of Us French, except Dr. Noel who acted as Interpreter. The Conversation of the French Gentlemen among themselves was lively enough: but to the rest of Us it was a dull and silent Scæne.... On the Quarter deck I was struck with the Capons, Cocks and Hens in their Coops the largest I ever saw and the Number was as remarkable

[3] The passage in the Diary of this date which JA is paraphrasing reads: "a few Months ago."

33

as their Size and beauty. While at dinner We saw a Pinnace, with half a dozen genteel People, go on board the Boston. Mr. Griffin one of our Petty officers, came in the Pinnace, with Captain Tuckers Compliments desiring to see me. We took leave and returned to our Ship, where we found very polite Company consisting of the Captain of another Ship bound to Martinique, and several of the Kings Officers bound out. One was the Commandant of that Island.

March 31. Tuesday. 1778. Captain Palmes was sent to Blaye, in the Pinnace, to the Officer at the Castle, in order to produce our Commission, and procure an Entry and Pass to Bourdeaux. Palmes returned full of the Compliments of the Officer to the Captain and to me. I shall not repeat the Compliments to me. But the earnest request to Captain Tucker was that he would salute the Fort with thirteen Guns, which was accordingly done.

All the Gentlemen We have seen to day agree that the American Commissioners Franklin, Deane and Lee, had been received in great pomp by the King, that a Treaty had been concluded. And they all expected War every moment.

This afternoon We ascended this beautiful River, the Villages and Country Seats appearing on each Side of Us all the Way, to within three Leagues of the Town.

April 1. Wednesday. 1778. This Morning Mr. J. C. Champage,[4] Merchant and Broker of the Marine at Blaye, came on board to make a Visit and pay his Compliments. I learned from him that of the first Grouths of Wine, in the Province of Guienne, there are four Sorts of Grapes, bearing the names of Chateau Margeaux, Hautbrion, La Fritte[5] and Latour.

This Morning I took Leave of the Frigate Boston, and excepting a short Visit or two on board, before I satt out on my Journey to Paris never saw her afterwards. She was injudiciously ordered to Charleston to defend that City, which a dozen such Ships would not have been able to effect, and was taken by the English.[6] I went up to the City of Bourdeaux with my Son and Servant, Mr. Vernon, Mr. Jesse Deane who were all my Suite, and Dr. Noel as an Interpreter, in the Pinnace. When We came up to the Town We had the good Luck to see Mr. McCreery and Major Fraser, on the Wharf. McCrery I had known in America. It had happened that I had ridden a long Journey with him. He came on board our Boat and conducted Us up to his Lodg-

---

[4] Diary entry of this date reads: "Champagne."
[5] Diary entry of this date reads: "La Fitte."
[6] In May 1780; see Sheppard, *Tucker*, ch. 7.

ings, where We dined, in the fashion of the Country. Among many other Things We had fish, and Salad, and Claret, Champaign and Mountain Wines. After Dinner Mr. Bondfield, whom I had known also in America, and who was agent at this place, invited me to a Walk. We went first to his Lodgings where We drank Tea, and then walked around the Town and went to see the new Comedy, a most splendid Building erecting for the Amusement of the Town. After this We went to the Opera, where the Scenery, dancing and Music aforded to my Curiosity a chearful and sprightly entertainment, having never seen any Thing of the kind before. Our American Theatres had not then existed even in Contemplation.

After the Opera We returned to Mr. McCrerys Lodgings where We supped.

April 2 Thursday. Walked round the Town to see the Parliament which was sitting, where We heard but understood not the Counsel, then to see the Council and chamber of Commerce. Then We went round to the Ship Yards, made many Visits, dined at the Hotel D'Angleterre, visited the Custom house, the Post Office, the Chatteau Trompette a famous Fortification of Vaubans and its Commandant. Then visited the Premier President of the Parliament of Bourdeaux. Here I met a reception that was not only polite and respectfull but really tender and seemingly affectionate. He asked Permission to embrace me A la francaise. He said he had long felt for me an Affection resembling that of a Brother. He had pitied me and trembled for me, and was cordially rejoiced to see me. He could not avoid sympathizing with every sincere friend of Liberty in the World. He knew that I had gone through many dangers and Sufferings in the cause of Liberty, and had felt for me in them All. He had reason he said to feel for the Sufferers in the Cause of Liberty, because he had suffered many Years in that cause himself. He had been banished for cooperating with Mr. Malsherbs, and the other Courts and Parliaments of the Kingdom in the time of Louis the fifteenth, for their Remonstrances against the arbitrary Conduct and pernicious Edicts of the Court &c. He envied the Count de Viralade his Son the pleasure, that he intended himself by accompanying me that Evening to the Commedy. But the Parliament was sitting and the press of Business rendered it impossible. Otherwise he should certainly attend me himself. Mr. Bondfield had to interpret all this Effusion of Compliments and I thought it never would come to an End. But it did and I concluded upon the whole there was a fund of Sincerity in it decorated and almost suffocated with French Compliments. Then We went to the Coffee House, then to the Comedie where We saw the two Misers (Les deux Avares). After which We supped with Messieurs Reuilles [Reculès] De Basmarein and Raimbeaux. Here I expected nothing but a common Supper and a small Company; but found myself much disappointed. Among many others in a large Company of both Sexes, were the Count de Viralade, the eldest Son of the first President whom I had just visited. Le Moine, the first Commissary of the Navy, Le Moine his Son a Commissary of the Navy. Cornie a Captain in the Navy and a Knight of Saint Louis. John Baptiste Nairac, a Deputy of commerce from La Rochelle. Paul Nairac a Merchant. Elisee Nairac a Merchant. La Tour Feger a Merchant; Menoire a Merchant, Conturier[7] a Merchant, and many others with their Ladies; and Mr. Bondfield and Major Fraser. The Company their dresses, Equipages, and the furniture were splendid and the Supper very sumptuous. The Conversation at and after Supper was very gay, animated, chearfull and good humoured as it appeared to my Eyes and Ears and feelings but my Understanding had no Share in it. The Language was altogether incomprehensible. The Company were more attentive to me, then I desired; for they often addressed Observations and questions to me, which I could only understand by the Interpretation of Mr. Bond [Bondfield], and the returns of civility on my part could only be communicated [to] me through the same Channel, a kind of conviviality so tædious and irksome, that I had much rather have remained in silent Observation and Reflection. One Anecdote I will relate, because among many others I heard in Bourdeaux it was Characteristic of the manners at that time.[8] One of the most elegant Ladies at Table, young and handsome, tho married to a Gentleman in the Company, was pleased to Address her discourse to me. Mr. Bondfield must interpret the Speech which he did in these Words "Mr. Adams, by your Name I conclude you are descended from the first Man and Woman, and probably in your family may be preserved the tradition which may resolve a difficulty which I could never explain. I never could understand how the first Couple found out the Art of lying together?" Whether her phrase was L'Art de se coucher ensemble, or any other more energetic, I know not, but Mr. Bondfield rendered it by that I have mentioned. To me, whose Acquaintance with Women had been confined to America, where the manners of the Ladies were universally characterised at that time by

---

[7] Diary entry of 3 April 1778 reads: "Coutourier."

[8] The following anecdote and the reflections thereon, which are not in JA's Diary, were omitted by CFA in editing his combined text of the Diary and Autobiography.

Modesty, Delicacy and Dignity, this question was surprizing and shocking: but although I believe at first I blushed, I was determined not to be disconcerted. I thought it would be as well for once to set a brazen face against a brazen face and answer a fool according to her folly, and accordingly composing my countenance into an Ironical Gravity I answered her "Madame My Family resembles the first Couple both in the name and in their frailties so much that I have no doubt We are descended from that in Paradise. But the Subject was perfectly understood by Us, whether by tradition I could not tell: I rather thought it was by Instinct, for there was a Physical quality in Us resembling the Power of Electricity or of the Magnet, by which when a Pair approached within a striking distance they flew together like the Needle to the Pole or like two Objects in electric Experiments." When this Answer was explained to her, she replied "Well I know not how it was, but this I know it is a very happy Shock." I should have added "in a lawfull Way" after "a striking distance," but if I had her Ladyship and all the Company would only have thought it Pedantry and Bigottry. This is a decent Story in comparison with many which I heard in Bourdeaux, in the short time I remained there, concerning married Ladies of Fashion and reputation. The decided Advances made by married Women, which I heard related, gave rise to many reflections in my mind which may perhaps be detailed hereafter on some similar Occasions. The first was if such a[re] the manners of Women of Rank, Fashion and Reputation [in] France, they can never support a Republican Government nor be reconciled with it. We must therefore take great care not to import them into America.

In Compliment to America this Company introduced a List of Toasts in our fashion which was an entire novelty at Bourdeaux. They gave Mr. Bondfield a Copy which he translated for me into English. The Toasts were announced by thirteen Guns in honor of the thirteen States, for then We had no more. Then the King of France twenty one Guns. The Congress, thirteen. General Washington Three. Mr. De Sartine, three. General Gates three. Marshall Broglie Three. The Count De Broglie his Brother, three. The Marquis de La Fayette three. The Glory and Prosperity of the thirteen United States, Thirteen. The Prosperity of France three. Eternal Concord between the two Nations now Friends and Allies, three. The State of Massachusetts and its Representative Mr. Adams. Mr. D'Estaing Vice Admiral. The City of Bourdeaux. Mrs. Adams three. The French and American Ladies Twenty one. The Departure of Mr. Adams when he ascended his Coach, was saluted by thirteen Guns. The Garden was beautifully illuminated, with an Inscription God Save the Congress, Liberty and Adams.

Amidst all these dissipations I was not unmindfull of my Obligations of Gratitude for the Preservations from Dangers in the late Voyage, nor my destination and future Prospects and Employments. I began to indulge hopes possibly too sanguine, that I had been saved for some valuable End and some important purpose for my Country.

April 3. Fryday. 1778. We Visited the Intendant, dined at Mr. Bondfields and supped at Mr. Le Texiers, a Duch Merchant from Amsterdam, long settled in Trade at Bourdeaux.[9] He was an inquisitive sensible Man with some considerable Information. He professed a regard for America, but seemed to be perplexed with many doubts and difficulties. He could not see how it was possible We could contend successfully against the Power of Great Britain, so irresistable by Sea and Land, with Armies and Navies so brave, experienced and disciplined and assisted with such Alliances. I answered that The Americans had no doubt of their Abilities. Very few entertained any doubt, and I had none at all, that We could defend ourselves as long as England could maintain the Contest even without Assistance; but I had hopes We should obtain Friends and perhaps Allies as powerful as Great Britain. We had more Men than she could ever send to America with the Assistance of all her Hessian and Anspach Allies who sold her their Subjects like Cattle to [be] slaughtered in America for the humane purpose of butchering Us.

Mr. Le Texier I found had a regard for England too. He said that they in Holland had regarded England as the Bulwark of the Protestant Religion and the most important Weight in the Ballance of Power in Europe against France. I answered that I had been educated from my Cradle in the same Opinion and had read enough of the History of Europe to be still of the same Opinion. There would therefore be no difference of Opinion between Us on these Points. We in America however, were not sufficiently acquainted with this subject, to see that the failure or the Weakening of the Protestant Cause, or a revolution in the ballance of Power in Europe would be the necessary consequence of our Liberty or even of our Independence. This would depend altogether upon the Conduct of England And her friends in Europe. If they should drive Us against our inclinations into permanent and indissoluble connections with one Scale of the ballance of Power, that would be the fault of Britain and her Friends that would

---

[9] The following conversation, since it is not in the Diary, must have been written by JA wholly from memory. CFA omitted it in his text.

be a misfortune to Us, but not our fault. Our Plan was to have no Interest, Connection or Embarassment in the Politicks or Wars of Europe, if We could avoid it. But it ought not to be expected that We should tamely suffer Great Britain to tear up from the foundations all the Governments in America, and violate thirteen solemn and sacred Compacts under which a Wilderness had been subdued and culti-vated, and submit to the unlimited domination of Parliament who knew little more of Us than they did of Kamshatska and who cared not half so much for Us, as they did for their flocks and herds. The In-humanity too, with which they conducted the War, betrayed such a Contempt of Us [as][1] human Nature could not endure. Not only hir-ing European Mercenaries, but instigating Indians and corrupting Do-mesticks as if We were fit for nothing but to be cutt to Pieces by Savages and Negroes. Americans would not submit to these Things, merely from Prophecies and precarious Speculations about the Prot-estant Interest and the ballance of Power in Europe. This Conversa-tion was extended into a much wider field of discussion and was main-tained on both Sides with entire civility and good humour, till I took leave of Mr. Le Texier and retired to my Lodgings. Twenty months afterwards passing through Bourdeaux in my Journey from Ferrol to Paris, Mr. Le Texier called upon me again And I found was still embarrassed with the same Prejudices and Scruples. But as I had not time to enlarge I only said I was surprized to find him still think it possible that We should ever come under the Government of England again when the Affections of the People were entirely alienated from it and We had pledged our Faith to France to maintain our Inde-pendence, an Engagement that would be sacredly fullfilled.

During my Delay at Bourdeaux, Mr. McCrery informed me in Con-fidence, that he had lately come from Paris where he had been sorry to perceive a dryness between the American Ministers Franklin, Deane and Lee. Mr. McCrery was very cautious and prudent but he gave me fully to Understand that the animosity was very rancorous, and had divided all the Americans and all the french People connected with Americans or American Affairs into Parties very bitter against each other. This Information gave me much disquietude as it opened a pros-pect of perplexities to me that I supposed must be very disagreable. Mr. Lee, Mr. Izard, Dr. Bancroft and others whom Mr. McCrery named, were entire Strangers to me, but by reputation. With Dr. Franklin I had served one Year and more in Congress. Mr. Williams I had known in Boston. The French Gentlemen were altogether un-

[1] MS: "and."

known to me. I determined to be cautious and impartial, knowing however very well the difficulty and the danger of Acting an honest and upright Part in all such Situations.

April 4. Saturday. 1778. About ten O Clock We commenced our Journey to Paris and went about fifty miles. Mr. Vernon chose to remain at Bourdeaux.

April 5th. Sunday 1778. Proceeded on our Journey more than an hundred Miles.

April 6. Monday 1778. Arrived at Poictiers, the City so famous for the Battle which was fought here. It is a beautiful Situation, and the Cultivation of the plains about it, appeared to me exquisite. The Houses were old and poor and the Streets very narrow. In the afternoon passed through Chattellerault, another City nearly as large as Poictiers, and as old and the Streets as narrow. When We stopped at the Post, to change our Horses, about twenty young Women came about the Carriage with their elegant Knives, Scissors &c., to sell. The Scæne was new to me and highly diverting. Their Eagerness to sell a Knife, was as great as I had seen before and have seen since in other Countries to obtain Offices. We arrived in the Evening at Orms, the magnificent Seat of the Marquiss D'Argenson. It is needless to make particular remarks upon this Country. Every Part of it is cultivated. The Fields of Grain, the Vineyards, the Castles, the Cities, the Parks, the Gardens, must be seen to be known. Every Thing is beautiful, yet except the Parks there is a great Scarcity of Trees. A Country of Vinyards without Trees, has to me always an Appearance of poverty: and every place swarms with Beggars, the Reason of which I suppose is because the Poor depend upon private Charity for Support, instead of being provided for by Parishes as in England or Towns in America.

April 7. Tuesday 1778. We travelled from Les Ormes, the splendid Seat of the Marquis D'Argenson, to Mer. We passed through Tours, Amboise and several small Villages. Tours was the most elegant Place We had yet seen. It stands on the River Loire which passes through Na[n]tes to the Sea. We rode upon a Causey made in the River Loire, for many miles. The Meadows and River Banks were very beautifull.

April 8th. Wednesday 1778. We rode through Orleans, and arrived at Paris about nine O Clock. For thirty miles from Paris the Road was paved and the Scænes were delightfull.

On our Arrival at a certain Barrier We were stopped and searched and paid the Duties for about twenty five Bottles, of Wine which were left, of the generous present of Mr. Delap at Bourdeaux. We passed the Bridge over the River Seine, and went through the Louvre. The

Streets crouded with Carriages with a multitude of Servants in Liveries.

At Paris We went to several Hotells which were full; particularly the Hotel D'Artois, and the Hotel Bayonne. We were then advised to the Hotel de Valois, Rue de Richelieu, where We found Entertainment, but We could not have it, without taking all Chambers upon the Floor, which were four in number, very elegant and richly furnished, at the small price of two Crowns and an half a day without any thing to eat or drink. I took the Apartments only for two or three days, and sent for Provisions to the Cooks. Immediately on our Arrival We were called upon for our Names, as We had been at Mrs. Rives's at Bourdeaux. My little Son had sustained this long Journey of nearly five hundred miles, at the rate of an hundred miles a day, with the utmost firmness, as he did our fatiguing and dangerous Voyage.

April 9. Thursday. 1778. Though the City was very silent and still in the latter part of the night, the Bells, Carriages and Cries in the Street, were noisy enough in the morning.

Went in a Coach to Passy with Dr. Noel and my Son. [We visited] [2] Dr. Franklin with whom I had served the best part of two Years in Congress in great Harmony and Civility, and there had grown up between Us that kind of Friendship, which is commonly felt between two members of the same public Assembly, who meet each other every day not only in public deliberations, but at private Breakfasts, dinners and Suppers, and especially in secret confidential Consultations, and who always agreed in their Opinions and Sentiments of public affairs. This had been the History of my Acquaintance with Franklin and he received me accordingly with great apparent Cordiality. Mr. Deane was gone to Marseilles to embark with D'Estaing for America. Franklin undertook the care of Jesse Deane, as I suppose had been agreed between him and the Childs Father before his departure. And he was soon sent, with my Son and Dr. Franklins Grandson Benjamin Franklin Bache, whom as well as William Franklin [3] whom he called his Grandson, the Dr. had brought with him from America, to the Pension of Mr. Le Cœur at Passy.

Dr. Franklin presented to me the Compliments of Mr. Turgot the late Controuler of the Finances and a very pressing Invitation to dine with him. Though I was not very well accoutered to appear in such

[2] Editorially supplied. The sentence as written is deficient in grammar and sense.

[3] William Temple Franklin, customarily called Temple, natural son of Sir William Franklin, late royal governor of New Jersey.

Company I was persuaded and concluded to go. I went with Dr. Franklin and Mr. Lee, and dined with this Ex Minister. The Dutchess D'Anville, the Mother of the Duke de la Rochefoucault, and twenty others of the Great People of France were there. I thought it odd that the first Lady I should dine with in France should happen to be the Widow of our Great Ennemy who commanded a kind of Armada against Us, within my Memory:[4] but I was not the less pleased with her Conversation for that. She appeared to be venerable for her Years, and several of her Observations at Table, full as I thought of bold, masculine and original Sense were translated to me. The House, Gardens, Library, Furniture, and Entertainment of the Table, appeared very magnificent to me, who had yet seen but little of France, and nothing at all of any other part of Europe. Mr. Turgot had the Appearance and deportment of a grave, wise and amiable Man. I was very particularly examined by the Company through my Colleagues and Interpriters Franklin and Lee concerning American Affairs. I should have been much better pleased to have been permitted to remain less conspicuous: but I gave to all their Inquiries the most concise and clear Answer I could and came off, for the first time I thought, well enough. Returned and supped with Franklin on Cheese and Beer.

Dr. Franklin had shewn me the Apartements and Furniture left by Mr. Deane, which were every Way more elegant, than I desired, and comfortable and convenient as I could wish. Although Mr. Deane in Addition to these had a House, furniture and Equipage in Paris, I determined to put my Country to no further expence on my Account but to take my Lodgings under the same Roof with Dr. Franklin and to Use no other Equipage than his, if I could avoid it. This House was called the The Basse Court de Monsieur Le Ray de Chaumont, which was to be sure, not a Title of great Dignity for the Mansion of Ambassadors though they were no more than American Ambassadors. Nevertheless it had been nothing less than the famous Hotel de Vallentinois, with a Motto over the Door Si sta bene, non se move, which

---

[4] Marie Louise Nicole Elisabeth de La Rochefoucauld was the widow of Jean Baptiste Frédéric de La Rochefoucauld de Roye, Duc d'Anville, who in 1746 had led the ill-fated French expedition to recapture Louisbourg and had died of mortification, perhaps by his own hand, at what later became Halifax, N.S.; her son was Louis Alexandre, Duc de La Rochefoucauld d'Anville (often spelled Enville), a *philosophe*, correspondent of Franklin and JA, and friend of the American cause, who was stoned to death by a Revolutionary mob in 1792 (*Dict. de la noblesse; La Grande Encyclopédie*). JA may have borrowed from Thomas Hutchinson the term "Armada" for the Duc d'Anville's fleet, which had caused wild apprehensions in New England; see Hutchinson's *Massachusetts Bay*, ed. Mayo, 2:325–328; also p. 67, below.

I thought a good rule for my Conduct. If you stand well do not move; or stand still.

April 10. Fryday. 1778. The first moment Dr. Franklin and I happened to be alone, he began to complain to me of the Coolness as he very coolly called it, between the American Ministers. He said there had been disputes between Mr. Deane and Mr. Lee. That Mr. Lee was a Man of an anxious uneasy temper which made it disagreable to do business with him: that he seemed to be one of those Men of whom he had known many in his day, who went on through Life quarrelling with one Person or another till they commonly ended in the loss of their reason. He said Mr. Izard was there too, and joined in close friendship with Mr. Lee. That Mr. Izard was a Man of violent and ungoverned Passions. That each of these had a Number of Americans about him, who were always exciting disputes and propagating Stories that made the Service very disagreable. That Mr. Izard, who as I knew had been appointed a Minister to the Grand Duke of Tuscany, instead of going to Italy remained there with his Lady and Children at Paris, and instead of minding his own Business, and having nothing else to do he spent his time in consultations with Mr. Lee and in interfering with the Business of the Commission to this Court. That they had made strong Objections to the Treaty, and opposed several Articles of it. That neither Mr. Lee nor Mr. Izard were liked by the French. That Mr. William Lee his Brother, who had been appointed to the Court of Vienna, had been lingering in Germany and lost his Papers, that he called upon the Ministers at Paris for considerable Sums of Money, and by his Connection with Lee and Izard and their party, increased the Uneasiness &c. &c. &c.

I heard all this with inward Grief and external patience and Composure. I only answered, that I was personally much a Stranger to Mr. Izard and both the Lees. That I was extreamly sorry to hear of any misunderstanding among the Americans and especially among the public Ministers, that it would not become me to take any part in them. That I ought to think of nothing in such a Case, but Truth and Justice, and the means of harmonizing and composing all Parties: But that I foresaw I should have a difficult, dangerous and disagreable part to Act, but I must do my duty as well as I could.[5]

<hr/>

[5] The following several paragraphs, including the two inserted letters and the comment concerning the second, were originally written by JA on a separate sheet and keyed to their place in the MS by the letter "A." From this it would appear that the idea of adverting to his letterbooks and copying selections from them was an afterthought on his part. Farther on in Part Two of his Autobiography JA indulged in this practice very freely.

When Mr. Lee arrived at my Lodgings ⟨in the⟩ one Morning, it was proposed that a Letter should be written to Mr. Dumas at the Hague to inform him of my Arrival and my Colleagues proposed that I should write it. I thought it an awkward thing for me to write an Account of myself, and asked Dr. Franklin to write it, after We had considered and agreed upon what should be written, which I thought the more proper as he was the only one of Us who had been acquainted with Mr. Dumas. Accordingly on the tenth of May [April] the Letter was produced in these Words, which I insert at full Length because it was the only public Letter I believe which he wrote while I was with him, in that Commission.

Sir   Passi April 10 1778
We received duely your dispatch of the third instant, and approve very much the care and pains you constantly take, in sending Us, the best Intelligence of public[6] Affairs.... We have now the Pleasure of acquainting you that Mr. John Adams, a Member of Congress appointed to succeed Mr. Deane in this Commission, is safely arrived here. He came over, in the Boston, a Frigate of thirty Guns, belonging to the United States. In the passage they met and made prize of a large English Letter of Mark Ship of fourteen Guns, the Martha, bound to New York, on whose Cargo, seventy thousand pounds Sterling was insured in London. It contains Abundance of Necessaries for America, whither she is dispatched, and We hope will get well into one of our Ports.

Mr. Adams acquaints Us, that it had been moved in Congress, to send a Minister to Holland, but, that, although there was the best disposition towards that country, and desire to have and maintain a good Understanding with their High Mightinesses, and a free commerce with their Subjects, the measure was respectfully postponed

---

Letters inserted in Part Two have been treated editorially like those in Part One. They are printed as found in the MS of the Autobiography but have been carefully compared with the versions (in Lb/JA/4–6, Adams Papers, Microfilms, Reel Nos. 92–94) from which JA copied them; significant variations have been noted, but trifling differences in punctuation, &c., have been disregarded, and small copying mistakes have been silently corrected. Other MS versions (notably drafts and recipients' copies) have also been compared, when known to the editors, but no attempt has been made to record all known versions of every letter, only those of prime textual value. The reader may once again be reminded that the suspension points JA sprinkled through the letter copies in his Autobiography seldom represent actual omissions.

CFA printed a few of the inserted letters in their places in the Autobiography, some elsewhere in JA's *Works,* but most of them not at all, with or without references to texts elsewhere available in print.

[6] LbC: "foreign."

for the present, till their Sentiments on it, could be known, from an Apprehension that possibly their connections with England, might make the receiving an American Minister, as yet inconvenient, and, if Holland should have the same good Will towards Us, a little embarrassing.[7] Perhaps, as our Independency begins to wear the Appearance of greater Stability, since our acknowledged Alliance with France, that difficulty may be lessened. Of this We wish you would take the most prudent methods privately to inform yourself. It seems clearly to be the Interest of Holland, to share in the rapidly growing Commerce of this young Sister Republick, and, as in the Love of Liberty, and bravery in the defence of it, she has been our great Example, We hope Circumstances and Constitutions in many respects so similar, may produce mutual benevolence: and that the unfavourable impressions made on the minds of some in America, by the rigour, with which Supplies of Arms and Ammunition were refused them in their distress may soon be worn off and obliterated, by a friendly Intercourse and reciprocal good offices.

When Mr. Adams left America, which was about the middle of February, our Affairs were daily improving, our Troops well supplied with Arms and Provisions, and in good order, and the Army of General Buorgoine, being detained for Breaches of the Capitulation, We had in our hands, above ten thousand Prisoners of the Enemy. We are Sir your most obedient Servants.[8]

The within Letter to you is so written that you may shew it, on Occasion. We send inclosed a proposed draft of a Letter to the Grand Pensionary, but as We are unacquainted with forms, and may not exactly have hit your idea, with regard to the matter and expression,

[7] On 2 July 1777 Congress instructed the Committee on Foreign Affairs "to prepare a commission to one or more of the commissioners appointed to foreign Courts, to empower him or them to represent the Congress at the States General of the United ⟨States of Holland⟩ Provinces" (JCC, 8:523). The Committee reported next day, and Congress voted that "the form of the commission and instructions ... be the same as those given to the commissioners to the Courts of Vienna, Berlin and ... Tuscany"; but later that day Congress tabled the proposed commission and instructions (same, p. 527, 531).

[8] Here ends the letter proper as it was signed by Franklin and Lee. RC has not been found. Dft (DLC:Franklin Papers) has two attachments, both of which appear below: (1) an additional note to Dumas and a postscript (the latter being in Lee's hand), and (2) a draft of the proposed communication to the Grand Pensionary, in Franklin's hand but heavily corrected by him. A copy of RC is in the Koninklijk Huisarchief, The Hague, and is docketed at head of text: "Communiqué à S.A.S. Monseigneur le Prince par Mr. le Conseiller Pensionaire de Bleiswyk"; at foot of text appears the following: "Adres / à Monsr: / Monsr: Dumas, chez Madame La Veuve Loder. / à / La Haÿe." From all this it seems clear that Dumas called on Van Bleiswyck with the original and waited while a clerk copied it.

We wish you would consult with our Friend[9] upon it, and return it, with the necessary corrections.

P.S. The Letters you mention coming to you from England, are from Mr. William Lee and you will be so good as to forward them, with his name circumscribed and inclosed to Messieurs Frederic Goutard and Fils, Banquiers a Frankfort sur la Maine.
A. M. Dumas

The draft of a Letter to the Grand Pensionary was in these Words.

Sir   Paris April 10. 1778
We have the honor of acquainting your Excellency, that the United States of North America, being now an independent Power, and acknowledged as such by this Court, a Treaty of Amity and Commerce, is compleated between France and the said States, of which We shall speedily send your Excellency a Copy, to be communicated if you think proper, to their High Mightinesses, for whom the United States have the greatest respect and the strongest desire, that a good Understanding may be cultivated and a mutually beneficial commerce established, between the People of the two nations, which, as will be seen, there is nothing in the above mentioned Treaty to prevent or impede. We have the Honor to be, with great respect, your Excellencys &c.[1]

I thought it most proper that this Letter should be signed by Mr. Franklin and Lee but as they insisted upon it, We all signed it.

It so happened or had been so contrived, that We Were invited to dine at Monsieur Brillons, a Family in which Mr. Franklin was very

[9] Doubtless the Duc de La Vauguyon (1746–1828), French ambassador to the Dutch Republic, 1776–1783, with whom JA was later to have a close and interesting diplomatic relationship during his own mission to the Netherlands (Hoefer, *Nouv. Biog. Générale*; JA, Diary, entry of July 1781, note 1).
[1] In Dft (see above, p. 45, note 8) the addressee is indicated at foot of text, by title only: "Grand Pensionnaire." The grand pensionary of Holland was Pieter van Bleiswyck, though versions of the present draft have been mistakenly catalogued and printed as if addressed to E. F. van Berckel, who was first pensionary of Amsterdam. The long and frequent letters of C. W. F. Dumas during April and May 1778 (in the Rijksar-chief, The Hague, Dumas Papers, I; microfilm in DLC:Dutch Reproductions) recite in great detail what was done concerning the draft. It was approved by La Vauguyon in the language proposed, but it had to be sent back to Paris, signed, and returned, and then La Vauguyon had second thoughts, doubtless prompted by Vergennes, that prevented its being delivered until 14 May, when Dumas presented it, with due ceremony, to Van Bleiswyck. For a running account of these events and of the complexities of Franco-Dutch-American relations at this time, see F. P. Renaut, *Les Provinces-Unies et la guerre d'Amérique* (1775–1784), Paris, 1924–1925, 5:129–134.

intimate, and in which he spent much of his Time. Here We met a large Company of both Sexes and among them were Monsieur Le Vailliant[2] and his Lady. Madam Brillion was one of the most beautifull Women in France, a great Mistress of Musick, as were her two little Daughters. The Dinner was Luxury, as usual in that Country. A large Cake was brought in with three flaggs flying. On one of them "Pride subdued": on another "Hæc dies, in qua fit Congressus, exultemus et potemus in eâ." Mr. Brillon was a rough kind of Country Squire. His Lady all softness, sweetness and politeness. I saw a Woman in Company, as a Companion of Madam Brillon who dined with her at Table, and was considered as one of the Family. She was very plain and clumzy. When I afterwards learned both from Dr. Franklin and his Grandson, and from many other Persons, that this Woman was the Amie of Mr. Brillion and that Madam Brillion consoled herself by the Amitie of Mr. Le Vailliant, I was astonished that these People could live together in such apparent Friendship and indeed without cutting each others throats. But I did not know the World. I soon saw and heard so much of these Things in other Families and among allmost all the great People of the Kingdom that I found it was a thing of course. It was universally understood and Nobody lost any reputation by it. Yet I must say that I never knew an Instance of it, without perceiving that all their Complaisancy was external and ostensible only: a mere conformity to the fashion: and that internally there was so far from being any real friendship or conjugal Affection that their minds and hearts were full of Jealousy, Envy, revenge and rancour. In short that it was deadly poison to all the calm felicity of Life. There were none of the delightful Enjoyments of conscious Innocence and mutual Confidence. It was mere brutal pleasure.

At Mr. Chaumonts in the Evening where We were invited to Supper, Two Gentlemen came in and advised me to go to Versailles, the next day. One of them was the Secretary of the Count de Noailles, the late French Ambassador in London. This Gentleman informed me that the Count De Vergennes had expressed to him his Surprize that I had not been to Court. They had been informed by the Police of my Arrival in Paris and had accidentally heard of my dining in Company at one place and another, but when any question was asked them concerning me, they could give no Answer. He supposed I was waiting to

[2] Possibly JA meant Louis Guillaume Le Veillard, who conducted the mineral baths in Passy and was a member of Franklin's intimate circle; but in the present passage JA was trusting heavily to a memory often faulty in these matters.

get me a french Coat, but he should be glad to see me in my American Coat.

April 11. Saturday 1778. Went to Versailles with Dr. Franklin and Mr. Lee, visited the Secretary of State for foreign Affairs, the Count de Vergennes and was politely received. He hoped I should stay long enough in France, to acquire the French Language perfectly.... Assured me that every Thing should be done to make France agreable to me. Hoped the Treaty would be agreable, and the Alliance lasting. Although the Treaty had gone somewhat farther than the System I had always advocated in Congress and further than my Judgment could yet perfectly approve, it was now too late to make any Objections, and I answered that I thought the Treaty liberal and generous, as indeed it was upon the whole, and that I doubted not of its speedy ratification. I communicated to him the resolution of Congress respecting the Suspension of Burgoins embarkation, which he read through and pronounced "Fort bon." We were then conducted to the Count Maurepas, the Prime Minister or the Kings Mentor, as he was often called. I was presented to him by Dr. Franklin as his New Colleague, and again politely received. This Gentleman was near fourscore Years of Age, with a fresh rosy Countenance, and apparently in better health and greater Vigour than Dr. Franklin himself. He had been dismissed from Office and exiled to his Lands by Lewis the fifteenth in 1748 and in his retirement if not before had obtained the Reputation of a Patriot, for which reason he had been recalled to Court by Lewis 16th, and placed at the head of Affairs.

I was then shewn the ⟨Pallace⟩ Castle of Versailles, and We happened to be present when the King passed through the Apartments to Council. His Majesty seeing my Colleagues, smiled and passed on. I was then shewn the Gallery, the Royal Appartments and the Kings Bed Chamber. The Magnificence of these Scænes, the Statues, the Paintings, the furniture, it may easily be supposed appeared to me sublime, or as the French more commonly phrase it, superb. We then returned to Passy, went into the City and dined with the Count where was the Count de Noailles, his Secretary and twenty or thirty others of the Grandees of France. After Dinner We went to see the Royal Hospital of Invalids, the Chapell of which was enriched and adorned with every Thing that most costly marble, and all the Arts of Architecture, Statuary and painting could at that time furnish in France. It was a monument of the Jealousy of Lewis the fourteenth, to emulate the Glory of Saint Pauls Church in London. After this We went a L'Ecole militaire, to the military School, went into the Chapell and Hall of Council. Here We saw the Statues of Conde, Turenne, Luxembourg and Saxe. Returned to Passy and drank Tea with Madam Brillion, who entertained Us again with her Musick and agreable conversation. She recommended to me Voyage Picturesque de Paris and lent me the Book.

Although my Ignorance of the Language was very inconvenient and humiliating to me, yet I thought the Attentions which had been shewn me from my first landing at Bourdeaux by the People in Authority of all ranks, and by the principal Merchants, and since my Arrival at the Capital by the Ministers of State and others of the first consideration, had been very remarkable and portended much good to our Country. They manifested as I thought, in what estimation the new Alliance with America was held.

April 12. Sunday. In the Course of the last Week, particularly on fryday, I was visited by a Number of American Gentlemen. Sir James Jay of New York, Brother of the then Chief Justice, who has since been President of Congress, Governor of the State, Ambassador abroad and Chief Justice of the United States, but is now in 1806 like so many others of our first and best Men in the Post of honor a private Station.... Mr. Joshua Johnson of Maryland Brother of my Friend Thomas Johnson, in some former Years Member of Congress with me, and at that time Governor of Maryland. Mr. Ralph Izzard of South Carolina, Dr. Bancroft, Mr. Livingston from Jamaica, Mr. Jonathan Loring Austin from Boston, Mr. Amiel from Boston. Mr. Johnson had been established in London in a lucrative Trade but finding a War approaching, and coinciding with his native Country in Principle and sympathizing in her feelings he had come over with his Family, that is his Wife and a Number of small Children, to France in his Way to America. He removed in a few days to Nantes, where finding some Encouragements in Commerce, and dreading the difficulties and dangers of a Voyage to America with a young family he remained during the War. One of his Children was destined to be my daughter.[3] Sir James Jay embarked soon for America but returned in a year or two to Europe, went to Holland and came again to Paris. Mr. Austin I received as my private Secretary. Congress had entrusted their Ministers with a few blank Commissions in the Navy: and We soon appointed Mr. Livingston and Mr. Amiel Lieutenants. Livingston served some time under Captain Tucker and Amiel under Captain Jones. I am not certain whether Dr. Smith was among these. But such a

[3] Daughter-in-law. Louisa Catherine Johnson married JQA in London, 26 July 1797.

Person came over to France with his Wife about that time and gave Dr. Franklin a great deal of Vexation, Mr. Lee not a little, to me he was always complaisant. Yet in 1800 he furnished Mr. Wood in New York with a part of the Billingsgate which composed his History of my Administration. Smith said he was honourably descended, his Father having been a Councillor in the Province of New York as his Brother William has also been. I am sorry that I shall be obliged to say something more of this Man hereafter.[4]

On this day April 12. Sunday I had the honor to dine with the Prince de Tingry Duke de Beaumont, one of the four Captains of the Kings Guards at Versailles. He was of the illustrious House of Montmorency and with a large Company of Dukes and Dutchesses, in all the Pomp and Splendor of France. By this time, I began to catch the Sense, now and then of the Conversation in Society, but very imperfectly. A Conversation between the Prince de Tingry and My Colleagues I understood so well as to perceive that he was harranguing upon Tolleration and Liberty of Conscience. With an Air of great Condescention and Self complacency for his great Liberality, he vouched safe to acknowledge that although he should ardently desire the Conversion of all Protestants to the Catholick Religion yet he would not persecute them &c. Under a Picture of Sir Robert Walpole, was written

> Edisti satis, lusisti satis, atque bibisti
> Tempus est abire tibi.

Some one made an Amendment of bribisti instead of bibisti.

Monday April 13. 1778. This morning the Dutchess Dayen and her Daughter the Marchioness de La Fayette came to Passy to visit me, and enquire after the Marquis.

This Morning Dr. Franklin, Mr. Lee and myself met in my Chamber and signed and sent the following Letters which I had written and had copied for Signature, in Answer to Letters received.

Mr. John Ross
Sir   Passi April 13. 1778
The Papers you mention are in the disposition of Mr. William Lee, who is gone to Germany. It is therefore not in our Power to comply with what you desire. Neither are We able to make you any further Advances. We wish you would send Us, with all convenient expedi-

---

[4] On Dr. James Smith see JA's Diary entry of 13 May 1778 and note; also the entries of 21 April and 9 May in the Autobiography, below.

tion, Copies of the Invoices and Bills of Loading, for those goods which were paid for, with the money, We formerly furnished You. We do not think it, within our Province, to make an entire Settlement with you. The Money in Mr. Sweighausers hands, which you say is under the direction and order of Mr. R. Morris, ought to be disposed of according to those orders. The Trade being now free from this country, it seems improper to Us, to give the passports you ask. We are Sir, your most obedient Servants.

B. Franklin, Arthur Lee, John Adams.

P.S. Mr. Wm. Lee is at Frankfort, where a Letter from you will possibly find him: but his stay there is very uncertain.

J. Williams Esqr.
Sir   Passi 13. April 1778.

We are sorry to inform you that the State of our Funds admits of no farther expenditure, without danger of bringing Us into great difficulties. It is therefore our desire, that you abstain from any farther purchases, and close your Accounts for the present, with as little expence as possible. We also desire to be informed, when the repair of the Arms is likely to be compleated. You judge right in not paying the Twenty Eight Louis, where there is the least Appearance of Trick, for that would encourage a thousand more. Enclosed you have a Copy of Merciers Agreement.[5] We have not yet been able to discover, that Mr. Deane has left among the Papers, any Agreement, with Mr. Monthieu, by which We can settle the difference you mention. Perhaps Mr. Monthieu may have it. We wish to avoid disputes, confusion and expence. We may now expect many American Vessells will come into the French Ports: We hope you may get them to take the Remainder of the Goods already bought on public Account, upon Freight, as is done at Bilbao. We are, Sir, your most obedient humble Servants.

Benjamin Franklin, Arthur Lee, John Adams.

John Bondfield Esqr.
Sir   Passi April 13 1778.

We thank you for the Civility of your favour of the 30th. Ulto.[6] and shall be obliged to you, for the earliest communication of any interest-

---

[5] Not recorded in JA's letterbook. Perhaps the agreement between the American Commissioners and one Mercier, 30 May 1777, for repairing arms, entered in *Cal. Franklin Papers, A.P.S.,* 3:504.

[6] From Bordeaux, 30 March 1778, to the American Commissioners, acknowledging his appointment as commercial agent for Congress at the ports of Bordeaux, Bayonne, Rochefort, and La Rochelle (PPAmP).

ing News that may reach your Port. We have the honor to be Sir, your most obedient humble Servants

Benjamin Franklin, Arthur Lee, John Adams.

John P. Merkle Esqr.

Sir   Passi April 13. 1778.

We have done by our Friends at Amsterdam, who have followed our Orders, every thing that We thought incumbent on Us to do relative to your Affairs, and We do not incline to have any farther concern with them. We are Sir, your most obedient Servants

B. Franklin, John Adams.[7]

I have inserted these Letters, apparently of little importance, not only because they were some of our first Essays in Business, but because these Transactions began to let me into the Secret of the disputes and Animosities among the Americans in general in France and especially between my Colleagues. Mr. Lee had as yet said nothing to me concerning these Controversies. I was informed afterwards by others that he had said he would be silent on this Subject and leave me to learn by experience the State and course of the public Business and judge for myself whether it had been or was likely to be done right or wrong.

Mr William Lee who had been a Merchant in London and I believe an Alderman had been appointed by Congress their Commercial Agent and a General Superintendant of all their Commercial affairs. Congress was our Sovereign Lawgiver, Prince and Judge, and therefore whatever was done by their express Authority, We, as I believed ought to respect and obey. Mr. William Lee had appointed Mr. Schweighauser commercial Agent for the United States, under him, and Mr. Schweighauser was a very solid Merchant highly esteemed by every body and highly approved by the Court. Mr. Jonathan Williams a relation of Dr. Franklin, whom I had known in Boston as well [as] his father, Unkle and Cousin who was a Clerk in my Office, I had the best disposition to favour as far as the public Service and my own Sense of propriety would permit. Dr. Franklin and Mr. Deane had employed him in transactions which appeared to me to be commercial and in this had differed with Mr. Arthur Lee and interfered with the

---

[7] Mercklé replied in a letter to JA from Amsterdam, 27 April (Adams Papers), detailing his efforts to procure arms for shipment to America via Dutch West Indies ports. He had evidently been one of Silas Deane's numerous agents, and the Lee brothers accordingly thought him contemptible; see *Deane Papers*, index, under his name.

Province of Mr. William Lee. I therefore united with Mr. Lee in this and many subsequent proceeding[s] requiring the Settlement of Mr. Williams's Accounts. Dr. Franklin finding that two of Us were agreed in Opinion, subscribed the Letter with Us.

Mr. Ross was neither appointed by Congress, by the public Ministers in France nor by Mr. William Lee, but I suppose was connected in Trade with Mr. Robert Morris, and might have orders from him to purchase Arms or Cloathing or other Articles for public Use, as Mr. Morris was then Chairman of the Commercial Committee of Congress and sometime after appointed Financier. Mr. Ross expected Us to advance him Money to pay for his Purchases and yet did not think him responsible to Us or obliged to send Us his Accounts, Vouchers or even his Powers or Orders. Whatever Mr. Deane or Dr. Franklin had done, before my Arrival, I thought this proceedure more irregular, more inconsistent with the Arrangement of Congress, and every Way more unjustifiable than even the Case of Mr. Williams. Mr. Arthur Lees Opinion and mine were perfectly in Unison upon this point, which Dr. Franklin perceiving, united with Us in subscribing the Letter. But these were grievous disappointments to Mr. Williams and Mr. Ross and all their Friends and consequently occasioned grumblings against Mr. Lee and Mr. Adams.

Merkle was a Dutchman and another Adventurer, who applied to Us for Assistance, without any fair Claim to it. Whether he had been employed by Mr. Morris or Congress to purchase any thing I know not. But We were not informed of any Authority he had to require Money of Us, and he was accordingly soon answered.

Mr. Monthieu had been very confidentially connected with Mr. Deane. The famous Contract for old Arms, so injurious to the United States and so dishonourable to all who had any part in it, had been made with Monthieu who was an humble friend of Mr. De Sartine. The Settlement of his Affairs became very troublesome to Us. I made a strict Enquiry of Dr. Franklin, Mr. Lee and others for the Books of Accounts, the Letter Books, the Letters received, the Copies of Letters sent, but no body knew of any. Mr. Lee said there had been no regular Accounts, nor any Letter Book. All agreed that Mr. Deane had done the Business, that he consulted Dr. Franklin only when he pleased, and Mr. Lee rarely if ever. And that all Accounts if any had been kept and all Letters, if any had been written, were carried off, or concealed by him.

Mr. Beaumarchais was another of Mr. Deanes confidential Friends. This Mans Character as a Writer of Dramas and Memoirs is public enough. His Intrigues as develloped by himself in some of his Writings are curious enough. There is one fact which came to my Knowledge which may be thought of more importance. The confidential Friend of Mr. Beaumarchais at Court was the Queens Treasurer. I was afterwards very formally introduced to him as a Personage of great Power and respectability, and with great solemnity informed that he was the Treasurer to the Queen and the intimate Friend of Mr. Beaumarchais.

Mr. Holker [was] the Father of the Mr. Holker who came to America with Mr. Deane, at the same time with Mr. Gerard and who passed in America for a Person of great Consequence, and as Consul General of France. The Holkers, Father and Son, were very intimate Friends of Mr. Deane, but neither had any appointment from King or Minister. Mr. Le Ray de Chaumont was their Patron, and their Occupation wholly as Merchants or rather as Manufacturers chiefly of Cotton, either in Partnership with Mr. Chaumont, or wholly under his direction.[8] Holker the Father often came to see me. And repeatedly related to me his History. He said he owed his ruin to his Grandfather, who as well as his Father was an Inhabitant of Manchester, and a Manufacturer there. Being in the Neighbourhood of Scotland, Manchester was greatly disaffected to the House of Hanover and his Grandfather a furious Jacobite. His grandfather was very fond of him and not less delighted with Porter and strong Beer, with which he regularly got drunk every night. When he began to grow mellow, it was his practice to take his Grandson then a little boy upon his Knee, and his Loyalty to the Steuarts glowing as the liquor inflamed him, he made the Child swear to stand by the Royal House of Stewart as long as he should live. Such was his love and veneration for his Grandfather,

---

[8] The remainder of the present paragraph was omitted by CFA in his edition. JA's remembered account of the Holker family appears to be in the main correct, though the incident of the attempted kidnapping of the Duke of Cumberland has not been and perhaps could not be verified. The elder John (or Jean) Holker, originally from Lancashire and a Jacobite, had been established since 1749 as a cloth manufacturer at Rouen, held the post of "Inspecteur Général des Manufactures du Royaume," and was on intimate terms with Le Ray de Chaumont. His son Jean (or John) was sent to America late in 1777 on a confidential mission for the French government; he held an appointment as "agent of the marine of France" and became the first French consul, later consul general, appointed under the Treaty of 1778; in 1781 he resigned to devote himself wholly to finance and land speculation in America. The younger Holker's extensive papers are in the Library of Congress. See André Rémond, *John Holker, manufacturier et grand fonctionnaire en France au XVIIIme siècle, 1719–1786*, Paris, 1946; Gérard, *Despatches and Instructions*, p. 131, note, and *passim*; Kathryn Sullivan, *Maryland and France, 1774–1789*, Phila., 1936, p. 46–47, 58–64; Howard C. Rice Jr., "News from the Ohio Valley . . . ," Hist. and Philos. Soc. of Ohio, *Bull.*, 16:267–292 (Oct. 1958).

that these Oaths thus imposed upon him every evening, although young as he was he knew the old Gentleman to be drunk, made such an impression upon him that he could not help joining in the Rebellion of the Year 1745 in favour of the Pretender. After their defeat by the Duke of Cumberland at Culloden he fled to London and concealed himself as it happened somewhere in the Neighbourhood of Kitty Fisher,[9] who was visited almost every Night by the Duke after his Return from Scotland. Kitty lived very near the Waters Edge, and he had laid a Scheme to seize upon the Duke when in the Arms of his Mistress and hurry him on board a Vessell to carry him directly to France. He had got his Vessel and his Men and every thing prepared, when he found he had been discovered and was obliged to fly to France without his Royal Prisoner. Here he found himself destitute and had subsisted by his Skill in the Manufactures of Manchester some of which he had endeavoured to introduce and establish in this Kingdom. He regretted his Error and his Folly as he always called it, but it was irretrievable. He had formerly endeavoured to obtain a Pardon, but so daring an Attempt upon the Liberty if not the Life of the Duke could not then be pardoned. Perhaps it might now but it was too late. He was too old and had become too much connected in France. The most important of his Connections however, were I believe those with Mr. Chaumont which were of little profit, and one with a French Wife, an old wrinkled Woman, the most biggoted superstitious Catholic in France always counting her Beads and saying her Pater Noster and believing her Salvation to depend upon them. Justice however requires that it should be acknowledged that he always spoke of her with respect and treated her with tenderness. She was possessed of some property, perhaps enough to subsist herself and him. Whether he was concerned with Mr. Chaumont in any Shipments of Merchandize to America particularly to Mr. Langdon of Portsmouth, upon Mr. Deanes recommendation, I know not. That Mr. Chaumont shipped Goods to a considerable Amount, I knew because he shewed me Mr. Langdons Account rendered, in which almost the whole Capital was sunk by the depreciation of Paper Money.

Holkers Conduct to me was always civil, respectful, social, frank and agreable, and as he spoke English so well and french so tolerably I was always glad to see him and converse with him. But he was al-

[9] Catherine Maria Fisher (d. 1767), a courtesan celebrated enough to have been several times painted by Sir Joshua Reynolds, memorialized in the *Dictionary of National Biography*, and written up in exhaustive detail by Horace Bleackley in *Ladies Fair and Frail*, London, 1909, p. 51-97.

ways making Apologies for Mr. Deane, and it was easy to see that he regretted very much the loss of his Friend, by whom he had expected to make his fortune, and although he had no other Objection to me, he found that I was not the Man for his Purpose.

Dr. Franklin, Mr. Lee and myself went to Versailles,[1] were introduced to the Levee of Mr. De Sartine, a vast number of Gentlemen were Attending, in one room after another, and We found the Minister at last, entrenched as deep as We had on a former day seen the Count de Maurepas. The Minister of the Marine, received Us very politely, and shewed Us into his Cabinet, where were all the Books and Papers of his Office. After he had finished the Business of his Levee, he came into the Cabinet to Us, and asked whether I spoke French, and whether I understood French? I should have answered malheureusement (miserably), or point du tout (not at all), but Mr. Franklin answered Un Peu, si l'on parle lentement et doucement (a little if one speaks slowly or moderately).[2] —He then made an Apology to each of Us, seperately in the name of his Lady, for her Absence, being gone into Paris to visit a sick relation. We were soon conducted down to dinner, which appeared [to] me as splendid as any I had seen, all Elegance and Magnificence. The Company of Gentlemen was numerous, and only four Ladies. During the dinner many other Gentlemen came in who I suppose had dined elsewhere, walked the room, leaned over the Chairs of the Ladies and Gentlemen at Table and conversed with them. After dinner the Company all arose as was usual in France, and went into another room, where a great Additional Number of Gentlemen came in. After some time We retired and went to make a Visit to Madam De Maurepas, the Lady of the prime Minister. The Countess was not at home, and Count Laurigais, who had conducted Us to her Apartments, wrote our Card for Us in the Porters Book "Messrs. Franklin, Lee and Adams, pour avoir l'honneur de voir (to have the honor to see) Madame De Maurepas." This I believe was the only time that I saw Laurigais. He spoke our Language so well, and seemed to have so much information that I wished for more Acquaintance with him: but finding that he was not a favourite at court and especially with those Ministers who had the principal management of our American Affairs, and hearing from Dr. Franklin and Dr. Bancroft that Mr. Lee and Mr. Izzard had given Offence by too much familiarity with him,

---

[1] On 13 April—for here JA has reverted to his Diary record after inserting, on separate sheets, the preceding letters and recollections.

[2] The words that are here placed (by the editors) in parentheses appear in the MS above their French equivalents.

I declined any farther Enquiry concerning him. And I never heard that those Gentlemen had any intercourse with him, after that time.[3]

We then proceeded to the Office of Mr. Rayneval, the first Secretary of Mr. De Vergennes and presented a Copy of my Commission. We then made a Visit to Madam De Vergennes and returned to Passi. My Commission, a Copy of which I presented to Mr. Rayneval, for the Count de Vergennes is in these Words

The Delegates of the United States of New Hampshire, Massachusetts Bay, Rhode Island and Providence Plantations, Connecticutt, New York, New Jersey, Pensylvania, Delaware, Maryland, Virginia, North Carolina, South Carolina and Georgia, to all who shall see these presents, send Greeting.

Wheras a Trade upon equal terms, between the Subjects of his most Christian Majesty, the King of France, and the People of these States, will be beneficial to both Nations, Know Ye, therefore, that We confiding in the Prudence and Integrity of Benjamin Franklin, one of the Delegates in Congress from the State of Pensylvania, Arthur Lee Esquire of Virginia, and John Adams, one of the Delegates, in Congress, have appointed and deputed, and by these presents do appoint and depute, them the said Benjamin Franklin, Arthur Lee and John Adams, our Commissioners, giving and granting to them, the said Benjamin Franklin, Arthur Lee and John Adams, or to any two of them, and in case of the death, absence or disability of any two, to any one of them, Full Power to communicate, treat, agree, and conclude, with his Most Christian Majesty, the King of France, or with such person or Persons, as shall by him be for that purpose authorised, of and upon a true and sincere friendship, and a firm, inviolable and universal Peace, for the defence, protection and Safety of the Navigation and mutual commerce of the Subjects of his Most Christian Majesty, and the People of the United States, and also to enter into and agree upon a Treaty with his Most Christian Majesty, or such Person or Persons as shall be by him authorised for such purpose, for Assistance in carrying on the present War between Great Britain and these United States, and to do all other Things which may conduce to those desirable Ends, and promising in good faith to ratify whatsoever our said Commissioners shall transact in the Premisses.

Done in Congress at York Town, this twenty seventh day of Novem-

[3] The Comte de Lauraguais, also known as Duc de Brancas, was a prolific author, wit, and patron of letters and the theater; he had known Arthur Lee in London and was consequently distrusted by Silas Deane and his friends. See Hoefer, *Nouv. Biog. Générale; Deane Papers,* 1:201; 2:402; 3:38–39.

ber, in the Year of our Lord, one thousand, seven hundred and seventy seven.

In Testimony whereof, the President, by Order of the said Congress, hath hereunto subscribed his Name and affixed his Seal.

Henry Laurens, and a Seal

Attest   Charles Thomson Secy.

On the Morning of this day, before I went to Versailles, I sent for Mr. Le Cœur, the Master of the Pension, or Accademy in Passi, who after shewing me his Conditions, agreed to take my Son, who accordingly packed up his Things, and went to the School, much pleased with his prospect, because he understood that rewards were given to the best Schollers, which he said was an Encouragement. Drawing, Fencing, Dancing and Musick, were taught at that Accademy as well as writing and Greek and Latin.

April 14. Tuesday 1778. I returned the Visits which had been made me by the American Gentlemen. This I found was an indispensable Punctilio, with my Countrymen in France. Great Offence had been taken by some of them, because Dr. Franklin had not very exactly performed this important Ettiquette, especially by those of them who had come over to Paris from England.

April 15. Wednesday. 1778. Dined with Madam Helvetius. One Gentleman and one Lady, besides Dr. Franklin, his Grandson and myself, made the Company. An elegant Dinner. This was a Lady of established Reputation also: The Widow of the famous Helvetius, who, as Count Sarsefield once said to me, if he had made a few millions of Livres the more as one of the Farmers General, and written a few Books the less as a Philosopher it might have been better for France and the World. She has erected a Monument to her Husband, a Model of which She has in her House. It is a Statue of herself, weeping over his Tomb with this Inscription.

> Toi dont l'ame sublime et tendre
> A fait ma gloire, et mon bonheur
> Je t'ai perdu: pres de ta cendre,
> Je viens jouer de ma douleur.

That She might not be, however, entirely without the Society of Gentlemen, there were three or four, handsome Abby's who daily visited the House and one at least resided there. These Ecclesiasticks, one or more of whom reside in allmost every Family of Distinction, I suppose have as much power to Pardon a Sin as they have to commit one, or to assist in committing one. Oh Mores! said I to myself. What Absurdities, Inconsistencies, Distractions and Horrors would these Manners introduce into our Republican Governments in America: No kind of Republican Government can ever exist with such national manners as these. Cavete Americani.

Here I saw a little Book of Fenelons, which I had never met before, "Directions for the Conscience of a King, composed for the Instruction of Louis of France, Duke of Burgundy."

We had here Grapes at this Season of the Year as fresh as if taken off the Vines. I asked how they were preserved. She said, "Sans Air." That is, the Air was exhausted by an Air Pump, from the Vessells in which they were kept, and excluded till they were wanted for Use. Apples, Pears and other fruits are preserved here in great perfection in the same Way.

April 16. Thursday 1778. From my first Arrival in France I had employed every moment of my time, when Business and Company would permit, in the Study of the French Language. I had not engaged any Master and determined to engage none. I thought he would break in upon my hours in the necessary division of my time, between Business, and Study and Visits, and might often embarrass me. I had other reasons too, but none were sufficient to justify me. It was an egregious Error and I have seen cause enough to regret it. In Stead of a Master I determined to obtain the best Advice of those who were Masters of the Language, and purchase the Books in which it was taught upon Principle. Two Abbys, De Chalut and Arnoux, the former a Brother of the Farmer General of that name, and himself a Knight of Malta, as well as of the Order of Saint Louis, and both of them learned Men, came early to visit me. They had a House in the City and another in the Country at Passi, in our Neighbourhood, where they resided in Summer. Whether they were Spies of the Court or not I know not. But I should have no Objection to such Spies for they were always my friends, always instructive, and agreable in conversation. They were upon so good terms however with the Courtiers that if they had seen any thing in my Conduct or heard any thing in my Conversation that was dangerous or very exceptionable, I doubt not they would have thought it their duty to give Information of it. They were totally destitute of the English language, but by one means and another They found a Way of making me understand them, and sometimes by calling an interpreter and sometimes by gibbering something like French I made them understand me. Dr. Franklin was reported to speak french very well, but I found upon attending critically to him that he did not speak it, grammatically, and upon my asking him sometimes whether a Phrase he had used was correct, he acknowledged to me, that he was wholly inattentive to the grammar. His pronunciation too, upon which the French Gentlemen and Ladies complemented him very highly and which he seemed to think pretty well, I soon found was very inaccurate, and some Gentlemen of high rank afterwards candidly told me that it was so confused, that it was scarcely possible to understand him. Indeed his Knowledge of French, at least his faculty of speaking it, may be said to have commenced with his Embassy to France. He told me that when he was in France some Years before, Sir John Pringle was with him, and did all his conversation for him, as his Interpreter, and that he understood and spoke French, with great difficulty, untill his present Residence, although he read it.

Finding that I should derive little advantage from Dr. Franklin in acquiring French, I determined to go to the fountain head, and I asked The Abbys Chalut and Arnoux, what Books they would recommend to me, as the best for teaching their Language upon Principle? They appeared to be much pleased with this question, and immediately named the true Principles of the French Tongue, and the French Synonimous Words of the Abby Gerard, The Dictionary of the Rules of the French Tongue in two Volumes, and The Dictionary of the Accademy. This they said was undoubtedly the most correct as an Authority, but there were other and larger Works such as the Dictionary of Richeley in three Volumes and the Dictionary of Trevoux in Eight Volumes in folio. I asked further what Writings were esteemed the best models. They said Pascalls provincial Letters, Madam de Sevinnes Letters, Hamiltons Memoirs, and even the Thousand and one Knights were as pure French as any in the language, but they would advise me to read The Cardinal De Retts and the Writers of that time but especially L'Esprit de la Ligue in three Volumes and L'Esprit de la Fronde in five, for these Books would lead me into the History of France and bring me acquainted with many of their Characters. They gave me the Names of Booksellers who would furnish me with any books I wanted. I soon went to Paris and purchased them all and many more.[4]

[4] Most of the titles listed can be identified among JA's books now in the Boston Public Library. See the following entries in the *Catalogue of JA's Library*: Girard, *Les vrais principes de la langue françoise* and *Synonymes françois* (p. 103); [Féraud,] *Dictionnaire grammatical, de la langue françoise* (p. 92); Institut de France, Académie française, *Dictionnaire de l'Académie françoise* (p. 127); Richelet, *Dictionnaire de la langue françoise*, 2 edns. (p. 212); *Dictionnaire universel françois et latin, vulgairement appelé Dictionnaire de Trévoux* (p. 74); Pascal, *Les provinciales, ou lettres écrites par*

This day We dined at Mr. La Fretés. A splendid House, Gardens and Furniture. The Family were fond of Paintings and exhibited a Variety of exquisite Pieces, but none of them struck me more than one Picture of a Storm and another of a Calm at Sea. I had not forgotten the Gulph Stream, the English Channel nor the Bay of Biscay.[5]

At this dinner the Conversation turned upon the Infrequency of Marriage in France. Go into any company they said and you would find very few who were married, and upon Examination of the numerous Company at Table I was found the only married Person in Company except the Heads of the Family. Here We were shewn a manuscript History of the Revolution in Russia in the Year 1762. The Author was asked why he did not publish it. He answered that he had no mind to be assassinated as he certainly should be if he printed it and was known to be the Writer. Mr. Franklin retired to another room and read it. When he returned it to the Author he made many Eulogies of the Style, Arrangement, Perspicuity &c. and added "You have followed the manner of Sallust, and you have surpassed him."—I thought this as good a french Compliment as the best of the Company could have made.

At Table there was much conversation about the Education of daughters at the Convents, and I found the discreetest people, especially among the Ladies, had a very bad Opinion of such Education. They were very bad Schools for Morals. It was then News to me that they were thought such in France.

The greatest part of the Conversation was concerning Voltaire. He was extolled to the Skies as a Prodigy. His Eminence in History, Epick Poetry, Dramatick Poetry, Phylosophy, even the Neutonian Phylosophy: His Prose and Verse were equally admirable. No Writer had ever excelled in so many Branches of Science and Learning, besides that

Louis de Montalte (p. 188); Marquise de Sévigné, *Recueil des lettres* (p. 226); Antoine, Comte Hamilton, *Œuvres,* which includes the *Mémoires du Comte de Grammont* (p. 113); Cardinal de Retz, *Mémoires* (p. 211). One other work, the author of which is not named by JA, remains in the Adams family library in Quincy (MQA): Louis Pierre Anquetil, *L'esprit de la ligue,* 2d edn., 3 vols., Paris, 1771.

JA's listing of specific authors and titles in this passage, for which there is no equivalent in his Diary, clearly indicates that he went to his shelves to refresh his memory about the French grammars, dictionaries, and literary and historical works he had acquired in Paris in order to learn French. But those named here are a more or less random selection from a much larger number of works of the same kind that he purchased in French and Dutch bookshops within the next few years. See another listing of French books in JA's Autobiography under 8 July, below.

[5] The following three paragraphs were begun by JA as an interlineation in the MS and then continued on a separate sheet marked for insertion ahead of the entry of 17 April, below.

astonishing multitude of his fugitive Pieces. He was the grand Monarch of Science and Litterature. If he should die the Republick of Letters would be restored. But it was now a Monarchy &c. &c. &c.

April 17. Fryday. We dined home with Company. Mr. Platt and his Lady, Mr. Amiel and his Lady, Mr. Austin, Mr. Alexander &c. There were two Alexanders, one a Batcheller, the other with a Family of several Daughters, one of whom Mr. Jonathan Williams afterwards married. They lived in a House not far from Us, were from Scotland, and had some connection with Mr. Franklin, which I never understood and took no pains to investigate.[6]

After dinner We went to see the Fete de long Champ, or the feast of the long Field. This was good Fryday. On this Week, all the Theatres of Paris are shutt up and the Performers forbidden to play. By this decree, whether of the Church or State, or both, All the fashionable People of Paris and its Environs are deprived of their daily Amusements and loose their ordinary topicks of conversation. The consequence of which is that they are si ennuiée, so weary of themselves that they cannot live. To avoid this direfull calamity they have invented this new Spectacle and have made it fashionable for every Person who owns a Carriage of any kind that rolls upon Wheels, and all those who can hire one to go out of Town and march their Horses slowly along one side of the great Road to the End of it, then they come about and return on the other Side, and in this manner the Carriages are rolling all day. It was asserted on that day that there was not a pair of Wheels left in the City. For some Years, the Ladies who were not acknowledged to have established reputations, were observed to appear in unusual splendor in these Processions, and the indecency increased from Year to Year till one of the most beautifull but one of the most infamous Prostitutes in Paris had sold her Charms to such profit that she appeared in the most costly and splendid Equipage in

[6] The Alexanders were a numerous and ubiquitous clan, some of whom Franklin had known in England and others apparently in Scotland, and all of whom were correspondents of his. William Alexander Jr. owned property in the West Indies and had had financial dealings with Franklin before the Revolution. He left England for France in 1776, welcomed Franklin from Dijon, and later established himself with his daughters (one of whom, Mariamne, married Franklin's grandnephew Jonathan Williams in 1779) at Auteuil. It is now known that Alexander was a secret agent of Sir William Pulteney, who in 1777–1778 tried to bring about peace by personal negotiations with Franklin. Alexander's career is described and his correspondence with Pulteney is quoted and abstracted by Frederick B. Tolles in "Franklin and the Pulteney Mission: An Episode in the Secret History of the American Revolution," *Huntington Libr. Quart.*, 17:37–58 (Nov. 1953). His letter of 26 May 1778 (p. 53–54) contains a vivid sketch of JA soon after his arrival in France.

the whole Row:[7] six of the finest horses in the Kingdom, the most costly Coach that could be built, more numerous Servants and richer Liveries than any of the Nobility or Princes. Her own Dress in Proportion. It was generally agreed to be the finest Shew that had ever been exhibited. This was so audacious an Insult to all modest Women and indeed to the national morality and Religion, that the Queen to her honor sent her a Message the next morning, that if she ever appeared again, any where, in that Equipage she should find herself in Bicêtre the next morning.[8] Yet even this was a modest fancy in comparison with the palace of Bellvue.[9] This was another Symptom of the pure virtuous manners which I was simple enough to think would not accord with our American Republican Institutions. To be sure it had never yet entered my thoughts, that any rational Being would ever think of demolishing the Monarchy and creating a Republick in France.

April 18. Saturday. 1778. This morning, the Father of General Conway, a venerable Personage from Ireland originally as I presume, came to visit me and enquire concerning his Son and American Affairs in General.

Dined at Mr. Bouffets, who spoke a little English. The Company consisted of Mr. Bouffets Brother, Mr. Veillard, Mr. Le Fevre, The Abbe des Prades, Mr. Borry and others.

On our return called and drank Tea, at Madam Brillions. We then made a Visit to M. Boulainvilliers, who is Lord of the Manor of Passi and a descendant of the celebrated Boulainvilliers who wrote many Books particularly on the States General and a Life of Mahomet &c. He had just come out with his Lady and daughter to his Country Seat at Passi, for the Season. His Daughter bore the Title of Mademoiselle De Passi, and was certainly one of the most beautiful young Ladies, I ever saw in France. She afterwards married The Marquis De Tonnere, a Gentleman of great Quality and fortune, since so famous for his tragical Catastrophy in the beginning of the Revolution.[1] This

[7] In JA's *Works* (3:133) the preceding passage reads as follows: "For some years, certain persons of equivocal reputation were observed to appear in unusual splendor in these processions, and the scandal increased from year to year, till one of the most notorious females in Paris appeared in the most costly and splendid equipage in the whole row"—a rare but striking instance of editorial bowdlerizing by CFA.

[8] A long letter from John Thaxter to AA, Paris, 18 April 1783 (Adams Papers), is very largely devoted to an account of the "Fête des longs Champs" that he had witnessed the day before.

[9] Bellevue, the splendid palace built for Mme. de Pompadour on the Seine near Meudon; it is described in Dezallier, *Environs de Paris*, 1779, p. 35-40. See JA's reflections on the role of Bellevue and its mistress in French history, in the entry of 2 June, below.

[1] The Comte de Clermont-Tonnerre, soldier, man of letters, and legislator, married Mlle. Boulainvilliers probably in 1779; he was killed by a mob in 1792 (Michaud, *Biog. Universelle*).

Noblemans Character was as amiable as that of his Father in Law was otherwise. Boulainvilliers held a superb hereditary office under the Crown which gave him very high Rank and great Emolument. But although he was very rich he was represented as oppressive, tyrannical and cruel as well as avaricious to a great degree. Mr. Franklin who at the age of seventy odd, had neither lost his Love of Beauty nor his Taste for it called Mademoiselle De Passy his favourite and his flame and his Love and his Mistress, which flattered the Family and did not displease the young Lady. After the Marquis had demanded Mademoiselle for a Wife and obtained her, Madam Chaumont, who was a Wit, the first time she saw Franklin cryed out "Helas! tous les Conducteurs de Monsieur Franklin, n'ont pas pu empeche le Tonnere de tomber sur Mademoiselle de Passi." A Year or two after this in conversation with Mr. De Marbois, Boulainvilliers happened to be mentioned, and Marbois said he had a most detestable Character. But said I, he has married a Daughter to a Man of good Character. Aye, says Marbois, I suppose you will say what signifies Character in France, when the worst cannot hinder a Man from marrying his Daughter to a Marquis De Tonnere?

April 19. 1778. Dined at home with Mr. Grand, our Banker, his Lady, his Niece and Ward Mademoiselle L'Abhard, his Sons, Mr. Austin, Mr. Chaumont and a great deal of other Company. Mr. Ferdinand Grand was a Protestant from Switzerland, who had a House in Paris and a small Country house near Us in Passi. Himself, his Lady, Niece and Sons composed as decent, modest and regular a Family as I ever knew in France. It was however by Mr. Chaumonts Influence with the Count De Vergennes and Mr. De Sartine that he obtained the Reputation and Emoluments of being the Banker to the American Ministers. Sir George Grand his Brother, might contribute something towards this favour, because he had kept an Inn at Stockholm when the Count de Vergennes was Ambassador of France in Sweeden, and accomplished the Revolution in that Kingdom to an absolute Monarchy. This was a mere measure of Economy in the French Court, because, before, it had cost them in Bribes to the States more money than they could well afford. The Meeting of De Vergennes with the heads of the Conspiracy had been held at Mr. Grands Inn, and he was rewarded with a Cross of Saint Louis, which gave him the Title of Sir, as I suppose, having never heard that he had any English Knighthood although he had lived in England where he married his Daughter to the Major or Colonel who was afterwards General Provost. This Lady as I presume is the same who afterwards married Colonel Burr of New York and was the Mother of Mrs. Alston of South Carolina.[2] Sir George was connected in Partnership with the House of Horneca Fizeaux & Co. in Amsterdam, a mercantile and Banking Company, and who had or were supposed to have the favour and Confidence of the French Ministers of State.

This Day Mr. David Hartley, a Member of the British House of Commons, with Mr. George [*i.e.* William] Hammond the Father of Mr. George Hammond who was afterwards Hartleys Secretary at the Negotiation of the definitive Treaty of Peace, and after that Minister Plenipotentiary to the United States, came to Visit Us, under pretence of visiting Dr. Franklin. This mysterious Visit, I did not at all admire. I soon saw that Hartley was ⟨*as great a Coxcomb*⟩ a Person of as consummate Vanity as Hammond was a plain honest Man: but I considered both as Spies, and endeavoured to be as reserved and as much on my guard as my nature would admit. Although I endeavoured to behave to both with entire civility, I suppose as I did not flatter Mr. Hartley with professions of confidence, which I did not feel, and of so much Admiration of his Great Genius and Talents as he felt himself, he conceived a disgust at me, and told Sir John Temple and others after his return to London "Your Mr. Adams that you represent as a Man of such good Sense, ⟨*I believe he may have that, but*⟩ If he has that, he is the most ungracious Man I ever saw." I had not expressed so much astonishment at his Invention of Fire Plates, and Archimides's Mirrors, as he thought they deserved. I knew him to be intimate with Lord North by his own confession as well as by the Information of Dr. Franklin and others: and although he was numbered among the Opposition in Parliament and professed to be an Advocate for the American cause, yet I knew very well that Opposition to the Ministry was the only solid Ground, on which all the Friendship for America, that was professed in England, rested. I did not therefore think it safe,

[2] This is garbled, but in view of the number of Prevosts who were British army officers, not surprisingly. Aaron Burr married in 1782 Theodosia (Stillwell) Bartow Prevost, whose second husband had been Col. Jacques Marc Prevost (d. 1777), brother of the Maj. Gen. Augustine Prevost (d. 1786) who commanded British forces in South Carolina during the Revolution and whose wife was Anna, daughter of Chevalier (usually called "Sir") George Grand of Amsterdam. The Burrs' daughter, also named Theodosia, married in 1801 Joseph Alston of South Carolina. Better known than either his father (Augustine) or his uncle (Jacques Marc) was Sir George Prevost (1767–1816), who at the time JA was writing was a major general and who became governor general of British North America and an unlucky figure in the northern campaigns of the War of 1812. See *DAB* under both Aaron Burr and Theodosia Burr; *DNB* under Sir George Prevost; Samuel H. Wandell and Meade Minnigerode, *Aaron Burr*, N.Y. and London, 1925, 1:88–91.

to commit myself to a Man, who came to Us without any pretence of Authority from his Sovereign or his Ministers. I say without any pretence of Authority because he made none. But I then supposed and still believe, that he came with the secret privity if not at the express request of Lord North to sound the American Ministers, and see if there were no hopes of seducing Us from our connection with France, and making a seperate Accommodation with Us, the very idea of which as the Treaty was already made appeared to me to be an Insult to our honor and good faith.[3] What were the Subjects or the Objects of his freequent private Conferences with Franklin I know not. If either or both of them ever made any minutes of them I hope they will one day appear in publick. I neither then nor ever since suspected any unfair practice in Franklin except some secret Whispers against Lee and possibly against myself, for he had by this time found that I was not to be ⟨his Tool⟩ sufficiently complyant with his Views. He had indeed seen enough of me in Congress, to know that [I] was not a Man to swear, in the Words of another at all times.

This Evening Mr. Chaumont took me in his Carriage to The Concert Spirituel, in the Royal ⟨Garden⟩ Pallace of the Tuilleries. A vast Number of Instruments were performing to an immense Crowd of Company. There were Men Singers and Women Singers. One Gentleman sung alone and then a young Lady. The Musick however did not entirely satisfy me. I had read that the French Ear was not the most delicate, and I thought the Observation verified. There was too much sound for me. The Gardens of the Tuilleries were full of Company of both Sexes walking.

April 20. Monday 1778. My Son had been with me since Saturday. This was delicious repast for me: but I was somewhat mortified to find that this Child among the Pupills at ⟨School⟩ the Pension and my American Servant among the Domesticks of the Hotel, learned more french in a day than I could learn in a Week with all my Books.

Dined with the Dutchess D'Anville, at the Hotel de Rochefaucault, with the Duke de la Rochefoucault her Son, her Daughter and Grand Daughter whom the Duke afterwards married, with a dispensation from the Pope, with a large Company of Dukes, Abbes and Men of Science and Learning among whom was Mr. Condorcet, a Philosopher

[3] The remainder of this paragraph was omitted by CFA in his text. Hartley's mission was unofficial, but it had the personal sanction of Lord North, who had been more or less persuaded by Hartley that Franklin held the key to reconciliation between Great Britain and America despite the new Franco-American alliance. See George H. Guttridge, *David Hartley, M.P., an Advocate of Conciliation, 1774–1783*, Berkeley, 1926, p. 280–287.

with a face as pale or rather as white as a Sheet of paper, I suppose from hard Study.[4] The Dutchess D'Anville and her Son, the great Friends [of] Monsieur Turgot, were said to have great Influence with the Royal Accademy of Sciences, to make members at pleasure, and the Secretary perpetuel Mr. D'Alembert, was said to have been of their Creation as was Mr. Condorcet afterwards. His Gratitude, a few Years after this, will be recorded in History. This Family was beloved in France, and had a reputation for Patriotism, that is of such Kind of Patriotism as was allowed to exist and be esteemed in that Kingdom, where no Man as Montesqueu says must esteem himself or his Country too much. Un homme capable de s'estimer beaucoup, was a dangerous Subject, in a Monarchy.

Recollecting as I did the Expedition of the Duke D'Anville against America, and the great Commotion in the Massachusetts, and the Marches of the Militia to defend Boston, when his Squadron and Army were expected to attack that Town, it appeared a very singular Thing that I should be very happy in his House at Paris at a splendid Dinner with his family. But greater Vicissitudes than this have become more familiar to me, since that time. The Lady appeared to me to possess a great Understanding and great Information.

In the Evening We visited Mr. Lloyd of Maryland, and his handsome English Lady. Here We saw Mr. Diggs.

April 21. Tuesday. 1778. Dined at Mr. Chaumonts, with the largest collection of great Company, that I had yet seen. The Marquis D'Argenson, The Count de Noailles, the Marshall de Mailbois, the B[r]other of Count de Vergennes, Mr. and Mrs. Foucault, the Son in Law and Daughter of Mr. Chaumont, who were said to have a fortune of four or five thousand Pounds Sterling a Year in St. Domingo, Mr. [Vilevault?][5] the first Officer, that is, a premier Comis under Mr. De Sartine, Mr. Chaumonts own Son and his other daughter with so many others that I found it impracticable to get their names and qualities.

But these incessant Dinners, and dissipations were not the Objects of my Mission to France. My Countrymen were suffering in America,

[4] M. J. A. N. de Caritat, Marquis de Condorcet (1743–1794), mathematician, early leader and eventual victim of the French Revolution, and advocate of the endless perfectibility of man and society (Hoefer, *Nouv. Biog. Générale*). JA owned several of Condorcet's published works and in the margins of his own copy of Condorcet's famous *Outlines of an Historical View of the Progress of the Human Mind*, London, 1795, wrote an angry running rebuttal. The debate between the French philosopher and the Yankee commentator is printed *in extenso* by Zoltán Haraszti in *JA and the Prophets of Progress*, ch. 12.

[5] See Diary entry of this date and note 1 there.

and their Affairs were in great confusion in Europe. With much Grief and concern, I received daily and almost hourly information, of the disputes between the Americans in France. The bitter Animosities between Mr. Deane and Mr. Lee: between Dr. Franklin and Mr. Lee: between Dr. Franklin and Mr. Izzard: between Dr. Bancroft and Mr. Lee and Mr. Izzard: and between Mr. Charmichael and all [of] them. Sir James Jay was there too, a Brother of Mr. John Jay, and an able Physician as well as a Man of Letters and information. He had lately come over from England, and although he seemed to have no Animosity against any of the Gentlemen, he confirmed many of the Reports that I had heard from several Persons before, such as that Mr. Deane had been at least as attentive to his own Interest, in dabbling in the English funds, and in trade, and in fitting out Privateers as to the Public, and said that he would give Mr. Deane fifty thousand Pounds Sterling for the fortune he had made here. That Dr. Bancroft too had made a fortune here, by speculating in the English Stocks and by gambling Policies in London. Mr. McCrery too, had adopted the Cry of Mr. Lees Ennemies, and said that the Lees were selfish, and that this was a Family misfortune. Dr. Franklin, Mr. Deane and Dr. Bancroft were universally considered as indissoluble Friends. The Lees and Mr. Izzard were equally attached in friendship to each other. The Friends and followers of each party both among the french and Americans were equally bitter against each other. Mr. Deane appeared to me, to have made himself agreable here, to Mr. De Chaumont, Mr. Beaumarchais, Mr. Monthieu, and Mr. Holker, Persons of importance and influence at that time, and with that Ministry, particularly the Count de Vergennes and Mr. De Sartine. Mr. Deane was gone home in great Splendor, with Compliments, Certificates and Recommendations in his favour from the King and Minister, and many other Persons French and American, among whom was Dr. Franklin who shewed me his Letter of recommendation in very strong terms.[6] Mr. Deane had been active, industrious, subtle and in some degree successfull, having accomplished some of the great purposes of his Mission. Mr. Gerard and Mr. Holker were also his Friends: and although he had little order in his Business public or private, had lived very expensively and spent great Sums of Money that no body could Account

<hr />

[6] Possibly this refers to Franklin's letter of 22 July 1778 to James Lovell, a member of the Committee on Foreign Affairs. Though it does not linger on the subject, this letter opens with a confident opinion that the "groundless" prejudices against Deane in Congress will soon be removed and that he will "come back with honour in the commission to Holland" (Franklin, *Writings,* ed. Smyth, 7:174–175).

for, and allthough unauthorised Contracts had well nigh ruined our Army, embarrassed Congress more than any thing that had ever happened and put his Country to a great and useless expence, I was still apprehensive there would be great Altercations excited by him in America, both in and out of Congress.

On the other hand it was said of Mr. Lee, that he had not the confidence of the Ministry, nor of the Persons of influence here, meaning as before Mr. Chaumont, Mr. Beaumarchais, Mr. Monthieu and Mr. Holker: that he was suspected of too much Affection for England, and of too much intimacy with Lord Shelbourne: that he had given Offence, by an unhappy disposition, and by indiscreet Speeches before Servants and others, concerning the French Nation and Government, despizing and cursing them.

I was extreamly sorry for these Altercations and Calumnies, knowing that Parties and divisions among Americans here, must have disagreable and pernicious Effects both at home and abroad. I was wholly untainted with these prejudices and unalterably determined to preserve myself from them. It was no part of my Business to quarrel with any one without cause, to differ with one Party or the other, or give offence to any body. But I must and would do my duty to the Public, let it give offence to whom it might.

In this place it is necessary to introduce a few portraits of Characters that the subsequent narration may be better understood.

Dr. Franklin one of my Colleagues is so generally known that I shall not attempt a Sketch of his Character at present.[7] That He was a great Genius, a great Wit, a great Humourist and a great Satyrist, and a great Politician is certain. That he was a great Phylosopher, a great Moralist and a great Statesman is more questionable.

Mr. Arthur Lee, my other Colleague, was a Native of Virginia. His Father had been long a Councillor under the Crown and sometime commander in Chief of the Colony and ancient Dominion of Virginia. He left several Sons, Thomas, Richard Henry, William, Francis Lightfoot and Arthur, with all of whom except Thomas I have been intimately acquainted. Their Father had given them all excellent Classical Educations and they were all virtuous Men. Arthur had studied and practiced Physick but not finding it agreable to his Genius he took Chambers in the Temple in England, and there was admitted to prac-

---

[7] Nevertheless, JA added the two sentences that follow, by interlineation, after he had written, or at least begun, his account of Arthur Lee which follows. And soon afterward he expressed his feelings respecting Franklin at greater length; see under 27 May, below.

tice as a Barrister, and being protected by several Gentlemen of Rank among the Opposition was coming fast into importance. Animated with great Zeal in the Cause of his native Country, he took a decided part in her favour and became a Writer of some Celebrity by his Junius Americanus and other publications. Becoming known in America as a zealous Advocate for our Cause, the two Houses of the Legislature of Massachusetts Bay appointed him provisionally their Agent to the Court of Great Britain, in case of the death, Absence or dissability of Dr. Franklin, in which capacity he corresponded with some of the Members of that Assembly, particularly with Mr. Samuel Adams, and with the Assembly itself, transmitting from time to time information of Utility and Importance. After a Congress was called in 1774, 5 and 6 He continued to transmit to Us some of the best and most authentic Intelligence, which We received from England. In 1786 [1776] when the Election of Ministers to the Court of France was brought forward and after I had declined the nomination,[8] and Mr. Jefferson had refused the Election and Appointment sent him by Congress, Mr. Arthur Lee was elected in his place. He came immediately over to Paris and joined his Colleagues in Commission. His manners were polite, his reading extensive, his Attention to Business was punctual, and his Integrity without reproach.

Mr. Ralph Izzard was a native of South Carolina. His Grandfather or Great Grandfather was One of Mr. Lockes Landgraves, and had transmitted to his Posterity an ample landed Estate. Mr. Izzard had his Education, I believe at Westminster or Eaton School, certainly at the University of Cambridge in England.[9] When he came to the Possession of his fortune he married Miss De Lancy a Daughter of Chief Justice De Lancy, who was so long at the head of the Party in New York in Opposition to the Livingstones, a Lady of great beauty and fine Accomplishments as well [as] perfect purity of conduct and Character through Life.[1] This accomplished Pair had a curiosity to Travel. They went to Europe, and passed through Italy, Germany, Holland and I know not how many other Countries. Mrs. Izzard, an excellent Domestic Consort, was very prolific, and it was often jocularly said that she had given Mr. Izzard a Son or a Daughter in every great City in

---

[8] No contemporary evidence concerning such a declination has been found.

[9] Izard attended a school at Hackney and Christ Church, Cambridge (Ralph Izard, *Correspondence . . . , Volume I,* ed. Anne Izard Deas, N.Y., 1844, p. v–vi).

[1] Alice (De Lancey) Izard was the daughter of Peter De Lancey and niece of James De Lancey, former lieutenant governor and chief justice of New York (Izard, *Correspondence,* cited in preceding note, p. vi; *DAB* under Ralph Izard).

Europe. When the American War commenced they were in England, and Mr. Izzard embracing the Cause of his Country with all the Warmth of his Character, passed with his Family over to France in his Way to America. Congress had been advised, by Persons who knew no better, to send a Minister to the Emperor and to the Grand Duke of Tuscany because they were Brothers to the Queen of France. In this measure there was less Attention to the Political Interests and Views of Princes than to the Ties of Blood and Family Connections. Congress however adopted the Measure, and Mr. Izzard was nominated by Mr. Arthur Middleton in the Name of South Carolina and highly recommended for his Integrity, good Sense and Information.[2] The Members from New York and other States supported the nomination and concurred in all the particulars of his Character. Mr. Izzard was accordingly appointed and when he arrived in Paris he found his Commission to the Grand Duke. With an high Sense of honor, and great Benevolence of heart as well as integrity of Principle, Mr. Izzard had a Warmth of Temper and sometimes a violence of Passions, that were very inconvenient to him and his Friends, and not a little dangerous to his Enemies.

Dr. Edward Bancroft was a Native of Massachusetts Bay in the Town of Suffield.[3] He had been a School Boy under Mr. Silas Deane,

[2] Izard's appointment was to the Court of Tuscany only; William Lee held commissions to the Courts of Berlin and Vienna.

[3] A mistake for Westfield. This "Native of Massachusetts Bay," as Julian P. Boyd has remarked in the most searching account yet written of Bancroft's character and fantastic career, "was destined to become one of the most remarkable spies of all time, achieving the astonishing feat of serving simultaneously as an intelligence agent for two nations at war while serving himself first of all, and mastering the art of duplicity so consummately as to conceal his treasons from some of the most astute men of his time and from historians for six decades after his death.... George Bancroft in 1866 made the first, briefest, and still valid appraisal of Edward Bancroft as a double spy. In 1889 Francis Wharton devoted twenty pages to refuting what he considered an aspersion, but the very next year Stevens' *Facsimiles* began to appear, making it certain that both

George III and Arthur Lee—the two contemporaries who trusted Bancroft least—were wrong only in underestimating the extent of Bancroft's perfidy" (Julian P. Boyd, "Silas Deane: Death by a Kindly Teacher of Treason?," *WMQ*, 3d ser., 16:165–187, 319–342, 515–550 [April, July, Oct. 1959], cited at p. 176 and note). JA considered Bancroft avaricious and immoral, and he disliked and distrusted him as a satellite of Franklin and a collaborator of Deane, but he clearly never suspected him of treason—even though he knew spying went on in the household of the American Commissioners at Passy (see his Autobiography under 27 April, below). It was Arthur Lee rather than JA who vetoed a proposal that Bancroft be sent on a confidential errand to England early in 1779. Addressing his fellow commissioners on this subject from Chaillot, 7 Feb. 1779, Lee said among other things: "The notorious character of Dr. Bancroft as a Stockjobber is perfectly known to you.... His living in open defiance of decency and religion when he was a Schoolmaster, whether in any Town of the Massachusetts or Connecticutt I do not recollect. After some Education at School he had been bound an Apprentice to a Trade: but being discontented he had ran away and gone to Sea, carrying away with him, some property of his master. After some years of Adventures, the history of which I have not heard, he had acquired Property enough to return to his native Town, made his Apologies to his master, paid him honourably all his demands, and went to Sea again. The next information I have of him, was that he was in England and had published his Essay towards a natural History of Guiana, which I have in a handsome Volume presented me with his own hand, and it is a Work, considering the Advantages of the Author, of great merit.[4] He wrote also in England The History of Sir Charles Wentworth, a Novel which no

you are no strangers to. . . . You know also that he is the creature and Agent of . . . Mr. Deane. . . . I have farther to inform you as one of your Colleagues, that I have evidence in my possession, which makes me consider Dr. Bancroft as a Criminal with regard to the United States, and that I shall have him charg'd as such, whenever he goes within their jurisdiction" (PPAmP: Franklin Papers). One may perhaps calculate the discount his colleagues regularly placed on Arthur Lee's allegations against individuals by the fact that neither Franklin nor JA took Lee's charge of treason seriously enough to do anything about it. To be sure, JA told Marbois on the voyage home to Boston in the summer of 1779 that Bancroft was too "irregular and excentric a Character" to be trusted (Diary, 2 July 1779). But soon after his return to Paris the following year he was willing to send dispatches by Bancroft's hand to Nantes on their way to America (JA to Bancroft, 26 Feb. 1780, LbC, Adams Papers); in 1782 he conversed freely with him about peace terms; and three years later, when minister in London where he saw Bancroft from time to time, he raised no objection to Jefferson's proposal (which did not work out) that Bancroft be employed by them as agent to Algiers (JA to Jefferson, 18 Aug. 1785, LbC, Adams Papers, printed in Jefferson, *Papers*, ed. Boyd, 8:400). In short JA never dreamt of Bancroft's true character.

That character was not yet known when CFA edited JA's *Works* in the 1850's. But among the Adams Papers are transcripts of two letters written by Bancroft to Lord North, London, 8 and 12 Aug. 1783, pressing in the name of "Justice and Humanity" for payment of the arrears in both Bancroft's salary as a spy in France ("£250 for the quarter of my allowance up to Midsummer last") and his "original permanent pension" of £500 agreed upon in Feb. 1777 before he went to France as a British spy. These letters add a few details to the now famous memorial that Bancroft addressed to Foreign Secretary Carmarthen in 1784 and are alluded to in that paper (which is printed from the original in the Public Record Office, F.O. 4, vol. 3, by Samuel F. Bemis as an appendix to his article "British Secret Service and the French-American Alliance," *AHR*, 29:474–495 [April 1924]). The transcripts are in a hand (not identified) and on paper of the mid-19th century and were apparently copied from the originals; but the editors do not currently know where the originals are or how the transcripts came into the Adams Papers.

[4] Published London, 1769. JA's copy, now in the Boston Public Library, is inscribed as follows: "To the Honble. John Adams Esqr. Minister Plenipotentiary from the United States of America to his Brittanic Majesty this Volume is very respectfully offered by the Author."

doubt was recommended to many readers, and procured a considerably better Sale, by the plentifull Abuse and vilification of Christianity which he had taken care to insert in it. He had also been in the Intimacy and Confidence of Dr. Franklin, who had recommended him to the Editors and Proprietors of the Monthly Review, in which his standing Share was to review all Publications relative to America. This Information I had from Dr. Franklin himself. I understood this very well, as I thought—to wit that Bancroft was the ostensible Reviewer, but that Franklin was always consulted before the publication. Bancroft was a meddler in the Stocks as well as Reviews, and frequently went into the Alley, and into the deepest and darkest retirements and recesses of the Brokers and Jobbers, Jews as well as Christians, and found Amusement as well perhaps as profit by listening to all the News and Anecdotes true or false that were there whispered or more boldly pronounced. This information I had from his own mouth. When Mr. Deane arrived in France, whether he wrote to Bancroft or Bancroft to him, I know not, but they somehow or other sympathised with each other so well that Bancroft went over to Paris and became a confidential associate with his old Friends Franklin and Deane. Bancroft had a clear head and a good Pen. He wrote some things relative to the Connection between France and America, with the Assistance of Franklin and Deane as I presume, which were translated into French by Mr. Turgot or the Duke de la Rochefaucault I forget which and printed in a Publication called Affaires de L'Angleterre et Amerique and which were very well done.[5] After the Peace he obtained a Patent in France for the exclusive Importation of the Bark of the Yellow Oak for the Dyers and then he went to England and procured a similar Patent there, by both which together he is said to have realised an Income of Eight hundred a Year.[6] He has resided in England to this time and has renewed his ancient connections with the Monthly Reviewers, as I conclude from several Circumstances, among others from the Review of my first Volume of The Defence &c. and from that of my Sons Travels in Silesia, in both which the Spirit of Franklin, Deane and Bancroft, is to me very discernible.[7]

[5] On the *Affaires de l'Angleterre et de l'Amérique* see JA's Diary entry of 3 March 1779, note, and references there.

[6] The remainder of JA's remarks on Bancroft in the present and following paragraphs were omitted by CFA in his text.

[7] The notice of the first volume of JA's *Defence of the Constitutions of Government of the United States of America* which appeared in the *Monthly Review* (76:394–399 [May 1787]) begins, "We have not met with a greater disappointment, in the course of our literary labours, than we have experienced with respect to the work now before us," and is hostile and patronizing

This Man had with him in France, a Woman, with whom he lived, and who by the french was called la Femme de Monsieur Bancroft. She never made her Appearance. She had several Children very handsome and promising whom I saw in France and two of whom I have since seen in America, with complexions as blooming as they had in their Childhood. One of them behaved very well—the other has been much censured, I know not how truly. Bancrofts intimacy with Franklin brought him daily to ⟨my⟩ our house, and he often came to my Appartment where I received him always with Civility for he was sensible, social and in several Things well informed. He often dined with Us especially when We had company. Here I was not so well pleased with his Conversation, for at Table he would season his food with such enormous quantities of Chayan Pepper, which assisted by a little generous Burgundy, though he drank not a great deal, would sett his tongue a running at a most licentious rate both at Table and after dinner, as gave me great paine. The Bible and the Christian Religion were his most frequent Subjects of Invective and ridicule, but he sometimes fell upon Poli[ti]cks and political Characters, and not seldom expressed Sentiments of the Royal Family and the Court of France, particularly of the Queen, which I thought very improper for him to utter or for Us to hear. Much as Mr. Lee was censured for freedoms of Speech, I never heard a tenth part so much from him as from Bancroft. The Queens Intrigues with Madame the Duchess of Polinac, her constant dissipation, her habits of expence and profusion, her giddy thoughtless conduct were for a long time almost constant Topicks of his Tittle Tattle.

Another Personage who must be introduced upon the Scene, was a Dr. Smith.[8] He told me he was a Native of New York, and of honourable descent for his Father had been a Member of his Majestys Council in that Province, and his Brother was William Smith who also had been a Royal Councillor. This Brother was afterwards Chief Justice in Canada. The Dr. had received a good Education in Letters,

---

throughout, though it must be admitted that the reviewer touched home in observing that, except for the passage JA quoted from Turgot, "the reader scarcely acquires any information concerning the constitution of the American States." In a letter to JA of 7 June 1787 AA said she had heard the review ascribed to "that poor envy ridden, contemptable, Ignorant self conceited Wretch Silas Dean" (Adams Papers).

A critical but not entirely hostile notice of JQA's *Letters on Silesia, Written during a Tour through That Country in the Years 1800, 1801,* London, 1804, appeared in the *Monthly Review,* 2d ser., 45:350–358 (Dec. 1804).

[8] James Smith; see Diary entry of 13 May 1778 and note; Autobiography entries of 12 April, above; 9 May, below. CFA omitted this entire passage on Smith.

I know not where, and was a tollerable Writer. He had been a Wanderer and an Adventurer in the West Indies and in England, but had not well succeeded in the practice of Physick. He had married a Lady, a most perfect Antithesis to beauty in the face and to Elegance in Person. She was however infinitely too good for him, for she had some property in the West Indies, enough I suppose to afford them a bare Subsistance, and she was what is much more, a discreet, decent, virtuous and worthy Woman. This Man was supposed to come over from England, either to solicit some Employment, or to embarrass and perplex the American Ministers, or to be a Spy both upon the Americans and the French. Which of the three was his Errand, or whether either of them I know not. When he first arrived in Paris he visited Franklin and brought him some English Newspapers containing a Number of Pieces upon Liberty which he said he had written. Franklin told me that he read them and found them to contain some good common place principles of Liberty and that they were moderately well written, but of very little value or consequence. Whether Franklin neglected to return his Visit or to answer his Letter or whether he had not expressed so much Admiration of Smiths Talents as he thought they deserved, or whatever was the offence, he soon became very Angry with Franklin and wrote him many petulant and offensive Letters, which he complained of to me, till at length he received one which [provoked?]⁹ him very highly. When [he] came in to Breakfast he said to Us at Table "This Envy is the worst of all distempers. I hope I shall never catch it. I had rather have the Pox and Dr. Smith for my Physician," and then gave Us an Account of an insolent Letter he had just received and read from Smith, which had thus put him out of Temper. For some time he continued to persecute Mr. Lee much in the same manner, and once when he asked an Audience of the three Commissioners together, he told Mr. Lee that if ever he found him out of commission he would call him out into the Field of honour. Lee only smiled at this, but Smith continued in such a Strain of provoking Insolence both to Franklin and Lee, although he had carefully avoided saying an offensive Word to me, that I thought it time for me to speak and I said Dr. Smith your Conduct and Language to Dr. Franklin and Mr. Lee are excessively abusive and insufferable, and if my Colleagues are of my Mind you shall commit no more such offences here without being turned out of the house. Perceiving the determined Tone and Air with which I spoke and easily believing that Mr. Franklin and Mr. Lee would not leave me in a minority in this resolution, he changed

⁹ MS: "proved."

his tone and said he did not mean to give Offence.—We had frequent Accounts of his violent invectives in Paris against my Colleagues and of his violent quarrells with the french at his Lodgings, cursing and swearing and raving as if he was beside himself: but concerning me he was always respectful in his Language and frequently said neither Deane, Franklin or Lee were fit to represent America at the Court of France: that Adams was the only Man that Congress had yet sent to Europe, who was qualified for his Station. Such Compliments from Dr. Smith, knowing so much of him as I did, although they were frequently repeated to me, were not very flattering to me. He continued as long as he staid in France to behave inoffensively to me. But he not long afterwards addressed Letters and remonstrances to Us all jointly as commissioners containing Remonstrances and misrepresentations, which only shewed his Ignorance of our Affairs, his Envy of our Situation and the iracible intemperance of his nature.

Another Character ought to be introduced here: although he was gone to America before my Arrival at Passi and I never had an Opportunity of seeing him.[1] A letter or two may have passed between him and me when he was Charge des Affairs at Madrid, but no misunderstanding ever occurred between Us, and I never received to my knowledge any Injury or Offence from him. He was a native of Maryland of Scotch Extraction; wherever he had his Education, he was in England or Scotland, when the Revolution commenced, and in this Year 1778 came over to Paris, and as I was informed commenced an Opposition to all the Commissioners Franklin, Deane and Lee, and indeed to all who had any Authority in American Affairs, and was very clamorous. Mr. Deane and Dr. Franklin and Dr. Bancroft, however a little before or after his departure found means to appease him in some degree, and after his Arrival in America he was chosen one of the Delegates in Congress for Maryland, where in a Year or two he got an Appointment as Secretary of Legation and Charge Des Affaires to Mr. Jay when in 1779 he was appointed Minister to the Court of Spain, where he remained many Years and finally died. He had Talents and Education, but was considered by the soundest Men who knew him as too much of an Adventurer. What was his Moral Character and

[1] William Carmichael is meant. JA's account of him is accurate except for its chronology. Carmichael came to Paris from London early in 1776 and was for some time an active and useful agent and collaborator of the American Commissioners, and especially of Silas Deane, in their efforts to obtain aid for America in Europe; but jealousies developed and Carmichael sailed for America early in 1778 (Floyd B. Streeter, "The Diplomatic Career of William Carmichael," *Md. Hist. Mag.*, 8:119-140 [June 1913]).

what was his Conduct in Spain I shall leave to Mr. Jay. But he was represented to me as having contributed much to the Animosities and Exasperations among the Americans at Paris and Passi. There were great divisions in Spain among the Americans and Mr. Jay had as much Trouble with his own Family Mr. Carmichael, Mr. Brokholst Livingston and Mr. Littlepage as I had at Paris. I shall leave this Scene to be opened by the memorials of the Actors in it, if any such should ever see the light.

I have now given a faint Sketch of the French and American Personages who had been concerned in our Affairs at and before the Time of my Arrival.

I may have said before, that Public Business had never been methodically conducted. There never was before I came, a minute Book, a Letter Book or an Account Book, or if there had been Mr. Deane and Dr. Franklin had concealed them from Mr. Lee, and they were now no where to be found. It was utterly impossible to acquire any clear Idea of our Affairs. I was now determined to procure some blank books, and to apply myself with Diligence to Business, in which Mr. Lee cordially joined me. To this End it was necessary to alter the Course of my Life. Invitations were sent to Dr. Franklin and me, every day in the Week to dine in some great or small Company. I determined on my part to decline as many as I could of these Invitations, and attend to my Studies of french and the Examination and execution of that public Business which suffered for want of our Attention Every day. An Invitation came from the Duke of Brancard[2] to dine with him at his Seat. I determined to send an Apology and on

April 22. Wednesday 1778 Dined at home and spent the day on Business with Mr. Lee.

April 23 Thursday. 1778. Dined at home with Company.

April 24 Fryday 1778. Dined at Mr. Buffauts with much Company.

April 25. Saturday. Dined at Mr. Chaumonts with Company.

April 26. Sunday 1778. Dined at home.

Monday April 27. 1778. Dined with Mr. Boulainvilliers, at his house in Passi, with Generals and Bishops and Ladies. In the Evening I went to the French Comedy, and happened to be placed in the Front Box very near to Voltaire, who was then upon his last Visit to Paris, and now attended the representation of his own Alzire. The Audience between the several Acts, called Out, Voltaire! Voltaire! Voltaire! and

---

[2] Not identifiable and probably a mistake of memory. CFA silently corrected the name to "Brancas," apparently assuming that JA meant the Comte de Lauraguais (see p. 57, note 3, above).

clapped and applauded him during all the intervals. The Aged Poet on Occasion of some extraordinary Applause arose and bowed respectfully to the Spectators. Although he was very far advanced in Age, had the Paleness of death and deep lines and Wrinkles in his face, he had at some times an eager piercing Stare, and at others a sparkling vivacity in his Eyes. They were still the Poets Eyes with a fine frenzy rolling. And there was yet much vigour in his Countenance. After the Tragedy, they acted the Tuteur, a Comedy or a Farce in one Act. This Theatre did not exceed that at Bourdeaux.

I had not been a month, as yet, in France, nor three Weeks in Passi, but I had seized every moment that I could save, from Business, company or Sleep to acquire the language. I took with me the Book to the Theatre, and compared it line for Line and word for Word, with the pronunciation of the Actors and Actresses, and in this Way I found I could understand them very well. Thinking this to be the best course I could take, to become familiar with the language and its correct pronunciation, I determined to frequent the Theatres as often as possible. Accordingly I went as often as I could and found a great Advantage in it as well as an agreable Entertainment. But as Dr. Franklin had almost daily Occasion for the Carriage and I was determined the public should not be put to the Expence of another for me, I could not go so often as I wished. Another project occurred to me to familiarise the language, which was to keep a Journal in French. This was accordingly attempted and continued for a few days,[3] but I found it took up too much of my time, and what was more decisive I was afraid to keep any Journal at all: For I had reason to believe, that the house was full of Spies, some of whom were among my own Servants, and if my Journal should fall into the hands of the Police, full of free remarks as it must be, to be of any value, it might do more Injury to my Country than mischief to me.

April 28. Tuesday. 1778. Breakfasted at home with Mr. C[h]aumont, Mr. Dubourg, Mr. Chaumont the Son, Mr. Franklin and his grandson.

Mr. Dubourg was a Physician, a Batcheller, a Man of Letters and of good Character but of little Consequence in the French World. Franklin had been introduced to him, in his first Visit to Paris, and Dubourg had translated his Works into French. He must have been in Years for he told me he had been acquainted with Lord Bolinbroke when he was in France. He told Us a Story of Cardinal Mazarine. An officer petitioned him, to make him a Captain of his Life Guard. The

[3] See Diary entries of 27 April 1778 and following.

78

Cardinal answered that he had no Occasion for any other Guard than his Tutelary Angell. Ah! Sir said the Officer your Ennemies will put him to flight with a few drops of holy Water. The Cardinal only replied that he was not afraid of that holy Water.—It was a wonder that some thing worse had not happened to the Officer, for his insinuation was nothing less than that the Devil was the Cardinals only tutelary Angell. Dubourg was a jolly Companion and very fond of Anecdotes. He told a great number, whenever I was in Company which were said to be excellent: but his Speech was so rapid that I could not fully understand them. One I remember, he told as an instance of the great presence of Mind, Self command and good nature of the Marshall De Turenne. He had chosen for his Valet, the stoutest Grenadier in his Army who frequently plaid at Hot Cockles with another of his Domesticks who was named Stephen. The Marshall one day stooped down to look out of a Window with one of his hands upon his back. The Grenadier, coming suddenly into the Chamber, raised his Gigantic Arm and with his brawny palm gave his master a furious blow upon his hand upon his back. The Marshall drew himself in and looked at the Grenadier, who the moment he saw it was his Master fell upon his Knees in despair, begging for Mercy "for he thought it was Stephen." Well, said the Marshall, rubbing his hand which was tingling with the Smart, "if it had been Stephen, you ought not to have struck so hard" and said no more upon the Subject.—This Story I understood, because I had read something like it in Rousseau.

Dined at home this day with Mr. Lee, who spent the day with me upon the public business. In the Evening We went to the Italian Comedy, where I saw a Harlequin for the first time.

April 29. Wednesday. 1778. Dined with the Marshall De Maillebois, with a great deal of Company. Here also We were shewn the Marshalls Amie seated at the Table, with all his great Company. Mr. Lee and I had a good deal of conversation with her. Mr. Lee spoke french with tolerable ease. I could say little: but I understood her as well as any one I had heard in french. It appeared to me that the Marshall had chosen her rather for her Wit and Sense than personal charms.... I was soon informed that this Marshall Maillebois and Marshall Brolie had the reputation of the two most intriguing Men in France; and I was the more disposed to believe it, of the former, because I knew of his Intrigue with Mr. Deane, to be placed over the head of General Washing[ton] in the Command in Chief of our American Army.[4] It

⁴ A double confusion. By "the former" in this sentence JA really meant "the latter" (i.e. not Maillebois but Broglie), but at the same time he confused the

is proper in this place to insert an Anecdote. Mr. Lee and I waited on the Count de Vergens, one day to ask a favour for our Country, I forget what it was. The Count said it was in the Department of War. It was on one of the Feasts of the Cordon blue, when the Count had been kneeling on marble Pavements in Church for some hours and his Knees aked to such a degree that he said he would take a Walk with Us to the Minister of War and ask the favour for Us. As We walked across the Court of the Castle of Versailles We met the Marshall Maillebois. Mutual Bows were exchanged as We passed, and Mr. Lee said to the Count de Vergennes That is a great General Sir. Ah! said the Count de Vergennes, I wish he had the Command with You! Mr. Lee's Observation was in French "C'est un grand General, Monsieur!" The Count de Vergennes's Answer was Ah! Je souhaite qu'il avait le Commandment chez vous. This escape was in my Mind a confirmation strong of the design at Court of getting the whole Command of America into their own hands, and a luminous Commentary on Mr. Deans Letters which I had seen and heard read in Congress, and on his mad Contract with Monsieur Du Coudray and his hundred Officers.[5] My feelings on this Occasion were kept to myself: but my reflection was, I will be buried in the Ocean or in any other manner sacrificed, before I will voluntarily put on the Chains of France when I am struggling to throw off those of Great Britain. If my Life should be spared to continue these memorials, more of this Marshall De Maillebois will be recorded. Puffers he had found who represented him as one of the greatest Generals of Europe, but in Holland where I saw him in Command he proved himself as mean and mercenary as he was imbecille and unskillfull.

After dinner We went to the Accademy of Sciences, and heard Mr. D'Alembert as Secretary perpetual, pronounce Eulogies on several of their Members lately deceased. Voltaire and Franklin were both present, and there presently arose a general Cry that Monsieur Voltaire and Monsieur Franklin should be introduced to each other. This was done and they bowed and spoke to each other. This was no Satisfac-

---

Duc de Broglie, who was a marshal of France, with his younger brother the Comte de Broglie, who was not. The Comte de Broglie did indeed set on foot a scheme in 1776 to assume command in America and persuaded Silas Deane to propose the idea to Congress; see Deane to the Secret Committee of Congress, 6 Dec. 1776 (*Deane Papers*,

1:404), and Gottschalk, *Lafayette*, 1: ch. 6, "The Broglie Intrigue."
[5] Deane's agreement with Tronson du Coudray, 11 Sept. 1776, preposterous as it was on some counts, did not provide for Congressional largesse to a hundred French officers, only a mere dozen (*Deane Papers*, 1:229–232). See JA's Diary, 18 Sept. 1777 and note.

tion. There must be something more. Neither of our Philosophers seemed to divine what was wished or expected. They however took each other by the hand.... But this was not enough. The Clamour continued, untill the explanation came out "Il faut s'embrasser, a la francoise." The two Aged Actors upon this great Theatre of Philosophy and frivolity then embraced each other by hugging one another in their Arms and kissing each others cheeks, and then the tumult subsided. And the Cry immediately spread through the whole Kingdom and I suppose over all Europe Qu'il etoit charmant. Oh! il etoit enchantant, de voir Solon et Sophocle embrassans. How charming it was! Oh! it was enchanting to see Solon and Sophocles embracing!

After the Secretary's Eulogies were finished, one of which if I remember well was upon Mr. Jurieu and another on Mr. Duhamel, a number of Memoirs were publickly read by their Authors, upon various Subjects. One was upon the Art of making good Wine. As soon as he had read the Title The Audience compelled him to stop, which he did I presume with pleasure, for it was to hear a loud Applause, for the Choice of his Subject before they knew how he had treated it. It seemed to be a chymical Analysis of all the ingredients which enter into the composition of Wine, and a proscess by which it might be made in its greatest perfection. It was much applauded as were the Eulogies and most of the other Memoires. I remarked in all these compositions a kind of affectation that surprized me. The Authors seemed to search for Opportunities to introduce hints and sa[r]castical Allusions to the frivolities, Vanity, Affectation, follies and prejudices of their own Nation. This I should have expected would have been hissed at least, if no more. But on the contrary nothing was more loudly applauded, and nothing seemed to produce more gaiety and good humour. Is this an honourable trait, or is it not? More Liberties of this kind were taken in France, I believe than in any other country. In America at that time they would not have been endured. In England some freedoms may be used with John Bull, but you must be very careful to respect his essential Characteristicks of Integrity, good Sense, sound Judgment, great Courage and humanity. If you touch these you touch an Englishman to the quick. I have somewhere read that it is a proof of the last degree of depravity: when a Nation will laugh at their own Vices and then go away and repeat them. But I have some doubt of this.

April 30. Thursday. 1778. Dined with the Marshall Duke de Mouchy, with the Duke and Dutchess D'Ayen, The Marchioness de la Fayette, their Daughter, The Vicountess de Maillebois, her Sister, another Sister unmarried, The Prussian Ambassador, an Italian Ambassador, and a vast Collection of other great Company. I saw at Table a handsome Lady and perceived that she spoke a little English. As I satt next to Madame de la Fayette I asked her who that Lady was. The Marchioness blushed and seemed in some confusion for some time: at length she assumed an Air of vivacity and said "C'est une Amie de Monsieur de Mouchy." "It is a friend of Mr. De Mouchy." The Personage with whom We dined was Phillip de Noailles, Marshall Duke de Mouchy, a Grandee of Spain of the first Class, a Knight of the orders of the King, and of the Golden Fleece, Grand Cross of the Order of Malta, named Lieutenant General of Guienne in 1768 and Commander in Chief of that province in 1775.... At Table, with an audible Voice, he addressed himself to me and asked me how I liked Bourdeaux? I answered that I found it a rich elegant City, flourishing in Arts And Commerce. The Duke then asked if I was contented with my reception there? I answered that they had done me too much honour. The Duke replied, he wished he had been there to have joined them in doing me honor. I saw a general Attention to this Dialogue and a sort of Admiration in all the Company at Table, which I did [not] [6] well understand. Count Sarsfield however and several others of the Company took care to inform me, that the Duke had made me a great Compliment at Table. This, to be sure was more than I knew at the time.... This Nobleman lived in all the Splendor and Magnificence of a Vice Roy, which is little inferiour to that of a King. The Prince de Poix was the eldest Son and the Viscount de Noailles the second Son of the Duke de Mouchy.

May 1. Fryday. 1778. Dined with the Duke D'Ayen, the Brother [7] of the Duke [de] Mouchy and the Father of the Marchioness de la Fayette. The House, the Gardens, the Walks, the Pictures and Furniture all in the highest Style of magnificence. The Portraits of the Family of Noailles, were ancient and numerous. Among them was a Picture of Noailles the Ambassador, in England at the time of the Regency when the Duke of Sommersett was at the head of it. The Negotiations of this Ambassador are in print and in my Possession.[8] We were shewn into the Library, which was very large, and into all the Rooms and first Suite of Chambers in the house. The Rooms were

---

[6] Inadvertently omitted by JA.

[7] A mistake of memory for "Nephew."

[8] Antoine de Noailles is meant. His mission to England and that of his brother François in the mid-16th century are dealt with in René Aubert de Vertot d'Aubeuf, *Ambassades de Messieurs de Noailles en Angleterre*, Leyden, 1763, 5 vols., which remains among JA's books in the Boston Public Library. The volumes bear marginal pencil markings and underlining in the text by JA.

very elegant and the furniture very rich. The Library was begun by the Ambassador and augmented by Cardinal Noailles in the Time of Lewis the fourteenth and Madame De Maintenon, who was his great friend. He is represented by Mr. Malesherbes in two Volumes which he wrote upon Toleration in the latter part of his Life to have contributed much to the revocation of the Edict of Nantes. The Cardinals Picture We also saw.

The Duchess D'Ayen had five or six Children contrary to the Custom of the Country, I saw no Amie there and this family appeared to be the most regular and exemplary of any that I had seen.

When I began to attempt a little conversation in french I was very inquisitive concerning this great Family of Noailles and I was told by some of the most intelligent Men in France, ecclesiasticks as well as others, that there were no less than six Marshalls of France of this Family, that they held so many Offices under the King that they received Eighteen millions of Livres annually from the Crown. That the Family had been remarkable for Ages, for their harmony with one another and for doing nothing of any consequence without a previous Council and concert. That, when the American Revolution commenced, a family Council had been called to deliberate upon that great Event and determine what part they should take in it, or what Conduct they should hold towards it. After they had sufficiently considered, they all agreed in Opinion that it was a Crisis of the highest importance, in the Affairs of Europe and the World. That it must affect France in so essential a manner, that the King could not and ought not to avoid taking a capital Interest and part of it. That it would therefore be the best policy of the Family, to give their Countenance to it as early as possible. And that it was expedient to send one of their Sons over to America to serve in her Army under General Washington. The Prince de Poix as the Heir apparent, of the Duke de Mouchy, they thought of too much importance to their Views and expectations to be risked in so hazardous a Voyage and so extraordinary a Service, and therefore it was concluded, to offer the Enterprize to the Viscount de Noailles, and if he should decline it, to the Marquis de la Fayette. The Viscount after due consideration, thought it most prudent to remain at home for the present. The Marquis, who was represented as a youth of the finest Accomplishments and most amiable disposition, panting for Glory, ardent to distinguish himself in military Service, and impatient to wipe out a slight imputation which had been thrown, whether by Truth or Calumny upon the Memory of his father who though he had been slain in Battle was suspected to have lost his Life by too much caution to preserve it,[9] most joyfully consented to embark in the Enterprize.[1] All France pronounced it to be the first page in the History of a great Man.

This Family was in short become more powerfull than the House of Bourbon. At least they had more influence in the Army, and when they afterwards united with the Duke of Orleans, the Le Rochefoucaults, the Le Moignons [Lamoignons] and a few others, the World knows too much of the Consequences. If they advised the calling of the Assembly of Notables The Wisdom of their Family Councils, had certainly departed.[2]

[9] Apparently quite untrue. Lafayette's father died gallantly in the battle of Minden, 1759. There was, however, a Noailles general in the 18th century who was somewhat notorious for his cautiousness in the field. See Gottschalk, *Lafayette*, 1:3, 26.

[1] As CFA points out in a note (JA, *Works*, 3:150), the story of a Noailles family council approving Lafayette's enlisting in the American cause is pure legend and contrary to fact. Gottschalk has narrated Lafayette's "escape" from his family and France in 1777 in definitive detail (*Lafayette*, 1:97 ff.).

[2] The members of the Noailles family bore so many different titles and offices, and JA's allusions to them are so casual and at times inaccurate, that it may be well to list and briefly identify in one place those whom JA knew or frequently mentioned. (This information is drawn from *Dict. de la noblesse,* Hoefer, *Nouv. Biog. Générale,* and *La Grande Encyclopédie,* which, however, vary slightly from one another in giving the forenames of some of the Noailles.)

At this time there were two branches of the Noailles family powerful at court and in the military and diplomatic affairs of France. They were headed by two brothers: (I) Louis, Duc de Noailles, and (II) Philippe de Noailles, Duc de Mouchy.

I

Louis, Duc de Noailles (1713–1793), known until his father's death in 1766 as the Duc d'Ayen, was a general and from 1775 a marshal of France; he was grandfather of Adrienne de Noailles, Lafayette's wife, and died of grief after the execution of Louis XVI.

His son was Jean Louis François Paul de Noailles (1739–1824), Duc d'Ayen from 1766 and Duc de Noailles after his father's death in 1793; like most of his family he had a military career, but he was also known as a wit and an amateur of science; during the Revolution he was an *émigré* in Switzerland, returning to France with the restoration of 1814. By his wife, Henriette Anne Louise (d'Aguesseau) de Noailles, he had five daughters, one of whom, Adrienne, married Lafayette. His wife died by the guillotine in July 1794, together with her mother-in-law and her daughter Anne, Vicomtesse de Noailles (see below).

A younger brother of the preceding was Emmanuel Marie Louis, Marquis de Noailles (1743–1822), successively French ambassador at The Hague, London (1776–1778), and Vienna.

Anne de Noailles (1758–1794), niece of the preceding, daughter of the Duc d'Ayen and sister of the Marquise de Lafayette, married in 1773 the Vicomte de Noailles (see under II, below), her first cousin once removed. Her death by the guillotine is mentioned above.

Her sister Adrienne (1759–1807) married in 1774 the Marquis de Lafayette.

II

Philippe de Noailles (1715–1794), long known as the Comte de Noailles and then as the Duc de Mouchy, in 1775 became a marshal of France; he was guillotined in June 1794.

The elder son of the Duc de Mouchy was Philippe Louis Marc Antoine de Noailles (1752–1819), Prince de Poix,

May 2. Saturday. 1778. Dined at Mr. Izzards, with Mr. Lloyd and his Lady, Mr. Francois [Francès] a French Gentleman who had served in England as Charge D'Affairs for so many Years, that the Language was become very familiar to him, which enabled him to be often usefull to the Americans in Paris. There was much other Company and after dinner We went to the French Comedy, where We saw the Brutus, a Tragedy of Voltaire, and after it the Cocher Supposée. As I was coming out of the Box, after the representation, a Gentleman seized me by the hand. I looked at him.—Governor Wentworth, Sir, said the Gentleman.—At first I was somewhat embarrassed, and knew not how to behave towards him. As my Classmate and Friend at Colledge and ever since, I could have pressed him to my Bosom, with most cordial Affection. But We now belonged to two different Nations at War with each other and consequently We were Enemies. Both the Governor and the Minister were probably watched by the Spies of the Police, and our Interview would be known the next morning at Versailles. The Governor however relieved me from my reverie by asking me questions concerning his Father and Friends in America, which I answered according to my Knowledge. He then enquired after the health of Dr. Franklin, and said he must come out to Passi and pay his Compliments to him. He should not dare to see the Marquis of Rockingham after his return, without making a Visit to Dr. Franklin. Accordingly in a day or two, he came and made Us a Morning Visit. Dr. Franklin and I received him together. But there was no conversation but upon Trifles. The Governors Motives for this Trip to Paris and visit to Passy I never knew. If they bore any resemblance to those of Mr. Hartley, his deportment and language were very different. Not an indelicate expression to Us or our Country or our Ally escaped him. His whole behaviour was that of an accomplished Gentleman. Mr. Hartley on the contrary was at least [to] me very offensive. In his conversation he seemed to consider our Treaty with France as a Nullity, that We might disregard at our pleasure and treat with England seperately, or come again under her Government at our Pleasure. This appeared to me offensive to our honor and an insult to our good faith, and although I

---

soldier and *émigré*.

The younger son of the Duc de Mouchy was Louis Marie, Vicomte de Noailles (1756–1804), who served under Rochambeau in America, 1780–1782, became a member of the Constitutional Assembly in 1789, took the popular side, and later continued his military career under Napoleon, being mortally wounded in a sea fight off Cuba. In 1773 he had married his first cousin once removed, Anne de Noailles, sister of Adrienne, who the following year married Lafayette.

always endeavoured to treat him with civility, I doubt not I sometimes received it somewhat "ungraciously."[3]

It is now high time to introduce some Facts, which occurred within the first Week or ten days of my residence at Passi. I have omitted them till this time because I was unable to ascertain the precise days, when they happened. I have before observed that Dr. Franklin, from my first Arrival had taken all opportunities to prejudice me against the Lees, Mr. Izzard &c., that Mr. Lee had been very silent and reserved upon the Subject of Parties &c. But within a few days after I had got settled in my Lodgings Mr. Izzard came out to Passi, and requested some private conversation with me. I accordingly attended him alone. Mr. Izzard began upon the Subject of the disagreable Situation of our Affairs in France and the miserable Conduct of them by Mr. Deane and Dr. Franklin, and their subordinate Agents, Adherents and Friends, upon the pillage that was committed upon Us, to gratify petty french Agents and Emissaries and Instruments, of whom nobody knew. Enlarged upon the Characters of Holker, Monthieu, Baumarchais and Chaumont. Represented the enormous Waste of Money by Mr. Deane, whom Dr. Franklin supported in all Things. Talked about the Money that was offered by Beaumarchais to Mr. Lee in London as a free Gift from the King, and for the Use of the United States in presence of Mr. Wilks and others: complained of foul play by intercepting dispatches, and of frauds in the qualities and Prices of Articles which had been purchased and shipped to America &c. &c. &c. He then introduced Dr. Bancroft, said he had known him in England and had there entertained an high Opinion of his Talents and had thought him an honest Man. But here, he found him a mere Tool and Dupe of Mr. Deane, Dr. Franklin and their French Satellites, and as unprincipled as any of them. Then he represented the whole Group of them as in a Conspiracy to persecute him and the two Lees and all their friends, and related to me an amazing number of Calumnies they had propagated concerning them at Court, in Paris, Passi and the Country. That they had not confined their Lies and Slanders to Americans in France, but had extended them to Mr. Richard Henry Lee in America and to Dr. Berkenhout in London &c.

As he enlarged upon the defamations and Persecutions against himself and his Friends he grew Warm. Mr. Izzard, with great honor and integrity, had irritable Nerves and very strong Passions. He either had or at least was reputed to have great pride. There was however more of the Appearance of this Vice in his external behaviour, than in his

---

[3] The following three paragraphs were omitted by CFA in his text.

heart. A hesitancy in his Speech and an appearance of impatience that was often occasioned by it, contributed very much to the Suspicion and imputation of hautiness. In enumerating the detractions against himself and his friends, his passions transported him beyond all bounds. He declared and with asseverations which I will not repeat but which all who knew Mr. Izard may easily imagine, that Dr. Franklin was one of the most unprincipled Men upon Earth: that he was a Man of no Veracity, no honor, no Integrity, as great a Villain as ever breathed: as much worse than Mr. Deane as he had more experience, Art, cunning and Hypocricy. Mr. Izzard dilated on many of these particulars and his harrangue was exten[d]ed to a great length.

I was thunderstruck and shuddered at the Situation I was in. By Dr. Franklins continual insinuations to me, I was convinced that the rancour in his heart was not less, though his Language had not been so explicit. I said nothing of this however to Mr. Izzard. I only observed to him, that Dr. Franklin, the two Mr. Lees and Mr. Izzard himself, all held Commissions from Congress and it was my duty to respect them all. That the conduct of Mr. Deane, I knew by his dispatches and contracts which had been read in congress before I left it, had been wild, irregular and pernicious, but that I had been desirous of imputing it to want of Judgment rather than any Thing worse. That my knowledge of Dr. Franklin personally had been only in Congress. That although I knew there had been great disputes in Pennsilvania formerly concerning his moral and political Character, as there had been in England, yet I knew at the same time that he had been in publick Life when Parties run high and that he had generally maintained an honourable Character in the World. That it was impossible for me to enter into any examination of what had passed before my Arrival, because I could find no books, Letters or documents of any kind to inform or guide me. That he must be sensible my Situation was delicate, difficult and dangerous in the extream, between two fires. I was a Stranger to the Country, the Language and the manners of the French: and not much less a Stranger to the Characters of the Americans in France. In this predicament I found myself necessarily an Umpire between two bitter and inveterate Parties, for in all questions that should come before the commissioners, if Dr. Franklin and Mr. Lee should differ in Opinion my Voice must decide. That it was easy to foresee that I should make both parties my Enemies: but no choice was left me, but to examine diligently every [question without]⁴ favour or affection to any man or party: and this course I was determined to pursue at all

⁴ Conjecturally supplied for words missing in the MS.

hazards. I entreated him to collect himself and by no means to allow himself to talk in the Style he had used to me to any other Person. That Dr. Franklin possessed the Confidence of the French Court and of his own Country, and held her Commission and Authority: and therefore it was the duty of all of Us, to treat him with respect.

May 3. 1778. The Business of the Commission had been delayed and neglected in a manner that gave me much uneasiness: Franklin and Lee had been reluctant to engage in it, as I suppose, knowing that they should differ in every thing and both of them as yet uncertain which Side I should take. I had now procured my blank Books, and I took the Letters which We had received into my own hands, and after making all the Enquiries into the Subjects which I could, I wrote in my blank book the following Answers. The Book is fortunately in my Possession and now before me with the Letters in my handwriting. I shall insert these Letters because they will serve among many others to shew the number of Persons who had their Eyes fixed upon our little Treasury, and under what a variety of pretences, and pretended Authorities they sett up their Claims upon Us for money. Dr. Franklin, after he found that Mr. Lee and I agreed in Opinion and were determined to sign and send them, did not choose to let them go without his name.

Monsr. Bersolle

Sir   Passi May 3. 1778
Your Bill upon our Banker was not paid, because it was drawn, without our leave; and before you had sent Us the Accounts to shew We were your Debtors, and he could not regularly pay a Bill on our Account, which he had not our orders to pay. We are Sir your most obedient Servants.   Benjamin Franklin
                                                                                            Arthur Lee
                                                                                            John Adams.

Mr. Moylan

Sir   Passi May 3. 1778
We received your several Letters of the 23d. and 30th. of March and the fifteenth and 17th of April.[5] We are obliged to you for the care you have taken respecting the sick Men. We shall apply as you advise for the discharge of Miggins, and hope to obtain it.

We have examined Mr. Bersolle's Accounts and find them approved by Captn. Jones, his Officers, and as you have paid his draft We shall

[5] Those of 30 March and 17 April are in PPAmP:Franklin Papers; the others have not been found.

repay you. But We wish that hereafter you would not engage Us in any considerable Expence without having received our orders, after acquainting Us with the Occasion. We are, Sir, your most obedient humble Servants

B. Franklin
Arthur Lee
John Adams.

Mr. Ross at Nantes.
Sir,   Passi May 3. 1778

In a former Letter, you wrote Us, that you would send Us, the Invoices &c. of the Goods shipped, on the public Account, if We thought it necessary. We wrote for those, which would answer for the money, We had advanced to you. The Reason given in yours of the 18th [6] for refusing it, does not appear to Us, at all sufficient. If it be unavoidable to seperate the part from the whole, We desire the whole may be sent agreable to your first proposal, which will also be of Use to Us, by shewing the nature and extent of the Supplies which have been sent. We therefore expect you will comply, without any farther delay, with what We desire, and which is indispensable.

You will be so good as to send Us a Copy of the order of the Commissioners, under which you say, the Ship Queen of France was purchased, as We find none such, here.

When you first applyed to Us for our Assistance, and represented that you had made Contracts for Goods, in pursuance of orders from the Committee of Congress, which contracts, if not fulfilled, would destroy your Credit, and, in consequence, hurt that of the Committee, it was agreed to furnish you with the Sum which you desired, and which you said would be sufficient to prevent those great inconveniences, on your promise to replace it. It is now near a Year since, and you have not performed that promise. The Disappointment has been very inconvenient to Us. Probably it was occasioned by your not receiving the Remittances you expected. However, We think you should have foreborne entering into any fresh contracts and Embarrassments; especially, as it was not required or expected of you, by the Committee, as appears by their Letter to you of Decr. 30. of which you have sent Us, an extract; nor have they ever desired it, of Us; nor did you inform Us, when you made your engagements, that you had any expectation of our Assistance, to discharge them. A little consideration will convince you, that it is impossible for Us, to regulate our own purchases and engagements, and discharge our debts with punctuality,

[6] Not found.

if other people, without our participation, allow themselves to run in debt, unnecessarily, as much as they please, and call upon Us for payment. By our complying with such unforeseen demands, We may soon, to prevent your discredit, become Bankrupts ourselves, which We think would be full as disreputable to Congress. We therefore now acquaint you, that We cannot give the permission you desire, of drawing on our Banker for the immense Sums you mention, and desire you would not have the least dependance on Aids, that We have it not in our power to grant. We are, Sir, your most obedient humble Servants   B. Franklin, Arthur Lee, John Adams.

This day May 3. 1778 We had Company to dine with Us, Mr. Izzard and his Lady, Mr. Lloyd and his Lady, Dr. Bancroft, and many others. Dr. Franklin and Mr. Izzard were upon such terms that the former would not invite the latter. I was determined that I would not enter into their Resentments, and therefore said to the Dr. that I would invite Mr. Izzard and his Family, which I did accordingly and they all came, Mr. Izzard and Mrs. Izzard, their little Son and two little daughters. We sent for all our young Gentlemen at Mr. Le Cœurs Accademy, and made a delightfull Show of young Americans.

May 4. Dined at Mr. Chaumonts with his Family, and other Company.

May 5. Tuesday 1778. Dined at home without company, which was a great rarity and esteemed by me a very great Blessing.

While I was at dinner alone, my Servant brought me a Letter addressed to Messieurs Franklin, Lee and Adams, Deputies of the United States of America at Passi, and endorsed De Vergennes. I opened it and found it in French, a litteral translation of which is as follows.[7]

Versailles May 4. 1778

I have taken the orders of the King, Gentlemen, on the Subject of the presentation of Mr. Adams, your new Colleague, and his Majesty will see him on fryday next, the eighth of this month. I hope you will be so good as to do me the honour, to dine with me, on that day; I shall be ravished to have that occasion, of passing some hours with you, and of renewing to you the assurances of the most perfect consideration, with which I have the honour to be Gentlemen your most humble and most obedient Servant   De Vergennes.
M[essieu]rs. Franklin, Lee and Adams.

I passed the whole of this day at home. Mr. Lee came in the After-

[7] The translation is from the French text JA copied into his Diary entry of 5 May 1778. The recipient's copy of Vergennes' letter has not been found.

noon to my Apartment and We sat down together, to a serious Examination of the public Papers, that is of all that We could find, and a close Attention to the public Business. In the Evening Mr. Chaumont came in and informed me of the destination of a Frigate of thirty two Guns from Marsailles to Boston and that I might write by her, if I pleased.

May 6. Wednesday. 1778. Franklin told Us one of his Characteristic Stories. A Spanish Writer of certain Vissions of Hell, relates that a certain evil Spirit he met with who was civil and well bred, shewed him all the Apartments in the place. Among others that of deceased Kings. The Spaniard was much amused at so illustrious a Sight, and after viewing them for sometime, said he should be glad to see the rest of them. The rest? said the Dæmon. Here are all the Kings who ever reigned upon earth from the creation of it to this day, what the Devil would the Man have?

This Anecdote was in the Spirit of those times for the Philosophers of the last Age had raised a king killing Spirit in the World. I wrote the Story down in the Evening with a Note upon it not less Characteristick of myself. It was this. This Fable is not so charitable as Dr. Watts, who in his view of Heaven says "here and there I see a King," which seems to imply that Kings are as good as other men, since it is but here and there that We see a King upon Earth.

The Truth is that neither then nor at any former time, since I had attained any maturity in Age, Reading and reflection had I imbibed any general Prejudice against Kings, or in favour of them. It appeared to me then as it has done ever since, that there is a State of Society in which a Republican Government is the best, and in America the only one which ought to be adopted or thought of, because the morals of the People and Circumstances of the Country not only can bear it, but require it. But in several of the great nations of Europe, Kings appeared to me to be as necessary as any Government at all. Nor had I ever seen any reason to believe that Kings were in general worse than other Men.

After Dinner We went to the field, where the King reviewed his Guards, French and Swiss, about eight thousands of them. The Show was pompous indeed as all other Shows are in this Country. The Carriages of the Royal Family were very magnificent. Returned and drank Coffee with Mr. Lee at his House in Challiot [Chaillot], about a mile from ours at Passi, walked home and drank Tea with Mr. Chaumonts Family, and spent the rest of the Evening in reading Cardinal Richelieu.

May 8. Fryday. 1778. Dr. Franklin and Mr. Lee went with me to Versailles to attend my Presentation to the King. We visited the Count de Vergennes at his Office, and at the hour of eleven, the Count conducted Us, into the Kings Bed Chamber, where his Majesty was dressing. One Officer putting on his Coat, another his Sword &c. The Count went up to the King and informed him that Mr. Adams was present to be presented to his Majesty, the King turned round and looked upon me and smiled. "Is that Mr. Adams," said his Majesty? Being answered in the affirmative by the Count, he began to talk to me, and with such rapidity that I could not distinguish one Syllable nor understand one Word. But it was observed by others as well as by me that he discovered a great inclination to have a dialogue with me, whether from mere curiosity, or a desire to impress upon his Courtiers, an unusual number of whom were collected upon that occasion, an idea of his Attention and Attachment to the American cause. It was agreed on all hands that the King was the best friend We had in France. The Count de Vergennes observing his Majestys Zeal went up to him and very respectfully, said, Mr. Adams will not answer your Majesty, for he neither speaks nor understands our Language as yet. . . . "Pas un mot" said the King. . . . In what he had said to me before, I thought he said among other things Y a-t-il long tems que vous avez ete dans ce pays ci? or Il n'y a pas long tems que vous avez été dans ce pays ci. But that was all that I even suspected that I understood. . . . The Count de Vergennes then conducted me to the Door of another Room, and desired me to stand there, which I did untill the King passed. After the usual Compliments of the King to the Ambassadors, his Majesty was preparing to retire when the Count de Vergennes again repeated to the King that I did not take upon me to speak french and the King repeated his question does he not speak it att all? and passing by all the others in the Row made a full Stop before me, and evidently intended to observe and remember my Countenance and Person as I certainly meant to remark those of his Majesty. I was deeply impressed with a Character of Mildness, Goodness and Innocence in his face. It seemed to me impossible that an ill design could be harboured in that breast. . . . This Monarch was then in the twenty fourth year of his Age, having been born the 23d of August 1754. He had the Appearance of a strong constitution capable of enduring to a great Age. His Reign had already been distinguished by two great Events. The first was the restoration of Harmony in his dominions, by the extinction of those Parties which had rent the Nation under his Predecessor, and the other was the Treaty with the United States of America an Epocha in the History of France which would have reflected Glory upon that Country in all future Ages, if she had known how to improve it. But for Want of Wisdom, it has proved fatal to the Monarch and many of his Family, torn France in Pieces by factions, and swelled her to an enormous and unnatural Power, dangerous to herself, destructive to Europe, and precarious in its duration.

The Ceremonies at this Court were very simple. On a certain day of every Week was called Ambassadors day,[8] when all the public Ministers whether Ambassadors, Ministers Plenipotentiary, Envoys or Residents, who all passed under the General Title of Ambassadors, went to Versailles, were presented to the King, Queen, Monsieur the Kings oldest Brother, the Count D'Artois the Kings youngest Brother, to Madam Elizabeth the Kings Sister and to the Kings two Aunts, who had Apartments in the Castle, though they lived at Bellvue. Neither the King or any of the Royal Family, commonly spoke to any of the Corps Diplomatique, except the first order, the Ambassadors. To them they said but a few Words. The Count de Mercy Ambassador from the Emperor said He had made his Court weekly in that Character to Monsieur for thirty Years, and had always been asked the same question "Have you come from Paris this morning?" Seven or Eight Years afterwards in England I found the Custom very different. The King and Queen must speak to every body. This has made the King the greatest Talker in Christendom, but it is a Slavery to which no human Being ought to be subjected. It is but Justice, to say that it was agreable and instructive to hear him, for let the insolent Peter Pindar say what he will, His Majesty said as many things which deserved to be remembered as any Sage I ever heard.[9]

We afterwards made Visits to Count Maurepas, Mr. De Sartine, to the Chancellor Miromenil, and to Mr. Bertin &c. The Chancellor had the Countenance of a Man, worn with severe Studies. When I was presented to him, he turned to Dr. Franklin and said, Monsieur Adams est un Personne celebre en Amerique et en Europe. We went afterwards to dinner, with the Count de Vergennes. There was a very long and a very full Table: No Ladies but the Countess. The Count's Brother who had lately signed the Treaty with Switzerland as Ambassador of France, and a Crowd of others, Dukes, Bishops and Counts. Mr. Garnier, the late Secretary to the Embassy in England was also

---

[8] Thus in MS.

[9] Under the pseudonym "Peter Pindar" the clergyman-physician-poet John Wolcot (1738–1819) published satires on George III in the 1780's, making a specialty of burlesquing the King's halting and vapid conversation (*DNB; The Works of Peter Pindar, Esqr. In Three Volumes*, London, 1794).

there. Mr. Garnier and a Mr.   asked me, with some Appearance of concern, whether there was any foundation for the Reports which the Ministry had spread in England of a dispute between Congress and General Washington? A Letter they said had been printed, from an Officer in Philadelphia to that purpose. My Answer was that no such dispute existed when I left Congress in November, that I heard of no such Thing after I left it, before my Embarkation in February, that I had no information of it, since my Arrival in France, and that so far from giving any Credit to the report, I believed it to be impossible. Mr. Garnier was the first French Gentleman, who began a serious political conversation with me, of any great length. I found him a sensible, well informed Man.

May 9. Saturday. 1778. This morning Mr. Joy, Mr. Johonnot, and Mr. Green Son of Mr. Rufus Green came to visit me. The American Ministers dined with Madam Bertin, at Passi.

This Lady is married to a Nephew of Mr. Bertin the Minister, and he holds some lucrative office under the Crown. She has a fine Person and an excellent Understanding. Her Husband is however said to be a great Libertine worn out with debauchery, and very far from treating her with the tenderness and fidelity which she merits. She is universally reputed to be a Woman of sincere Piety and spotless virtue, and has inflexibly rejected the many Advances which have been made to her by Gentlemen who had every Advantage of Power, Person and fortune to recommend them, preferring the consciousness of Innocence and the Esteem of the very few, to all other considerations. This Lady is said by Dr. Smith to have been a Spy employed by the Court to watch the American Ministers. I cannot contradict this, because it is possible, but I have no reason to believe it, any more than that every Man and Woman in France were so employed. Dr. Smith says too, that she adored Franklin as much as she despized me. That she respected Franklin is very true, and that she respected Mr. Lee and Mr. Izzard is also true. And if she did not respect me she was the greatest hypocrite in France: for not one Lady in the Kingdom ever made me so many professions and gave me so many proofs of her invariable Esteem as Madam Bertin, and there was not one for whom I had and have still so great a regard. Her Attentions to Mr. Izzards Family and to me, were very particular, and the reason she assigned for it, to other Persons, was that she understood We were domestic People. I have heard nothing about her for more than twenty Years, and whether death by the Guillotine or otherwise has removed her I know not:

but her Memory ought to be vindicated from the Aspersions of this Dr. Smith.[1]

May 10. Sunday. 1778. Messieurs Brattle, Waldo, Joy, Johonnot, Green and Austin, dined with Us, at Passi. After dinner We walked in the Bois de Boulogne, as far as the new Seat of the Count D'Artois, which he called Baggatelle, where We saw Mr. Turgot, Mr. and Madam La Frété and much other Company, Sunday in this Country being devoted to diversions, Exercises and Amusements. There were more Games, Plays and Sports of every kind on that day than on any other in the Week. Some of these American Gentlemen I suspect came over from England, with hopes of Employment by the Commissioners or of recommendations to Congress. Mr. Waldo was however the only one who applied explicitly to me for that purpose. But in the first place We had no Employments to bestow, and in the next place, I thought as Mr. Waldo had left America and resided in England so long before the War broke out, it would be doing Injustice to others who had born the burthen in the heat of the day, to appoint him to any place worth his accepting. The Answer I gave him, I do not remember, and should have forgotten the Conversation, had not Sir John Temple told me, several Years afterwards that Mr. Waldo was much offended and took great exceptions to what I had said to him. He reported to Sir John that I told him I would set my face against him tooth and nail. These are very vulgar Expressions and were very unnecessary, if I said them, which I doubt. But although Mr. Waldo had been esteemed a good Whigg in Boston, when he left it, yet he had never any particular merit that I knew of, he had left his Country for six Years of her great-

[1] The "Aspersions" in question, intended for JA rather than Mme. Bertin, are in John Wood, *The History of the Administration of John Adams ...*, N.Y. [1802], p. 324–325, in a chapter that deals at large with JA's jealousy of Franklin:

"During the embassy of Franklin, Adams and Lee at Paris, a fete was given in honor of America, by a Mrs. Bertand, the Lady of a Nobleman, who acted in capacity of Lord in waiting to the King. Mrs. Bertand was one of those celebrated female politicians, who used to be in the employ of the Court, for the purpose of discovering, by her intrigues, the secret springs and intentions of foreign cabinets. . . . [S]he was also a lady of science, and the principal patroness of the arts in Paris. Her veneration for Franklin was equal to her contempt for Mr. Adams; but Adams and Lee, with almost every American of education then at Paris, were of course invited to partake of the pleasures of an entertainment, intended as a compliment to their country. During the performance of a theatrical piece, the portrait of Franklin was introduced on the stage. . . . an universal burst of applause ensued, which wounded the feelings of Adams to such a degree, that he feigned sickness and left the performance."

A footnote states that "Dr. James Smith, now in New-York, was present, and seated near Mr. Adams at the above fete."

est distress, and had never discovered any inclination to return to it, till after the Conquest of Burgoine and the Treaty with France and therefore I thought there was a meanness in his Wishes to take the bread out of the mouths of Men, who had done, suffered and merited much more than he had.

May 11. Monday. Dined at Mr. Sorins, at Passi.[2] Here, if I mistake not I dined with a Bishop, and another Gentleman and Lady. The Lady was known by the Husband to be the Mistress of the Bishop, and it was no Secret to any body. The Bishop was reported to have made some compensation to the Husband, by procuring him some little Employment and by contributing some what largely to the Expences of the family. The Countenances of the Bishop, the Husband and the Wife were watch'd by me with more marked Attention, than was perhaps compatible with good Breeding in France. No notice of it, however was taken by any of the Company. The Jesuitical face of the Bishop, who was said too, to be one of the most sensible Men in France, The conscious humiliation in the Faces of both Husband and Wife, convinced me, that misery was in the hearts of them all: that they saw and approved better Things, but followed the worse. Such are the manners of France, said I to myself. Our Republican Governments in America, must exclude all these Examples or We shall be soon undone.

May 12. Tuesday. 1778. Mr. Deane had left the care of his Son Jesse with Dr. Franklin and Dr. Bancroft, so that I had no longer any responsibility, on his Account. Mr. Vernon had chosen to remain at Bourdeaux, although I had proposed to him to come to Passi and assist me as my private Secretary, a Situation which would at least have borne all his Expences, and initiated him very early, into the Knowledge of the foreign Affairs of his Country: but as his Fathers Views were commercial rather than political, I could not disapprove of his Choice. In Answer to a Letter from him I wrote him the following

My dear Sir   Passi, near Paris May 12. 1778

Your favour of the tenth of last month came to my hands some days ago, and I believe that your determination to reside at Bourdeaux, in preference to any other commercial City is judicious, because it is generally agreed to be the most oppulent and flourishing; and its proximity to Spain may give you a fairer Opportunity of gaining Knowledge of the Trade of both Kingdoms, than you could have, in any other.[3]

---

[2] The Diary entry of this date ends at this point. The remembered incident and comment that follow were omitted by CFA in his text.

[3] Vernon's letter, dated 10 April, is in the Adams Papers. He did not remain

I can say nothing of your choice of a House, because the Gentlemen are wholly unknown to me; for which reason I believe it will be better for me, to refer you to Mr. Bondfield the American Agent, than to write directly to Messieurs Feyers.

Give my Compliments to Mr. Bondfield, and ask the favour of him to assist you in settling the terms with those Gentlemen or any other with whom you may determine to agree. Mr. Bondfield may be assured that he will be doing much good, by assisting you, for that you are sprung from a Family of much merit, in America. That your Father who was a Merchant of large property and excellent reputation, in the Town of Newport in Rhode Island, has had the Virtue to abandon his property to the fury of a British Army, and take his Lot with his Countrymen, in their hardy Struggle for Liberty. That he is a Gentleman in high Trust and Esteem, being the first of the three Members of the Continental Navy Board, established at Boston, for the Eastern District of North America.

If these things are decently represented to those Gentlemen, I doubt not, they will agree to take you into their family: and Mr. Bondfields Goodness of heart I am convinced, will be gratified by the Opportunity of rendering this Service to a young Gentleman of liberal Education and promising hopes, and to a Father, whose Sufferings and Services, have deserved this friendship of his Countrymen. Shew this Letter to Mr. Bondfield, who may shew it, to whomsoever, he will. I am, Sir, with much Esteem, your Friend and humble Servant   John Adams
Mr. William Vernon Jur. at Bourdeaux.

This day We dined at Mr. Duprés, at the   Montagne. The Gardens and the prospects were very fine. The Place lies adjoining to the Seat of the First President of the Parliament of Paris. We met his Lady in our Walks, and she desired the Gentlemen to shew Us the Grounds, but not the whole of them, for she wished to enjoy the Company of the American Ministers, At her house, at her own invitation, and she chose to reserve a part of the Curiosities of the place as an inducement to Us to accept it. Compliments are so essential a branch of the Science of Life, the Savoir vivre, in France, that it is astonishing how prompt and ingenious, they are in producing them.

From this Hill We had a fine View of the Country, and of the Kings Castle at Vincennes. My little Son and the other young Americans at the Pension, were invited and dined with Us.

May 13. Wednesday. 1778. Dined at Mr. Chaumonts, with a great

---

in Bordeaux; see JA's Diary entry of 13 Feb. 1778 and note 3 there.

deal of Company. After Dinner took a Walk to Chaillot to see Mr. Lee, who had a large Company of Americans to dine with him, among the rest, Mr. Fendell of Maryland and Dr. Smith, Brother of Mr. William Smith of New York the Historian. This Gentleman has been occasionally mentioned before.

May 14. Thursday. 1778. Under this date, I find in my private Letter Book, the following in Answer to Letters received from Mr. McCreery

Dear Sir   Passi near Paris May 14. 1778.

Your two Letters of April 25, and May 3 [4] are before me. I thank you for the trouble you have taken in searching for the Breeches. I have no suspicion of the Servants at your house. I rather conjecture that once, upon the road, when a few Things were taken out of my Trunk, this Article might slip aside. The Gold could not have been the temptation for it was hid in the Waistband. However, whether it is in the hands of a Thief or an honest finder, I wish he knew of the Gold for it might be of Service to him. So much for that. [5]

I am not disposed to find fault with any thing I meet with, in this Country. Such a disposition, in any Traveller, in any Country, I should esteem a Mark of a littleness of Mind: but in a Person situated as I am, and sustaining the public trust, that has been committed to me, I should hold it, not only an Absurdity, but a Misdemeanor.

The Gentleman you allude to, [6] I hope has been more upon his guard, because from a long Acquaintance, with his Character and conduct, I know he has Abilities and merit, and, from all that I have seen of him here, I am convinced that he is actuated by great Zeal and Anxiety for the public good.... A fatal Misunderstanding, between some Characters, of importance, has given rise to reflections upon each others Conduct that must have hurt the reputation of our Country. The Gentleman you allude to, thinks that our Affairs have been mismanaged and the public Interest imprudently dissipated: and that many Persons have been improperly admitted to the public Purse. Another Gentleman, who has had the principal direction of the Purse,

---

[4] In the Adams Papers.

[5] The "Breeches" belonged to JQA, contained eight guineas in gold sewed into the waistband, and were never found. See McCreery to JA, Bordeaux, 3 May, and an entry in JA's Accounts, 1778–1779, printed in his Diary at the end of 1778 (vol. 2: 326).

[6] "Some People will fly into a violent Passion for what [a] Frenchman sees no harm in, or for the least mistake made by a Servant, and immediately Curse the whole Nation. This I'm credibly inform'd has been the Rule of a Gentleman in Paris, whom I have already mention'd to you, and has been the means of procuring him many Enemies" (McCreery to JA, 25 April). This unnamed "Gentleman" was undoubtedly Arthur Lee.

1. "JOHN ADAMS — PRÉSIDENT DES ÉTATS-UNIS, D'APRÈS NATURE AU
PHISIONOTRACE 1800 À 1801," BY SAINT-MÉMIN

PARIS, May 18, 1778.

199

GENTLEMEN,

CERTAIN Intelligence having been received, that eleven British Ships of War, viz. One of 90 Guns, nine of 74, and one of 64 Guns, are in the Road of St. Hellens, near Portsmouth, bound for North-America, and the United States being in Alliance with France, you are requested, as speedily as possible, to convey this Information to the Commanders of any French Fleet, or Ships of War in America, by sending them this Letter, and also to publish the Contents of it in all the Continental News-Papers.

We have the Honor to be, Gentlemen,

Your most obedient humble Servants,

FRANKLIN,

JOHN ADAM.

To the Governor, or any Counsellor, or Senator, or Member of any House of Representatives, in any of the Thirteen United States of America.

Read in Congress, July 8, 1778,

And ordered to be published.

CHARLES THOMSON, Secretary.

2. FIRST PAGE OF JOHN ADAMS' "TRAVELS AND NEGOTIATIONS"

3. CIRCULAR LETTER OF THE AMERICAN COMMISSIONERS

complains of reflections upon the French Nation and Government, Customs, manners &c. I wish there were no ground for any of these reflections: But one thing I know, that an immense Sum of Money is gone, that a great Sum of Money is still due. And another thing I know, that I am at a loss to discover what America has received as an equivalent for all these Sums and Debts.

As to Mr. Delap, whom you recommend for Agent, I have not a Sentiment but of respect for that Gentleman: but, Sir, the Appointment of continental Agents and the Management of commercial Affairs, is now in a new Channel under the orders of Congress, and I believe the Commissioners will not think themselves at Liberty to interfere in it. Mr. Bondfield I believe has a regular appointment, and for any thing I have ever heard behaves well. If any complaints should arise, the Commissioners will undoubtedly attend to them, with the utmost impartiality.

If you should determine homewards, be so good as to let me know as early as you can, and the part of the Continent to which you shall go. . . . Whether you go or stay, I wish you all happiness and prosperity, being with sincere Esteem your friend and Servant.
Mr. William McCreery at Bourdeaux.

I find written under this Letter, in my private Letter Book, the Words "Not Sent." Upon more mature deliberation, I thought it improper and dangerous, to lay open so much of the State of our Affairs and the Altercations of the Parties, to any private Gentleman in France, especially at the distance of Bourdeaux: and therefore resolved to withhold the Letter, though it contained nothing but the exact truth.

The public Business of this day May 14 included the following Letter

Sir   Passi May 14. 1778
In the several Cruises made by Captains Wicks, Johnson, Cunningham, Thompson and others, of our armed Vessels, on the Coasts of Great Britain, it is computed that between four and five hundred Prisoners have been made, and set at Liberty, either on their landing in France, or at Sea, because it was understood that We could not keep them confined in France. When Captain Wicks brought in, at one time, near an hundred, We proposed to Lord Stormont, an Exchange for as many of ours confined in England: but all Treaty on the Subject was rudely refused, and our People are still detained there, notwithstanding the liberal discharges, We had made of theirs, as abovementioned. We hear that Captain Jones has now brought into

Brest, near 200, which We should be glad to exchange for our Seamen who might be of Use in our Expeditions from hence: but as an Opinion prevails that Prisoners of a Nation with which France is not at War, and brought into France by another Power, cannot be retained by the Captors, but are free, as soon as they arrive, We are apprehensive that these Prisoners may also be sett at Liberty, return to England, and serve to man a Frigate against Us, while our brave Seamen, with a number of our Friends of this nation, whom We are anxious to sett free, continue useless and languishing in their Goals. In a Treatise of one of your Law Writers, entituled A Treatise of Prises or Principles of French Jurisprudence concerning the Prizes, which are made at Sea[7] printed in 1763 We find the above Opinion controverted page 129 §. 30. in the following Words. "This seems to shew, that it is not true, as some Persons pretend, that as soon as a Prisoner, making his escape or otherwise, has sett his foot on Land, in a neutral Power, he is absolutely free from that moment. Indeed it will not be permitted to retake him, without the consent of that Power; but she would be wanting to the Laws of Neutrality, if [s]he should refuse her Consent. This is a Consequence of the Assylum due to the Ship in which was the Prisoner or the Hostage."

We know not of what Authority this Writer may be, and therefore pray a moment of your Excellencys Attention to this matter, requesting your Advice upon it, that if it be possible some means may be devised to retain these Prisoners, till as many of ours can be obtained in exchange for them. We have the Honor to be &c.

To Mr. De Sartine.   Benjamin Franklin
                                                      Arthur Lee
                                                      John Adams

May 15. Fryday. 1778. Dined at Mr. Grands with all the Americans in Paris.

We received a Letter from the Count De Vergennes, a litteral Translation of which is in these Words.

Versailles the 15th. of May 1778

I have the honour, Gentlemen, to send you the Copy of a Letter, written to Mr. De Sartine, by the Consul of France at Madeira. You will see, in it, all the Circumstances of the Conduct, which an American Privateer, named John Warren has held, towards a French Snow or Brigantine, Captain Rochell,[8] which he seized, near enough to the

---

[7] LbC gives this title and the following quotation in French.
[8] LbC: "Rochel."

Land and in Sight of the City of Madeira. Proceedures so reprehensible, cannot remain unpunished, and I doubt not Gentlemen, that you will make to Congress such representations, as will produce the most efficacious measures, not only that the Captain John Warren may receive the punishment his conduct merits but also to procure for the French Vessell, the Satisfaction and indemnification which are due to her. I rely, in this respect, on the Necessity, of which you must undoubtedly be convinced, of restraining such Excesses, the Consequences of which will not be less felt by the Congress, than they are by Us. I have the honour to be, most perfectly, Gentlemen your most humble and most obedient Servant   De Vergennes.
Messrs. les Deputes des Etats Unis

[*Enclosure*]

Copy of a Letter written to Mr. De Sartine, by Mr. De La Ruilliere [Tuelliere], Consul at Madeira the 15. February 1778.

I have the honour to inform you, that on the fourth of this month, a French Snow or Brigantine, which is believed to be the Prudent Captain Rochell of about one hundred and fifty tons, coming from London with a Cargo of Commodities, and some flour, for this Island, was met, visited and captured, near enough to the Land and in Sight of this City by an American Privateer, which is said to be from Boston and is named the Lyon Captain John Warren, and finally sent to Boston, under the prætext that the Cargo belonged to Englishmen. The Circumstances which accompanied this Capture, render the Action of this Cruiser not only extremely blameable but they characterize him rather as a Pirate, than as a Privateer authorized by any Government.

Following the directions of a Portuguese Fisherman, whom the said Vessell had taken for a guide to conduct her into the Road, the Privateer entered into this Vessell as into a Prize, taking immediate possession, and even ill treating the People, and after having transported them by violence on board the Privateer, taken and kept all the Papers, which could prove to whom the Vessell belonged, and of what Nation he was, she put on board an American Crew with whom she sent her to America, naturally in the Intention of selling there, the Cargo, and perhaps the Vessell, with the Ventures of the french Captain and Seamen, and all that might belong to Merchants of Neutral Nations, with the Insurgents in some of our American Islands, where the said Cargo of Commodities, ou bien de Pipes en bote, would sell to great Advantage whereas they would be of very little Value, if sold in the English Colonies of the Insurgents, which abound in such Merchandizes. I have made haste, my Lord to inform you of this fact, persuaded, that after having reflected upon its importance, you will condescend to take all the measures necessary, to obtain restitution of so irregular a Capture, to cause the Captain of the Privateer to be punished for his Crime, and to prevent in future all similar Outrages, so prejudicial to our navigation and commerce, and so inconsistent with the Safety, and the respect, which all nations preserve, for our flagg, in the present Circumstances.[9]

May 17. 1778. Dined at home. Dr. Dubourg, Mr. Parker and another Gentleman dined with me.

May 18. 1778. We wrote the following Circular Letter to all the Seaports.

Gentlemen   Paris May 18. 1778

Certain Intelligence having been received, that Eleven British Ships of War, vizt. one of 90 Guns, nine of 74 and one of sixty four Guns, are in the road of St. Hellens near Portsmouth, bound for North America, and the United States being in Allyance with France, you are requested as speedily as possible to convey this information to the Commanders of any French Fleet or Ships of War in America, by sending them this Letter, and also to publish the Contents of it, in all the Continental Newspapers. We have the honor to be, Gentlemen, your most obedient humble Servants.

Twenty Copies of this Letter, signed by B. Franklin and John Adams were sent on the day of the date of it.[1]

This day, May 18, We dined at Mr. La Frété's country Seat, at the foot of Mount Calvare. The House, Gardens and Walks were very spacious. The Seat is upon the River Seine, nearly opposite to that Castle, whimsically called Madrid, built by Francis the first, and called by that name, to quiet his conscience and save his honour by a Punn, for violating his Parol given to Charles the fifth.

---

[9] At several points JA's translation from the French text in his letterbook leaves something to be desired. See, further, JA's Autobiography under 19 May, below.

[1] This notation follows the text of the letter in JA's letterbook. The circular was addressed "To the Governor, or any Counsellor, or Senator, or Member of any House of Representatives, in any of the Thirteen United States of America." On receipt of a text, Congress ordered it to be published, 8 July (JCC, 11:675); it was printed as a broadside, and three copies are in Arch. Nat., Marine, Paris, B4, vol. 146, one of which is reproduced as an illustration in the present volume.

May 19. 1778. We wrote to Congress, and to the Count De Vergennes.

To the President of Congress
Sir   Passi May 19. 1778
We have the Honor to inclose a Copy of a Letter received from Monsieur the Count De Vergennes, the Secretary of State for foreign Affairs, with a Copy of a Letter inclosed in it, for the Consideration of Congress, not doubting that Congress will give it all the Attention, that an Affair of so much importance demands. We have the Honor to be &c.   B. Franklin, Arthur Lee, John Adams.[2]

Sir   Passi May 19. 1778
We have had the Honor of your Excellencys Letter of the fifteenth instant, inclosing a Copy of a Letter from Mr. De La Rouilliere, Consul at Madeira of the 15th. of March [*i.e.* February?] 1778.

We have inclosed to Congress a Copy of your Excellencys Letter with a Copy of its Inclosures, and have recommended to Congress, the earliest attention to the Subject, and have no doubt that Justice will be speedily done. We have the Honor to be &c.
                        B. Franklin, Arthur Lee, John Adams.
His Excellency Le Compte De Vergennes.

I find this Note of this date, in my book.

                                                        May 19. 1778.
Mr. A. returns his respectfull Compliments to Mr. Hyslop, and informs him with much pleasure, that Dr. Chancey and his Family were well, the beginning of February and as he supposes Mr. Hyslops Family likewise, having never heard any thing to the contrary. As to Advice, what Mr. Hyslop had best do, Mr. A. is not able to give any, but wishes Mr. Hyslop to follow his own Judgment which is much better. Hopes the Storms will blow over in time, and that he shall have the pleasure of again seeing Mr. Hyslop in fair Weather.[3]

[2] No recipient's copy of this letter has been found, and probably none was received by Congress. Copies of both the letter and its enclosures (the letters inserted in the Autobiography under 15 May, above) are in PCC, No. 85, made by Henry Remsen Jr. from "a Volume of the Commissioners Letters kept by Mr. [Arthur] Lee."
[3] This was in answer to a third-person note from Hyslop, London, 8 May, inquiring about his own and Dr. Chauncy's families in Boston (Adams Papers). The writer was doubtless William Hyslop, a Boston merchant who was a connection by marriage of the eminent clergyman Charles Chauncy (Thwing Catalogue, MHi; *NEHGR*, 8 [1854]: 128r–u).

May 19. Tuesday. 1778. We dined with Mr. De Challut, one of the Farmers General.... We were introduced into the most superb Gallery I had yet seen. The Paintings, Statues, and Curiosities, were as rich and costly as they were innumerable. The Old Marshall Richelieu, and a vast number of other great Company dined with Us. After dinner Mr. De Challût invited Dr. Franklin and me to go to the Opera and take Seats in his Logis, which We did. The Musick and dancing were very fine. The French Opera is a very pleasing Entertainment for a few times. There is every Thing, which can please the Eye or the Ear. But the Words are unintelligible, and if they were not, they are said to be very insignificant. One always wishes in such an Amusement to learn something. The Imagination, the Passions and the Understanding have too little Employment in the Opera.

May 20. Wednesday. 1778. I wrote the following Letter

Sir   May 20. 1778

Your Favour of the 26 of April I duely received, and it is with the utmost pleasure, that I am able to inform you, that an Officer of the name of De Fleury, whom I suppose to be your Son, having never heard of more than one of that name, is in the American Army under General Washington, to whom he has recommended himself, by his signal Valour And Activity upon several Occasions.[4] He has also recommended himself, so far to Congress, that they have, twice I think, acknowledged his Bravery, by Votes upon their Journal, in which they have presented him, with two horses, he having had so many shot under him in Battle. I have not the honor, personally to know this worthy Officer, but I know enough of his fame to felicitate you, Sir, and his Mother, upon the honor of having such a Son, and to wish that his Life and health may be preserved for the Comfort of his Parents and for the honor and Advantage of the two Countries, now so happily united as Friends and Allies, France and the United States of America.

I believe, Sir, you may be perfectly easy, about your Sons Subsistance: because his Pay and Appointments, I believe are sufficient to supply all his Wants of that kind. I am, Sir, with much respect your most obedient Servant   John Adams.

A Monsieur De Fleury Conseignieur de la Ville de St. Hippolite.

Dined this day at Dr. Dubourg's, with a small Company, very

[4] The letter from Fleury *père* is in the Adams Papers. His son was François Louis Teissèdre de Fleury, a French officer who had a very distinguished military career in America, 1777–1782, at first as a volunteer and later under Rochambeau (Lasseray, *Les français sous les treize étoiles*, 2:425–433).

handsomely but not amidst those Signs of Wealth and grandeur that I see every where else. I saw, however more of Sentiment, and therefore more of genuine Taste than I had seen in other places where there was ten times the magnificence. Among his Pictures were a devellopement of the Interiour decorations, and of the Paintings on the Cieling of the Gallery of Versailles. The Physician Erasistratus discovering the Love of Antiochus. The Continence of Scipio. The Adieus of Hector and Andromache, in which the Passions were so strongly marked that I must have been made of Marble, not to have felt them and been melted by them. I had not forgotten Adieus, as tender and affecting as those of any Hector or Andromache that ever existed, with this difference, that there were four Astyanaxes instead of one in the Scene. With Feelings too exquisite to produce tears or Words, I gazed in Silence at every Line, at every light and shade of this Picture, and could scarcely forgive Homer for introducing the Gleam of the Helmet and its Effect upon Astyanax, or any circumstance which could excite a Smile and diminish the Pathetic of the Interview.

After dinner We went and drank Tea, with Madame Foucault, and took a view of Mr. Foucaults House. A very grand Hotel it was, or at least appeared so to me. The Furniture, the Beds, the Curtains, the every Thing was as rich as Silk and Gold could make it.... But I was wearied to death with gazing wherever I went, at a profusion of unmeaning Wealth and Magnificence. The Adieus of Hector and Andromache, had attracted my Attention and given me more pleasure melancholly as it was, than the sight of all the Gold of Ophir could.... Gold, Marble, Silk, Velvet, Silver, Ivory and Alabaster, made up the Show every where.

I shall make no Scruple to violate my own rule of Criticism, by introducing on the same page with Hector and Andromache, a Story of Franklins which he gave Us in the same day. Franklin delighted in New Gate Anecdotes and he told us one of a Taylor who stole a horse, was detected and committed to New Gate, where he met another Felon, who had long followed the Trade of Horse Stealing. The Taylor told his Story to the other who enquired, why he had not taken such a road, and assumed such a disguise and why he had not disguised the Horse? I did not think of it. Did not think of it? Who are You? and what has been your Employment? A Taylor.... You never stole a Horse before I suppose in your Life? Never.... ——————— What Business had you with Horse Stealing? Why did not you content yourself with your Cabbage?

May 21. Thursday 1778. The disputes between the Parties had by this time become so well known to me, and their violence had arisen to such rancour, that what ever was done or said by Dr. Franklin or by me, when I agreed with him in Opinion was censured and often misrepresented by one Party, and whatever was done or said by Mr. Lee or Mr Izzard, and by me when I thought they were in the right was at least equally censured and misrepresented by the other. I was so thoughrougly disgusted with the Service and so fully convinced, that our whole System was wrong and that ruin to our Affairs abroad and great danger and confusion in those at home, must be the Consequence of it, that I thought it my indispensable duty to represent my Ideas in America. To Congress I had no Justification to write but in conjunction with my Colleagues. It was impossible that We could agree in any thing, I therefore determined to write to a confidential Friend in Congress, who I knew would communicate it to others, who might make such Use of it as the public good might require. I accordingly wrote to Mr. Samuel Adams as follows.

My dear Sir   Passi May 21. 1778
I have never yet paid my respects to you, since my Arrival in Europe, for which seeming Neglect of Duty, the total Novelty of the Scænes about me, and the incessant Avocations of Business and Ceremony and Pleasure, for this last I find in Europe, makes an essential part of both the other two, must plead my excuse.

The Situation of the general Affairs of Europe, is still critical and of dubious Tendency. It is still uncertain, whether there will be War, between the Turks and Russians; between the Emperor and the King of Prussia; and indeed between England and France, in the Opinion of many People; my own Conjecture however is, that a War will commence and that soon.

Before this reaches you, you will be informed, that a strong Squadron of thirteen Capital Ships and several Frigates, has sailed from Toulon, and that another Squadron is ordered to sail from Spithead. Whatever I may have heard of the destination of the first, I am not at Liberty to mention it. We have yet no intelligence that the latter has sailed.

Chatham the great is no more: but there is so much of his wild Spirit in his last Speech, yet left in the Nation, that I have no doubt but Administration will put all to the hazard.

We are happy to hear, by the Frigate Le Sensible, which has returned to Brest, that the Treaty arrived safe at Casco Bay. We hope to have the earliest Intelligence of the ratification of it. . . . The Commissioners from England, who sailed about the twenty second of April, will meet as We suppose with nothing but ridicule.

Prussia is yet upon the reserve concerning America, or rather, forgetting his Promise has determined not to acknowledge our Independance, at present. His Reason is obvious. He wants the Aid of those very German Princes who are most subservient to Great Britain, who have furnished her with Troops to carry on the War against Us, and therefore he does not[5] choose to offend them by an Alliance with Us, at present. Spain is on the reserve too: but there is not the least doubt entertained here, of her intentions to support America. In Holland there is more Friendship for Us, than I was aware before I came here. At least, they will take no part against Us.

Our Affairs in this Kingdom, I find in a State of confusion and darkness, that surprizes me. Prodigious Sums of money have been expended and large Sums are yet due. But there are no Books of Account, or any Documents, from whence I have been able to learn what the United States have received as an Equivalent.

There is one Subject, which lies heavily on my Mind, and that is the expence of the Commissioners. You have three Commissioners at this Court, each of whom lives at an Expence of at least Three thousand Pounds Sterling a Year, I fear at a greater Expence. Few Men in this World are capable of living at a less Expence, than I am. But I find the other Gentlemen have expended, from three to four Thousand a Year each, and one of them from five to six. And by all the Enquiries I have been able to make, I cannot find any Article of Expence, which can be retrenched.

The Truth is, in my humble Opinion, our System is wrong in many Particulars.   1. In having three Commissioners at this Court. One in the Character of Envoy is enough. At present each of the Three is considered in the Character of a Public Minister; a Minister Plenipotentiary, which lays him under an absolute Necessity of living up to this Character. Whereas one alone would be obliged to no greater Expence, and would be quite sufficient for all the Business of a Public Minister.   2. In Leaving the Salaries of these Ministers at an Uncertainty. You will never be able to obtain a satisfactory Account, of the public Monies, while this System continues. It is a Temptation to live at too great an Expence, and Gentlemen will feel an Aversion to demanding a rigorous Account.   3. In blending the Business of a public Minister with that of a Commercial Agent. The Businesses of various departments, are by this means so blended and the public and private Expences so confounded with each other, that I am sure no Satisfaction can ever be given to the Public, of the disposition of their

---

[5] LbC (and also RC, in NN:Bancroft Coll.): "dont."

Interests and I am very confident that Jealousies and Suspicions will hereafter arise against the Characters of Gentlemen, who may perhaps have Acted with perfect Integrity and the fairest Intentions for the public Good.

My Idea is this, seperate the Offices of Public Ministers from those of commercial Agents.... Recall, or send to some other Court, all the Public Ministers but one, at this Court. Determine with Precision, the Sum that shall be allowed to the remaining one, for his Expences and for his Salary, i.e. for his Time, Risque, Trouble &c., and when this is done see that he receives no more than his allowance.

The Inconveniences arising from the Multiplicity of Ministers and the Complications of Businesses are infinite.

Remember me, with the most tender Affection to my worthy Colleagues, and to all others to whom you know they are due. I am your Friend and Servant   John Adams
The Honourable Samuel Adams [6]

This Letter was received by Mr. Adams in due Season, and by him communicated to Mr. Richard Henry Lee and others. Mr. R. H. Lee wrote me immediately that he had seen it and was entirely of my Opinion.[7] It was communicated to so many members of Congress that it produced the Revolution which followed, My Friends and the Friends of Mr. Arthur Lee uniting with those of Dr. Franklin, Mr. Deane and Mr. Izzard, in introducing the new Plan.[8]

The representation in my Letter of the Expences of the Commissioners, related only to the State of Things before my Arrival. My Expences were very trifling. I had no House rent to pay seperate from Dr. Franklins. I kept no Carriage and used none but that of Dr. Franklin and that only when he had no Use for it. I had very little Company more than Dr. Franklin would have had, if I had not been there. But before my Arrival, Mr. Deane had his House and Furniture and Establishment of Servants as well as his Carriage in Paris, and another Establishment for his Appartments in the Country at Passy and another Carriage and Set of Horses and Servants, besides his

[6] RC has a postscript: "This will be delivered you by a young Gentleman, by the Name of Archer, who appears to have a good Head and an honest Heart.—He fights as a Voluntier on the side of America, because his Conscience would not permit him to fight on the other side, with a Commission."

[7] R. H. Lee to JA, 29 Oct. 1778 (Adams Papers; R. H. Lee, *Letters,* ed. Ballagh, 1:447–448).

[8] The "new Plan" of Sept.–Oct. 1778 left Franklin sole American minister plenipotentiary to France; see JA's Diary entry of 12 Feb. 1779, note 4.

Libertine Expences. Mr. Lee had an House, furniture, Carriage and organization of Servants at Challiot. Dr. Franklin had his in the Basse Court de Monsieur Le Ray de Chaumont at what rent I never could discover, but from the Magnificence of the Place it was universally expected to be enormously high. Making the best Estimate I could from the representations that were made to me I wrote as I then believed. But after a longer Residence, more experience and further Inquiry, I was convinced that I had admitted much exaggeration into the Account. Nevertheless the Expences of Mr. Deane never have been known and never I presume can be known.

I had taken pains to perswade my Colleagues to take a House in Paris, and have but one establishment for Us all. Mr. Lee, whose Opinion was that We ought to live in Paris, readily consented but Dr. Franklin refused. I proposed that Mr. Lee should take Appartements with Us at Passi, and there was room enough for Us all, and I offered to resign my Appartments to him and take others which were not so convenient: but he refused to live together unless it were in Paris, where the Americans in General and the French too, seemed to think We ought to live. All my proposals were therefore abortive.

Before I wrote the Letter to Mr. Adams I had many Things to consider. What would be the Consequence if my Plan should be adopted? Dr. Franklins Reputation was so high in America, in the Court and Nation of France and all over Europe, that he would undoubtedly as he ought to be left alone at the Court of Versailles. Mr. Lee held two Commissions, one to the Court of France and one to the Court of Spain. If that to the Court of Versailles should be annulled, the other to the Court of Madrid would remain in force. It would therefore make little Odds to him. I had but one and that to the Court of Versailles. If this were annulled, what would become of me. There was but one Country to which I thought it possible Congress would send a Minister at that time, and that was Holland. But there was no hope that Holland would then receive a Minister, and I thought Congress ought not to send one there as yet. I thought therefore that there was no Alternative for me, but to return to America: and I very deliberately determined, that I had rather run the Gauntlett again through all the British Men of War in the Bay of Biscay, the British Channel and the Gulph Stream with all their Storms and Calms than remain where I was under a System and in Circumstances so ruinous to the American Cause. I expected however that Congress would make some provision for my return by giving me orders to receive Money enough for my Expences, and give me a Passage in a Frigate if any one should be in France. In this last expectation alone I was disappointed.

May 21. Thursday. 1778. Dined at home.

May 22 Fryday. We sent the following Letter.

To the Honourable the Council and the Honourable the House of Representatives of the State of Massachusetts.

May it please your Honours   Passi May 22. 1778

Mr. Joseph Parker of London has made Application to Us concerning a Claim, that he has of Property in a certain Vessell, which has been as he informs Us, in the Custody of the Public, since the Spring of the Year 1775, requesting Us to write to your honours, on the Subject.

From what some of Us know and all of Us have heard of Mr. Parker, We have reason to think him a worthy Man, who has always been a Friend and connected with the Friends of America in England, by whom he is strongly recommended: and from his representations to Us, his present Circumstances render it very necessary for him to obtain this Property from America, if it is practicable, as the longer detention or confiscation of it, will be inevitable Ruin to him and his Family.... As the Affair is represented to Us, the Ship was detained by an order of the Honourable General Court, before the tenth of September 1775.... If this is the Case, it may be perhaps justly thought an hard one upon Mr. Parker, and therefore We cannot but become petitioners for Mr. Parker, that his case may be taken into consideration and determined as soon as possible; which We hope may be in his favour.

It is to be observed, that though considerable Property belonging to Americans, was in the hands of Merchants in England, and in the public Funds, before and at the time of the commencement of the War, there is no instance come to our Knowledge, that the Government have seized and confiscated such property, or made any Inquiry after it: and perhaps it may be prudent in Us not to be the first, in giving an Example of such Severity: especially as by the common practice in Europe, frequently confirmed by Treaties, so as to have become in a manner part of the Law of nations, no such Advantage is taken, but at least six months is allowed after a War commenced, for the Subjects on both Sides, to withdraw their Effects. We have the honor to be with great respect.   Signed by Franklin, Lee and Adams.[9]

[9] What is apparently the recipient's copy of this letter is in MiU-C:Presidents Coll., and is remarkable for the fact that the first paragraph is in JA's

Dined at home this day, with a great deal of Company. Went After dinner to see the Microscope[1] of Moliere, which was followed by The Heureusement. Mr. Amiel went with me. We called at the Microcosme and at Mr. Amiels at the Pension.

May 23. Saturday. We wrote this Letter[2]

Sir   Passi May 23. 1778

A Pilot being wanted to conduct an Advice Boat to America, if you have in your Ship, a suitable Person that can be spared, the Commissioners request, that you would permit him to go on that Service. We have the honour to be, Sir your most obedient humble Servants

B. Franklin, Arthur Lee, John Adams

Dined at home with Company.

May 24. Sunday 1778. I was so uneasy at the difficulty of getting any Business done and at the distracted Condition of our Affairs, that I thought it my duty to write in a private Capacity to the Commercial Committee of Congress.

Sir   Passi May 24. 1778.

I find that the American Affairs, on this Side of the Atlantick, are in a State of disorder, very much resembling that, which is so much to be regretted on the other.[3] Our Resources are very inadequate to the demands upon Us, which are perhaps unnecessarily increased, by several irregularities of Proceeding. We have, in some places, two or three Persons, who claim the Character of American Agents; Agents for commercial Affairs; and continental Agents, for they are called by all these different Appellations.

In one quarter, one Gentleman claims the Character from the Appointment of Mr. William Lee, Another claims it from the Appointment of the Commissioners at Passi, and a third from the Appointment of the commercial Committee of Congress. This introduces a tripple Expence and much Confusion and delay. These Evils have been accidental, I believe, and unavoidable, but they are Evils still, and ought to be removed.

---

hand, with improvements and additions interlined by Franklin, while the second paragraph is entirely in Franklin's hand. See illustration in this volume.

[1] A mistake for "Misanthrope"; see Diary entry of this date.

[2] To "Capt. [John Paul] Jones," as LbC indicates. RC (DLC: John Paul Jones Papers) is in Franklin's hand.

[3] LbC continues this sentence as follows: "and arising as I suppose from the same general Causes, the Novelty of the Scænes, the Inexperience of the Actors, and the Rapidity with which great Events have succeeded each other." This omission was a mere copyist's inadvertence.

One Person at Bourdeaux, another at Nantes, and a third perhaps at Havre de grace or Dunkirk, would be amply sufficient for all public Purposes; and to these Persons all Orders from Congress, or the commercial Committee, or the Commissioners at Passi, ought to be addressed: To the same Persons all public Ships of War, and all other Ships belonging to the United States, and their Prizes ought to be addressed. And all Orders for Supplies of Provisions, Cloathing, Repairs of Vessells &c. as well as all orders for shipping of Merchandizes or Warlike Stores for the United States, ought to go through their hands.

We have such Abuses and irregularities, every day occurring, as are very allarming. Agents of various Sorts are drawing Bills upon Us, and the Commanders of Vessells of War are drawing upon Us, for Expences and Supplies, which We never ordered, so that our resources will soon fail, if a speedy Stop is not put to this Career. And we find it so difficult to obtain Accounts from Agents of the expenditure of Monies, and of the Goods and Merchandizes shipped by them, that We can never know either the true State of our Finances, or when and in what degree, We have executed the orders of Congress, for sending them Arms, Cloaths, Medicines or other Things.

In order to correct some of these Abuses, and to bring our Affairs into a little better order, I have constantly given my Voice, against paying for Things which We never ordered, against paying Persons who have never been authorized, and against throwing our Affairs into a multiplicity of hands in the same place: but the Consequence has been the refusal of so many demands and requests, that I expect much discontent will arise from it, and many Clamours.

Whether the Appointment by Congress of one or more Consuls for this Kingdom would remedy these inconveniences, I must submit to their Wisdom. Signed John Adams
The Hon. The Commercial Committee of Congress.

May 25. Monday. Business as well as disputes increased and multiplied upon Us, and there was nobody to do any Business but me so that I found it necessary to decline invitations abroad and dine at home as much as possible, to answer the public Letters, but after I had written them I had trouble and delay enough in getting them signed by my Colleages. This day the following were written

Sir   Passi May 25. 1778
    Your favours of May 9. and 16 from Brest We duely received.[4] We
    [4] That of the 9th is in PPAmP: Franklin Papers and is endorsed in JA's hand;

congratulate you, on your Success, and safe Arrival at Brest, as well as on the honour you have acquired by your Conduct and Bravery in taking one of the Kings Ships.

As We have some expectation of obtaining an Exchange of Prisoners from England, We would advise you to keep those you have made, securely confined, tho' in the manner most consistent with humanity, till We have an Answer from thence. For if We can get an equal number of our own Seamen, to man the Drake, she will be an additional Strength to you, in a future Expedition; whereas sending her, with the Prisoners to America, will not only weaken you, by the hands you must spare to navigate her, and to keep the Prisoners in Subjection, but will also hazard their being retaken.

We should have been happy to have been early informed of the particulars of your Cruise, and of the Prizes you have made, of which We have no authentic Advice to this hour.

Your Bill of Exchange in favour of Mr. Bersolle, for twenty four Thousand Livres, which you inform Us you mean to distribute among the brave Officers and Men to whom you owe your late Success, has been presented to Us, by Mr Chaumont.

We are sorry to inform you, that We have been under the disagreable necessity of refusing Payment; and that for several reasons; first, because your Application should have been made to Mr. Schweighauser, who is the Person, regularly authorized to Act as Continental Agent at Brest, and We are determined that all American Concerns, within our department shall go through his hands, as long as he shall continue in the Character of American Agent, or at least till We shall find it necessary to order otherwise. Secondly because the Bill is drawn for an expence, which We have no right or authority to defray. We have no Authority to make presents of the public Money, to Officers or Men, however gallant or deserving, for the purpose of providing their Families with Cloathing, or for any other purpose. Nor to advance them money upon the Credit of their Shares of Prizes, nor have We Authority to advance them any part of their Pay or Bounties: All these Things belong to Congress alone, and must be done by the proper Boards, in America.

Our Authority extends no farther, than to order the necessary Repairs to be made to your Ship, to order her to be furnished with necessary Victuals, which We are ready to order Mr. Schweighausser to do, as soon as We shall be informed by you, what repairs and

that of the 16th has not been found. JA's draft of the present letter is in the Adams Papers and does not differ in language from LbC.

Victuals are wanted, with an Estimate of the Amount of the Expence.

There is one Thing further, which We should venture to do, for the benefit of your Men. Upon a representation from you of the quantity of Slops, necessary for them, We should order Mr. Schweighausser to furnish your Ship with them, not more however, than one Suit of Cloaths for each Man, that you may take them on board of your Ship, and deliver them out to the Men, as they shall be wanted, charging each Man upon the Ships Books, with what he shall receive, that it may be deducted out of his Pay.

Lt. Simpson has stated to Us, your having put him under Arrest for disobeying orders. As a Court Marshall must by order of Congress, consist of three Captains, three Lieutenants, and three Captains of Marines, and these cannot be had here, it is our desire, that he may have a Passage, procured for him, by the first Opportunity to America, allowing him whatever may be necessary for his defence. As the Consequences of an Arrest in foreign Countries, are thus extreamly troublesome, they should be well considered before they are made.

If you are in Possession of any Resolution of Congress, giving the whole of Ships of War, when made Prizes, to the Captors, We should be obliged to you for a Copy of it.

We should also be obliged to you for a particular Account, in whose hands the Prizes made by you, are, and in what forwardness, the Sale of them. We have the honor to be, Sir your most obedient humble Servants   B. Franklin, Arthur Lee, John Adams
John Paul Jones Esqr. Commander of the Ranger.

Sir   Passi May 25. 1778.

Your Favours of May 11. and 18. are now before Us.[5] We shall this day acquaint Captain Jones, how far it is in our Power to comply with his desires and in what manner.

Your Letter of the Eighteenth informs Us, of a dispute between Mr. Schweighausser and you, concerning the disposal of the Rangers Prizes, and you are still of Opinion that you have Authority to interfere in the disposal of Prizes, and that you should be chargeable with neglect of Duty, if you did not, untill your former Orders are recalled.[6]

The Necessities of our Country, demand the Utmost Frugality,

[5] Both in PPAmP:Franklin Papers, and both endorsed by JA. A draft of the present letter to Williams, in JA's hand, is in DLC:Franklin Papers; see the following note.

[6] In the draft this sentence ends as follows: ". . . and that you should be chargeable with Neglect of Duty, if you should not." This is the only variation in language between the draft and the letterbook copy.

which can never be obtained, without the utmost Simplicity, in the management of her Affairs. And as Congress have Authorised Mr. William Lee, to superintend the commercial Affairs in general, and he has appointed Mr. Schweighausser, and as your Authority is under the Commissioners at Paris only: We think it, prudent and necessary for the public Service to revoke, and We do hereby revoke, all the Powers and Authorities heretofore granted to you, by the Commissioners Plenipotentiary of the United States of America at Paris or any of them, to the End, that hereafter, the Management of the Affairs maritime and commercial, of America, may be under one sole Direction, that of Mr. Schweighausser, within his district. As to the Merchandizes and Stores of every kind, which you have on hand at present, We leave it to your Choice, either to ship them to America yourself, or to deliver them over to Mr. Schweighausser, to be shipped by him.

It is not from any Prejudice to You, Mr. Williams, for whom We have a great respect and Esteem, but merely from a desire to save the public Money, to prevent the Clashing of Claims and Interests, and to avoid Confusion and delays, that We have taken this Step.

We have further, to repeat our request, that you would lay your Accounts before Us, as soon as possible, because untill We have them, We can never know, either the State of our Finances, or how far the Orders of Congress for Stores and Merchandizes to be shipped to America, have been fullfilled. We are Sir with great respect, your most obedient, humble Servants   B. Franklin, Arthur Lee, John Adams. Jonathan Williams Esqr.   Nantes.

Sir   Passi May 25. 1778
We enclose you Extracts, from our Letters of this Days Date, to Mr. Williams and Captain Jones, which We recommend to your Attention, and We hope this Arrangement will produce the Order and Œconomy so necessary to the proper conduct of public Business. Our Wish is, that you will give Us previous notice of any extraordinary proposed Expence, that We may determine, before it is incurred, how far it is consistent with our Finances, it being our determination to avoid running in Debt, or pledging ourselves for what We cannot perform. You will be so good, as to send Us an Account every month, and We will direct your Bills upon Us, for the ballance to be paid by our Banker. We are with great respect, Sir, your most obedient Servants   B. Franklin, Arthur Lee, John Adams. Mr. Schweighauser.

In the foregoing Letter was inclosed an Extract of the foregoing Letter to Mr. Williams, beginning with the Words "Your Letter of the 18 informs Us" and ending with these "We have taken this Step." Also an Extract of the foregoing Letter to Captain Jones, beginning with the Words "Your Application should have been made" &c. and ending with these, "deducted out of their Pay."[7]

Sir   May 25. 1778

Your favours of the 12 and 17 of May are before Us.[8] They contain Information of an interesting nature, which We shall attend to as soon as Circumstances will admit.

We thank you for the punctuality, with which you, from time to time, furnish us with Intelligence, as it arises in your City; and wish for a continuance of your favours in that Way.

You desire We should write you, that your Bills on Us, will be duely honoured.... We request that you would transmit Us, an Account of your disbursements, and after We shall have received and examined your Accounts, your Bills for the ballance shall be duely honoured.

We must request you, as We do every other American Agent for the future, to transmit Us your Accounts monthly, that We may know the State of our Affairs, and not run deeper in debt, than We shall be able to pay, which there is no small danger of. We have the honour to be, with great respect, Sir &c.   Signed B. Franklin, Arthur Lee, John Adams.

John Bondfield Esq.   Bourdeaux.

By these Letters, the Die was cast, and one great Scene of Controversy closed for the present. I had written all of them myself, and produced them to my Colleagues as soon as I could get them together. I was doubtfull whether Mr. Franklin would sign them, but when he saw that Mr. Lee and I would sign them without him, if he refused, with his habitual Wisdom he very composedly put his Signature to them all. Whether from a conviction in his Conscience, that the decision was right, or from an Apprehension, that upon a representation of it to Congress it would be there approved, or from both these motives together, is none of my concern. The Bruit was however spread, from this time, at Nantes and Brest, and Bourdeaux and else-

[7] This note was copied by JA from his letterbook.

[8] Two letters from Bondfield to the American Commissioners of 12 May are in PPAmP:Franklin Papers, both endorsed by JA; that of 17 May has not been found.

where, that Mr. Adams had joined with Mr. Lee against Dr. Franklin. Hence some of the subsequent Letters to America, that Monsieur Adams n'a pas reussi, ici, que de raison parce qu'il a se joint a Monsieur Lee, contre Monsieur Franklin. I made as great a Sacrifice of my personal Feelings upon this Occasion as Mr. Franklin. Mr. Williams, his Father, Unkle and Cousins I considered as my Friends. Mr. Schweighauser was to me an entire Stranger, but by the Acknowledgment of every Body French, Americans and Dr. Franklin himself, his House was established in Reputation for Integrity, for Capital, for Mercantile Knowledge, and for an entire Affection to the American cause, being a Protestant and a Swiss, though long established and universally respected in France. Mr. Williams was a young Gentleman, without Capital, and inexperienced in the Commerce of France, and liable to be imposed upon, by french Merchants and Speculators, who might be envious of Mr. Schweighausers Superiority of Wealth and Credit, and who I well knew were looking with longing Eyes to our little deposit of Money in Mr. Grands Bank. But abstracted from all these Considerations Congress and Mr. William Lee had lawfully and regularly settled the question, and I could not reconcile it to public or private Integrity to disturb it.

May 26. Tuesday. 1778. Dined at the Seat in the Country of Monsieur Bertin, a Secretary of State. Madam Bertin, the Lady of the Ministers Nephew, invited Dr. Franklin, Mr. William Temple Franklin and me to ride with her in her Coach with four Horses, which We did. This was one of the pleasantest rides, I had seen. We rode near the Backside of Mount Calvare, which is the finest Hill near Paris, though Mont Martre is a very fine Elevation. The Gardens, Walks and Waterworks of Mr. Bertin were in a Style of magnificence, like all other Seats of the Gentlemen in this Country. He was a Batchelor. His House and Gardens were situated upon the River Seine. He shewed his Luxury, as he called it, which was a collection of misshapen Rocks, at the End of his Garden, drawn together, from great distances, at an Expence of several Thousands of Guineas. I told him I would sell him a thousand times as many for half a Guinea. His Water Works were curious, four Pumps going by means of two horses. The Mechanism was simple and ingenious. The Horses went round as in a Mill. The four Pumps empty themselves into a square Pond, which contains an Acre. From this Pond the Water flows, through Pipes, down to every Part of the Garden.

I enquired of a certain Ecclesiastick, who sat next to me at dinner, who were the purest Writers of French. He took a Pencil and gave me in Writing, The Universal History of Bossuet, La Fontaine, Moliere, Racine, Rousseau, Le petit Cærene [Carême] of Massillon, and the Sermons of Bourdaloue.

May 27th. Wednesday.[9] I must now, in order to explain and justify my own Conduct give an Account of that of my Colleague Dr. Franklin. It is and always has been with great reluctance, that [I] have felt myself under the Necessity of stating any facts which may diminish the Reputation of this extraordinary Man, but the Truth is more sacred than any Character, and there is no reason that the Character of Mr. Lee and Mr. Izzard not to mention my own, should be sacrificed in unjust tenderness to that of their Ennemy. My quondam Friend Mrs. Warren is pleased to say that "Mr. Adams was not beloved by his Colleague Dr. Franklin."[1] To this Accusation I shall make no other Answer at present than this, that "Mr. Deane was beloved by his Colleague Dr. Franklin."

I found that the Business of our Commission would never be done, unless I did it. My two Colleagues would agree in nothing. The Life of Dr. Franklin was a Scene of continual discipation. I could never obtain the favour of his Company in a Morning before Breakfast which would have been the most convenient time to read over the Letters and papers, deliberate on their contents, and decide upon the Substance of the Answers. It was late when he breakfasted, and as soon as Breakfast was over, a crowd of Carriages came to his Levee or if you like the term better to his Lodgings, with all Sorts of People; some Phylosophers, Accademicians and Economists; some of his small tribe of humble friends in the litterary Way whom he employed to translate some of his ancient Compositions, such as his Bonhomme Richard and for what I know his Polly Baker &c.; but by far the greater part were Women and Children, come to have the honour to see the great Franklin, and to have the pleasure of telling Stories about his Simplicity, his bald head and scattering strait hairs, among their Acquaintances. These Visitors occupied all the time, commonly, till it was time

[9] This entire entry, dealing with the conduct of Franklin and JA's relations with him during the joint commission of 1778–1779, was omitted by CFA in his text. There is no entry in JA's Diary under this date.

[1] Mercy Warren, *History of the Rise, Progress and Termination of the American Revolution*, Boston, 1805, 3:176, q.v. for a remarkably penetrating sketch of JA as a diplomat. While writing his "Travels" JA was reading this work with rising indignation, and in July and August 1807 he was to address a much longer "Answer" directly to Mrs. Warren protesting what he thought were sneers and aspersions upon him in her *History*. His ten letters, with her answers to some of them and an introductory note by CFA, are printed in MHS, *Colls.*, 5th ser., 4 (1878):317–491.

to dress to go to Dinner. He was invited to dine abroad every day and never declined unless when We had invited Company to dine with Us. I was always invited with him, till I found it necessary to send Apologies, that I might have some time to study the french Language and do the Business of the mission. Mr. Franklin kept a horn book always in his Pockett in which he minuted all his invitations to dinner, and Mr. Lee said it was the only thing in which he was punctual. It was the Custom in France to dine between one and two O Clock: so that when the time came to dress, it was time for the Voiture to be ready to carry him to dinner. Mr. Lee came daily to my Appartment to attend to Business, but we could rarely obtain the Company of Dr. Franklin for a few minutes, and often when I had drawn the Papers and had them fairly copied for Signature, and Mr. Lee and I had signed them, I was frequently obliged to wait several days, before I could procure the Signature of Dr. Franklin to them. He went according to his Invitation to his Dinner and after that went sometimes to the Play, sometimes to the Philosophers but most commonly to visit those Ladies who were complaisant enough to depart from the custom of France so far as to procure Setts of Tea Geer as it is called and make Tea for him. Some of these Ladies I knew as Madam Hellvetius, Madam Brillon, Madam Chaumont, Madam Le Roy &c. and others whom I never knew and never enquired for. After Tea the Evening was spent, in hearing the Ladies sing and play upon their Piano Fortes and other instruments of Musick, and in various Games as Cards, Chess, Backgammon, &c. &c. Mr. Franklin I believe however never play'd at any Thing but Chess or Checquers. In these Agreable and important Occupations and Amusements, The Afternoon and Evening was spent, and he came home at all hours from Nine to twelve O Clock at night. This Course of Life contributed to his Pleasure and I believe to his health and Longevity. He was now between Seventy and Eighty and I had so much respect and compassion for his Age, that I should have been happy to have done all the Business or rather all the Drudgery, if I could have been favoured with a few moments in a day to receive his Advice concerning the manner in which it ought to be done. But this condescention was not attainable. All that could be had was his Signature, after it was done, and this it is true he very rarely refused though he sometimes delayed.

From the 26 I remained at home, declining all invitations abroad, arranging the public affairs, and reading french Litterature till

May 29. Fryday. 1778. When I dined again at Monsieur La Fretés at the foot of Calvare. And, We saw a great Rarity in France, Madam

La Frete had four Sisters who dined with Us. Monsieur Rulier [Rulhière] who had always dined with Us at that House, the same Gentleman who wrote the History of the Revolution in Russia, and who also had written an History of the revolutions in Poland, dined there to day. He offered me the reading of these Histories. I asked him who was the best Historian of France, he said Mezeray: and added that the Observations upon the History of France by the Abby de Mably were excellent.

The Disposition of the People of this Country for Amusements, and the Apparatus for them, was remarkable in this House, as indeed it was in every genteel House that I had seen in France. Every fashionable House had compleat Setts of Accommodations for Play, a Billiard Table, a Bacgammon Table, a Chesboard, a Chequer Board, Cards, and twenty other Sorts of Games, that I have forgotten. I often asked myself how this rage for Amusements of every kind, and this disinclination to serious Business, would answer in our republican Governments in America. It seemed to me that every Thing must run to ruin.

May 30. Saturday 1778. Dr. Franklin, who had no Business to do, or who at least would do none, and who had Mr. William Temple Franklin for his private Secretary, without consulting his Colleagues and indeed without saying a Word to me, who lived in the same house with him and had no private Secretary, though I had all the Business to do, thought fit to take into the Family a French private Secretary, a young Man of civil deportment however and good Understanding. He had some Knowledge of the Italian, German and English Languages. For what reason or for what Purpose he was introduced I never knew. Whether it was to be a Spy upon me, or whether Franklin was persuaded by some of his French Friends to give him Employment, or whether it was to save Mr. William Temple the trouble of Copying the Letters when I had written them, I gave myself no trouble to enquire. I thought his Salary and his Keeping an unnecessary expence. The young Man however continued with Us, as long as I remained at Passi, and conducted himself with propriety. This day I dined at home, with this young Gentleman only. Having some Inclination to look a little into the Italian Language, I asked him which was the best Dictionary and Grammar of it. He said those of Veneroni: and the best Dictionary and Grammar of the German, were those of Gottshed. I asked many questions about French books, and particularly enquired about their Prosody, as I wished to understand something of their Versification. He said the best Treatise of French Prosody was The Poetique Francoise of Mr. Marmontell.

June 2. Tuesday. 1778. Went to Versailles, and found it deserted, the Court being gone to Marli.... We went to Marli, met the Count de Vergennes and did some Business with him, then went to Mr. De Sartine and after doing some business dined with him. His Lady was at home and dined with the Company. The Prince de Monbarry [Montbarey], then Secretary of War, dined there. After dinner went to the Spanish Ambassadors, the Count D'Aranda's Caffee, as they call it, where he gives Coffee, Ice Creams and Cakes to all the World. Marli was the most curious and beautiful place I had yet seen. In point of Magnificence it was not equal to Versailles but in Elegance and Taste, superiour. The Machinery, which conveys such a great body of Water from the Seine to Versailles, and through the Gardens of Marli is very complicated, and magnificent. The Royal Palace is handsome and the Gardens before it are grand. There are six Pavillions, on each side of the Garden, that is six Houses for the Residence of the Kings Ministers, while the Royal Family is at Marli, which is only for three Weeks. There is nothing prettier than the play of the fountains in the Garden. I saw a Rainbow in all its glory in one of them. The Shades, the Walks, the Trees were the most charming I had yet seen.

We had not time to visit Lucienne [Louvecienne], the elegant retreat for devotion, Penitence and Mortification of Madam Dubarry: and indeed I had been in such a Reverie in the morning in passing Bellvue, that I was not averse to postpone the Sight of another Object of the same kind to a future Opportunity.

On the Road from Paris and from Passi to Versailles, beyond the River Seine and not far from St. Cleod [Cloud] but on the opposite side of the Way, stood a pallace of uncommon beauty in its Architecture, situated on one of the finest Elevations in the neighbourhood of the River, commanding a Prospect as rich and variegated as it was vast and sublime. For a few of the first times that I went to Versailles I had other Things to occupy my Attention: but after I had passed through my Ceremonies and began to feel myself more at Ease, I asked some Questions about this place and was informed that it was called Bellevue and was the Residence of the Kings Aunts Adelaide and [Victoire,] [2] two of the surviving Daughters of Louis the fifteenth. That this palace had been built and this Establishment made by that Monarch for Madame Pompadour, whom he visited here, almost every night for twenty Years, leaving a worthy Woman his virtuous Queen

[2] Blank in MS.

alone at Versailles, with whom he had sworn never to sleep again.[3] I cannot describe the feelings, nor relate half the reflexions which this object and history excited. Here were made Judges and Councillors, Magistrates of all Sorts, Nobles and Knights of every order, Generals and Admirals, Ambassadors and other foreign Ministers, Bishops, Archbishops, Cardinals and Popes, in the Arms of a Strumpet. Here were directed all Eyes that wished and sought for Employment, Promotion and every Species of Court favour. Here Voltaire and Richelieu and a thousand others of their Stamp, obtained Royal favour and Commissions. Travellers of all Ranks and Characters from all Parts of Europe, were continually passing from Paris to Versailles and spreading the Fame of this House, its Inhabitants and Visitors and their Commerce, infamous in every point of view, civil, political, moral and religious, all over the World. The Eyes of all France had been turned to Bellevue, more than to Paris or Versailles. Here Letters de Cachet, the highest Trust and most dangerous Instrument of arbitrary Power in France were publickly sold, to any Persons who would pay for them, for any the vilest Purposes of private Malice, Envy, Jealousy or Revenge or Cruelty. Here Licences were sold to private Smugglers to contravene the Kings own Laws, and defraud the public Revennue. Here were sold Dukedoms and Peerages, and even the Cordon blue of the Knights of the Holy Ghost. Here still lived the Daughters of the last King and the Aunts of the present. Instead of wondering that the Licentiousness of Women was so common and so public in France, I was astonished that there should be any Modesty or Purity remaining in the Kingdom, as there certainly was, though it was rare. Could there be any Morality left among such a People where such Examples were set up to the View of the whole Nation? Yes there was a Sort of Morality, there was a great deal of humanity, and what appeared to me real benevolence. Even their politeness was benevolence. There was a great deal of Charity and tenderness for the poor. There were many other qualities that I could not distinguish from Virtues.... This very Monarck had in him the Milk of human Kindness, and with all his open undisguised Vices was very superstitious. Whenever he met the Host, he would descend from his Coach and [fall?][4] down upon his Knees in the Dust or even in the Mud and compell all his Courtiers to follow his Example. Such are the Inconsistencies in the human Character.

[3] This sentence (among others in the present paragraph) was silently emended by CFA. As he printed it, it reads: "... Madame de Pompadour, whom he visited here for twenty years, leaving a worthy woman, his virtuous queen, alone at Versailles, from whom he had sworn an eternal separation" (JA, *Works*, 3:170).

[4] Word omitted in MS.

From all that I had read of History and Government, of human Life and manners, I had drawn this Conclusion, that the manners of Women were the most infallible Barometer, to ascertain the degree of Morality and Virtue in a Nation. All that I have since read and all the observations I have made in different Nations, have confirmed me in this opinion. The Manners of Women, are the surest Criterion by which to determine whether a Republican Government is practicable, in a Nation or not. The Jews, the Greeks, the Romans, the Swiss, the Dutch, all lost their public Spirit, their Republican Principles and habits, and their Republican Forms of Government, when they lost the Modesty and Domestic Virtues of their Women.

What havock said I to myself, would these manners make in America? Our Governors, our Judges, our Senators, or Representatives and even our Ministers would be appointed by Harlots for Money, and their Judgments, Decrees and decisions be sold to repay themselves, or perhaps to procure the smiles ⟨and Embraces⟩ of profligate Females.

The foundations of national Morality must be laid in private Families. In vain are Schools, Accademies and universities instituted, if loose Principles and licentious habits are impressed upon Children in their earliest years. The Mothers are the earliest and most important Instructors of youth.... The Vices and Examples of the Parents cannot be concealed from the Children. How is it possible that Children can have any just Sense of the sacred Obligations of Morality or Religion if, from their earliest Infancy, they learn that their Mothers live in habitual Infidelity to their fathers, and their fathers in as constant Infidelity to their Mothers. Besides the Catholic Doctrine is, that the Contract of marriage is not only a civil and moral Engagement, but a Sacrament, one of the most solemn Vows and Oaths of Religious devotion. Can they then believe Religion and Morality too any thing more than a Veil, a Cloak, an hypocritical Pretext, for political purposes of decency and Conveniency?

June 3. Wednesday. 1778. On this Day We sent the following Letters.

Sir   Passi June 3. 1778
We have received sundry Letters from Lt. Simpson, and sundry Certificates from Officers and others, concerning his Behaviour in General, and particularly upon that Occasion, in which he is charged with disobedience of Orders.... Without giving or forming any decided Opinion concerning his guilt or innocence of the Crime laid to his charge, We may venture to say that the Certificates We have received

are very favourable to his Character, and at least afford reason to hope, that he did not mean to disobey his orders.

Be this however, as it may, We are constrained to say, that his confinement on board any other Ship than the Ranger, and much more his Confinement in a Prison on Shore, appears to Us to carry in it, a degree of Severity, which cannot be justified by reason or Law.

We therefore, desire, you would release Mr. Simpson, from his imprisonment, and permit him to go at large, on his Parole to go to Nantes, there to take his passage to America, by the first favourable Opportunity, in order to take his Tryal by a Court Marshall.

We request you to transmit Us, as soon as possible, an Account of what is due to Lt. Simpson, according to the Ships Books for Wages.

An Application has been made to Us, in behalf of Mr. Andrew Fallen, one of the Prisoners lately made by you, and his case represented, with such Circumstances, as have induced Us to request you, to let Mr. Fallen go, where he will, after taking his Parole in Writing, that he will not communicate any intelligence which may be prejudicial to the United States, that he will not take Arms against them during the War, and that he will surrender himself Prisoner of War whenever called upon by Congress, or their Ministers at Paris. We are, Sir, your most obedient Servants. Signed B. Franklin, Arthur Lee, John Adams. John Paul Jones Esqr. Captain of the Ranger.

Sir   Passi June 3. 1778

We have received several Letters from you,[5] and several Certificates from Officers and others, respecting your Behaviour in general, as well as particularly relative to the Charge of Disobedience of orders, for which you have been confined.

It would be improper for Us, to give any Opinion concerning this charge, which is to be determined only by a Court Marshall: But We have requested Captain Jones to sett you at Liberty upon your Parol to go to Nantes, there to take your Passage to America, by the first favourable Opportunity, in order to take your Tryal by a Court Marshall. We are, Sir, your humble Servants

                    B. Franklin, Arthur Lee, John Adams.
Lt. Simpson of the Ranger.

The Representations in favour of Simpson and against Jones, were

---

[5] Simpson's letters of 8 and 25 May are in PPAmP:Franklin Papers, both endorsed by JA. On the case of Thomas Simpson, lieutenant of the *Ranger* and prizemaster of the *Drake,* see the letters and comment under 16 July, below; also S. E. Morison, *John Paul Jones,* Boston, 1959, p. 160–172.

very strong. His whole Ship was against the Captain, with a surprizing Unanimity, and although Jones was evidently one of Franklins Party both among the French and Americans, yet his Conduct was so evidently wrong in some Instances, and so dubious in others that Franklin could not refuse his Signature, to all the decisions of his Colleagues concerning him.

Jones had obtained the Command of the Ranger, under the Auspices of Mr. Robert Morris in Philadelphia, and I understood carried Letters to Mr. Deane and Dr. Franklin, which upon his first Arrival in France he carried to Paris. They introduced him to their friends among the French and Americans, particularly to Mr. Williams, and he was so universally considered as the Partisan of Deane and Franklin, that as soon as he had made a Prize of an English Ship of War the Drake, the Cry of Versailles and the Clamour of Paris became as loud in favour of Monsieur Jones as of Monsieur Franklin and the Inclination of the Ladies to embrace him almost as fashionable and as strong.[6] Jones's personal Behaviour to me was always, to the time of his Death as civil and respectful as I could wish: But I suppose that means were found to insinuate into him that the refusal of his Draught and the Lenity to Lt. Simpson were the Effects of my Uniting with Mr. Lee against Mr. Franklin, although Franklin had agreed to both. The Impressions he received from that Party I suppose were the cause of his impertinent Enquiries after my Conduct in Holland and his Wish that I was in America expressed in a Letter to Mr. Dumas which was published in the Portfolio at Philadelphia a few Years ago.[7] What became of Lt. Simpson I know not, but I have always thought that the arbitrary Conduct of Jones was the cause of great Injustice to him.

To his Excellency Monsieur De Sartine at Versailles.

Passi June 3. 1778

We have the honour of inclosing to your Excellency, an Account of Duties paid by the Agent for necessary Supplies to the Ship of War the

[6] This is to some extent anachronistic. The adulation of Jones by French ladies and others did not occur after his *Ranger* cruise in 1778 but upon his return to Paris two years later following his more spectacular cruise with the *Bonhomme Richard* squadron. See S. E. Morison, *John Paul Jones*, Boston, 1959, ch. 15.

[7] "Let me know how Mr. Round Face, first letter, that went lately from Paris to the Hague, is proceeding? I understand he is gone to Amsterdam. I wish he may be doing good. If he should, inadvertantly, do evil, as a stranger, I shall, as his fellow-citizen, be very sorry for it, but you, being a native, will hear of it. I confess I am anxious about his situation. The man has a family, and these troublesome times, I wish he were at home to mind his trade and his fireside, for I think he has travelled more than his fortune can well bear" (Jones to Dumas, *Ariel*, Road of Croix, 8 Sept. 1780, *Port Folio*, 1st ser., 4 [1804]:43).

Boston, in the Port of Bourdeaux. As these duties are very heavy, and the payment of any Duties on mere Supplies to Ships of War, as on Merchandizes exported, appears to Us uncommon, We beg the favour of your Excellency to give such orders, relative to it, in all his Majestys Ports, as may regulate this, for the future.

The Captain of the Ship of War the Ranger, belonging to the United States, has We understand, put his Prizes into the hands of the Intendant or Commandant at Brest, and no Account has been rendered of them, to the Public Agent or to Us. We are also given to understand, that in Consequence of this proceeding, very heavy Fees are to be paid upon the Sale of them. As the Transaction is altogether improper, We must trouble your Excellency for an order to the Commandant to deliver them, without delay, or extraordinary Charges to the Public Agent, Mr. Schweighauser of Nantes or to his order.

It would give Us Satisfaction to annoy our Ennemies, by granting a Letter of Marque, as is desired, for a Vessell fitted out at Dunkquerque, and as it is represented to Us, containing a mixed Crew of French, Americans and English: But if this should seem improper to your Excellency, We will not do it. We have the Honour to be &c. Signed B. Franklin, Arthur Lee, John Adams.

40 Coats for Marines—Do. Waistcoats and Breeches—260 Outside Jacketts—250 inside—260 Pair of Breeches—66 Blankets—330 Pr. of Shoes—108 Hatts—108 Caps—Duties paid on the whole seven hundred and ninety Livres.

Sir   Passi June 3. 1778

Two days ago I had the pleasure of your Letter of the 26 May[8] inclosing an Account of Cash and Payments made to and for me, at Bourdeaux, amounting to 1404 Livres, in which Sum it ought to be remembered, are included the Expences of Captain Palmes, Dr. Noel and Mr. Jesse Deane at Bourdeaux and from thence to Paris, as well as my own, excepting 231 Livres and six Sous paid to Dr. Noel by an order on the Banker at Paris, for the ballance of all Expences.

Your Letter incloses also an Account of sundry Articles of Merchandizes shipped by you in a Trunk for my Family, to the Amount of 888 Livres and twelve Sous, which Sum together with your Commissions please to charge to the public Account, as you propose, and I will be responsible for the Money here. I am much obliged to you, Sir, for your Care in this Business and am your most obedient Servant

John Adams

John Bondfield Esqr.

[8] Not found.

Sir   Passi June 4. 1778

Your Letters of the 26th and 30th. of May, We have received:[9] the first accompanying the Accounts of Supplies &c. for the Boston; the last inclosing an Affidavit of a Plott against her Safety. Upon looking over the Accounts, We find some Articles, particularly fresh Beef, charged at a very high rate; but We suppose this Article must be dearer at Bourdeaux, than it is at Paris or Nantes, as We depend upon your Attention to procure every Thing, at the most reasonable rate. By the Rangers Account, she was supplied with fresh Beef, at five Sols and an half a pound, whereas in your Account fifteen Sols are charged.... Your Bills will be honoured as you have drawn them. We hope, the Boston, before this time is gone. As the Expence of supporting such Ships is very great, they ought not to be in port one moment longer than is necessary.

As to the Plott: We shall communicate the Affidavit to the Ministry: But in the mean time, We depend upon it, that Captain Tucker will make some Example among the Guilty, on board of his Ship, if there are any, and that the Government at Bourdeaux, will punish any Person, at Land, who shall be found guilty of this Conspiracy or any other like it.

By all that We can learn there is a Junto of Ennemies in that Neighbourhood, who must be brought to reason by Severity, if nothing else will do. We have the Honor to be, with very great respect, Sir, your most obedient Servants   Signed B. Franklin, Arthur Lee, John Adams. John Bondfield Esqr.

P.S. Your Bills are accepted.

Sir   Passi June 4. 1778

We have the Honor of inclosing to your Excellency, a Copy of a Letter from Captain Whipple of the Providence Ship of War, of Thirty Guns, in the Service of the United States.[1] As she brought no dispatches for Us, the Letter from the Captain, is all her Intelligence. We have the Honor to be with the greatest respect, your Excellencys most obedient &c.   Signed B. Franklin, Arthur Lee, John Adams
Mr. Le Comte de Vergennes.

On the same day We wrote to Lord North

My Lord

The Fortune of War, having again made a Number of British Sea-

[9] Not found.
[1] Abraham Whipple to Franklin, Paimboeuf Harbor, 31 May (PPAmP); see the Commissioners' answer of 6 June, below.

men Prisoners to the United States, it is our Duty to trouble you with a renewal of our former request, for an immediate Exchange of Prisoners in Europe. To detain unfortunate Men, for months in Prison, and send them, three thousand Miles to make an Exchange, which might take place immediately and on the Spot, is a most grievous and unnecessary Addition to the Calamities of War, in which We cannot believe the British Government will persist.

It is, with the utmost regret, that We find ourselves compelled to reitterate, to your Lordship, our Remonstrances against your treating the Citizens of the United States, made Prisoners by the Arms of the King of Great Britain, in a manner unexampled, in the practice of civilized Nations. We have received late and authentic Information, that numbers of such Prisoners, some of them Fathers of Families in America, having been sent to Africa, are now in the Fort of Senegal, condemned, in that unwholesome Climate, to the hardest labour, and most inhuman Treatment. It will be our indispensable Duty, to report this to the Congress of the United States of America, and Retaliation will be the inevitable Consequence, in Europe as well as America, unless your Lordship will authorize Us to assure Congress that these unhappy Men, as well as all others of our Nation, who have been treated in a similar manner, shall be immediately brought back and exchanged.

Most earnestly We beseach your Lordship, no longer to sacrifice the essential Interests of Humanity, to the Claims of Sovereignty,[2] which your Experience must by this time have convinced you, are not to be maintained. We have the Honor to be &c.   Signed B. Franklin, Arthur Lee, John Adams
To Lord North.

June 6. 1778 We wrote the following Letter

Sir   Passi June 6. 1778
We had Yesterday the favour of your Letter of 31st. of May, from the Harbour of Paimbeuf, and We congratulate you, on your safe Arrival in France, as well as your fortunate Passage through the dangers at Rhode Island; but more especially on the honor, which You, your Officers and Men have acquired, in your gallant Rencounter with the Enemies Ships on that Station.

You will address yourself, as well as your Prize, on her Arrival, to Mr. Schweighauser at Nantes, who will assist you in the necessary Repairs of your Ship, of which We must leave you to judge, furnish

---

[2] LbC: "to Claims of Sovereignty."

you with necessary Victuals and Slops for your Men, not more than one Suit of Cloaths for each Man of the Ships Compliment, and such munition of War as you may want, in all which We recommend to you, the strictest possible frugality, which the distressed Circumstances of our Country, demand of all her Officers. We leave it to You and Mr. Schweighausser to repair the Ship either at Nantes or at Brest, as you shall judge best for the public Service. Signed B. Franklin, Arthur Lee, John Adams.
To Abraham Whipple Esq. Commander of the American Frigate the
    Providence at Painbeuf.

Sir   Passi June 6. 1778
    We had the Pleasure of yours of the first instant, Yesterday.[3] We have directed Captain Whipple to address himself, as well as his Prize on her Arrival to you, for the necessary Repairs of the Providence, of which We must leave him to judge, to furnish him with necessary Victuals and Slops for his Men, not more than one Suit of Cloaths for each Man of the Ships Compliment, and such munition of War as he may want, in all which We recommend to him and to you the strictest Frugality, which the distressed Circumstances of our Country demand.
    You request directions relative to the part you are to act, on such Occasions towards the Custom House. All that We can say, at present, is, that the American Men of War must comply with the Laws: but We will endeavour to obtain explicit directions from his Majesty, concerning this Subject.
    We are &c.   B. Franklin, Arthur Lee, John Adams.
Mr. Schweighauser.

    This Letter must be inserted.[4] We received it in French: but the following is a litteral translation of it.

                     Marli the 6. of June 1788
    I am informed Gentlemen, that the Sieur Bersolle, after having made very considerable Advances to Captain Jones, Commander of the Frigate of the United States of America, the Ranger, made this Captain give him a Bill of Exchange, which you have refused to discharge the Amount. As the Sieur Bersolle finds himself by this means under Embarrassment, and as you will perceive, no doubt, that it is interesting for the conservation of your Credit, that he be promptly relieved

---

[3] Not found.
[4] The following letter and the comment thereon were copied by JA on a separate leaf and keyed by a cross for insertion ahead of the entry dated 7 June.

from it, I am persuaded that you will not delay, to cause to be paid not only the Bill of Exchange in question, but also that which is due by Captain Jones to the Treasury of the Marine at Brest, both for those Effects which have been delivered to him, from the Magazines of the King, and for his personal Subsistence, and that of his Crew.

Upon a representation which he has made, that the Men of his own Crew had pillaged from the Ship Chatham, many Effects, one part of which consisting of Silver Plate, had been sold to a Jew, Information has been obtained, by which the Plate and other Effects have been discovered; but the whole has been deposited, to remain, untill the Captain shall be in a Condition to reimburse what has been paid for these Effects.

I think, moreover, that it is important that you should be informed that this Captain who has quarrelled with his Officers and all his Crew has caused to be committed to Prison, Mr. Simpson, his second in Command. You will perhaps judge it proper, to procure the necessary Information, to know whether this principal Officer has merited to suffer such a punishment. I have the honnour to be with the most perfect Consideration, Gentlemen, your most humble and most obedient Servant   De Sartine.
Messieurs Franklin, Lee et Adams Deputés des Etats Unis de L'Amerique   Passy.

I might leave the Reader to make his own reflections upon this interposition of a Minister who had certainly no right to meddle in this Business. But the Secret was that the Officers of our own Ships and every Body else, were to be countenanced in violating the Laws and Orders of Congress, in doing the most arbitrary Things of their own heads, without consulting the Commissioners, and in trampling on the most equitable orders of the Commissioners merely to throw the American Business and Profits into the hands of the Tools of the Minister and his Understrappers and to give them Opportunities of Pillage.

June 7. 1778. Went to Versailles in Company with Mr. Lee, Mr. Izard and his Lady, Mr. Lloyd and his Lady and Mr. Francis [Francès], a Gentleman who spoke the English Language very well, having resided many Years in England in some diplomatique Character, and who undertook upon this Occasion to conduct Us. Our Objects were to see the Ceremonies and the Procession of the Knights of the Holy Ghost, or the Chevaliers of the Cordon blue, and in the Evening the public Supper of the Royal Family at the grand Couvert. The Kneelings, the Bows, and the Curtesies of the Knights of the Saint Esprit, the Dresses

NOUVEAU VOYAGE DE FRANCE;

AVEC

UN ITINÉRAIRE, ET DES CARTES faites exprès, qui marquent exactement les routes qu'il faut suivre pour voyager dans toutes les Provinces de ce Royaume.

Ouvrage également utile aux François & aux Etrangers.

Nouvelle Edition, revue, corrigée & augmentée.

PAR M. PIGANIOL DE LA FORCE.

TOME PREMIER.

A PARIS,

Chez BAILLY, Libraire, Quai des Augustins.

M. DCC. LXXX.

Avec Approbation, & Privilege du Roi.

5. JOHN ADAMS' FRENCH GUIDEBOOK

ITINERARIO ESPAÑOL, O GUIA DE CAMINOS,

PARA IR DESDE MADRID à todas las Ciudades, y Villas mas principales de España;

Y PARA IR DE UNAS Ciudades à otras; y à algunas Cortes de Europa.

AÑADIDO, Y CORREGIDO en esta tercera Impresion, por Joseph Mathias Escrivano. Se hallarà en su Libreria, frente de la Aduana, Calle de Athocha.

CON PRIVILEGIO, Y LAS Licencias necessarias.

EN MADRID: En la Imprenta de Miguel Escrivano, Calle Angosta de San Bernardo. Año de 1767.

4. JOHN ADAMS' SPANISH GUIDEBOOK

6. THE AMERICAN COMMISSIONERS AT WORK IN 1778: LETTER BEGUN BY JOHN ADAMS AND CORRECTED AND COMPLETED BY BENJAMIN FRANKLIN

and Decorations, The King seated on his Throne, his investiture of a new created Knight with the Badges and Ornaments of the Order, and his Majesty's profound and reverential Bow before the Altar as he retired, were Novelties and Curiosities to me, but surprized me much less, than the Patience and Perseverance with which they all kneeled for two hours together upon the hard Marble, of which the Floor of the Chapel was made. The distinction of the blue ribbon, was very dearly purchased at the price of enduring this painful Operation, four times in a Year. The Count De Vergennes confessed to me, that he was almost dead, with the pain of it. And the only insinuation I ever heard, that the King was in any degree touched by the Philosophy of the Age was, that he never discovered so much impatience under any of the Occurrences of his Life, as in going through those tedious Ceremonies of Religion to which so many hours of his Life were condemned by the Catholic Church.

The Queen was attended by her Ladies to the Gallery opposite to the Altar, placed in the Center of the Seat, and there left alone by the other Ladies, who all retired. She was an Object too sublime and beautiful for my dull pen to describe. I leave this Enterprize to Mr. Burke. But in his description there is more of the orator than of the Philosopher.[5] Her Dress was every Thing that Art and Wealth could make it. One of the Maids of honor told me, she had Diamonds upon her Person to the Value of Eighteen millions of Livres, and I always thought her Majesty much beholden to her Dress. Mr. Burke saw her probably but once. I have seen her fifty times perhaps and in all the Varieties of her Dresses. She had a fine Complexion indicating perfect health, and was an handsome Woman in her face and figure. But I have seen Beauties much superiour both in Countenance and form, in France, England and America. After the Ceremonies of this Institution are over there is a collection for the Poor and that this closing Scene may be as elegant as any of the former, a young Lady of some of the first Families in France is appointed to present the Box to the Knights. Her dress must be as rich and elegant in Proportion as the Queens, and her Air, motions and Curtesies must have as much Dignity and Grace as those of the Knights. It was a curious Entertainment to observe the Easy Air, the graceful Bow and the conscious Dignity of the Knight in presenting his contribution, and the correspondent Ease, Grace and Dignity of the Lady in receiving it were not less charming. Every Muscle, Nerve and Fibre of both seemed perfectly

---

[5] In Burke's *Reflections on the Revolution in France,* London, 1790 (Burke, *Works,* Bohn's British Classics edn., London, 1876, 2:347–348).

disciplined to perform its functions. The Elevation of the Arm, the bend of the Elbow and every finger in the hand of the Knight, in putting his Louis Door [d'Or] into the Box, appeared to be perfectly studied because it was perfectly natural. How much devotion there was in all this I know not, but it was a consummate School to teach the rising Generation the Perfection of the French Air and external Politeness and good Breeding. I have seen nothing to be compared to it, in any other Country. The House of Lords in England I thought the most likely to rival this: But seven Years afterwards when I had seen that Assembly on two extraordinary Occasions, the first the Introduction of the Prince of Wales to his Seat in Parliament and the second the Tryal of Mr. Hastings, I concluded the Peers of Great Britain were too intent on the great Interests of the Nation, to be very solicitous about the Charms of the exteriour Exhibition of a Spectacle. The Procession of the Peers and the Reverences they made to the Throne in conformity to the Usage of their Ancestors, as they passed to their Seats in Westminster Hall, were decent and graceful enough.

At nine O Clock in the Evening We went to the grand Couvert, and saw the King, Queen and Royal Family at Supper. Whether Mr. Francis had contrived a plott to gratify the Curiosity of the Spectators, or whether the Royal Family had a fancy to see the raw American at their leisure, or whether they were willing to gratify him with a convenient Seat, in which he might see all the Royal Family and all the Splendors of the Place, I know not. But the Scheme could not have been carried into Execution certainly without the orders of the King. I was selected and summoned indeed from all my Company, and ordered to a Seat close beside the Royal Family. The Seats on both Sides of the Hall, arranged like the Seats in a Theater, were all full of Ladies of the first Rank and Fashion in the Kingdom and there was no room or place for me but in the midst of them. It was not easy to make room for one more Person. However Room was made and I was situated between two Ladies, with Rows and Ranks of Ladies above and below me, and on the right hand and on the left [h]and Ladies only. My Dress was a decent French Dress, becoming the Station I held, but not to be compared with [the] Gold and Diamonds and Embroidery about me. I could neither speak nor understand the Language in a manner to support a Conversation: but I had soon the Satisfaction to find it was a silent Meeting, and that nobody spoke a Word but the Royal Family to each other, and they said very little. The Eyes of all the Assembly were turned upon me, and I felt sufficiently humble and mortified, for I was not a proper Object for the criticisms of such a Company. I [found] [6] myself gazed at, as We in America used to gaze at the Sachems who came to make Speeches to Us in Congress, but I thought it very hard if I could not command as much Power of face, as one of the Chiefs of the Six Nations, and therefore determined that I would assume a chearful Countenance, enjoy the Scene around me and observe it as coolly as an Astronomer contemplates the Starrs. Inscriptions of Fructus Belli were seen on the Ceiling and all about the Walls of the Room among Paintings of the Trophies of War, probably done by the order of Louis the fourteenth, who confessed in his dying Hour as his Successor and Exemplar Napoleone will probably do, that he had been too fond of War. The King was the Royal Carver for himself and all his Family. His Majesty eat like a King and made a Royal Supper of solid Beef and other Things in Proportion. The Queen took a large spoonful of Soupe, and displayed her fine Person and graceful manners, in alternately looking at the Company in various parts of the Hall, and ordering several kinds of Seasoning to be brought to her, by which she fitted her Supper to her Taste. When this was accomplished, her Majesty exhibited to the admiring Spectators, the magnificent Spectacle of a great Queen swallowing her Royal Supper in a single Spoonful, all at once. This was all performed like perfect Clockwork, not a feature of her face, nor a Motion of any part of her Person, especially her Arm and her hand could be criticised as out of order. A little and but a little Conversation seemed to pass among the Royal Personages of both Sexes, but in so low a voice that nothing could be understood by any of the Audience.

The Officers about the Kings Person brought him many Letters and Papers from time to time, while he was at Table. He looked at these, some of them he read or seemed to read, and returned them to the same Officers who brought them or some others.

These Ceremonies and Shows may be condemned by Philosophy and ridiculed by Commedy, with great reason. Yet the common Sense of Mankind has never adopted the rigid decrees of the former, nor ever sincerely laughed with the latter. Nor has the Religion of Nations in any Age, approved of the Dogmas or the Satyrs. On the Contrary it has always overborne them all and carried its Inventions of such Exhibitions to a degree of Sublimity and Pathos which has freequently transported the greatest Infidels out of themselves. Something of the kind every Government and every Religion has and must have: and the Business and Duty of Lawgivers and Philosophers is to endeavour to prevent them from being carried too far.

[6] MS: "find."

133

June 8. 1778. Dined with Mr. Alexander, and went to the Concert. There were two Gentlemen of the Name of Alexander, originally from Scotland, who came to France and took a house in the Neighbourhood of Passi. One was a Bachelor who had lived in the West Indies and was supposed to be a Man of Property. The other had a Family consisting of several Daughters one of whom Mr. Williams afterwards married. There had been some former Connections between Mr. Franklin and this family in England, which was carefully concealed as a Mystery and I had no Curiosity to enquire into it. Franklin however several times said to me that they had been under great Obligations to him in former times. And one of them now and then dropped to me, some of Franklins former confessions to him, concerning his Amours which were curious enough. The Ostensible Purpose of their residence in France was a Lawsuit of great importance to them in which they expected and I believe received Assistance from Franklin. The Alexanders were sensible Men, and their daughters were well behaved and agreable young Ladies, which made their Situation in the neighbourhood a pleasant Circumstance.

June 10. 1778.

Sir   Passi June 10. 1778

We have received your Letter of the fourth instant,[7] and in answer to it We beg leave to say, that We approve of your refusal of the twelve hundred Livres to Mr. William Morris, and for the future, We expect that you pursue the same line of Conduct and advance Money to no Person whatsoever upon our Account or in expectation that we shall repay it, without our express orders.

You are not entituled to pay any Captains orders, or Bills, upon any Occasion whatsoever, without our previous instructions.... Goods not Money are to be provided for the Captains: and these goods are to extend no further, than necessary repairs of their Ships, necessary Victuals for their Companies, and one Suit of Cloaths for each Person, to be delivered to the Captain, or such Officer as he shall direct, to be delivered to the People as they shall want, and charged to the Individuals on the Ships Books, that they may be deducted out of their Pay.

As to the Prize, if she should arrive, you will dispose of her, in concert with Captain Whipple, as he and you shall think best, for the Interest of the Public and the Captors.[8]

Mr. Monthieu has offered Us, the Flammand to go to America, upon

[7] Not found.

[8] In LbC a paragraph follows which is crossed out: "The Fuses from Berlin, the Druggs from Marseilles, and the Remittances from London being Sub-jects which We in our Capacity of Commissioners at this Court have nothing to do with, our Mr. Arthur Lee will write you in particular concerning them."

Freight to carry the goods which We have now on hand. We desire you, to inform Us, what freight We ought to give for this Ship, that We may know whether it is for the public Interest to hire this Vessell or not. We have the honor to be &c.   Signed B. Franklin, Arthur Lee, John Adams.

P.S. Captain Jones's Expences to and from Paris, you will please to pay and charge to the Public Account.
Mr. Schweighauser.

Sir   Passi June 10. 1778
We desire you will send Us, a Return of the Prisoners in your Possession, with their Rank and Names, to exchange them agreably to a Proposition of the British Court.

Your Account of the disagreement among your Ships Company has reached Us, on which We shall give you our Opinion, soon. We are &c.   Signed B. Franklin, Arthur Lee, John Adams
Captain Jones of the Ranger.

To any Captain bound to America
Sir   Passi June 10, 1778
Advices from London of the fifth of June, mention that the Squadron under Admiral Byron, which sailed from Portsmouth the 20th of May, had put into Plymouth the 27th and still continued there: and that orders had been sent down to that Squadron, not to proceed at present to America, as had been intended. Of this you will be pleased to inform those, whom it may concern.
We are &c.   B. Franklin, Arthur Lee, John Adams.

Sir   Passi June 13. 1778
Mr. Hezekiah Ford, Chaplain to the third and fifth Regiments of North Carolina Forces, in the Service of the United States of North America, having been made Prisoner in America, and sent to Europe, has found his Way to Paris and is now with Us. . . . He desires to do what Service he can to the Public, and We have determined to recommend him to You to officiate on board your Frigate as Chaplain, untill he shall return to America; and We do hereby recommend him Accordingly. We are Sir, your most &c.   Signed B. Franklin, Arthur Lee, John Adams.
Captain Abraham Whipple

Sir   Passi June 15. 1778
We beg leave to inform your Excellency, in Answer to the Com-

plaint of Mr. Bersolle, that he had formerly taken the Liberty, himself to draw upon our Banker for Advances, made to Captain Jones, before his last Cruise, and was much displeased, that his draft was refused payment.... We acquainted him, then, with the reason of this refusal, vizt. that he had sent Us, no Account of his disbursements or Advances, by which We might judge, whether his Draft was well founded, and he never had any Permission to draw upon our Banker. However, Afterwards, when We had seen his Accounts, Payment was made to him.

In the present Case, it is said, he has advanced to Captain Jones, 1000 Louis immediately on his Arrival, for which the Captain has drawn on Us, in Mr. Bersolles favour: but as Captain Jones had not previously satisfyed Us, of the necessity of this Advance, nor had our permission for the Draft, his Bill was also refused Payment. And as Captain Jones writes Us, that upon the News of our refusal, he was reduced to Necessity, not knowing where to get Victuals for his People, We conclude that the Advance was not actually made, as it was impossible he should in so short a time have spent so large a Sum. And We think it extreamly irregular in Merchants to draw Bills before they send their Accounts, and in Captains of Ships of War, to draw for any Sums they please, without previous notice and express Permission. And our Captains have the less Excuse for it, as We have ever been ready to furnish them, with all the Necessaries they desired. And Captain Jones in particular has had of Us, near one hundred thousand Livres for such Purposes, of which twelve thousand were to be distributed among his People to relieve their Necessities, the only purpose mentioned to Us for which this draft was made, and which We thought sufficient.—If this Liberty assumed of drawing upon Us, without our knowledge or Consent, is not checked and We are to be obliged to pay such drafts, it will be impossible for Us to regulate our own Contracts and Engagements so as to fullfill them with Punctuality, and We might in a little time become Bankrupts ourselves.... If therefore Mr. Bersolle has brought himself into any Embarrassment, it is not our fault but his.... We are ready to discharge all Debts We contract, but We must not permit other People to run us in Debt, without our Leave, and We do not conceive it can hurt our Credit, if We refuse Payment of such Debts.

Whatever is due for Necessaries furnished to Captain Jones by the Caisse de La Marine at Brest either from the Magazine, or for the Subsistance of his People, We shall also readily and thankfully pay, as soon as We have seen and approve of the Accounts. But We conceive, that regularly, the Communication of Accounts should always precede Demands of Payment.

We are much obliged by the Care that has been taken, to recover the Goods pillaged from the Chatham, and We think the Charges that have arisen in that Transaction ought to be paid, and We suppose will be paid out of the produce of the Sales of that Ship and her Cargo.

We understand Lieutenant Simpson is confined by his Captain for Breach of Orders: He has desired a Tryal, which cannot be had here, and therefore at his request, We have directed that he should be sent to America for that purpose.

We shall be obliged to your Excellency, for your Orders to permit the immediate Sale of the Chatham and other Prizes, that the part belonging to the Captors may be paid them, as they are very uneasy at the delay, being distressed for Want of their Money to purchase Cloathing &c. and We wish to have the Part belonging to the Congress, out of which to defray the Charges accruing on the Ships. The Difficulties our People have heretofore met with in the Sale of Prizes, have occasioned them to be sold, often for less than half their Value. And these difficulties not being yet, quite removed, are so discouraging, that We apprehend it will be thought adviseable, to keep our Vessells of War in America, and send no more to cruise on the coast of England.

We are not acquainted with the Character of Captain Botsen. But if your Excellency should have Occasion for a Pilot, on the coast of America, and this Person, on examination should appear qualified, We shall be glad that he may be found Useful in that quality: And We are thankfull to the Consull at Nice, for his rediness to serve our Countrymen. With the greatest respect and Esteem, We have the honor to be, your Excellency's &c.

B. Franklin, Arthur Lee, John Adams.

M. De Sartine

June 16. 1778.

To Captain Jones

Sir   Passi June 16. 1778

Upon the Receipt of this Letter, you will forthwith make Preparations with all possible dispatch, for a Voyage to America.... Your own Prudence will naturally induce you, to keep this your destination secret, least measures should be taken by the Ennemy to intercept you.

If, in the course of your passage home, Opportunities should present of making Prizes, or of doing any material Annoyance to the Ennemy, you are to embrace them, and you are at Liberty to go out of your Way, for so desireable a purpose. The Fishery at the Banks of New-foundland, is an important Object, and possibly the Ennemy's Men of War may have other Business than the Protection of it.... Transports are constantly passing and repassing from Rhode Island, New York and Philadelphia to Hallifax, and from all those Places to England. You will naturally search for some of these as Prizes.

If the French Government should send any dispatches to you, or if you should receive any from Us, to carry to America, you will take the best care of them, and especially that they may not fall into improper hands.—You are not however to wait for any dispatches, but to proceed upon your Voyage, as soon as you can get ready.

If there is any room on board your Ship, where you could stow away a Number of Chests of Arms, or of Cloathing for the Use of the United States, you will inform Mr. Schweighauser of it, that he may send them to you before your departure. We do not mean to incumber you with a Cargo, which shall obstruct the sailing of your Ship, or which shall impede you in fighting her: but if, consistent with her sailing and fighting she can take any quantity of Arms or Cloathing, it would be a desirable Object for the Public.   Signed B. Franklin, Arthur Lee, John Adams.

Sir   Passi near Paris June   1778[9]

We[1] received yours of the fifth instant, acquainting Us, that the Ministers have at length agreed to an Exchange of Prisoners.[2]—We shall write to Captain Jones, for the List required, which will be sent you, as soon as received. We understand there are at least two hundred. We desire and expect that the Number of ours, shall be taken from Fortune[3] and Plymouth in Proportion to the Number in each place, and to consist of those who have been longest in confinement, it being not only equitable that they should be first relieved, but this Method will prevent all Suspicion, that you pick out the worst and weakest of our People to give Us in Exchange for your good ones. If you should think proper to clear your Prisons at once, and give Us all our People, We will give you our solemn Engagement, which We

[9] From its position in the letterbook this letter must have been written on 16 June or very soon thereafter.

[1] LbC: "I." The same mistake was made in the next sentence but one below and was there corrected by overwriting to "We." Was JA subconsciously taking over the business of the American Com-

mission for himself?

[2] Hartley's letter, addressed to Franklin, is in PPAmP and is printed in Edward E. Hale and Edward E. Hale Jr., *Franklin in France*, Boston, 1887–1888, 1:203.

[3] LbC: "Forton"; i.e. Forton Prison, Portsmouth, England.

are sure will be punctually executed, to deliver to Lord Howe in America, or his order, a Number of your Sailors equal to the Surplus, as soon as the Agreement arrives there. There is one thing more, which We desire may be observed: We shall note in our List the names and Number of those taken in the Service of the King, distinguishing them from those taken in the Merchants Service; that in the exchange to be made, you may give adequate numbers of those taken in the Service of the States and of our Merchants. This will prevent any Uneasiness among both your Navy Men and ours, if the Seamen of Merchantmen were exchanged before them.

As it will be very troublesome and expensive, as well as fatiguing to them, to march your People from Brest to Calais, We may endeavour to get leave for your Ship to come to the Road of Brest to receive them there, or if that cannot be, We must desire from your Admiralty a Passport for the Ship that is to convey them from Brest to Calais.

If you have any of our People still Prisoners on board your Ships of War, We request they may be put into the Prisons, to take their Chance of exchange with the rest. &c.   Signed B. Franklin, Arthur Lee, John Adams

Mr. David Hartley.

This Letter to Mr. Hartley was superscribed to   Hodge Esqr.[4]

Sir   Passi June 17. 1778

Mr. Archer a young English Gentleman of Parts and Spirit, who is going to America to serve as a Volunteer, will deliver you this. The English Fleet had not sailed the tenth. We have no News yet, of its sailing. The Spanish Flota has not arrived as We have learned.... *The Dutch are more friendly to Us, than I was aware.*[5] ... Appearances indicate an immediate Rupture in Germany, between the Emperor and the King of Prussia. Ireland is very discontented and tumultuous. The English Fleet, after the most violent impresses for two Years, is miserably manned, and after all their Puffs in wretched Repair. The Stocks never were so low. In short, without an Army, Navy, Money, Allies or confidence in the Justice of their cause, England is like to have France

[4] A double mistake. The superscription (name of addressee at head of letter) had been inserted in the letterbook by John Thaxter, JA's private secretary, when making copies of these letters for the files of Congress, but Thaxter wrongly inserted the name of the addressee of the letter that *follows* this one to Hartley, and JA incorporated this piece of misinformation in his Autobiography. (JA's clerical untidiness, especially his inconsistency in placing names of recipients sometimes above and sometimes below the texts of letters in his letterbooks, led his secretaries and himself into errors and may well have led his editors into others.)

[5] Italics (underscoring) not in LbC.

and America, at least to contend with, and I have no doubt Spain too. Even Portugal, by late Letters to Us, and by late Examples of their treatment of American Vessells, is more friendly to Us than We thought. &c.   John Adams.
Isaac Smith Esq.

Sir   Passi June 23 1778
    As We have a Prospect of an Exchange of Prisoners, you are desired to send Us with all possible dispatch, a List or Return of all the Prisoners you have in your Custody, and We shall give orders concerning them as soon as We shall be informed, to what place they are to be sent to be exchanged.

    As to your future destination, We desire you, to take on board, your Frigate, as many Arms and Cloaths, or other merchandizes, as you can without impeding her in Sailing or Fighting, and no more: with which you are to acquaint Mr. Schweighauser, who will send them on board. If Mr. Schweighauser should have a Vessell bound to America with Stores for the Public, you are to take her under your Convoy.

    You are to use your best Endeavours to make Prizes, in the Course of your Passage, and in all respects to annoy the Enemy as much as you can, and are at Liberty to go out of your Way for so good a Purpose. If you can take or destroy any of the Enemies Fishery on the Banks of Newfoundland, you are not to omit the Opportunity.

    As Transports are continually passing between England and Hallifax, Rhode Island, New York and Philadelphia, and from each of these Places to all the others, you will use your best Endeavours to intercept some of them.

    If you should have Dispatches committed to your Care, either from the Government of this Kingdom, or from Us, you are to have them carefully encased in Lead, and, in case of Misfortune which God forbid, you are to take effectual Care, by sinking them, that they may not fall into the Enemies hands. We wish you a prosperous Cruise and Voyage and are &c.   B. Franklin, Arthur Lee, John Adams
Captain Abraham Whipple of the Providence Frigate.[6]

Sir   Passi June 23. 1778
    We had this day the honour of your Letter of the 18th. of June,[7] and are obliged to you for the Information you have given Us, concerning the freight of Ships.

    [6] RC (CtY:Franklin Coll.) is in JA's hand; a note below the signatures in RC reads: "Recd from Paris the 30th Instant by M [Lee?] from Schweighausers House Nantes."
    [7] Not found.

We have ordered Captains Whipple and Jones to prepare their Frigates forthwith to return home, and have ordered them to take on board, as many Arms or other Stores as they can, without Obstructing them in sailing or fighting, And no more, of which they are to inform you, that you may order them on Board accordingly. There are some Arms repaired, which We wish to have sent on board those Ships, if they can take them, or any of them.

We inclose you, Resolutions of Congress concerning the distribution of Prizes,[8] by which you will govern yourself in the distribution of those of the Providence and the Ranger. The Drake belongs wholly to the Captors. The Bounties upon Men and Guns are not to be paid by Us or by you, but by Congress in America, untill they shall order otherwise. That part of the other Prizes, which by the Resolutions of Congress, belongs to the United States, you will receive, and giving Us notice of the Value or amount of it, will carry to the Credit of the United States subject to our orders.

We have a prospect of exchanging the Prisoners, and have ordered returns of them all to be made to Us, that We may transmit them to England.   Signed B. Franklin, Arthur Lee, John Adams.
Mr. Schweighauser.

N.B. Admiral Byrons Fleet, having sailed, and probably for America, it is desired that the Notice sent of its having been countermanded, may not be sent to America.

Sir   Passi June 23. 1778

Mr. Joy Castle of Philadelphia has represented to Us, that a Barque called The Jane, William Castle Master, with her Cargo belonging to him, has been seized at Bourdeaux, by order of his Majesty as English Property, that he is a Citizen of the United States, and having been necessarily absent from America, for some time, on Account of the Sickness of his Family, but always intending to return thither, where he has an Estate, as soon as possible. That he took in a Cargo of Provisions in Ireland, sent his Vessell to Bourdeaux, in order there to load her for the United States.

We hereby certify, that the said Joy Castle has taken the Oath and subscribed the Declaration of Allegiance to the United States, and that We believe his Declaration to be true and sincere; and accordingly request your Excellency's Attention to his Case, and that his Property may be restored to him, as likewise his Vessel cleared out for

[8] This was presumably a copy of Congress' resolutions of 23 March 1776 (JCC, 4:229–232).

the said States. We have the honor to be with the greatest respect, your Excellencys &c.   Signed B. Franklin, Arthur Lee, John Adams.
M. De Sartine

Gentlemen [9]   Passi near Paris June 24. 1778
   We beg the favour of you to send Us an Account of the Prize mentioned in the inclosed Letter; that We may direct a distribution of the Produce, agreable to the resolutions of Congress.   Signed B. Franklin, Arthur Lee, John Adams.

[Enclosure]

   Copy of Captain Jones's Letter to the Commissioners.

Gentlemen   Ranger Brest 10 June 1778
   One of the Prizes taken last Winter by the Ranger, arrived at Bourdeaux, and was I understand sold by Messieurs S. and J. H. Dunlap.[1] On my return to Nantes from Paris, I wrote to that House requesting that the Captors Part of that Prize, might be immediately remitted to Mr. Williams of Nantes, so that a division might be made before the Departure of the Ranger. That House hath paid no Attention to my request, nor even condescended to answer my Letter. Therefore to remove the Uneasiness of my Officers and Men, I beg the favour of you to give orders that the Captors Part may be forth with remitted, agreable to my first Intention &c.

Sir   Passi June 26. 1778.
   We have had the honor of your Letters of June 18 and 19[2] referring to a former Letter respecting a Surgeons Bill, which We have received.
   As to the Surgeons Bill, We leave it wholly to you, to settle with him and allow him what you shall think just. The Account appears to Us to be too high, and We think with you, that the deduction you mention ought to be made.
   We are obliged to you, Sir, for the Articles of Intelligence you have sent Us, and wish for further favours of that kind, and approve much of your Proposal of transmitting Intelligence to America by every Opportunity.

---

[9] S. and J. H. Delap, merchants at Bordeaux; see the enclosure, below, and note there.
[1] RC (PPAmP:Franklin Papers) has the correct spelling "Delap."

[2] Both dated from Dunkerque, signed "Frans. Coffyn," endorsed by JA, and in PPAmP:Franklin Papers. See Commissioners to Coffyn, 13 July, below.

The Whalemen and other Seamen you mention, We wish may be sent to Brest or to Nantes, to serve on board our Frigates, where they will find many of their Countrymen and Comrades. At Nantes or Brest they will find Mr. Schweighauser or his Agent, who will find them Employment immediately; unless they should be willing to engage with Mr. Amiel, which We should prefer.

Inclosed with this, you have a Commission, Instructions and a Bond. The Bond We wish you to see executed with the usual Formalities, and when executed transmit it to Us. The Commission and Instructions you will deliver to Mr. Amiel.[3] We are, Sir your most humble Servants.   Signed B. Franklin, Arthur Lee, John Adams.
Francis Coffin Esq.

This Mr. Coffin was a Friend and Correspondent of Mr. Chaumont and conducted our Affairs always, as far as I ever heard with Candour, Intelligence and Fidelity.

To His Excellency Mr. De Sartine
Sir   Passi June 30. 1778
We have the Honor of inclosing to your Excellency a Protest,[4] relative to one of our Vessells, which was made Prize of, by the English, when under the Protection of the French Coast. As they have always reclaimed the Prizes made by our Cruisers in such Circumstances, We hope your Excellency will think it just, that We should be indemnified[5] out of their Effects in this Kingdom. We have the Honor to be &c.   B. Franklin, Arthur Lee, John Adams.

July 4. 1778. This being the Anniversary of the Declaration of American Independence, We had the honour of the Company of all the American Gentlemen and Ladies, in and about Paris, to dine with Dr. Franklin and me, at Passi, together with a few of the French Gentlemen in the Neighbourhood, Mr. Chaumont, Mr. Brillon, Mr. Vaillant, Mr. Grand, Mr. Beaudoin, Mr. Gerard De Rayneval, the Abby's Challut and Arnoud &c. Mr. Izzard and Dr. Franklin were upon such Terms, that Franklin would not have invited him, and I know not that Izzard would have accepted the Invitation if he had. But I said to Mr. Franklin that I would invite him, and I believe Dr. Smith and all the rest that he omitted and bring them all together and compell them if

---

[3] The "Instructions" to Amiel, i.e. a MS copy of Congress' instructions to commanders of private ships of war, adopted 3 April 1776 (*JCC*, 4:253–254), are in ViU:Arthur Lee Papers, with a covering note to Amiel, 23 June 1778, in JA's hand, signed by Franklin, Lee, and JA.
[4] Not found.
[5] LbC: "dedammaged."

possible to forget their Animosities. Franklin consented, and I sent Cards to them in my name only. The others were invited in the Names of both of Us. The Day was passed joyously enough and no ill humour appeared from any quarter: Afterwards Mr. Izzard said to me, that he thought We should have had some of the Gentlemen of that Country: He would not allow those we had to be the Gentlemen of the Country. They were not Ministers of State, nor Ambassadors, nor Princes, Nor Dukes, nor Peers, nor Marquises, nor Cardinals, nor Archbishops, nor Bishops. But neither our Furniture, nor our Finances would have born Us out in such an Ostentation. We should have made a most ridiculous figure in the Eyes of such Company. Besides the Ministers of State never dine from home unless it be with one another at the Castle: And We were not yet acknowledged, as public Minister[s,] by any Sovereign in Europe, but the King of France: therefore no Ambassador or other public Minister could have accepted our invitation. I know very well that the Company We had and the Society with which Dr. Franklin generally associated were disliked and disapproved by a great Body of the first and soundest People in the Kingdom. Some of them had been *"fletris,"* by a grand Court Martial or Court of Inquiry, which had been appointed on the Beginning of this Reign, or the latter End of the last consisting of the Marshalls of France whose Report I have read. These great People I now speak of, were, I know, very much disgusted, at our living at Passi and in the house of Mr. Chaumont. But this Step had been taken before my Arrival, and what could We do? The Circle in question, revolved round Mr. De Sartine and the Count de Vergennes, and were countenanced probably by Count Maurepas, whose departure from the first Intention of the present King had disgusted and driven from Court, first Mr. Malesherbes and next Mr. Turgot. I have not at present the Books and Papers, which I have seen and read, and if I had it would be endless as well as useless, to devellope the State of Parties in France at the Close of the Reign of Louis the 15th, and at the Commencement of that of Louis the Sixteenth. By those Revolutions of Parties We were thrown into the hands of a Sett of People, whose Intrigues, and mercenary Views, involved the first Years and indeed days of the Alliance with Suspicion and Want of confidence. The Persons and Parties are all dead, I believe, and no Man will probably ever look into the Memorials of those times with sufficient care to distinguish the Springs of Action. But I know what I say and I know it was regretted and lamented by many of the greatest and best Men in the Kingdom.

July 5. 1778. I have neglected to introduce, in the proper time, because I cannot precisely ascertain the Day, an Anecdote which excited my Grief, my Pitty and somewhat I confess of my resentment. Mr. Deane had left orders with Dr. Bancroft to receive and open all Letters which might arrive, addressed to him, after his departure. Among others he brought one to me addressed to Mr. Deane from Mr. Hancock, highly complimentary to Mr. Deane, professing great Friendship and Esteem for Mr. Deane, lamenting his Recall, complaining of the cruel Treatment he had received, and assuring him that it was not Congress that had done it. I pitied the weakness, grieved at the meanness and resented the Malice of this Letter. He had left Congress long before I did. He must have been ignorant of the most urgent motives of Congress to the Measure. He must have been blind not to have seen the egregious faults and Misconduct of Mr. Deane before this. If Congress had not done it, who had done it? Congress was unanimous in his Recall. In short the whole Letter was the Effect of a miserable Jealousy and Envy of me. I felt no little Indignation, at the ill Will, which had instigated this Persecution against me across the Atlantic, from a Man who had been under great Obligations to me for defending him and his Fortune, and whom I had never injured nor justly offended. The Letter was a fawning flattery of Deane, a Calumny against Congress, and had a tendency to represent me in an unfavourable light in foreign Countries and to embarrass and obstruct me in the discharge of the Duties of my Mission.[6]

July 6. 1778. Dined with the Abbys De Chaillut and Arnoud. Mr. De Chaillut the Farmer General and Brother of the Abby was there, Mr. and Mrs. Izzard, Mr. Lee, Miss Gibbs and Miss Stevens, and Mr. and Mrs. Lloyd. After dinner the Abby invited Us to the French Comedy, where We saw The Malheureux imaginaire, and the Parti de Chasse d'Henri Quatre.

July 7. 1778. Dined at St. Lu, with the Farmer General De Chaillut. The aged Marshall Duke Richelieu, and many others Marquisses, Counts and Abbys were there.

July 8.[7] I had long since determined to look at France, with a steady Eye and obtain as much Information as I could of her Manners, Institutions and History: but there was another branch of Enquiry in which all America at this time was compleatly uninformed, I mean the Ne-

---

[6] This incident, not mentioned in the Diary, was told by JA entirely from memory and was omitted by CFA in his text. The letter from Hancock to Deane has not been found.

[7] This entry (for which there is no corresponding entry in the Diary) was omitted by CFA in his text.

gotiations and Dispatches of Ambassadors. The Powers of Europe in general have kept the Letters and Memorials of their Ambassadors locked up in the Cabinetts of their Courts: very few of them have ever been collected and published. The Policy of France has been different. There are extant more Publications of their negotiations, than of all the rest of Europe.... I purchased D'Avaux, D'Estrades, Dossat, Jeannot,[8] Torcy, Noailles, The Diplomatick Dictionary, The Principles of Negotiation of the Abby De Mably, the Public Law of Europe founded on Treaties by the same Author, The Corps Diplomatique, and all other Books I could find relative to the office of an Ambassador as Wickefort &c. Grotius, Puffendorf, Vattell &c. I had read before in America. An Historical Collection of the Acts, Negotiations, Memorials and Treaties from the Peace of Utrecht, to the Year 1742 by Mr. Rousset in   Volumes, The History of the Congress and of the Peace of Utrecht as also of that of Rastadt and of Bade in Volumes.

These Writings contain a great deal of the History of France, especially of her foreign Relations, but as I wished to know as much of their internal Concerns as possible I purchased Veilly, Mezerai, De Thou and other Histories of France, and especially all the memoirs I could find of the civil Wars in France, among many others The Memoirs to Serve for the History of Ann of Austria, the Consort of Louis the Thirteenth King of France, by Madam De Motteville one of her Favorites in   Volumes, and the Memoirs of Mademoiselle de Montpensier, Daughter of Gaston of Orleans Brother of Louis the thirteenth in   Volumes, and all the original Memorials I could find of the Times of the League and the Fronde.[9]

[8] Doubtless a mistake for Jeannin; see the following note.

[9] This listing appears to have been compiled by JA partly by consulting the shelves of his library and partly from memory. Like the books he mentions earlier in his Autobiography (16 April, above) as having been acquired to teach himself French, most of the works he lists here can still be found among his books in the Boston Public Library, together with a great many others on French history and government and on European diplomacy generally. See the following entries in the *Catalogue of JA's Library*: Avaux, *Négociations de Monsieur le Comte d'Avaux en Hollande*, 2 copies (p. 17); Estrades, *Lettres, mémoires et négociations ... en Italie,* *en Angleterre & en Hollande,* 2 copies (p. 86); Arnaud, Cardinal d'Ossat, *Letres* (p. 186); Jean Baptiste Colbert, Marquis de Torcy, *Mémoires* (p. 54); Vertot d'Aubeuf, *Ambassades de Messieurs de Noailles en Angleterre* (p. 255); Mably, *Des principes des négociations* and *Le droit public de l'Europe*, 2 edns. (p. 154); Dumont, comp., *Corps universel diplomatique du droit des gens* (p. 79); Rousset de Missy, *Recueil historique d'actes, négociations, mémoires et traitéz* (p. 217); [Freschot,] *Histoire du congrès et de la paix d'Utrecht* (p. 98); Velly, *Histoire de France* (p. 254); Mézeray, *Abrégé chronologique de l'histoire de France*, 2 edns. (p. 167); Jacques Auguste de Thou, *Histoire universelle*, 2 edns. (p. 244); Fran-

It will be easily understood, that with my superficial Knowledge of the French Language, and with all the Business on my hands and Amusements that were inevitable, these Writings were not to be read in a short time. I resolved however to read as much of them as I could, and in fact I did read a great deal and endeavoured to get as good a general Idea of their Contents as possible. The Information obtained from these Books and the Observations I there made on the Manners and Character of the French People, together with my general Reading on the Nature and forms of Government, enabled me Eight or ten Years afterwards to form a pretty correct Judgment of the wild Project of demolishing the Monarchy and instituting a Republick, especially a Republic in one Representative Assembly, in France. But more, much more of this hereafter.

July 9. 1778. We wrote the following Letters

Mr. Schweighausser

Sir   Passy July 9. 1778

Inclosed you have an order on Messrs. Desegray, Beaujard Junr. and Co., Merchants at L'orient for 1520 Bags of Saltpetre, which you will please to receive, and ship for America, as Opportunities may serve. We are with Esteem yours &c.   Signed B. Franklin, Arthur Lee, John Adams

July 10. We also forward you herewith an order upon Mr. Cassoul [Cossoul], drawn by Mr. Williams for sundry Articles, which you will dispose of in the same manner with the Salt petre.

Messrs. Desegray, Beaujard and Co. Merchants L'orient

                                                          Passy July 9. 1778

Please to deliver to Mr. Schweighauser, Merchant at Nantes, or to his order, Fifteen hundred and twenty Bags of India Salt Petre belonging to the United States, and marked as follows—(here follow the Marks which are not necessary to transcribe[1]) in all 1520 Bags weighing 216475 nt. We are Gentlemen yours &c.   Signed. B. Franklin, Arthur Lee, John Adams

---

çoise Bertaut de Motteville, *Mémoires* (p. 174); Duchesse de Montpensier, *Mémoires* (p. 172).

Two other works listed here by JA are still in the family library at Quincy (MQA), bearing JQA's bookplate but quite likely having first belonged to JA. These are Pierre Jeannin, *Les négociations de M. le Président Jeannin,* 4 vols.

in 2, Amsterdam, 1695 (see JA's Diary, 16 July 1779 and note 3 there); and Abraham van Wicquefort, *L'ambassadeur et ses fonctions,* 2 vols., The Hague, 1681 (also another copy, 2 vols., Cologne, 1715).

[1] In LbC a list of the marks follows the text of the letter.

These two Letters are in the hand Writing of Mr. Arthur Lee, in my Book and are the first that were so.

I began now to think it high time to attend to my Friends in America and on this day I wrote the following private Letters. The first to Mr. James Lovell a Member of Congress.

My dear Friend   July 9. 1778

I had yesterday the honour of receiving the Dispatches from Congress which were sent by the Saratoga from Baltimore, arrived at Nantes, convoyed in by the Boston Captain Tucker, who has returned from a short cruise and has brought[2] in four Prizes, and those by the Spy, from New London arrived at Brest; and the inexpressible Pleasure of your private Letters by the same Vessells.

You acquaint me that you had written to me before Eight or nine times, which has given me some Anxiety, as these Letters are the first I have received from you or from any Member of Congress, since my Arrival in France.

The Ratification of the Treaty gives universal Joy to this Court and Nation, who seem to be sincerely and deeply rejoiced at this Connection between the two Countries.

There is no Declaration of War, as yet, at London or Versailles: but the Ships of the two Nations are often fighting at Sea, and there is not the smallest doubt but War will be declared, unless Britain should miraculously have Wisdom given her to make a Treaty with The Congress like that which France has made. Spain has not made a Treaty: but be not deceived, nor intimidated: All is safe in that quarter.

The Unforeseen dispute in Bavaria has made the Empress Queen and the King of Prussia, cautious of quarrelling with Great Britain, because her connection with a Number of the German Princes, whose Aid, each of those Potentates is soliciting, makes her Friendship, or at least her Neutrality in the German War which is threatened, of importance to each. But this will do no hurt to America.

The Brest Fleet alone is greatly superiour to Keppells, who seems to discover much dread of them. Indeed they are in excellent order, well manned and eager for Battle.

You have drawn so many Bills of Exchange upon Us, and send Us so many Frigates, every One of which costs Us a vast Sum of money; so many Merchandizes and Munitions of War have been sent, whether arrived or not; and We expect so many more Draughts upon Us, that I

[2] LbC: "sent."

assure you, I am very uneasy concerning our Finances here. We are labouring to hire Money and have some prospect of Success, but I am afraid not for such large Sums as will be wanted.

I find it less difficult to learn French than I expected, but I have so many Persons to converse with, and so many papers to read and write in English that I can scarce obtain a few minutes every day to study my Lesson, which I should otherwise do like a good Lad.

Let me intreat you to omit no Opportunity of writing me. Send me All the Newspapers, Journals, &c. and believe me your Friend and Servant   John Adams
Mr. Lovell.

Mr. Gerry a Member of Congress.
My Dear Friend   Passi July 9. 1778
I was disappointed in my Expectations of receiving Letters from You by the two Vessells, The Saratoga and the Spy, which have arrived. Although I know your time is every moment of it, wisely and usefully employed, yet I cannot but wish for a little of it, now and then. Europe is eager, at all times, for news from America, and this Kingdom in particular enjoys every Syllable of good News from that Country.

Great Britain is really a Melancholly Spectacle.... Destitute of Wisdom and Virtue to make Peace; burning with malice and revenge; yet affrighted and confounded at the Prospect of War.... She has reason; for if she should be as successfull in it, as she was in the last, it would weaken and exhaust her, and she would not, even in that Case recover America, and consequently her Superiority at Sea.... But humanly speaking it is impossible, she should be successful.

It is with real Astonishment that I observe her Conduct.... After all Experience, and altho' her true Interest, and her only safe plan of Policy is as obvious as the Sun, yet she cannot see it.... All Attention to the Welfare of the Nation seems to be lost, both by the Members of Administration and Opposition, and among the People at large.... Tearing one another to Pieces for the Loaves and Fishes, and a universal Rage for gambling in the Stocks, seem to take up all their Thoughts.

An Idea of a fair and honourable Treaty with Congress, never enters their Minds. In short Chicanery seems to have taken Possession of their hearts so entirely, that they are incapable of thinking of any Thing fair.

We had an Example, here last Week.... A long Letter, containing a Project for an Agreement with America, was thrown into one of our Grates.... There are Reasons to believe, that it came with the Privity of the King.... You may possibly see it, sometime.... Full of Flattery, and proposing that America should be governed by a Congress, of American Peers, to be created and appointed by the King.... And of Bribery, proposing that a Number not exceeding two hundred American Peers should be made, and that such as had stood foremost, and suffered most, and made most Enemies in this Contest, as Adams, Handcock, Washington and Franklin by Name, should be of the Number.... Ask our Friend, if he should like to be a Peer?

Dr. Franklin, to whom the Letter was sent, as the Writer is supposed to be a Friend of his, sent an Answer, in which they have received a Dose that will make them sick.   John Adams
Mr. Gerry

This Letter requires a Commentary.... The Reasons for believing that it came with the Privity of the King, were derived wholly from Dr. Franklin, who affirmed to me that there were in the Letter infallible Marks, by which he knew that it came from the King, and that it could not have come from any other without the Kings Knowledge. What these Marks were he never explained to me. I was not impertinently inquisitive, and he affected to have reasons for avoiding any more particular devellopement of the Mystery. Many other hints have been dropped by Franklin to me, of some Mysterious Intercourse or correspondence between the King and him, personally.... He often and indeed always appeared to me to have a personal Animosity and very severe Resentment against the King. In all his conversations and in all his Writings, when he could naturally and sometimes when he could not, he mentioned the King with great Asperity. He wrote certain Annotations on Judge Fosters discourse on the Legality of the Impressment of Seamen, in the Margin of the Book, and there introduced his habitual Accrimony against his Majesty. A thousand other Occasions discovered the same disposition. Among the ancient disputes between Franklin and the Proprietary Governors of Pensilvania, I have read, that Franklin, upon hearing of a report in Circulation against his Election as Agent for the Province at the Court of St. James's that he had no Influence with the Ministry, and no Acquaintance with Lord Bute, broke out into a Passion and swore, contrary to his usual reserve, "that he had an Influence with the Ministry and was intimate with Lord Bute." It is not generally known that the Earl of Bute was a Philosopher, a Chymist and a natural Historian. That he printed seven

or Eight Volumes of natural History of his own Composition, only however for the Use of his particular confidential Friends. This kind of Ambition in the Earl might induce him to cultivate the Acquaintance with
Franklin, as it did afterwards Rochefoucault, Turgot and Condorcet
in France. And at the Earl of Butes some mysterious Conferences between the King and Franklin might have been concerted: and in these
Interviews Franklin might have conceived himself deceived or insulted.
I mention this merely as conjecture, Suggestion or Surmise. Franklins
Memorials, if they ever appear may confirm or confute the Surmise,
which however after all, will be of very little Consequence. Without
the Supposition of some kind of Backstairs Intrigues it is difficult to
account for that mortification of the pride, affront to the dignity and
Insult to the Morals of America, the Elevation to the Government of
New Jersey of a base born Brat.[3]

Franklin consulted with me, and We agreed first to do nothing without previously informing the French Court. Secondly as the Letter was
supposed to come from a Friend of Franklin, at the desire or by the
orders of the King, it was agreed that Franklin should write the Answer. He produced his draught to me and it was very explicit, decided
and severe, and in direct terms asserted that by certain Circumstances
in the Letter Franklin knew that it came from the King. We sent a
Copy of the Answer to the Count de Vergennes as well as the original
Letter and Project and asked his Excellencys Advice, whether We
should send it or not.

In the Letter the Writer proposed that We should meet him at
twelve O Clock precisely in a certain Part of the Church of Notre
Dame, on a certain day in order to have a personal Conference upon
the Subject. I know not that the Papers were ever returned from Ver-
sails. We received no Advice to send the Answer. The Day after the
One appointed to meet the Messenger at Notre Dame the Count De
Vergennes sent Us the Report of the Police of Paris, stating that at the
Day, Hour and place appointed a Gentleman appeared and finding
nobody wandered about the Church gazing at the Statues and Pictures and other Curiosities of that magnificent Cathedral, never loosing Sight however of the Spot appointed and often returning to it,
looking earnestly about at times as if he expected Somebody: His Person, Stature, figure, Air, Complexion, Dress and every Thing about
him was accurately and minutely described. He remained two Hours
in the Church and then went out, was followed through every Street

---

[3] This sentence, interlined as an afterthought in the MS, was omitted by CFA
in his text.

and all his motions watched to the Hotel where he lodged. We were told the Day he arrived there, the Name he assumed, which was Colonel ⟨Mc⟩ Fitz——something an Irish name that I have forgotten, the Place he came from and the time he sett off to return.

In my Letter to Mr. Gerry it is inaccurately said that Dr. Franklin sent an Answer. It was written and I supposed would be sent but it was not.

Whether the Design was to seduce Us Commissioners, or whether it was thought that We should send the Project to Congress and that they might be tempted by it, or that disputes might be excited among the People, I know not. In either case it was very weak and absurd and betrayed a gross Ignorance of the Genius of American People.[4]

An Aristocracy of American Peers! hereditary Peers I suppose were meant, but whether hereditary or for Life, nothing could be more abhorrent to the general Sense of America at that time, which was for making every Magistrate and every Legislator eligible and that annually at least.

An Aristocracy of American Peers! But this could not be simple: the King must have been intended to have a Negative upon the Laws no doubt: but was this Authority to have been executed by a Vice Roy to reside in Philadelphia? And were this Vice Roy and these two hundred Peers to have made all the Laws, without a Representation of the People by annual or other Elections? Even if there were to have been three Branches to the general Government, what was to become of State Governments? All abolished? Or all continued under some kind of Subordination to the General Government? Any of these Projects would have appeared to the People of America, at that time as extravagant and as tyrannical as any Thing the English had done. The English were strangely infatuated with an Idea, that Adams and Hancock, Washington and Franklin with a few others in the several States,

[4] This affair, related fairly accurately by JA from memory, still remains mysterious. The letter to Franklin, purportedly from Brussels, 16 June 1778, was signed "Charles de Weissenstein" and is reproduced, with its bulky enclosures, from the originals in the Archives des Affaires Etrangères, Paris, in Stevens, *Facsimiles*, Nos. 835–837. Franklin's (ultimately unsent) answer, 1 July, is printed from the original in the same repository in his *Writings*, ed. Smyth, 7:166–172. In MH:Arthur Lee Papers (photoduplicate in Adams Papers Editorial Files) is a paper which is apparently the report of the police charged with observing "Weissenstein's" emissary (who was to wear a rose in his hat or waistcoat and pick up a packet from Franklin in the choir of the Cathedral of Notre Dame). The report is dated 7 July and is captioned "Copie pour M. fr. . . ." It identifies the emissary as "M. *Jennings* qui étoit Capitaine aux Gardes du Roi d'Angleterre il y a quatre ou cinq ans; son Pere a été Ministre en quelque Cour étrangere."

as they had Influence enough to throw off the Authority of Great Britain, would have Influence enough to put it on again, as a Man who has Strength enough to throw off his Cloak may be supposed able to throw it again over his Shoulders. Nothing could be more erroneous: For none of these Leaders had any Influence but that which was given them by the Folly and Temerity of Great Britain: and if any of them had adopted and advocated any such Projects as these, he would not only have lost all Influence in America, but been obliged to fly to England for Protection among the Royalists and Refugees. These Speculations were however, all rendered unnecessary. Independence had been declared two Years, and all America, in a manner had renounced every modification of Government under Great Britain forever, fully convinced that no cordial Confidence or Affection could ever be restored on either Side. Besides a Treaty with France had been solemnly made. America was then a Virgin and her Faith sacred. And it would have been ridiculous to suppose that France would now consent that We should make a seperate Treaty and become subject again to England, that the reunited Empire might immediately fall upon France in a new War.

We thought the whole Subject so futile that I think We never transmitted any Account of it to Congress.

To Governor Henry of Virginia
Dear Sir   Passi July 9. 1778
I had the honour of a Letter from you, some time ago,[5] which I have never had an Opportunity of answering 'till now.

Immediately after the Receipt of it, I went with Mr. Arthur Lee to Versailles in order to obtain the Articles you wrote for. It gave me pleasure to do any thing in my Power to serve the State of Virginia or its worthy Governor: but my Assistance was not necessary, as Mr. Lee sollicited the Business with great Spirit and with good Success as he will inform you.

We have received Yesterday, by two Vessells, the Saratoga and the Spy, very agreable Accounts from America.... The Ratification of the Treaty, with such perfect Unanimity, and in such handsome terms, is very agreable here, and will be so in other parts of Europe.

The Resolutions of Congress for detaining General Burgoine's Army, those upon the conciliatory Bills, and their late Address to the People, are exceedingly admired and applauded all over Europe.

[5] From Williamsburg, 5 March 1778 (Adams Papers). Henry requested JA's assistance for Arthur Lee, "Agent for our State," in procuring credit for arms in France to be sold to Virginia.

Hostilities having commenced between France and England, without any formal declaration of War, it is this day said that the Brest Fleet has put to Sea.... If they meet Keppell there will be a sublime Battle. But if Keppell should beat D'Orvilliers, which one would think however to be impossible, as the French Fleet is certainly superiour in number, fuller manned, in better repair and in higher Spirits, Britain would not be much the better for it. For their Fleet will be disabled, their Seamen destroyed, losses which they cannot repair. Whereas Spain remains to bring up the rear: and France is better able to repair her losses. It is a Connection with America, which must in future decide the Ballance of maritime Power, in Europe.

What Events will take place in America, is uncertain. D'Estaing's Fleet is there before now: but what he will do, time must discover. Byron is twenty or thirty days behind him. But I think it is probable, that some part of the American Seas, will also have the honour of a magnificent Sea fight, for the first time.

The English Papers received this day, announce the Evacuation of Philadelphia. But it is not perfectly understood, how the Army could march through the Jersies without molestation. Surely America will not suffer that remnant of an Army to plague them much longer.

The same Papers affirm that a Committee of Congress is appointed to treat or confer, with the Commissioners from London, and mention the names, but We can conceive here, of no Use for such a Conference, but to ask the question, Have you Power and Will to acknowledge the Sovereignty of our States? The Answer must be, No.

I should esteem myself, at all times honoured, by a Letter from You. The Anxiety here, for Intelligence from America is indeed surprizing. Indeed Sir, you would be flattered with the Attention that is shown to our States, and with the high Eulogiums, that are every where bestowed, by learned and ingenious Men, upon our Constitutions, our Laws, our Wisdom, Valour and Universal Virtue. Partial as I am to my Country, and dearly as I love it, I cannot but say that I think they do Us, rather more honour than We deserve. But We are Combattants for Liberty, and it is a fashionable Saying in this Country, that every Man who combats for Liberty is adorable. There is more Liberality of Sentiment in every part of Europe, except England, but especially in France, than former Ages have known, and it will increase every day.

I am &c.   John Adams

Patrick Henry Esqr. Governor of Virginia.

July 10. 1778.

Mr. Williams

Passi July 10. 1778

We approve of the Directions given by you to stop the Reparation of the Arms at Nantes, paying the Workmen their Wages, Gratifications and Conduct Money, according to Agreement, of which you inform Us in your Letter July 3. 1778.[6]   Arthur Lee, John Adams

Passi July 10 1778.

Mr. Williams is desired to send the Commissioners an order for the Goods remaining on hand, including the sixty three Barrells of Beef to be delivered to Mr. J. D. Schweighauser of Nantes or to his order.
                              Arthur Lee, John Adams

These two Letters are also in the Hand Writing of Mr. Arthur Lee, in my Book. The Reason why Dr. Franklin did not sign them I do not remember. He might be absent, or might disapprove them.

Sir   Passi July 10. 1778

I had Yesterday the pleasure of your Letter from Nantes,[7] and am much obliged to you for the agreable Intelligence contained in it.... I had no letters by the Sarratoga, later than the thirtieth of April, but the Spy has arrived at Brest, and brought a full and unanimous Ratification of the Treaty, and an handsome Resolution of Congress expressing their high Sense of the Friendship of the French King. The Treaty was ratified in less than forty eight hours, after its Arrival.[8]

The English have affirmed in their Papers of the fourth of this month, that their Army has evacuated Philadelphia, and got safe to New York.... I think they ought not to have got there without broken Bones. However, I have little dependence on these paragraphs of English Newspapers.... Gates commands at Peeks Kill. An ominous Name, to the British Army in New York.

I am glad to learn that a Vessell has arrived to your Address, in which you are also an Owner. I wish you much pleasure and profit in the disposition of her Cargo. And as Rochefoucault and Swift inform Us, that in all good fortune of our Friends We first consult our private Ends, if you have received among the Cargo, any good News, I wish you would let your Friends at Passi, come in for a Share of it.

[6] In PPAmP:Franklin Papers; endorsed by JA.
[7] Dated 4 July, endorsed by Arthur Lee?, and in PPAmP:Franklin Papers.
[8] LbC has an additional sentence, omitted here doubtless by mere inadvertence: "Our latest Letters however by this Vessell are of the 15 of May."

You will possibly see a Part of your Letter in the Affairs De L'Angleterre et de L'Amerique. The Anecdote of the M. De La Fayette, will please in this Country, which takes a great Interest in all the Actions of that gallant and amiable young Nobleman.[9] His Lady is gone to Bourdeaux, or I would have sent your Letter to her.

The Brest Fleet is sailed, as I was told last night, so that We may expect soon to hear of a Rencounter. I think it probable too, that We may soon hear of a splendid Sea Fight in America, the first that will grace the History of that Country. God grant it may be prosperous to it.

I am, dear Sir, your Friend and Servant.   John Adams
Mr. William McCreery at Nantes.

Dear Sir   Passi July 10 1778
I received, the day before Yesterday, your Letter by the Saratoga[1] And I thank you for it, and for the Packett of Newspapers. Pray continue this goodness.... Pack up every Newspaper you can lay your hands on, by themselves, and write upon the Outside of the Package "Not to be thrown Overboard," for in that case, if they are taken, the News gets published by the Enemy, which is an Advantage. Pray send me also, a Sett of the Journals of the Congress, by every Opportunity for some time. Mr. Thompson will have the goodness (my Respects to him) to furnish you with these, without expence, and a Volume of the Journals, is a great Curiosity here, and an handsome Present. Inclose them in Carthrige Paper and direct them to me. Before this reaches you, great Events will have taken place in America, I presume, and very probably a Battle in Europe, between D'Orvilliere's Fleet, and Keppells, in which if England should get the better, which seems not very probable, she will still be the Looser in the End, because the War she has before her with France, Spain and America, must exhaust her, how many gallant Exploits soever she may perform in the course of it. Your Friend.   John Adams
Mr. John Thaxter, in the Secretary's Office of Congress.

Sir   Passi July 10. 1778
I had the Honour of a Letter from you,[2] by the French Frigate which

---

[9] JA probably submitted to Edmé Jacques Genet the passage in McCreery's letter about Lafayette's action on the Schuylkill, 19 May, but since Genet soon had the news in a more official form, McCreery's remarks were not used in the *Affaires de l'Angleterre et de l'Amérique*.
[1] Dated "York Town" (York, Penna.), 30 April (Adams Papers).
[2] Dated "Head Quarters," Boston, 14 May (Adams Papers).

gave me the more pleasure, as no other Person in the Massachusetts thought proper to take any notice of me, by that Opportunity.... I laid your Letter immediately before the People in Power here, and an Extract of it has crep'd into a Publication called Affaires de L'Angleterre et de L'Amerique.[3]

We received the day before Yesterday, a very handsome Ratification of the Treaty, which is extreamly pleasing to the Ministry, and will give fresh Vigour to their Operations, as Hostilities are already commenced.

Great Britain has before her a very chearing Prospect.... Stripped of the best Branch of her Commerce, her Navy is like a girdled Tree. Without Soldiers, without Sailors, without Ships indeed in sufficient numbers and in suitable repair, without commerce, without Revenue, and without Allies, she has the united Forces of France, Spain and America to meet by Land and by Sea. She seems to be chiefly occupied at present with concerting Measures for the defence of the Kingdom, and is agitated with an apparent dread of another Conquest like that of William the Norman. France has an hundred Thousand Men in Normandie, Picardie and Brittany, and a Fleet compleatly ready to go out of Brest, if not already at Sea, greatly superiour to that of Keppell. —I mention Spain among the Ennemies of Britain, because, although she has not as yet made a Treaty with Us, yet I am well assured in my own mind, that she will have neither Inclination nor Ability to preserve a Neutrality, if a War is openly avowed between France and England as it very soon will be.

I am very easy in my own Mind, concerning the British Commissioners, because, after the Resolutions of Congress upon the Conciliatory Bills, which you sent me,[4] which are admired and applauded all over Europe, and after an Unanimous Ratification of the Treaty with France, I am sure there can be nothing to fear from a Conference.

Britain has but one wise plan of Policy, which is as obvious, as it is prudent, and that is, instantly to make with America, such a Treaty as France has made. But she will not see it. She is yet too proud and vain, and the Consequences of her blindness must be, that instead of the dominant Power of Europe, which she has been but for a little while,

---

[3] This was a paragraph describing the amazement of the British officers who were prisoners in Cambridge upon hearing that France had recognized American independence. It is translated and printed in the *Affaires*, vol. 10: p. cclxxxvi (No. 46).

[4] Congress' reply to the British commissioners' proposals was voted on 17 June (JCC, 11:614–615); it was soon afterward published, with relevant correspondence and other papers, in the newspapers.

she will dwindle down into a Power of the second order: as Spain, which under Charles the fifth was the first Power in Europe, by a similar quarrell with her Provinces, weakened herself to such a degree as to fall down into the middle Class of Powers, and has never yet been able to regain her Ascendancy. This is the established order of Things, when a Nation has grown to such an height of Power as to become dangerous to Mankind, she never fails to loose her Wisdom, her Justice and her Moderation, and with these she never fails to loose her Power; which however returns again, if those Virtues return.

I shall be under great Obligations to you, Sir, if you will continue your favours by every opportunity. Your Newspapers, tho' badly printed, are very valuable here. I am with great respect &c.

John Adams.

Hon. Major General Heath   Boston.

July 11. 1778

To His Excellency Monsieur De Sartine.
Sir   Passi July 11. 1778
We have had the honour of your Excellencys Letter of the Fifth Instant relative to Captain Jones,[5] and We redily consent that he should be at your Excellencys disposition and shall be happy if his Services may be in any respect Usefull to the designs your Excellency may have in Contemplation. We have the honour to be with the greatest respect, your Excellency's &c.

B. Franklin, Arthur Lee, John Adams.

The Letter to which this is an Answer, marks the first conception of the Plan which was afterwards carried into Execution under Jones in the Bonhomme Richard.

This day July 11. 1778 We received from Mr. Williams the following order,

Mr. Cassoul
Sir   Passi July 10. 1778
Deliver to Mr. J. D. Schweighauser the following Goods taking his Receipt for the same, on Account of the Honourable Ministers Plenipotentiary of the United States, viz. one hundred and Ninety Six Swivels, Forty nine Cases of Arms, one Case of Duck, two Bales of

[5] In MH:Arthur Lee Papers; endorsed by JA. Sartine stated that he needed Jones "pour quelqu'expédition particuliere" and therefore requested that he be permitted to stay in France and that his second in command be ordered to take the *Ranger* to America.

Linnen, Eight Cases of Medicines, Two Barrells of Do. According to Bills of Lading from Holland. . . . Fifty Five Cases of Sabres according to Bills of Lading from Dunkirk, Two Thousand Eight hundred and forty Six Suits of Soldiers Cloaths, according to my Invoice, Four Bales of Do. according to Mr. Monthieu's Invoice. One hundred and seventy one Sheets of Copper to be weighed. Forty five Casks of Flints. All the Arms and Furniture repaired and unrepaired in the Magazine, taking an Inventory of the same, and sixty three Barrells of Beef. Those of the above Articles which stand in my name in the Bureau D'Entrepot you will see transferred to Mr. Schweighauser, and me discharged therefrom, at the time of Delivery.

I am your humble Servant   Signed J. Williams Jr.[6]

Sir   Passi July 13. 1778

We have received several late Letters from you, and two this morning by the hand of Captain Amiel, containing abundant Testimonies of your good Character.

As We have never entertained the least doubt, of your Probity or Honor, or of your unblemished reputation, you have given yourself much trouble without necessity, and used as the Saying is, In Re non dubiâ, testibus non necessariis.

It is true We received a Letter, in which some regret was expressed that We had addressed Mr. Amiel and his Papers to you, and the reason assigned was, because the Letter Writer thought you had made yourself "somewhat too busy, in some particular matters," but this you may be assured never made the least Impression upon Us, to your disadvantage.[7]

In one of those Letters We received the Bond, Instructions and Commission returned.

If you should write to America, the News as it occurs, you may write to the Honourable James Warren Esqr., Speaker of the House of Representatives of Massachusetts Bay, at Boston,—or to The Honourable Committee of foreign Affairs, at Congress, or to both. If you can send any English Newspapers they will be always acceptable. But We would wish You to observe one Rule, which is, not to write any News to America that is not well authenticated, because there are so

[6] The text from which JA copied this letter is a copy entered by Arthur Lee in Lb/JA/4.

[7] See Commissioners to Coffyn, 26 June, above; also Coffyn to Commissioners, 7, 9, 10 July; Poreau, Mackenzie & Co. to Commissioners, 7 July; Peter Amiel to Commissioners, 9 July (all from Dunkerque and all in PPAmP: Franklin Papers; endorsed in various hands, including Arthur Lee's but not JA's).

many Misrepresentations floating about in the World, that if these should be written as they occurr, to a distant Country, they would tend to confound and mislead the People.

The American Seamen you mention, We wish to have put into some Employment, by which they may earn their Bread and save Expences to their Country, as soon as possible, and it is indifferent to Us, whether it is at Dunkirk, Brest, or Nantes. We are &c.

B. Franklin, Arthur Lee, John Adams

Mr. Francis Coffyn at Dunkirk.

Sir   Passi July 13. 1778

As We understand the Boston in her last Cruise, did not sail so well as formerly, We apprehend this Alteration has been made, by some change in her Ballast: for which reason, you are directed, if you judge it necessary, to take out your present Ballast; to apply to Mr. Schweighauser at Nantes, and take from him such Articles, as he may have to send to America, which may be stowed away in your Ship, without hindrance to her sailing or fighting, and to take from him also, a quantity of Lead, to be used as Ballast untill you arrive in America, and then delivered to the Continental Agent, informing Congress or the Navy Board by Letter.

Upon the Receipt of this Letter, you are then to join Captain Whipple and to pursue his orders, respecting your future Cruises and Voyage to America. If Lieutenant Simpson of the Ranger should apply to you for a Passage to America, in the Boston, you will afford him Accommodations according to his Rank. We are &c.

B. Franklin, Arthur Lee, John Adams

Captain Tucker

Sir   Passi July 13. 1778

You will putt on board the Boston Frigate such Articles as Captain Tucker shall inform you he can take to America, and among other Things you are desired to furnish him, if it is in your Power, with a quantity of Lead.... As this Article is much wanted in America, and is excellent for Ballast, you are desired to furnish him as much as he can carry and you can conveniently supply. We are &c.

B. Franklin, Arthur Lee, John Adams.

Mr. J. D. Schweighauser.

Sir   Passi July 13. 1778

We have ordered Captain Tucker, to join you, in your future

Cruises and Voyage to America.—You will get to Sea, with all possible Expedition.[8]   B. Franklin, Arthur Lee, John Adams.
Captain Whipple

July 14. 1778. Dined at Chatou with Mr. Bertin, the Minister of State. Went to see the Park where We rambled till We were weary. We received from Mr. De Sartine the following Letter, in french.

Versailles the 14. July 1778

Notwithstanding the Precautions I have taken, Gentlemen, to assure the Subsistance of the Inhabitants of the Islands of St. Pierre and Miquelon, who, in the present Circumstances, will receive little or no Supplies sent by the Commerce of France, it may happen that the Interception of one or more, of the Vessells which I have caused to be expedited to those Islands, with Cargoes of Provisions, may reduce their Inhabitants to the greatest distress. And there will no longer be an Opportunity to provide a remedy when We shall be informed of the Event. . . . I have thought that We might depend upon the Assistance of the United States of America, and I have pointed them out, for the case of a pressing Necessity, to the Administrators of the Islands of St. Pierre and Miquelon.—It will be very agreable to his Majesty, if you concurr, in whatever may depend on you, in procuring such Succour, by recommending to the United States of America and particularly to the Government of Boston, to encourage if it is possible, some Expeditions to those Islands, to carry Eatables to their Inhabitants and supply their Necessities. I have the Honor to be, most perfectly, Gentlemen your most humble and most obedient Servant

De Sartine

The Gentlemen The Deputies of the Congress of the United States of America.

The next day We received another Letter of which the following is a litteral Translation.

Versailles 15 July 1778

Among the English Prisoners detained at Belle Isle, Gentlemen, and proceeding from Vessells detained in the Ports of France, are found the Persons named James Niggins and John Selby, who call themselves Americans, the first of Charlestown in South Carolina, and the other of Baltimore in Maryland: They demand their Liberty, and

---

[8] In LbC the following clause was added to this sentence and then inked out: "and remember that the great Jamaica Fleet sails for Europe the 26th. of this Month."

the means of returning home. According to their declaration, they made heretofore a part of the Crew of the Ship Hancock, arrived from America at the Port of Nantes, in the month of December last, and that Ship having sailed from that Port to return to Charlestown, was taken, at thirty Leagues from Belle Isle by an English Privateer and carried to Falmouth, where to avoid the Press, they consented to remain, on board the Englishman who had made them Prisoners. I pray you to signify to me, whether these Men are known to you, whether you consider them as belonging to the United States of America, whether they have made, or caused to be made any representation to you, and whether you consider them, as entitled, to obtain their demand. I have the honour to be, with the most perfect Consideration, Gentlemen, your very humble and most obedient Servant

De Sartine

Messrs. Franklin Lee and Adams Deputys of the United States of America.

Lieutenant Simpson
Sir   Passi July 16. 1778
We have long wished to accommodate Disputes among the Officers of the Ranger, and have at length the Pleasure to inclose you a Letter from Captain Jones, which has given Us much Satisfaction for several Reasons, one of which is that it has given Us an opportunity to reinstate you on board the Ranger.[9]

You are accordingly, upon the receipt of this Letter, forthwith to take the Command of the Ranger as her first Lieutenant, and to join Captain Whipple of the Providence, and observe his orders, relative to your future Cruises and Voyage to America.

As to the British Prisoners you will leave them in such place and in the Custody of such Persons, as Mr. Schweighauser shall advise.

B. Franklin, Arthur Lee, John Adams

Delivered Captain Jones a Copy of the above Letter the 5. of August, 1778.[1]

Captain Whipple
                                                              Passi July 16. 1778
We have ordered Lieutenant Sympson to whom the Command of the Ranger devolves, by the destination of Captain Jones to another

[9] The text of Jones' letter of this date, which was enclosed, is copied into JA's Autobiography farther on under the present date.

[1] This memorandum is added in Arthur Lee's hand following the text of the letter (which has no indication of signatures) in JA's letterbook.

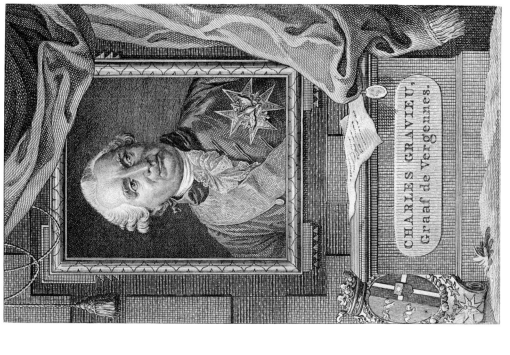

8. VERGENNES, FRENCH MINISTER OF FOREIGN AFFAIRS

7. HÔTEL DE VALENTINOIS, RESIDENCE OF THE
AMERICAN COMMISSIONERS AT PASSY

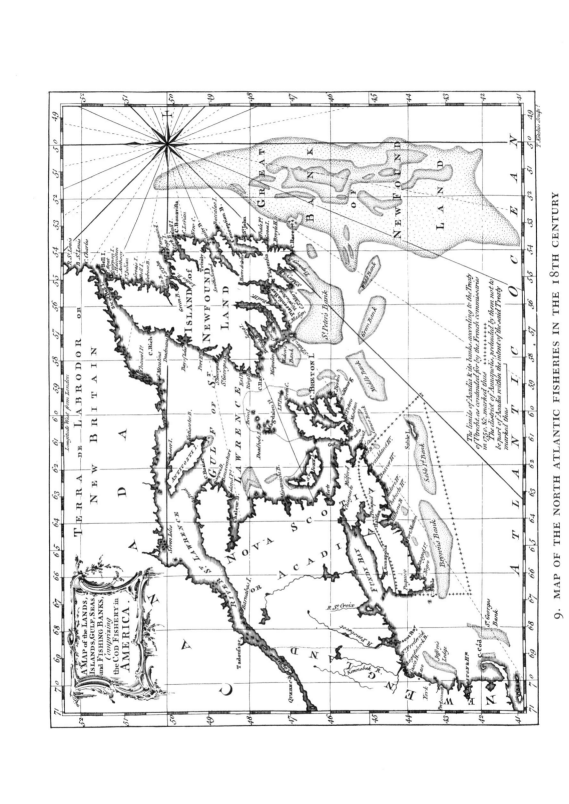

9. MAP OF THE NORTH ATLANTIC FISHERIES IN THE 18TH CENTURY

Service, to join you and obey your orders, respecting his future Cruises and Voyage to America. We wish you to Use all possible dispatch, in getting to Sea, with the Providence, Boston and Ranger.

You are to Use your utmost Endeavours, to take, burn, sink and destroy all Privateers of Jersey and Guernsey, and all other British Cruisers, within the Command of your Force, as you may have Opportunity.

You are to leave all the Prisoners in such place, and in the Custody of such Persons, as Mr. Schweighauser shall advise. We are &c.

B. Franklin, Arthur Lee, John Adams.

Mr. Schweighauser

Passi July 16 1778

We have ordered the Ranger under the command of Lieutenant Simpson to put to Sea with all possible Expedition: You will be so good as to furnish her, with the Necessaries Mr. Simpson may demand, with as much dispatch as possible.

The British Prisoners, on board of all these Frigates, are to be left behind, but We will endeavour tomorrow to obtain directions from the Ministry, in whose hands and in what place they shall be lodged. We have directed the Captains to leave them in such place and in the Custody of such Persons as you shall advise. Signed B. Franklin, Arthur Lee, John Adams.

The Honourable the Council of the Massachusetts Bay

May it please your Honours   Passi July 16. 1778

We have the Honour to inclose a Copy of a Letter just received from Monsieur De Sartine, the Minister of State for the Marine of this Kingdom, in answer to which We have had the honour to assure his Excellency that We would embrace the first Opportunity of communicating it to your honours.[2]

We have not the smallest doubt of the good Inclinations of the People in America to supply the Necessities of their Friends at Saint Peters and Miquelon, nor of the Abilities of those in the Northern States to do it effectually, provided the British Men of War are withdrawn from the Hallifax and Newfoundland Stations. Perhaps it may be done notwithstanding the dangers of Men of War. We hope however it will be attempted. There is no doubt that a good Price may be ob-

---

[2] The enclosure was a copy of Sartine's letter to the Commissioners of 14 July, q.v. under that date above. The Commissioners' answer to Sartine is inserted below under the present date.

tained, at the same time that an acceptable Act of Friendship and of Humanity, will be performed.

We have the Honour to request that this Letter and its Enclosure may be laid before the General Court, and that such Measures may be taken as their Wisdom shall dictate, for the accomplishment of so desirable a purpose. We have the Honour to be

B. Franklin, Arthur Lee, John Adams.

To the President of Congress

Sir   Passi July 16. 1778

We have the Honour of inclosing a Copy of a Letter from his Excellency Monsieur De Sartine, The Minister of State for the Marine of this Kingdom in Answer to which We have had the Honour to assure his Excellency that We would embrace the first Opportunity of communicating it to Congress.[3]   B. Franklin, Arthur Lee, John Adams.

Monsieur De Sartine

Passi July 16. 1778

We have the Honour of your Excellencys Letter of the fourteenth instant, and We shall embrace the first Opportunity of writing to Congress and to the Government of The Massachusetts Bay, And inclosing Copys of your Excellencys Letter to Us, which We are persuaded will have the most powerfull Influence with them to exert themselves and to recommend to their Fellow Citizens to engage in Expeditions for the relief of the Inhabitants of St. Peters and Miquelon. There is not the smallest doubt of their Ability to supply the Wants of their Friends at those places provided the British Men of War should be withdrawn from the Newfoundland and Hallifax Stations, but if there should remain as many Ships of War on those Stations as there have been for the last two Years, the difficulty will be very great.

We have the honour to inclose to your Excellency a Copy of a Letter just received from Mr. Schweighauser, whereby your Excellency will see the difficulties that still embarrass our Frigates, in relation to their Prizes.[4] We entreat your Excellencys further Attention to the

---

[3] In LbC JA began an additional paragraph with the words "We have not the smallest doubt," and then broke off. The letter was never completed and never sent. Instead, the Commissioners simply enclosed a copy of Sartine's letter to them of 14 July in their next letter to Congress and drew Congress' attention to Sartine's plea; see Commissioners to Congress, 20 July, copied into JA's Autobiography under that date, below.

[4] This enclosure has not been found.

Subject and that orders may be given for the Releif of our Officers and Men from their Embarrassments.

We have the Honour to request your Excellencys Attention to another Subject, that of the British Prisoners made by our Frigates, the Providence, Boston, and Ranger and all others in future. As it is necessary for those Frigates forthwith to proceed to Sea, and as We have some hopes of an Exchange of Prisoners in Europe We request your Excellency that We may have leave to confine them in your Prisons, to be maintained there at our Expence untill exchanged or sent by Us to America and that your Excellency would give the necessary Directions accordingly. We have the Honor to be with the greatest respect, your Excellencys most humble and obedient Servants

B. Franklin, Arthur Lee, John Adams.[5]

Gentlemen   Passi July 16. 1778

At the time when I took Lieutenant Simpsons Parole I did not expect to be long absent from America, but as Circumstances have now rendered the time of my return less certain, I am willing to let the dispute between Us drop forever, by giving up that Parole, which will entitle him to command the Ranger. I bear no Malice. And if I have done him an Injury, this will be making him all the present Satisfaction in my Power. If, on the contrary he hath injured me, I will trust to himself for an Acknowledgment.—I have the Honor to be, with Sentiments of due Esteem and respect Gentlemen your obliged, very obedient and humble Servant.   Signed Jno. P. Jones.
Honble. Commissioners.[6]

By the preceeding Papers it will be seen that Jones had been so elevated by his Success in taking Prizes and especially by the Glory of capturing the Drake that he had acted a very high handed and presumptuous Part upon many Occasions, which gave Us a great deal of trouble, from several Sources.[7] One of the greatest was, that We most heartily applauded his Bravery, and were desirous of avoiding every thing that might disgrace, or discourage him or any other Officer or Man of the Navy. Another was, he was manifestly one of the Deane party and countenanced, perhaps stimulated by the whole Corps of Satelites of Mr. De Sartine at least, perhaps of the Count de Vergennes, perhaps of the Treasurer of the Queen. Chaumont, Monthieu, Beau-

[5] LbC is in Arthur Lee's hand and does not indicate who signed the copy sent.

[6] JA copied this letter from a copy in Arthur Lee's hand in Lb/JA/4.

[7] The comments on Jones in this and the following paragraph were omitted by CFA in his text.

marchais and Bancroft and Holker and all their Subordinates in Nantes, L'Orient, Brest, Paris, and every where were blowing the Trumpets of Fame for Le Capitaine Jones, and a refusal of the most unreasonable demand he made or could make, would be unpopular with the Cabal of Paris. His Conduct however was so compleatly unjustifiable that Franklin could not approve it, nor excuse it. He accordingly assented to all our measures. With a great Exercise of Patience, We prudently brought him at last to write Us the above Letter, which terminated all Difficulties for the present.

The true Source of the dispute on board the Ranger, I suppose was the same which produces most of the Quarrells among Naval Officers, the division of the Glory. The Captain was thought to be desirous of monopolizing the honor of conquering the Drake. The Officers and Men, although they allowed that the Captain was a Man of desperate Courage, yet unanimously affirmed that the Lieutenant was an abler Seaman and more skillful in Battle, and that the Victory was in a greater degree due to him. The partiality of the Crew for their Countryman the Lieutenant was natural enough: but I have no doubt the Captain had his full share of Merit, in that Action.

This day[8] We received the Letter of which the following is a Translation.

Versailles the 18 July 1778

I receive, Gentlemen, Letters from L'Orient, on the Subject of Differences, which have arisen, between the Commander of the American Frigate the Boston and some Frenchmen who made a part of his Crew, some in the Character of Volunteers, and others in the quality of Sailors. According to what is written to me, upon this Subject, whatever means have been employed to effect a reconciliation, they have not been able to obtain it. And they have been obliged to disembark a Number of twenty Eight, twenty five of whom are volunteers and three Novices. It appears that the discontent of these People was not against the Captain of the Ship, nor against that of the Volunteers, but that it was not the same with the first Lieutenant, and two other Officers, from whom, it appears, they had received very ill Treatment. These are Facts which have come to the Knowledge of the Commissary of the Classes at L'orient, as well as of Monsieur De La Touche de Treville Chef D'Escadre, who being at L'orient on Occasion of the Operations, with which he is charged, went on board the Frigate. This General

---

[8] JA should either have said "Two days later" or else have inserted a new date heading for 18 July.

Officer has had, even, personally Subjects of Complaint, which have obliged him to enter into Explanations with the Captain. Moreover, when the People disembarked were put on Shore, the Captain employed himself, in causing to be restored to them, all he could of their property, which during their Absence had been in part pillaged by some of the Crew; but it appears that they experience difficulties about their Pay and Subsistence; that they pretend to have a right to Shares in two Prizes sent into L'orient, but renouncing all Pretentions to two others, which have been sent to America. They pretend that they did not engage themselves at Bourdeaux, but for one Cruise, as their Engagement mentions, but the Captain asserts that it ought not to finish, till after the Arrival of the Vessell at Boston, although this is not explained in the Engagement. It will be convenient, Gentlemen, that you give orders upon this Subject to avoid the Expence to which this Contest will give rise, if it should be carried to the Admiralty. I pray you to signify to me, what you would wish to have done upon this Subject, that I may communicate it to the Commissary of the Classes. This Commissary writes me, that he has offered the Captain of the Frigate, all the facilities, which may depend upon him, for the Inlistment of new Volunteers, to replace the others. I have the honour to be, with a perfect Consideration, Gentlemen, your most humble and most obedient Servant De Sartine.

P.S. Mr. Schweighauser has written me from Nantes, that his Correspondent at Brest, meets with difficulties on the Part of the Admiralty relative to the Sale of the Prizes, made by the Frigate the Ranger. I write to the Officers of the Admiralty, to cause those difficulties to cease, and I give Notice of it to Mr. Schweighauser. D.S.
M[essieu]rs. Franklin, Lee, et Adams Deputys of the United States of North America.

Versailles 18 July 1778

I see, Gentlemen, by my Correspondence, that there are in the Ports of France, several American Vessels, which might be usefully employed for the common cause, and which, nevertheless, appear to remain inactive. I doubt not that the reciprocal Interest will engage you to give such orders as you shall believe necessary, in the present Circumstances. I have the honour to be with great Consideration, Gentlemen, your most humble and most obedient Servant De Sartine.
Mrs. The Deputies of the United States of America.

To the Honourable the President of Congress[9]
Sir   Passi July 20. 1778

We have the honour to inform Congress, that the Spy Captain Niles, has arrived at Brest, and brought Us Ratifications of the Treaties with his Most Christian Majesty, which have given much Satisfaction to this Court and Nation. ... On the Seventeenth instant, We had the honor of exchanging Ratifications, with his Excellency the Count de Vergennes. The Treaties, ratified, signed by his Majesty, and under the Great Seal of France, are now in our Possession, where, perhaps, considering the dangers of Ennemies at Sea, it will be safest to let them remain for the present.[1] —Copies of the Ratifications, We shall have the honour to transmit to Congress by this Opportunity.

War is not yet declared, between France and England by either Nation: but hostilities at Sea, have been already commenced by both, and as the French Fleet from Brest under the command of the Count D'Orvilliere and the British Fleet under Admiral Keppell, are both at Sea, We are in hourly expectation of Intelligence of a Rencounter between them. The Jamaica Fleet, the Windward Islands Fleet, and a small fleet from the Mediterranean, have arrived at London, which has enabled them to obtain, by means of a violent Impress, perhaps a thousand or fifteen hundred Seamen, who will man two or three Ships more; in the whole, making Admiral Keppells Fleet somewhat nearer to an Equality with the French. In the mean time, the Spanish Flota has arrived, but the Councils of that Court, are kept in a Secrecy so profound, that We presume not to say, with Confidence, what are her real Intentions. We continue however to receive from various quarters encouraging Assurances: and from the Situation of the Powers of Europe it seems highly probable, that Spain will join France, in Case of War.

A War in Germany, between the Emperor and the King of Prussia, seems to be inevitable, as it is affirmed, that the latter has marched his

---

[9] Henry Laurens. This important dispatch was copied on a separate sheet by JA and keyed by the letter "A" for insertion at its proper place in the MS of the Autobiography. LbC is obviously a draft, in JA's hand with corrections by himself and a few more in Arthur Lee's hand (one of which is indicated in the next note but one below). The recipient's copy has not been found and probably never reached Congress; the version on file in PCC, No. 85, is a

copy in Henry Remsen Jr.'s hand, taken from "a Vol. of the Commissioners Letters kept by Mr. [Arthur] Lee." For the enclosures see below.

[1] There remain in the Adams Papers texts of both the Treaty of Amity and Commerce and the separate secret article (reserving the right of Spain to become a party to the Franco-American treaties), as ratified by Congress and signed and sealed by Pres. Laurens, 4 May 1778.

Army into Bohemia: so that We apprehend that America has at present nothing to fear from Germany.

We are doing all in our Power to obtain a Loan of Money: and have a prospect of procuring some in Amsterdam: but not in such quantities as will be wanted.

We are constrained to request Congress to be as sparing as possible in their Draughts upon Us.... The Draughts already made, together with the vast expence arising from the Frigates which have been sent here, the Expences of the Commissioners, the Maintenance of your Ministers for Vienna and Tuscany,[2] and of Prisoners who have made their Escapes, the Amount of Cloaths and Munitions of War already sent to America: All these Things considered,[3] We are under great Apprehensions, that our Funds will not be sufficient to answer the Draughts, which We daily expect, for the Interest of Loan Office Certificates, as well as those from Mr. Bingham.

We have the honour to inclose a Copy of a Letter from Mr. De Sartine, the Minister of State for the Marine, and to request the Attention of Congress to the Subject of it.[4]

We are told in several Letters from the Honourable Committee of foreign Affairs, that We should receive Instructions and Authority, for giving up, on our part, the whole of the Eleventh Article of the Treaty of Commerce, proposing as a Condition, to the Court of France, that they on their part should give up the whole of the Twelfth. But unfortunately those Instructions and that Authority were omitted to be sent with the Letters, and We have not yet received them. At the time of the Exchange of Ratifications however, We mentioned this Subject to the Count De Vergennes, and gave him an Extract of the Committees Letter. His answer to Us was, that the Alteration would be readily agreed to, and he ordered his Secretary not to register the Ratification untill it was done. We therefore request that We may be honoured with the Instructions and Authority of Congress, to sett aside these two Articles, as soon as possible, and while the Subject is fresh in memory.[5]

The Letter to Mr. Dumas is forwarded: and in Answer to the Committees Inquiry What is proper for Congress to do for that Gentleman,

---

[2] In LbC the preceding nine words are interlined in the hand of Arthur Lee—a fact not without significance since the ministers in question were Lee's brother William and the Lee brothers' close friend Izard.

[3] Preceding four words not in LbC;

JA added them in his copy in order to improve his sentence structure.

[4] This was Sartine's letter of 14 July, q.v. above under that date; also the answer under 16 July.

[5] See Miller, ed., *Treaties*, 2:10–11, 32–33.

We beg leave to say, that his extream Activity and Dilligence, in negotiating our Affairs, and his Punctuality in his Correspondence with Congress, as well as with Us, and his Usefulness to our cause in several other Ways, not at present proper to be explained, give him in our Opinion, a good title to two hundred Pounds Sterling a Year, at least.

The other Things mentioned in the Committee's Letters to Us, shall be attended to as soon as possible.

We have received also, the Resolution of Congress of Feb. 9. and the Letter of the Committee of the same date, impowering Us to appoint One or more suitable Persons to be commercial Agents for conducting the Commercial Business of the United States in France and other Parts of Europe.... But as this Power was given Us, before Congress received the Treaty, and We have never received it, but with the Ratification of the Treaty; and as, by the Treaty Congress is impowered to appoint Consuls in the Ports of France, perhaps it may be expected of Us, that We should wait for the Appointment of Consuls. At present Mr. John Bondfield of Bourdeaux, and Mr. J. D. Schweighauser at Nantes, both by the appointment of Mr. William Lee, are the only Persons, authorized as Commercial Agents. If We should find it expedient to give Appointments to any other Persons, before We hear from Congress, We will send Information of it, by the next Opportunity.... If Congress should think proper to appoint Consuls, We are humbly of Opinion, that the Choice will fall most justly as well as naturally on Americans, who are in our Opinion better qualified for this Business than any others; and the Reputation of such an Office, together with a moderate Commission on the Business they may transact, and the Advantages to be derived from Trade, will be a sufficient Inducement to undertake it, and a sufficient Reward for discharging the Duties of it.   Signed B. Franklin, Arthur Lee, John Adams

In this Letter We inclosed the following Paper.

The Function of Consuls

Is to maintain in their departments, the Priviledges of their Nation according to Treaties

To have Inspection and Jurisdiction [6]

[6] JA broke off here without copying this paper farther. A complete text, in Arthur Lee's hand, is in Lb/JA/4, following the letter to Congress of 20 July in which it was to be enclosed. The full text is printed in Wharton, ed., *Dipl. Corr. Amer. Rev.*, 2:652–653, evidently from the copy by Remsen in PCC, No. 85.

July 25. 1778. I was much amused, among some People here who understand a little English, to hear them puzzling each other with Samples of English Sentences, very difficult to be pronounced by a Frenchman. Among many others I remarked the following and very curious indeed were the Attempts to pronounce them. "What think the chosen Judges?" "I thrust this Thistle through this Thumb." "With an Apple in each hand and a third in my Mouth." But of all the Words I ever heard essayed by a French Man, the Words "General Washington" produced the greatest Variety of difficulties. I know not that I ever heard two Persons pronounce them alike, except the Marquis de La Fayette and his Lady. They had studied and practised them so long that they had mastered the great Subject. In my second Voyage to France, I carried with me a Friend as a private Secretary, Mr. John Thaxter. His name was a new Problem of Pronunciation. I could have filled a Sheet of Paper with the Varieties of Sounds, which these two Names suggested to my French Friends. "VAUGSTAINGSTOUNG" was one of the Sounds for Washington: and "TAUGISTEY," was another for Thaxter. But enough of this in this place.

This day I wrote the following private Letter to Richard Henry Lee Esqr. a Member of Congress from Virginia.

My Dear Sir   Passi July 25. 1778

Your Favour of the 13 of May was brought me this day,[7] with the Dispatches by Captain Barns. Am much obliged by your friendly Congratulations on my Arrival in France, which was a pleasant Event, after having more than once the prospect of going to the Bottom in the Gulph Stream, and half a dozen times a prospect very nearly as gloomy, that of going Prisoner to England, where I assure you, notwithstanding their then pretences of wishing an Accommodation, I should not have failed to have been treated with great Contempt, Indignity and Insult. . . . We took a fine Prize upon the passage, by which I sent Letters and large bundles of Pamphlets and Newspapers to Congress: but within a few days I have had the Mortification to learn she has been retaken and carried into Hallifax. Tucker, however, in the Boston has taken four other Prizes since, of smaller Value.

In this Quarter of the World, an unforeseen Event, the Death of the Duke of Bavaria, has probably prevented the Courts of Vienna, Berlin and Tuscany, from acknowledging our Independence: but I rather think it will do Us a greater Service than such an Acknowledgment would have been, by keeping from Great Britain all Recruits from

---

[7] In Adams Papers; R. H. Lee, *Letters*, ed. Ballagh, 1:405–407.

other parts of Europe. In the present State of Europe I think it impossible that she should obtain a Regiment from Russia or Germany.

The Démarchés of Spain are misterious. . . . She has sent a fresh Ambassador to London, and yet is arming in all her Ports with double dilligence. The Tardiness of this Power, however, may have disagreable Consequences to the Count D'Estaing. . . . The States General are making their Fleet respectable, but you may be assured, it is not to join Great Britain against America.

In this Kingdom, I have the pleasure to assure you, that I have found an universal favour to America. . . . I have never seen a French Tory. They tell me, it is the first Time the French Nation ever saw a Prospect of War, with Pleasure.

The only disagreable Circumstances are the vast demands for Money and the slender Funds: and the difficulties of conversing in a language, which is far from being familiar to me. . . . But with a little English, a little Latin and a constant Application at all Leisure times, which however do not happen so often as I wish, to the French: I make it out to understand and be understood.

I have never yet seen Mr. Beaumarchais, but his Account will be carefully attended to.

Remember me in the most respectfull and affectionate manner, to all good Men, and believe me to be your sincere Friend and most obedient Servant   John Adams.

R. H. Lee

Autobiography of John Adams

Part Three: 1779–1780

PEACE.[1]

The following is a litteral Translation of a Letter I received from His Excellency the Chevalier De La Luzerne, His Most Christian Majestys Minister Plenipotentiary to the United States of America.[2]

Sir   Philadelphia 29th. of September 1779

I sincerely applaud myself, for having foreseen that your Residence in America would not be of long duration; and I congratulate your Fellow Citizens, on the choice they have made of you to proceed on the negotiation of that peace, which is to assure the repose of the Thirteen States. You will carry with you, that moderation and Equity which have appeared to me to constitute the foundation of your Character;

[1] Unlike the other two fragments of JA's Autobiography, "Peace" has no date of composition prefixed, but it was with little doubt begun, and, as far as it goes, entirely written in 1807. The preceding part, "Travels and Negotiations," is dated at the beginning 1 Dec. 1806, but not even JA in the full flush of enthusiasm for his task of self-vindication was likely to have written some 160 quarto pages in a fine hand in a single month. Clearly his enthusiasm had waned by the time he reached July 1778 in the course of his documentary narrative, and so he broke off his "Travels" abruptly, supposing, no doubt, that he would come back later to fill the gap between the summer of 1778 and that of 1779, when he returned from France to Braintree. He never did, though his Diary entries are fortunately quite full for portions of that period. At some point in 1807 he began his narrative anew with his appointment as sole American peace commissioner in the fall of 1779, the year 1807 being mentioned as the current year in the seventh folded sheet of the present MS (see p. 202, below).

This time, however, his autobiographical fervor evaporated even sooner. "Peace" is only half as long as either

Part One or Part Two of the Autobiography. It hardly more than gets its narrator to Paris (though the trip there overland through northern Spain was strenuous enough) before it breaks off in mid-sentence after JA had copied in a few lines of his letter to Vergennes dated 21 March 1780. JA was not through writing autobiography, but he never returned to this MS.

[2] JA translated this letter from a copy he had made in his letterbook in 1779 from the recipient's copy (Adams Papers), which is in Marbois' hand, signed by La Luzerne, and printed in JA, *Works*, 7:115.

Editorial treatment of letters inserted in Part Three of the Autobiography is the same as that for those in the earlier parts; see above, p. 43, note 5. The letters that JA inserted in "Peace" were drawn from Lb/JA/5, 8, 10, 11, Adams Papers, Microfilms, Reel Nos. 93, 96, 98, 99. None of the letters except those between JA and Vergennes beginning 12 Feb. 1780 were included by CFA in his combined edition of JA's Diary and Autobiography. Nor did CFA use anything else from "Peace" until he reached the entry dated 20 Jan. 1780, p. 237, below.

and you are already sure to find in France the Ministry of the King, in the same dispositions. The Choice of Congress is approved by all Persons of honest Intentions in America, and it will be equally applauded in Europe, and I will be answerable for the Suffrages and the Confidence of all Men by whom you shall be known. You, Sir, will labour to give Peace to your Country: and my cares will have for their Object, to draw closer the ties, which unite your Nation to mine. Our Occupations then will have some Analogy, and I pray you to be well persuaded, that I shall take an immediate Interest in your Success.

The Frigate, The Sensible, is still in the Port of Boston: it will depend upon You, Sir, to consult with Mr. De Chavagne, in case you should determine to go with him. I am persuaded, beforehand, that the Minister of the Marine, will be of Opinion that We could not make a better Use of this Vessel, than by employing her to carry You to Europe. I have the honour to be with the most inviolable Attachment, Sir, your most humble and most obedient Servant

Le Che de La Luserne.

To Mr. John Adams Minister Plenipotentiary of the United States.

Sir   Philadelphia the 29. of September 1779

I have only time to inform you, how much interest I have taken in the Choice which your Countrymen have made of you, to go and negotiate the Peace in Europe. I have been really touched, by that Unanimity and Zeal, with which all Minds have united, in the Opinion which they have conceived of you; and in the Persuasion, that a Minister, without Prejudices and without any other Passion than that for the Happiness of his Country, and the conservation of the Alliance, was the Man the most proper to conduct the important Work of Peace.

I desire very much, Sir, that you would carry with you again to Europe, the young Gentleman your Son, notwithstanding the Aversion he has to Navigation. He will learn of you the means of being, one day, usefull to his Country; and your Precepts and your Sentiments will teach him to cherish my Nation, who perceive more and more from day to day, how much her Union with You is natural and reciprocally advantageous. I am, with respect, Sir your most humble and most obedient Servant   De Marbois

To Mr. John Adams &c.[3]

The following Letter was sent at the same time to the Captain of the Frigate.

[3] Translated by JA from a copy in his letterbook that he had earlier made from the recipient's copy (Adams Papers), printed in JA, *Works*, 7:116–117.

The Mission, Sir, with which the Congress has charged Mr. John Adams, is of such importance, that Mr. Gerard and I have thought it necessary to take measures the most prompt and the most certain to assure his Passage. We have accordingly proposed to Congress to take Advantage of your Frigate, for the conveyance of that Minister; and our Proposition has been accepted: Nevertheless the Congress have of their own Accord, inserted the Condition, that Mr. Adams should make the convenient Arrangements for his Departure, in a reasonable time, so that your Frigate may not be detained too long. I therefore reitterate the prayer, which I have already made to you, Sir, to concert with Mr. Adams, concerning the measures, which he shall judge convenient to take for his departure. . . .[4] I hope, considering the nature of the circumstance, The Minister will entirely approve the delay which you may be obliged to make, of your departure; and I am persuaded on the other hand that Mr. John Adams will make with all possible celerity the preparations for his Embarkation. &c. &c. Compliments &c. Signed Le Chevalier De La Luserne.

I think entirely, Sir, as Mr. The Chevalier De La Luserne thinks, and I unite my Requests with his, and Compliments &c. &c. Signed Gerard

To the Captain Chavagne Commander of the Frigate the Sensible.[5]

To these Letters I sent the following Answers

Sir   Braintree October 17. 1779
I have the honour of your Letter from Philadelphia of the 29th. of September, and return you my sincere Thanks for your kind congratulations, on the honor which has been done me, in my Election to an important Negotiation in Europe. The Sentiments your Excellency is pleased to express of my Character, and of the good Opinion of my own Countrymen, in general, are exceedingly flattering to me.

There is no Character, in which I could Act, with so much pleasure, as in that of a Peacemaker. But Alass! When I reflect upon the Importance, Delicacy, Intricacy and danger of the Service, I feel a great deal of diffidence in myself.[6] Yet when I consider the remarkable Unanimity with which I was chosen, after Congress had been so long

[4] Suspension points in MS, as elsewhere in Part Three of the Autobiography. They seldom if ever indicate omissions in the text.

[5] Translated by JA from a copy in his letterbook that he had made in 1779 from an undated copy, presumably furnished to him by La Luzerne, which is also in Adams Papers and is printed in JA, *Works*, 7:115–116.

[6] LbC, which is a draft, reads: "But alass! Sir, when I reflect upon the ⟨Weight and⟩ Importance ⟨of the Subject, the⟩ Delicacy, Intricacy and Danger of ⟨it⟩ the Service, ⟨the Difficulty of accomplishing so great a Work, and at

distressed with the Appearance of their foreign Affairs, and so divided in Sentiment about most other Characters, I am penetrated with a Sense of the honor done to me, more than I can express.

Your Excellency may be assured, that wherever I go, I shall carry with me, the highest Opinion of the Wisdom, the Equity and Policy, of the present Minister from France, and the fullest persuasion, that his negotiations will be reciprocally advantageous to the Allies, incessantly tending to strengthen the tyes of Interest and good Will, which at present unite them.

Your Excellency will be pleased to accept of my thanks, for the favour of a passage in the Frigate the Sensible.... I have not yet received from Congress any dispatches: As soon as they arrive I shall immediately wait on Captain Chavagne, and the Frigate shall not be unnecessarily detained on my Account. I will either embark immediately, or inform the Captain that I cannot have the pleasure to go with him.

I must also request your Excellency to present my respectful Compliments and Thanks to Mr. Gerard, for so obligingly joining his instances with yours to the Captain of the Frigate, for my Passage in her.

I have the Honor to be, with the sincerest Attachment &c.

John Adams

His Excellency The Chevalier De La Luserne.

My dear Sir   Braintree Octr. 17. 1779

I had the Honour of your favour of the 29. Septr. by express, and I thank you for your kind Congratulations and Compliments on my Election to the Momentous Office of Peace maker. I am really Sir, much affected with the Unanimity, with which Congress have conferred this Honour upon me.

I cannot be sufficiently sensible of the favourable Opinion you express of me. But I feel myself agitated with too many very strong Passions, relative to myself and my Family, besides those which regard the Prosperity of my Country, and the conservation of the Allyance, to subscribe entirely to that Opinion.

My little Son, Sir, is very sensible of the honour you have done him in mentioning his Name upon this Occasion: but I believe it will be my duty to leave him at home, that his education may be, where his

---

the same Time giving Satisfaction to my Countrymen and my Sovereign,⟩ I feel a great deal of Diffidence ⟨of⟩ in myself."

Other small revisions in LbC have been disregarded here.

Life is to be spent. He has already learned to esteem and respect the French Nation, and these Sentiments I hope will never leave him.[7]

In whatever Country I may be, I shall never forget the agreable hours I have passed with Mr. Marbois, nor cease to hope for his honor and prosperity. I hope you have found every Thing as agreable at Philadelphia as you could expect, and that all Circumstances will become from day to day, more and more so.—I am very ambitious of carrying with me to Europe any dispatches which his Excellency the Chevalier may think proper to entrust to my care, especially Letters to his Friends, among whom, I have particularly in my Eye Mr. Malserbs. I request also the same favour from you, Sir, and have the honor to be with an affectionate respect &c.   John Adams.

Mr. Marbois Secretary to the French Embassy in America.[8]

To the President of Congress

Sir   Braintree November 4. 1779

I had Yesterday the Honour of receiving your Letter of the twenty-eth of October inclosed with two Commissions, appointing me, Minister Plenipotentiary, from the United States, to negotiate Peace and Commerce with Great Britain; together with Instructions for my Government in the Execution of those Commissions; Copies of Instructions to the Ministers Plenipotentiary, at Versailles and Madrid; and two Acts of Congress, of the fourth and fifteenth of October.[9]

Peace is an Object of such vast importance; the Interests to be adjusted, in the Negotiations to obtain it, are so complicated and so delicate; and the difficulty of giving even general Satisfaction is so great: that I feel myself more distressed at the prospect of executing the Trust, than at the Thoughts of leaving my family and Country; and again encountering the dangers of the Seas and of Enemies.

[7] As things turned out, both JQA and his younger brother CA accompanied their father on his second mission to Europe. See the summary of JA's letter to Bidé de Chavagnes, 5 Nov. 1779, below.

[8] RC (Bibliothèque Nationale, Paris, Fonds Français, vol. 12768) varies at several points slightly but not materially from LbC and the present copy.

[9] RC (Adams Papers, printed in JA, *Works*, 7:119–120) has the enclosures here listed, all of which JA inserted in full below except the instructions to Jay (just appointed to Madrid) of 29 Sept. and 15 Oct. and the two resolves of Congress. Jay's instructions are printed in Wharton, ed., *Dipl. Corr. Amer. Rev.*, 3:352–353, 375. The resolve of 4 Oct. fixed the salaries of the ministers plenipotentiary, "in full for their services and expences," at £2500 per annum and those of their secretaries at £1000; while that of 15 Oct. ordered Franklin to make payments to them for their subsistence upon arriving in Paris.

For the circumstances of these new diplomatic appointments, see JA's Diary entry of 13 Nov. 1779, note 1; also his Autobiography, p. 180, note 4, and p. 242, note 3, below.

Yet when I reflect on the general Voice in my favour; and the high honour that is done me by this Appointment: I feel the warmest Sentiments of Gratitude to Congress; shall make no hesitation to accept it; and devote my self without reserve or loss of time, to the discharge of it.

My Success however, may depend in a very great degree, on Intelligence and Advices that I may receive from Congress; and on the punctuality with which several Articles in my Instructions may be kept secret. It shall be my most earnest endeavour to transmit to Congress, the most constant and exact information in my power, of whatever may occur; and to conceal those Instructions which depend, in any measure, on my Judgment.

I hope I need not suggest to Congress the necessity of communicating to me from time to time as early as possible, their Commands; and of keeping all the discretionary Articles an impenetrable Secret: a Suggestion, however, that the Constitution of that Sovereignty, which I have the honor to represent, might excuse.

As the Frigate has been sometime waiting, I shall embark in Eight or ten days, at farthest.... Your Excellency will be pleased to present my most dutifull respects to Congress; and accept my Thanks for the polite and obliging manner, in which you have communicated their commands. I have the Honour to be, with great Esteem and respect, your Excellencies most obedient humble Servant   John Adams.
His Excellency Samuel Huntington Esqr. President of Congress.[1]

The Commissions acknowledged in the foregoing Letter to have been received were two; one for Peace and the other for Commerce, exact Copies of both here follow.

1. For Peace.

The Delegates of the United States, of New Hampshire, Massachusetts Bay, Rhode Island and Providence Plantations, Connecticut, New York, New Jersey, Pennsylvania, Delaware, Maryland, Virginia, North Carolina, South Carolina, and Georgia
To all who shall see these Presents, send Greeting
It being probable, that a Negotiation will soon be commenced, for putting an End to the Hostilities, between his Most Christian Majesty, and these United States on the one Part, and his Britannic Majesty, on the other Part, and it being the sincere desire of the United States,

[1] RC (PCC, No. 84, I); endorsed by Charles Thomson: "Letter from J. Adams Novr. 4. 1779   Read 22.—accepts his Commissns." Slight variations in wording between LbC and RC have been disregarded here.

that they may be terminated, by a Peace, founded on such solid and equitable Principles, as reasonably to promise a Permanency of the Blessings of Tranquility, Know Ye, therefore, that We, confiding in the Integrity, Prudence and Ability of The Honourable John Adams Esquire, late Commissioner of the United States of America at the Court of Versailles, late Delegate in Congress, from the State of Massachusetts Bay, and Chief Justice of the said State, Have nominated and constituted, and by these Presents Do nominate and constitute him the said John Adams, our Minister Plenipotentiary, giving him full Power general and special, to Act in that Quality, to confer, treat, agree and conclude, with the Ambassadors or Plenipotentiaries of his Most Christian Majesty, and of his Britannic Majesty, and those of any other Princes or States, whom it may concern, vested with equal Powers, relating to the Reestablishment of Peace and Friendship, and whatever shall be so agreed and concluded, for Us, and in our Name to sign, and thereupon make a Treaty or Treaties, and to transact every Thing that may be necessary for compleating, securing and strengthening the great Work of Pacification, in as ample form and with the same Effect, as if We were personally present and Acted therein, hereby promising in good Faith, that We will accept, ratify, fulfill and execute, whatever shall be agreed, concluded and signed by our said Minister Plenipotentiary, and that We will never Act nor suffer any Person to Act, contrary to the same, in the whole or in any part. In Witness whereof We have caused these Presents to be given in Congress at Philadelphia, the twenty Ninth day of September in the Year of our Lord One Thousand Seven hundred and Seventy Nine, and in the fourth Year of the Independence of The United States of America.
Signed by the President and sealed with his Seal.
Samuel Huntington President, And a Seal.
Attest   Cha Thomson Secy.[2]

2. The Commission for making a Treaty of Commerce with Great Britain was in these Words

The Delegates of the United States of New Hampshire, Massachusetts Bay, Rhode Island and Providence Plantations, Connecticutt, New York, New Jersey, Pennsylvania, Delaware, Maryland, Virginia, North Carolina, South Carolina and Georgia, in Congress assembled,
To all who shall see these Presents send Greeting

[2] The original commission for treating of peace, engrossed on parchment, signed, sealed, and attested, is in Adams Papers under the date it bears on its face. JA's name and dignities and the date of issue were filled in after the text of the commission had been engrossed. See illustration in this volume.

It being the desire of the United States, that the Peace which may be established between them and his Britannic Majesty, may be permanent and accompanied with the mutual Benefits derived from Commerce, Know Ye therefore, that We, confiding in the Integrity, Prudence and Ability of Honble. John Adams esqr., late Commissioner of The United States of America at the Court of Versailles, late Delegate in Congress from the State of Massachusetts Bay and Chief Justice of said State, Have nominated and constituted, and by these Presents Do nominate and constitute him the said John Adams, our Minister Plenipotentiary, giving him full Power general and special to Act in that quality to confer, agree, and conclude with the Ambassador, or Plenipotentiary of his Britannic Majesty, vested with equal Powers, of and concerning a Treaty of Commerce, and whatever shall be so agreed and concluded, for Us and in our Name to sign and thereupon make a Treaty of Commerce, and to transact every Thing that may be necessary for compleating, securing and strengthening the same, in as ample form and with the same effect, as if We were personally present and acted therein, hereby promising in good Faith, that We will accept, ratify, fulfill and execute whatever shall be agreed, concluded, and signed by our said Minister Plenipotentiary and that We will never Act, nor suffer any Person to act, contrary to the same, in the whole nor in any Part. In Witness whereof, We have caused these Presents to be given in Congress at Philadelphia the twenty ninth day of September in the Year of our Lord One Thousand Seven hundred and Seventy nine, and in the fourth Year of the Independence of the United States of America.

Signed by the President and sealed with his Seal
Samuel Huntington President And a Seal.

Attest   Cha Thomson Secy.[3]

With these Commissions, I received the following Instructions respecting Peace.[4]

[3] The original commission for negotiating a treaty of commerce, engrossed on parchment, signed, sealed, and attested, is in Adams Papers under the date it bears on its face. JA's name and dignities and the date of issue were filled in after the text of the commission had been engrossed.

[4] Copied here from the original Instructions (Adams Papers), signed by Huntington and enclosed in his letter to JA of 20 Oct.; endorsed: "Instructions to me. 16 Octr. 1779. Peace." These instructions had been adopted by Congress on 14 Aug. (JCC, 14:956–960), after intermittent debate on foreign affairs and especially on the minimum peace terms acceptable to America, since the preceding February. Because of irreconcilable divisions in Congress over who should represent America in the peace mission and the closely related mission to Spain, the elections did not take place until six weeks had elapsed,

Sir   16 October 1779

You will herewith receive a Commission giving you full Power, to negotiate a Treaty of Peace with Great Britain, in doing which you will conform to the following Information and Instructions.

First. The United States are sincerely desirous of Peace and wish, by every means consistent with their Dignity and Safety, to spare the further Effusion of Blood. They have therefore, by your Commission and these Instructions laboured to remove the Obstacles to that Event, before The Enemy have evidenced their Disposition for it.... But as the great Object of the present defensive War on the part of the Allies is to establish the Independence of the United States, and as any Treaty, whereby this End cannot be obtained, must be only ostensible and illusory, You are therefore to make it a preliminary Article, to any proposition,[5] that Great Britain shall agree to treat with the United States as sovereign, free And independent.

Secondly. You shall take especial Care also, that the Independence of the said States be effectually assured and confirmed by the Treaty or Treaties of Peace, according to the form and Effect of the Treaty of Alliance with his Most Christian Majesty; and You shall not agree to such Treaty or Treaties, unless the same be thereby so assured and confirmed.

Thirdly. The Boundaries of these States are as follow, vizt. These States are bounded North, by a line to be drawn from the Northwest Angle of Nova Scotia, along the highlands, which divide those Rivers which empty themselves into the River St. Lawrence, from those which fall into the Atlantic Ocean, to the Northwestermost head of Connecticut River, thence down along the middle of that River to the forty fifth degree of North Latitude, thence due West, in the Latitude of Forty five degrees North from the Equator, to the Northwestermost Side of the River St. Lawrence or Cadaraqui, thence straight to the South end of Lake Nipissing and thence straight to the Source of the River Mississippi: West, by a Line to be drawn along the middle of the River Mississippi, from its Source to where the said Line shall intersect the thirty first degree of North Latitude: South, by a Line to be drawn due East from the Termination of the Line last mentioned in the Latitude of Thirty one degrees North from the Equator, to the Middle of the River Appalachicola, or Catahouchi, thence along the Middle thereof, to its Junction with the Flint River, thence straight to the

---

and there was a further delay of nearly a month before JA's Instructions were copied and sent to him.

[5] A copying error by JA for "Negotiation."

head of St. Mary's River, and thence down along the Middle of St. Mary's River to the Atlantic Ocean: And East by a Line to be drawn along the Middle of St. Johns River, from its Source to its Mouth in the Bay of Fundy, comprehending all Islands within twenty Leagues of any part of the Shores of the United States and lying between Lines to be drawn due East, from the Points where the aforesaid Boundaries between Nova Scotia on the one Part and East Florida on the other Part, shall respectively touch the Bay of Fundy and Atlantic Ocean. You are therefore strongly to contend, that the whole of the said Countries and Islands lying within the Boundaries aforesaid And every Citadel, Fort, Post, Place, harbour and Road to them belonging, be absolutely evacuated by the Land and Sea Forces of his Britannic Majesty, and yeilded to the Powers of the States to which they respectively belong, in such Situation as they may be, at the termination of the War. But notwithstanding the clear right of these States, and the importance of the Object, yet they are so much influenced by the Dictates of Religion and Humanity, and so desirous of complying with the earnest requests of their Allies, that if the Line to be drawn from the mouth [6] of the Lake Nipissing to the head of the Mississippi, cannot be obtained without continuing the War for that purpose, You are hereby empowered to agree to some other Line between that Point and the River Mississippi, provided the same shall in no part thereof be to the Southward of Latitude Forty five degrees North: And in like manner, if the Eastern Boundary above described cannot be obtained you are hereby empowered to agree, that the same shall be afterwards adjusted by Commissioners to be duely appointed for that purpose, according to such Line as shall be by them settled and agreed on as the Boundary between that part of the State of Massachusetts Bay formerly called the Province of Maine and the Colony of Nova Scotia agreably to their respective Rights: And You may also consent that the Enemy shall destroy such Fortifications as they may have erected.

Fourthly. Although it is of the Utmost Importance to the Peace and Commerce of the United States, that Canada and Nova Scotia should be ceded and more particularly that *their equal and common Right to the Fisheries should be guarantied to them, Yet a desire of terminating the War, hath induced Us not to make the Acquisition of these Objects an Ultimatum on the present Occasion.*[7]

[6] This word is underlined in the original Instructions.

[7] Emphasis added by JA in copying the Instructions into his Autobiography. Having been deleted upon French insistence from the American peace ultimata, a British guarantee of American rights in the North Atlantic fisheries was included, as a sop to the New England delegates, in JA's Instructions for ne-

Fifthly. You are empowered to agree to a Cessation of Hostilities during the Negotiation, provided our Ally shall consent to the same, and provided it shall be stipulated that all the Forces of the Enemy shall be immediately withdrawn from the United States.

Sixthly. In all other matters not above mentioned You are to govern yourself by the Alliance between his most Christian Majesty and these States; by the Advice of our Allies, by your Knowledge of our Interests, and by your own discretion, in which We repose the fullest Confidence.

Done at Philadelphia, the Sixteenth day of October, in the Year of our Lord one Thousand Seven hundred and Seventy nine, and in the fourth Year of our Independence.

By The Congress of the United States of America
Saml. Huntington President

Attest Cha Thomson Secy.

The Honble. John Adams Esq. Minister Plenipotentiary, appointed to negotiate a Treaty of Peace.

Instructions as to a Treaty of Commerce with Great Britain, 16. October 1779 [8]

Sir

You will herewith receive a Commission giving you Full Power, to negotiate a Treaty of Commerce with Great Britain, in doing which you will consider Yourself bound by the following Information and Instructions.

First. You will govern yourself principally, by the Treaty of Commerce with his most Christian Majesty, and as on the one hand, you shall grant no Priviledge to Great Britain not granted by that Treaty to France, so on the other you shall not consent to any particular restrictions or Limitations whatever in favour of Great Britain.

Secondly. In Order that you may be the better able to act with propriety on this occasion, it is necessary for you to know that We have determined 1st. That the common Right of Fishing shall in no case be given up. 2d. That it is essential to the Welfare of all these United States that the Inhabitants thereof, at the Expiration of the War should

---

gotiating a treaty of commerce with Great Britain. See the following document; also the separate instruction to Franklin, which follows thereafter, and JA's Diary entries of 4 Nov. 1782 *et seq.*

[8] Copied here from the original Instructions (Adams Papers), signed by Huntington and enclosed in his letter to JA of 20 Oct.; endorsed: "Instructions to me. 16 Octr. 1779. Commerce." These Instructions had also been voted by Congress on 14 Aug. (JCC, 14:960–962), six weeks before JA was chosen to carry them out.

continue to enjoy the free and undisturbed exercise of their common Right to fish on the Banks of Newfoundland and the other Fishing Banks and Seas of North America preserving inviolate the Treaties between France and the said States. 3d. That Application shall be made to his most Christian Majesty to agree to some Article or Articles for the better securing to these States, a Share in the said Fisheries. 4th. That if after a Treaty of Peace with Great Britain she shall molest the Citizens or Inhabitants of any of the United States, in taking Fish on the Banks and Places herein after described, such molestation being in our Opinion a direct violation and breach of the Peace, shall be a common cause of the said States, and the Force of the Union be exerted to obtain redress for the Parties injured, and 5th. That our Faith be pledged to the several States, that without their unanimous consent, no Treaty of Commerce shall be entered into, nor any Trade or Commerce carried on with Great Britain, without the explicit Stipulation herein after mentioned. You are therefore not to consent to any Treaty of Commerce, with Great Britain, without an explicit Stipulation on her part, not to molest or disturb the Inhabitants of the United States of America in taking Fish on the Banks of Newfoundland and other Fisheries in the American Seas, any where excepting within the distance of three Leagues from the Shores of the Territories remaining to Great Britain at the Close of the War, if a nearer distance can not be obtained by Negotiation: And in the Negotiation you are to exert your most strenuous endeavours to obtain a nearer distance in the Gulph of St. Lawrence and particularly along the Shores of Nova Scotia, as to which latter We are desirous that even the Shores may be occasionally used for the purpose of carrying on the Fisheries by the Inhabitants of these States.

Thirdly. In all other matters you are to govern yourself by your own discretion as shall be most for the Interest of these States, taking care that the said Treaty may be founded on Principles of Equality and Reciprocity, so as to conduce to the mutual Advantage of both Nations, but not to the Exclusion of others.

Done at Philadelphia, this Sixteenth day of October, in the Year of our Lord one Thousand Seven hundred and Seventy nine, and in the fourth Year of our Independence.

By The Congress of the United States of America,
Saml. Huntington President

Attest   Cha. Thomson Secretary

The Honourable John Adams Esqr. Minister Plenipotentiary appointed to negotiate a Treaty of Commerce with Great Britain.

It may be proper here, also to insert the following Instructions

To the Honble. Benjamin Franklin Esqr. Minister Plenipotentiary of
The United States of America at the Court of France 16. Oct. 1779 [9]

Sir

Having determined, in order to put a Period to the present War
conformably to the humane dispositions which sway the Allied Powers,
that We would not insist on a direct Acknowledgment by Great Britain
of our Right in the Fisheries, this important matter is liable to an
incertitude, which may be dangerous to the political and commercial
Interests of the United States, We have therefore agreed and resolved,
that our Right should in no case be given up. That We would not form
any Treaty of Commerce with Great Britain, nor carry on any Trade
or Commerce whatsoever with her, unless she shall make an express
Stipulation on that Subject, and that if she shall after a Treaty of
Peace, disturb the Inhabitants of these States in the exercise of it, We
will make it a common cause to obtain redress for the Parties injured.
But notwithstanding these precautions, as Great Britain may again
light up the flames of War and use our exercise of the Fisheries as her
pretext; and since some doubts may arise, whether this Object is so
effectually guarded by the Treaty of Alliance with his Most Christian
Majesty, that any molestation therein, on the part of Great Britain is
to be considered as a Casus Fœderis, you are to endeavour to obtain of
his Majesty an explanation on that Subject, upon the Principle that
notwithstanding the high Confidence reposed in his Wisdom and Justice, Yet considering the Uncertainty of human Affairs, and how
doubts may be afterwards raised in the Breasts of his Royal Successors,
the great importance of the Fisheries renders the Citizens of these
States very solicitous to obtain his Majesty's Sense with relation to
them, as the best Security against the Ambition and Rapacity of the
British Court. For this purpose you shall propose the following Article, in which never the less such Alterations may be made as the Circumstances and Situation of Affairs shall render convenient and proper.
Should the same be agreed to and executed you are immediately to
transmit a Copy thereof to our Minister at the Court of Spain.

"Whereas by the Treaty of Alliance between the Most Christian

[9] Presumably copied here from a version in Lb/JA/15, a volume containing
records of the joint American Peace
Commission at Paris, 1781–1783, copied
by William Temple Franklin (Adams
Papers, Microfilms, Reel No. 103). A
copy without date of this instruction had
been enclosed in Huntington's letter to
JA of 20 Oct. (Adams Papers); it had
actually been adopted by Congress on
14 Aug. (JCC, 14:962–966).

King and the United States of North America, the two Parties guaranty mutually from that time and forever against all other Powers, to wit, The United States to His Most Christian Majesty, the Possessions then appertaining to the Crown of France in America, as well as those which it may acquire by the future Treaty of Peace; And his Most Christian Majesty guaranties on his part to the United States their Liberty, Sovereignty and Independence, absolute and unlimited as well in matters of Government as Commerce, and also their possessions and the Additions or Conquests that their Confederation might obtain during the War, according to said Treaty; and the said Parties did further agree and declare that in Case of a Rupture between France and England, the said reciprocal guaranty should have its full Force and Effect, the moment such War should break out: and whereas doubts may hereafter arise how far the said Guaranty extends to this, to witt, that Great Britain should molest or disturb the Subjects and Inhabitants of France or of the said States, in taking Fish on the Banks of Newfoundland, and other the Fishing Banks and Seas of North America, formerly and usually frequented by their Subjects and Inhabitants respectively: And whereas the said King and the United States, have thought proper to determine with Precision the true interest and meaning of the said Guaranty in this respect; Now therefore as a farther demonstration of their mutual good Will and Affection it is hereby agreed, concluded and determined as follows; to witt, That if after the conclusion of the Treaty or Treaties which shall terminate the present War, Great Britain shall molest or disturb the Subjects or Inhabitants of the said United States, in taking Fish on the Banks, Seas, and Places formerly used and frequented by them so as not to encroach on the territorial rights, which may remain to her after the termination of the present War as aforesaid, and War should thereupon break out between the said United States and Great Britain; or if Great Britain shall molest or disturb the Subjects and Inhabitants of France, in taking Fish on the Banks, Seas and Places formerly used and frequented by them, so as not to encroach on the territorial Rights of Great Britain as aforesaid, and War should there upon break out between France and Great Britain; in either of these Cases of War as aforesaid, His Most Christian Majesty and the said United States shall make it a common cause, and aid each other mutually with their good offices, their Councils and their Forces, according to the Exigence of Conjunctures, as becomes good and faithfull Allies: Provided always that nothing herein contained, shall be taken or understood as contrary to or inconsistent with the true intent and meaning of the Treaties already subsisting between His Most Christian Majesty and the said States, but the same shall be taken and understood as explanatory of and conformable to those Treaties."

Done at Philadelphia this Sixteenth day of October in the Year of our Lord one Thousand, Seven hundred and Seventy nine, and in the Fourth Year of our Independence, by the Congress of the United States of America   Signed Saml. Huntington President
Attest   Cha Thomson Secy.

What measures Mr. Franklin pursued, in Obedience to these Instructions to obtain from the Court of France, any farther Stipulations for the Security of the Fisheries, or whether he ever gave himself any trouble about them I never knew. But one Thing is certain, that he never had any Success: for instead of giving Us any additional Assurances of the Fisheries, The Count De Vergennes in Europe, and the Chevalier De La Luserne and Mr. Marbois in America in subordination to him, entered into many insidious Intrigues to deprive Us of them. This base and injurious Policy will be detailed, devellopped and placed in its true Light hereafter, in the Course of these Papers.[1]

As it is uncertain what Questions may hereafter be started, and What Pretensions may be advanced between France, England and America, concerning The Fisheries, it may be usefull to preserve in this Place some Papers which I obtained in 1778, I believe from Mr. Lee or Mr. Izzard.[2]

Copy of a Letter from Sir Stanier Porteen to Lord Weymouth respecting the Newfoundland Fishery.

My Lord
In Obedience to your Lordships commands, I have perused the Correspondence to and from Mr. Stanley and The Duke of Bedford, during their Stay at Paris, previous to the last Treaty of Peace, from which it appears, that in their different Projects and Counter Projects, the Articles concerning the Newfoundland Fishery, chiefly referred to what was stipulated in the Treaty of Utrecht. The French Ministers pressed at first, to have Cape Breton ceded to them, and when that was refused, they insisted that they must have some place, as an "Abri" to secure themselves. After many discussions, the Isle of Miquelon was

[1] JA did not return to this subject in his Autobiography, but he dealt with it at great length and with massive documentation in his later communications to the *Boston Patriot*, especially those written in May 1811, published in the following August, and never reprinted. See the Introduction on this "second autobiography" by JA.

[2] According to his Diary, 26 Nov. 1782, JA obtained copies of these papers from Ralph Izard; they are in the Adams Papers under the assigned date of Nov. 1782.

offered to them, and then St. Pierre was added to it, and the fifth and sixth Articles were agreed upon as they stand in the Definitive Treaty signed the tenth of February 1763. . . . On the first of March following, the Duke De Nivernois held a very extraordinary and unexpected Language with the late Lord Egremont, which cannot be so well expressed, as by sending your Lordship the inclosed Extract from Lord Egremonts Letter to the Duke of Bedford, by which it appears, that the Duke De Nivernois insisted "that the French had an exclusive Right to the Fishery from Cape Bonnavista, to Point Riche, and that they had, on ceding the Island of Newfoundland to Great Britain by the thirteenth Article of the Treaty of Utrecht, expressly reserved to themselves such an exclusive Right, which they had constantly been in Possession of, till they were entirely driven from North America in the last War." Many successive Letters passed on the same Subject, but the inclosed extract sufficiently explains what your Lordship wished to know, whether the French claimed the exclusive right, or solicited to be indulged in it. If your Lordship should want any further Ecclaircissement I will endeavour to obey your Commands. I am, with the greatest Respect, My Lord, your Lordships most humble and most obedient Servant.   Signed S. Porteen
Right Honourable Viscount Weymouth.

N.B. Porteen was Secretary to Lord Weymouth.[3]
Extract of a Letter from the Earl of Egremont, Secretary of State, to his Grace the Duke of Bedford, Ambassador at the Court of France, dated White Hall, March 1st. 1763 respecting Newfoundland Fishery.

I did not expect to have had Occasion to trouble your Grace, with another Messenger so soon; but his Majesty has judged it highly expedient, that I should, without loss of time, acquaint you with a very extraordinary Conversation, I had on Saturday last with the Duke De Nivernois, on the Subject of the Fishery at Newfoundland.

In order that your Grace may understand what gave rise to this Conversation I must observe, that, since the Success of his Majesty's Arms in North America, the British Fishermen have resorted more than they used formerly to do, to the Northern Parts of Newfoundland, where by the thirteenth Article of the Treaty of Utrecht, a Liberty had been left to the French to fish, and to dry their Fish on Shore; and for that purpose to erect the necessary Stages and Buildings, but with an express

[3] Sir Stanier Porten held various minor diplomatic and civil posts (*DNB*). It was perhaps in his capacity of keeper of state papers at Whitehall that he corresponded on this subject with Weymouth, a secretary of state in Grafton's and North's cabinets.

Stipulation, "De ne pas sejourner dans la ditte Isle, au dela du tems necessaire, pour pêcher, et sêcher le Poisson." And as by the fifth Article of the Definitive Treaty the same Priviledge is renewed and confirmed to the French, it was apprehended some disagreable Altercations might arise, between the Subjects of the two Nations, in case the French should find the best fishing Stations preoccupied by the English, who, from their Situation might be able to reach Newfoundland first, and would probably exert themselves for that purpose, in order to avail themselves of the received Law among Fishermen, that whoever arrives first, shall have the choice of the Stations, and that France would complain of this, as in effect excluding them from the Fishery, and consequently eluding what it was certainly meant by the Treaty they should enjoy. His Majesty therefore, firmly resolved to observe religiously every Engagement he had entered into, and whose earnest Wish is to avoid every Thing, that could possibly create the least Uneasiness between the two Courts, thought it the most agreable to the open and candid manner in which the whole Negotiation has been conducted, that I should speak to the French Ambassador on this Subject, and to obviate any dispute on this matter, that I should make him sensible of the clear meaning of the Treaty of Utrecht, which expressly cedes to Great Britain, the Absolute Property of the whole Island of Newfoundland, without any exception whatever; at the same time granting to the French Subjects, a Liberty to resort to a limited part thereof for the purpose of taking and curing Fish only, and this Liberty is confined to the Season of the Year, proper for that occupation. But on my opening this matter to the Duc De Nivernois I was greatly surprized to find his Excellency insisting, with more warmth than I have hitherto observed in him on any one point, that by the Treaty of Utrecht, the French had an exclusive right to the Fishery from Cape Bonavista to Point Riche, and that they had, on ceding the Island of Newfoundland to Great Britain, by the thirteenth Article of that Treaty, expressly reserved to themselves, such an exclusive Right, which they had constantly been in possession of, till they were entirely drove from North America, in the late War.—It was needless to make Use of any other Argument to refute this weak Reasoning, than a bare reference to the Treaty of Peace of Utrecht, and on my producing the same to the French Ambassador he seemed much struck with it, and desired to look on the Treaty of Commerce, but on turning over this last, and not finding the least mention of Newfoundland therein, he endeavoured to distinguish between the Spirit and the Letter of the Treaty, and tho' he would not support his assertion of an exclusive right by any Stipulation in any Treaty, he still insisted on it with so much Warmth as even to let drop some insinuations, as if it might occasion the Renewal of the War. On finding the Duc De Nivernois in this temper, I thought it better not to push the Altercation further at that time, but to reserve myself to make a report to the King of what had passed, which having done, I am in consequence thereof, commanded by his Majesty to despatch this Messenger to your Grace, and to signify to you the Kings Pleasure, that you should lose no time in explaining this matter to the French Ministers and shewing them the impossibility of his Majestys departing from the express Letter of a Treaty, the Stipulations whereof are so explicit and clear, that they will furnish you with ample Arguments to refute the unjustifiable Pretensions of France, and to support the indisputable Rights of his Subjects, who, altho they may not in times past have frequented the Northern Parts of the Island of Newfoundland so much as the French, yet they have from time to time resorted to and exercised the Fishery on every part of the Coasts of that Island agreably to the most undoubted Right they have by the Words of the Treaty of Utrecht, to which the Commodores, who have commanded at Newfoundland, have been constantly referred by their Instructions, and which Treaty must still continue to be their Guide, with respect to such parts to which both Nations have a Liberty to resort. The King, however, thought it consistent with that Candor he has always professed, that the French Ambassador should be apprized of what is above mentioned, but the unreasonable manner in which he received what I said to him, and the Pretension he has attempted to set up of an exclusive Right of the French to fish and dry on the Northern Parts of Newfoundland make it highly necessary to come to an Ecclaircissement with the Court of France. It is therefore the Kings Pleasure, that your Grace should forthwith state to the French Ministers, with the utmost precision, the express Stipulations of the Treaty of Utrecht, letting them see that the King must support his Subjects in the Rights they have thereby acquired, but at the same time, that his Majesty, far from entertaining the most distant Thought of rendering illusory the Liberty of Fishing and drying he has agreed to leave to the French, will be ready to concur in any Arrangement, the Court of France may think proper to propose, provided such Arrangements be not inconsistent with the undoubted Rights of his Majestys Subjects according to the thirteenth Article of the Treaty of Utrecht, renewed and confirmed by the fifth Article of the Definitive Treaty, in order to prevent all future disputes, and thereby to put it out of the Power of a Number of illiterate Fishermen to involve the two Nations in fresh Troubles by any unreasonable and unequitable Pretensions.

Your Grace will be so sensible of the Incident which has given Occasion to this dispatch, that I need only Add that the King will expect with the Utmost Anxiety to hear from your Grace, the Result of your Conference with the French Ministers, in Consequence of the orders I now transmit to you.

On the fifth of November 1779 I wrote to the Chevalier De Chavagne the Captain of the French Frigate The Sensible, that I had received all my dispatches from Congress and would be ready to embark and sail in Eight days. That the Persons who were to go with me, would be Mr. Dana who was Secretary to my Commission and Chargé D'Affaires, Mr. Thaxter my private Secretary, my two Sons, John, twelve Years old, and Charles nine, and one Servant for me and another for Mr. Dana, in all seven Persons. That Mr. Dana was a Gentleman of principal Rank in this Country, a Member of Congress and of the Council of Massachusetts Bay and now in a very important Commission, which made it necessary for me to request, that a particular Attention might be paid to his Accommodation, and at least as much as to mine.

On the Thirteenth day of November 1779, I had again the melancholly Tryal of taking Leave of my Family, with the Dangers of the Seas and the Terrors of British Men of War before my Eyes, with this additional Aggravation that I now knew by Experience, how serious they were, much better than I had when I embarked in Nantasket Road in 1778. We went to Boston and embarked on Board the Frigate whose Yards were manned, in Honour of the Passengers. We found the Ship crouded, full 350 Sailors, a great number of whom had been recruited in America: and a great many Passengers, among whom were Mr. Jeremiah Allen and Samuel Cooper Johonnot, Grandson of Dr. Cooper.

I shall not consume much time in the Narration of this second Voyage to Europe though it was attended with as much danger as the first. We met indeed no British Men of War, which in my Estimation were the Worst of all Evils. We had but one very violent Gale of Wind, and that was so much inferiour to those I had encountered the Year before in the Bay of Biscay, in the English Channel and above all in the Gulph Stream, that it appeared to me to have no terror in it. It was nevertheless furious enough to allarm the Officers and People, and their Apprehensions were increased by the foundering or at least by the sudden and final disappearance of a Chasse Maree, that had hitherto sailed under our Convoy from L'Orient.[4] Their Fears as well as mine were increased by another Circumstance, which very seriously threatened destruction to Us all. We had not been two days at Sea before I perceived that the Pumps were going and that a Leak in the Ship was constantly admitting a great deal of Water. At first it was said to be a steady Leak, and not attended with much danger, but it constantly increased from day to day, till our Arrival in Spain. During all the latter part of the Voyage, a large Stream of Water was constantly pouring over each Side into the Sea, from the Pumps which were worked by day and by Night, till all the People on board, Passengers and Officers as well as Seamen were almost exhausted with fatigue. The Sensible was an old Frigate, and her Planks and timbers were so decayed, that one half the Violence of Winds and Waves which had so nearly wrecked the new and strong Ship the Boston the Year before, would have torn her to pieces. Or had We been chased by a superiour British Force, and obliged to spread all our Sails, it is highly probable that the Leak would have been increased and the Ship foundered.

November 24 1779. We were on the Grand Bank of Newfound Land, and about this time, We spoke with an American Privateer, The General Lincoln Captain Barnes. He came on board and our Captain supplied him with some Wood and other Articles he wanted. We all wrote Letters by him to our Families.

Since I came on board I found that even the French Officers had heard more News, or at least more Title Tattle than I had. This was the first time that I heard that Envy and Calumny had been busy with the Character of my Friend General Warren and his Family. That his Son had made a great Fortune, by Privateering, by Trade, by purchasing Sailors Shares and by Gambling: That he had won of C, whom Nobody pittied, a great Sum of Money. That he had made great Profits by buying, in great quantities what he knew was wanted for the Navy and then selling it to the Board. That the Agent too had made a great fortune, that his Wife was a Tory and many Anecdotes of her Conversation &c. These Reports which were mentioned as undoubted and notorious Truths gave me great Uneasiness, because, though I gave very little Credit to them, It was not in my Power to contradict them. There are no Appearances remaining I believe of the Great fortunes, and probably the Accusations were greatly exaggerated, if not merely invidious Suspicions. Indeed I had found that the Passions of Envy, Jealousy, hatred and Revenge engendered by Democratical Licentiousness, had encreased in a great degree by the political Competi-

[4] The *Courrier de l'Europe*; see Diary entry of [5] Dec. 1779, note.

tions in many other Instances, and was not a little allarmed at the Prospect they opened of still greater Evils.[5]

November 25. 1779. The Wind was fair and the Weather pleasant. We had passed the Grand Bank, and found ourselves on the Eastermost Edge of it. On sounding We found Bottom in thirty fathoms of Water.

The Captain and all his Officers and Passengers were so much alarmed at the increasing danger of the Leak and at the fatiguing Labour of all hands in keeping the Pumps in play, that it was concluded to make for one of the Western Islands as the first Friendly Land We could possibly reach: but We missed them and some day in the beginning of December 1779 We found ourselves, as was supposed within one hundred Leagues of Ferrol or at least of Corunna, to one or the other of which places We determined to direct our Course with all the Sail, the Ship could prudently bare. The Leak which kept two Pumps constantly going, having determined the Captain to put into Spain. This Resolution was a great Embarrassment to me. Whether I should travel by Land to Paris a Journey of twelve or thirteen hundred miles, or Wait for the Frigate to be examined and repaired, which might require a long time? Whether I could get Carriages, Horses, Mules or any other Animals to convey Us? What Accommodations We could get upon the Road? How I could convey the Children, and what the Expences would be? were all questions which I could not answer: nor could I find any Person on board, who was able to give me any satisfactory Information. It was said however by some that the Passage of the Pyranees was very difficult: that there was no regular Stage or Post: that We must purchase Carriages and Horses &c.... I could not help reflecting how much greater these inconveniences had been rendered, and how much more our perplexity if the rest of my Family had been with me. With Ladies and young Children and Additional Servants Male and Female We should have been in more distress on Land than at Sea.

December 7. 1779. Tuesday. About Eleven O Clock We discovered Land. Two large Mountains, one sharp and steep, the other large and broad, made their Appearance. We passed three Capes, Finisterre, Tortanes and Veillane. The Chevalier de La Molion gave me some Accajou Nutts. In handling the outside Shell, which has a corrosive Oil in it, in order to come at the meat, I got a little of this juice on my fingers and afterwards inadvertently rubbing my Eyes, I soon found the Lids swelled and inflamed up to my Brows.

[5] See Diary entry of 24 Nov. 1779 and note 3 there.

December 8. 1779. Wednesday. We got into Ferrol, where We found a Squadron of French Ships of the Line under the Command of the Count De Sade. We went on Board, the General as they called him, that is The Commodore, to make our Compliments. We then went on Shore, visited the Spanish General Don Joseph St. Vincent, and then took a Walk about the Town, saw a great Number of Spanish and French Officers, who all congratulated Us on our narrow Escape and applauded Captain Chavagne for making the first Port. When We returned on board the Sensible We found she had made seven feet of Water in her Hold, within the first hour of her coming to Anchor when the Pumps had been abandoned from the fatigue of every Body worn out by pumping.

December 9. 1779. Thursday. Went on Shore with all my Family, and took Lodgings. Dined with the Spanish Lieutenant General of the Marine with twenty four French and Spanish Officers. Don Joseph, though an old Officer had a great deal of Vivacity and good humour as well as Hospitality. The difference between the Faces and Airs of the French and Spanish Officers was more obvious and striking than that of their Uniforms. Gravity and Silence distinguish the latter: Gaiety, Vivacity and Loquacity the former. The Spanish Uniforms were ornamented with a very broad and even Gold Lace, the French with a narrow and scolloped one. The French Wiggs and Hair had several Rows of curls over the Ears: The Spanish only one. The French Bags were small, the Spanish large: Many of the Spaniards had very long hair quieued, reaching down to their hams almost. All the Officers of both Nations had new Cockades, made up of two, a red and a white one in token of the Union of the two Nations.

In the Evening We went to the Comedy or rather the Italian Opera; where We saw many Officers, and very few Ladies. The Musick and dancing were tolerable; but the Actors and Actresses very indifferent, at least it was a dull Entertainment to me. Perhaps it might have been more pleasing, if I had Understood the Italian Language: but all the Knowledge I ever had of this, which was not much, was acquired after that time.

This Evening the French Consul, whose Name was De Tournelle Consul of France at Corunna, arrived at Ferrol, and was introduced to me at my Chamber, by the French Vice Consul. Both made me the politest Offers of Assistance of every Sort. Supped and lay down, but I cannot say I slept or rested, at my Lodgings. We had too many Companions in Bed, in whose Society I never could sleep, much more than if I had been buried in hot embers.

The Delegates of the United States

of New Hampshire. Massachusetts Bay. Rhode Island and Providence Plantations. Connecticut. New York. New Jersey. Pennsylvania. Delaware. Maryland. Virginia. North Carolina. South Carolina.

& Georgia

To all who shall see these Presents send Greeting

It being probable that a Negotiation will soon be commenced for putting an end to the Hostilities between his most Christian Majesty and these United States on the one part, and his Britannic Majesty on the other part; and it being the sincere desire of the United States that they may be terminated by a Peace founded on such solid and equitable principles as reasonably to promise a permanency of the Blessings of tranquility: Know Ye therefore, that We confiding on the integrity, prudence and ability of the honorable John Adams esquire late Commissioner of these United States at the Court of Versailles, have nominated and constitute, and by these Presents do nominate and constitute the said John Adams ... our Minister Plenipotentiary ...

... his Britannic Majesty and these ... of ... ...

In Witness whereof we have caused these presents to be given in Congress at Philadelphia the twenty ... day of September in the year of our Lord one thousand seven hundred and seventy nine and in the fourth year of the Independence of the United States of America.

Signed by the PRESIDENT and sealed with his Seal.

Sam.l Huntington President

Attest Cha Thomson secy

10. JOHN ADAMS' COMMISSION TO TREAT OF PEACE WITH GREAT BRITAIN, 1779

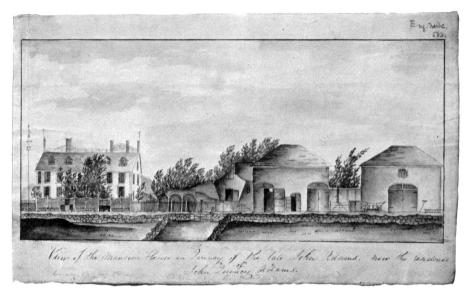

11. SKETCH, WASH DRAWING, AND WOODCUT OF THE "OLD HOUSE,"
RESIDENCE OF THE ADAMS FAMILY IN QUINCY FROM 1788 TO 1927

1779 December 10 Fryday. Breakfasted for the first time on Spanish Chocolate which fully answered the fame it had acquired in the World. Till that time I had no Idea that any thing that had the Appearance of Chocolate and bore that name could be so delicious and salubrious.

Every Body now congratulated Us, on our safe Arrival at this place. The Leak in the Sensible had increased since she had been at Anchor; and all agreed that We had escaped a very great danger.

1779 December 11. I wrote to Congress the following Letter and prepared a Duplicate and Triplicate to go by different Opportunities.

Sir   Ferrol December 11. 1779

I have the Honour to inform Congress, that on the thirteenth day of November I embarked on Board the French Frigate Le Sensible, and on the fourteenth came on Board The Honourable Francis Dana Esq., the Secretary to my Commission, when We fell down to King Road, and on the fifteenth sailed for France.

A Leak was soon discovered in the Ship, which obliged Us to ply the Pumps. As it seemed a steady Leak, it gave little Alarm at first: but continuing to increase, to such a degree, as to make two Pumps, incessantly necessary night and day, obliging the Passengers to take their turns in common with the Ships People, the Captain judged it necessary to make the first Port he could find. ... Accordingly on the Seventh day of December, We happily discovered Cape Finisterre, and on the Eighth arrived at the magnificent Spanish Port of Ferrol, where We found a Squadron of French Ships of the Line, the Officers of which think We were very happy in making this Port, as the Frigate, since she has been in Harbour, is found to make Seven or Eight feet of Water in an hour.

The Advice of all the Gentlemen here to me is to make the best of my Way to Paris by Land: As it is the Opinion of many that the Frigate will be condemned. But if not, she certainly will not be ready to sail again from this Port, in less than four or five Weeks. This is unfortunate to me, because by all the information I can obtain, Travelling in this Kingdom is attended with many difficulties and delays, as well as very great expence, there being no regular Posts as in France and no possibility of passing over the mountainous parts of this Country in Carriages.

I find there has been no Engagement in the European Seas, between the English and the combined Fleets of France and Spain, as was reported in America. There has been an epidemic Sickness, on board the French Fleet, which obliged them to return to Brest rather sooner than was intended. There are twenty five Spanish Ships of the Line in Brest Harbour with the French. It is reported that Monsieur Du Chaffault is appointed Commander in Chief of the French Fleet and that the Comte D'Orvilliere has retired.

Captain Jones has done another brilliant Action, by taking a Forty four Gun Ship, after an obstinate Engagement, and carried her into the Texell. But I cannot learn the particulars with much Certainty or Exactness.

I have been treated with the utmost Politeness and Attention since my Arrival in this place, both by the Spanish and French Officers, particularly by the Spanish Lieutenant General of the Marine, Don Joseph Saint Vincent, who is Commander in Chief of the Marine, by Monsieur De Sade, the French Chef D'Escadre, and by the French Consul and Vice Consul, who have all obligingly offered me every Assistance in their Power.

I shall endeavour to inform Congress of every Step of my Progress, as I may find Opportunity. I have heard nothing as yet, which makes it probable to me, that I shall have any Thing to do openly and directly, in pursuance of my Commission, very speedily. There is a confused Rumour here of a Mediation of Russia and Holland: but I am persuaded without foundation. It seems to be much more certain that the English continue in their old ill Humour and insolent Language, notwithstanding their Impotence grows every day more apparent. I have the honour to be with the greatest respect and Esteem, Sir your most obedient and most humble Servant   John Adams.

His Excellency Samuel Huntington Esqr. President of Congress.[6]

1779 December 12 Sunday. Walked about the Town, but there was nothing to be seen, excepting two Churches, and the Arsenals, dry Docks, Fortifications and Ships of War.

1779 December 13. Monday. The great Inconvenience of this Harbour is, the Entrance is so narrow, there is no possibility of going out, but when the Wind is in one Point, that is the South East.... I was surprized to find so important a Place as this is to the Spanish Naval Power, surrounded by Heights which might easily be possessed by an Enemy, and which entirely overlooked and commanded the Town, the Ships, the Arsenals and Docks.

[6] RC (PCC, No. 84, I); in John Thaxter's hand; at head of text: "Duplicate"; unsigned; endorsed in several hands: "No. 1. J. Adams [...] original by Capt. Trash from Corunna to New- bury Port, Mass. Bay. Duplicate of Decembr. 11th:1779   Original receivd.— Recd. May 15. 1780—orig read March 27."

The Three French Ships of the Line here were the Triomphant of Eighty Guns, M. Le Comte De Sade Chef D'Escadre or General, M. Le Chevalier de Grasse Preville, the Capitaine de Pavillon.

The Souverain of Seventy four Guns, M. Le Chevalier De Glandevesse Captain

The Jason of Sixty four Guns, M. de La Marthonie, Commander.

We dined one day with the Comte De Sade on Board the Triomphant, with all the principal Officers of the Fleet in all the Luxury of the French Navy.

A very fine Turkey was brought upon Table, among every Thing else that Land, Sea or Air could furnish.[7] One of the Captains, as soon as he saw it, observed that he never saw one of those Birds on a Table but it excited in him a deep regret for the Abolition of that order of Ecclesiasticks the Jesuits to whom We were he said, indebted for so many Excellent Things, and among the Rest for Turkeys. These Birds he said were never seen or known in Europe till the Jesuits imported them from India. This occasioned much Conversation and some Controversy: but the majority of the Officers appeared to join in this regrett. The Jesuits were represented as the greatest Masters of Science and Litterature: as practising the best System of Education, and as having made the greatest improvements, the happiest Inventions and the greatest discoveries for the Comfort of Life and the Amelioration of Man and Society. Till this time I had thought that although millions of Jesuits, Pharisees and Machiavilians still existed in the World, yet that the Word Jesuit as well as that of Pharisee and Machiavilian, had become so odious in Courts and unpopular with Nations that neither was ever advocated in good Company. I now found my Error, and I afterwards perceived that even the Philosophers were the principal Friends left to the Jesuits.

The French Names Dindon and Poulet D'Inde, indicate that the Fowl was imported from India: But the English Name Turkey and Turkey fowl, seems to imply that the Bird was brought from the Levant. But if I am not mistaken, the English pretend that Sir Walter Raleigh first imported this Luxury from America. These important Questions of Natural History I shall leave to the Investigation and Discussion of those who have nothing else to do, nor any thing of more Taste and Consequence to contemplate.

I was highly entertained however with this Conversation and not a

---

[7] The following conversation, including that on the important subject of American naval prospects, was recorded in the Autobiography wholly from memory. Compare, or rather contrast, JA's Diary entry of this date.

little delighted to find that I could so well understand a Conversation so rapid and lively in French.

As the Count De Sade placed me next to himself at Table, his chief and indeed his whole Conversation was with me. He was very inquisitive about every Thing in America, but the Subject which most engaged his Attention was the Commerce and especially the Naval Power of America. This Subject I always found most prevalent in the Minds of all the Naval Gentlemen both of France and Spain. The Count said that no Nation in Europe had such Advantages for Naval Power as America. We had Timber of the best Kinds in the World, our Oaks and Cedars especially the Live Oaks and Red Cædars, which America Possessed in such Abundance, were an Advantage that no Nation ever enjoyed before in such Perfection. That We had inexhaustible Mines of Iron Oar and all the Skill and Apparatus necessary to prepare it, work it and refine it. That our Soil produced Flax and Hemp of good quality, and our Agriculturalists knew how to raise it and preserve it. We have a Maxim among Us in the Marine, said the Count, That with Wood, Hemp and Iron, a Nation may do what it will. And you may do what you will, and you will do what you will. For No Nation has, and No Nation that ever existed ever had such Advantages for raising a formidable Navy in a short time as you have. For to all the Materials you add all the Skill and Art. You have already learned of the English, all the Skill in Naval Architecture and all the Art and Enterprise of Navigation, which was ever possessed by the most commercial and most maritime People that ever existed. In fine his Conversation was in the same Strain with that of Monsieur De Thevenot [Thevenard] at L'Orient, in the Spring of the same Year, but more in detail. As the Count de Sade understood no English and my organs were not very flexible to the French, my part of the Conversation could not be very fluent. I made him however to understand, that I thought our People had so much Employment at home upon their Lands, which would be more comfortable and less hazardous if not more profitable that it would be a long time before they would turn their Attention to a Naval military Power. I must however now confess that I did not then believe that French, Spanish, Dutch and English Emissaries, would obtain so much influence in America as to cast a mist before the Eyes of the People and prevent them from seeing their own Interest and feeling their own Power for seven and twenty Years, to such a degree as to suffer their own Coasts and harbours to be insulted and their Commerce plundered even in the West Indies by Pirates, which a few Frigates might send to their [own?] place. The

Count presented to me The Chevalier De Grasse, as his Captaine De Pavillon and as the Brother of the Count de Grasse, the Commander in America,[8] and as a Gentleman of large and independent Fortune, who had no Occasion to go to Sea but chose to expose himself to the rough Life of a Sea Officer, from pure Zeal for the Kings Service.

1779 December 14. Tuesday. Walked once more to the Barracks and dry Docks. The Stones with which these Works were constructed, were far inferiour to our Quincy North Common Granite. They were not better than the South Common Stone. We went into the magnificent Church of St. Julien, where We saw Numbers of Devotees upon their Knees, some before the Altar and some before one Statue or Picture and some before another. This kind of Devotion was much more fashionable in Spain than in France.

We had lodged en la Calle de La Madalena, junto coca, en casa de Pepala Botoneca, i.e. in the Street of the Magdalen near the head, in the House of Pepala Botoneca.

I spent several Evenings with the French Consul Monsieur Detournelle, whom I found a well bred and well informed Man. He was well read, and had been conversant with the Writers on the Law of Nations, particularly in the Titles of those Laws relative to Ambassadors and Consuls. He quoted several Writers on the Rights and Duties of Ambassadors and Consuls and some on Ettiquette and the Formalities and Ceremonies required of those Offices. He told me that the Office of French Consuls was regulated by an ordinance of the King, but that some Nations had entered into particular Stipulations with the King. That the Consuls of different Nations were differently treated by the same Nation. That as Consul of France he had always claimed the Priviledges of the most favoured Nation. That he carefully enquired what Priviledges were enjoyed by the Consuls of England, Germany and Italy and demanded the highest Priviledges of the Gentis amicissimæ.

The Chief Magistrate of the Town of Ferrol, is The Corregidor. For the Province or Kingdom of Gallicia, there is a Souvereign Court of Justice, which has both civil and criminal Jurisdiction. In all criminal Cases it is without Appeal, but in some civil Cases an Appeal lies to the Council at Madrid. There is no time allowed in criminal Cases for an Application for Pardon, for they execute forthwith. Hanging is the Capital Punishment. They burn sometimes but it is after death. There was lately a Sentence for Parricide. The Law required that the Crimi-

---

[8] This is with little doubt a mistake of JA's memory; see Diary entry of this date and note.

nal should be headed up in a hogshead, with an Adder, a Toad, a Dog and a Cat and cast into the Sea. But I was much pleased to hear that Spanish humanity had suggested and Spanish Ingenuity invented a Device to avoid some part of the Cruelty and horror of this punishment. They had painted those Animals on the Cask, and the dead body was put into it, without any living Animals to attend it to its watery Grave. The ancient Laws of the Visigoths are still in Use, and these, with the Institutes, Codes, Novelles &c. of Justinian, the Cannon Law and the Ordinances of the King, constitute the Laws of the Kingdom of Gallicia.

The Bread, the Colliflowers, the Cabbages, Apples, Pears, Beef, Pork and Poultry were good. The Fish of several Sorts were good, excellent Eels, Sardines, and other Species, and the Oysters were tolerable, but not equal to ours in America.

I had not seen a Chariot, Coach, Phaeton, Chaise or Sulky, since I had been in the Place, very few Horses and those very small and miserably poor; Mules and Asses were numerous but small. There was no Hay in the Country: The Horses, Mules &c. eat Wheat Straw.

There had been no frost. The Verdure in the Gardens and Fields was fresh. The Weather was so warm that the Inhabitants had no Fires, nor Fire Places, but in their Kitchens. We were told We should have no colder Weather before May which is the coldest Month in the Year. We found however, when We travelled in the Month of January in the Mountains, Frost and Snow and Ice enough. But at this time and in this Neighbourhood of the Sea, Men, Women and Children were seen in the Streets, with naked Legs and feet, standing on the cold Stones in the mud, by the hour together. The Inhabitants of both Sexes have black hair and dark Complexions, with fine black Eyes. Men and Women had long hair ramilied down to their Waists and sometimes down to their Knees.

Though there was little Appearance of Commerce or Industry, except about the Kings Docks and Yards and Works, yet the Town had some Symptoms of Growth and Prosperity. Many new Houses were building of a Stone which comes from the rocky Mountains round about, of which there are many. There were few goods in the Shops, little Show in their Marketts, or on their Exchange. There was a pleasant Walk a little out of Town, between the Exchange and the Barracks.

There were but two Taverns in the Town. Captain Chavagne and his Officers lodged at one, at six Livres each a day. The other was kept by a Native of America, who spoke English and French as well as

Spanish, and was an obliging Man. Here We could have lodged at a dollar a day each: but where We were We were obliged to give an hundred and twenty nine dollars for six days besides a multitude of other Expences, and besides being kept constantly unhappy by an uneasy Landlady.

Finding that I must reside some Weeks in Spain, either waiting for the Frigate or travelling through the Kingdom, I determined to look a little into the Language. For which purpose I went to a Bookseller and purchased Sobrino's Dictionary in three Volumes in Quarto, The Grammatica Castillana an excellent Spanish Grammar in their own Tongue, and a Lattin Grammar in Spanish. My Friend Captain De Grasse made me a present of a very handsome Grammar of the Spanish Tongue by Sobrino....[9] By the help of these Books, the Children as well as the Gentlemen of our little Company were soon employed in learning the Language. To one who understood the Latin it seemed to be easy and some of Us flatter'd ourselves, that in a Month We might be able to read it, and understand the Spaniards as well as be understood by them. But experience taught Us our Error and that a Language is very difficult to acquire especially by Persons in middle Life.

Mr. Linde an Irish Gentleman, and Master of a Mathematical Accademy here, as well as Mr. De Tournelle, says, that the Spanish Nation in general have been of Opinion that the Revolution in America is a bad example to the Spanish Colonies, and dangerous to the Interests of Spain, as the United States if they should become ambitious and be seized with the Spirit of Conquest, might aim at Mexico and Peru. The Consul mentioned the Opinion of Raynalle, that it was not for the Interest of the Powers of Europe, that America should be independent.

To the Irish Gentleman I observed, that Americans hated War: that Agriculture and Commerce were their Objects, and it would be their Interest, as much as that of the Dutch to keep peace with all the World, untill their Country should be filled with People, which could not be for Centuries. That War and the Spirit of Conquest were the most diametrically opposite to their Interests, as they would divert their Attention, Wealth, Industry, Activity, from a certain Source of Prosperity and even Grandeur and Glory, to an uncertain one; nay to one, that it was certain never could be to their Advantage. That the Government of Spain over her Colonies had always been such, that she never could attempt to introduce such fundamental Innovations, as those by which England had provoked and compelled Us to revolt. And the Spanish

[9] For two of the works mentioned here see Diary entry of this date and note.

Constitution was such, as could extinguish the first Sparks of discontent, and quell the first risings of the People. That it was amazing to me, that a Writer so well informed as Raynalle, could ever give an Opinion that it was not for the Interest of the Powers of Europe, that America should be independent, when it was so easy to demonstrate, that it was for the Interest of every one of them except England. That they could loose nothing by it, but certainly every one of them would gain something, and many of them a great deal.

Wee can see but a little Way into Futurity. . . . If, in 1807, We look back for seven and twenty Years, and consider what would have been the Consequence to Mexico and Peru and all South America, and all the French and Spanish West India Islands, had the United States remained subject to Great Britain, Mr. Linde and the Consul and the whole Spanish Nation might be convinced, that they owe much to the American Revolution. The English love War as much as We abhor it, and if they had now the American Cities for Places of Arms, the American Harbours for Shelter, American Provisions for Supplies and American Seamen and Soldiers for Reinforcements, by what tenure would France and Spain hold their American Dominions?

1779 December 15. Wednesday. This Morning We arose at five O Clock, went over the Water in a Boat and mounted our Mules, thirteen in Number, and two Mulateers, one of whom went before for a Guide, and the other followed Us, to pick up Stragglers. We rode over very bad roads and very high Mountains where We had the View of a very extensive Country, appearing to be a rich Soil and well cultivated, but there were very few plantations of Trees. We saw some Orange Trees, some Lemmon Trees, many Madeira Nut Trees, and a few, but very few Oaks. We dined at Hog Bridge, about half Way to Corunna upon Provision made by the Consul whose Attention and Politeness as well as that of the Vice Consul at Ferrol had been very conspicuous. We arrived at Corunna about seven O Clock and allighted at an Inn kept by Persons who spoke French. An Officer who spoke English held open the Gate for Us to enter, attended Us to our Lodgings, and then insisted on our visiting the General, who is Governor of the Province, and a Colonel, who commands under him and is military Governor of the Town. These are both Irish Gentlemen; and made many Professions of Friendship to our Cause and Country. The Governor of the Province, told me he had orders from Court to treat all Americans as the best Friends of Spain. They were all very inquisitive about Mr. Jays Mission: to know who he was, where he was born, whether he had ever been a Member of Congress, and Whether President. When he embarked—in what Frigate—Where he was destined, whether to France or Spain, and to what Port of France, Brest, L'orient or Nantes.

The General politely invited me to dine. Said that Spaniards made no Compliments but were very sincere. He asked me, when this War would finish? I answered not yet; but when the Kings of France and Spain would take the Resolution to send twenty or thirty more Line of Battle Ships to reinforce the Count D'Estaing and enable him with the Cooperation of Americans to take all the British Forces and Possessions in America.

December 16. 1779. Thursday. This Morning the Governor of the Province of Gallicia and the Governor of the Town of Corunna came to my Quarters at the Hotel du grand Amiral, to return the Visits I made them the last Evening. His Excellency repeated his Invitation to me to dine with him the next day with all my Family. He insisted on seeing my Sons. Said I ran a great risque in taking my Children with me: He had once passed very near my Country in an Expedition in a former War, which he had made against the Portuguese; that himself and every Thing in his Power, were at my Service; that he did not speak English.... I knew not how to answer all this politeness, better than by saying that I was engaged in the Study of the Spanish, and hoped that the next time I should have the Honour of seeing his Excellency, I should be able to speak to him in his own Language. At this he smiled and made a low bow, made some further Enquiries concerning American Affairs and took Leave. Mr. Dana and I took a Walk about the Town, to see the Fortifications, the Shipping, the Marketts, Barracks &c.

After dinner Captain Trask and his Mate of a Schooner belonging to the Tracys of Newbury Port, who had been obliged by bad Weather and contrary Winds to put in here from Bilbao, came to visit me and I gave them Letters to Congress as well as to my Family.

Mr. Detournelle came in and We walked with him to see the Tour de Fer, i.e. The Tower of Iron, a very ancient Monument, intended probably for a Light House as it commands a very wide Prospect of the Sea, and descries all Vessells coming from the East and from the West. There is no Record or memorial of the original of it, nor of the Nation by whom it was built. It is conjectured that it was created by the Phenicians. There is a smaller Building near it, by an Inscription on which it appears, that it was built or repaired by the Romans in the time of Augustus Cesar, but this has indubitable Marks of its being a modern Work in comparison of the Grand Tower. This is all of Stone an hundred feet in height. The mortar with which the Stones were cemented is as hard as the Stones themselves, and appears to have a large mixture of powdered Stone in it. There was formerly a magnificent Stair Case winding round it in a Spiral from the Ground, to the top of it, and it is said that some General once road in a Coach or on Horseback to the highest Step of the Escalier. But now the Stairs and railings are all taken away and the Stones employed to pave the Streets of Corunna. They are large, square and smooth, and would make beautifull Streets if well laid: but they lie in much irregularity, and with out any order. In going to this monument and returning from it We passed by two noble Windmills very large and all of Stone, which lay in a State of desolation that astonished Us. Neglected and forsaken, falling fast into total Ruin. We anxiously enquired why so fine an Estate was suffered to decay in this manner, and were told that a Law Suit had been depending above forty Years to determine the Tittle disputed between two Claimants and that neither would repair the Buildings till it should be decided to which of them they belonged. Very grievous reproaches were added concerning the Delay of the Law in Spain.

There are in this Little Town Three Convents of Monks and two of Nuns. One of the Nunneries is of Capuchins, a very austere order. The Girls eat no meat, wear no linnen, sleep on the floor, never on a bed, their faces are always covered with a Veil and they never speak to any body.

On this day I wrote the following Letter to Congress and sent it together with the Letters from Ferrol by Captain Trask, but neither were received till the 15th. of October 1780 and then in a Triplicate.[1]

Sir   Corunna December 16 1779

By the Opportunity of a small Vessel, accidentally in this harbour, bound to Newbury Port, I have the honour to inform Congress, that I have been detained by violent Rains and several Accidents in Ferrol untill Yesterday, when I set out with my Family for this place, and arrived last Evening without any Accident. I waited immediately on the Governor of the Province, and on the Governor of the Town and received many Civilities from both: and particularly from his Excellency the Governor of the Province of Gallicia an Assurance, that he was not only personally disposed to render me every hospitality and Assistance in his Power, but that he had received express orders from

---

[1] A triplicate of this dispatch, sent later with triplicates of others, was received by Congress on that date, according to a note in JA's letterbook; but the original recipient's copy (PCC, No. 84, I, in Thaxter's hand, signed by JA), is endorsed in Thomson's hand: "No. 2 Letter from J. Adams Corunna Decr. 16. 1779 Read March 27. 1780." There are trifling variations in wording among the extant texts.

his Court to treat all Americans that should arrive here, like their best Friends.

These Personages were very inquisitive about American Affairs, particularly the Progress of our Arms and the Operations of the Count D'Estaing; and more particularly still concerning the Appointment of a Minister Plenipotentiary to the Court of Madrid. They requested his Name, Character, Nativity, Age; whether he was a Member of Congress, and whether he had been President, with many other particulars.

To all these questions I made the best Answers in my Power: and with respect to his Excellency the Minister Plenipotentiary to the Court of Madrid, I gave them the most exact information, and such a respectable Character as the high Offices he has sustained, and his own personal merit, require.

It is the prevailing Opinion here, that the Court of Madrid is well disposed to enter into a Treaty with the United States, and that the Minister from Congress will be immediately received, American Independence acknowledged, and a Treaty concluded.

The Frigate the Sensible, is found to be in so bad a Condition, that I am advised by every body to go to France by Land.—The Season, the Roads, the Accommodations for travelling are so unfavourable, that it is not expected I can get to Paris in less than thirty days. But if I were to wait for the Frigate it would probably be much longer. I am determined therefore to make the best of my Way by Land. And it is possible that this Journey may prove of some Service to the Public, at least I hope the Public will sustain no loss by it, though it will be tedious and expensive to me.

There are six Battalions of Irish Troops in Spain, in three Regiments, several of whose Officers have visited me, to assure me of their respects to the United States.

I have been this Afternoon to see the Tower de Fer, and the Island of Cezarga which was rendered famous in the Course of the last Summer, by being appointed the Rendezvous of the French and Spanish Fleets. The French Fleet arrived at this Island on the ninth day of June last, but were not joined by the Spanish Fleet from Ferrol untill sometime in July, nor by that from Cadiz till much later; so that the combined Fleets were not able to sail for the English Channel, untill the thirtyeth of July. To prevent a similar inconvenience, another Campaign, there are about five and twenty Spanish Ships of the Line, now in Brest, which are to winter there, and be ready to sail with the French Fleet, the approaching Summer, at the first Opening of the Season. God grant them Success and tryumph!

Although no Man wishes for Peace more sincerely than I, or would take more pleasure or think himself more highly honoured by being instrumental in bringing it about; yet I confess I see no prospect or hope of it, at least before the End of another Summer. America will be amused with rumours of Peace, and Europe too: but the English are not yet in a temper for it.

The Court of Russia has lately changed its Ambassador at the Court of London, and sometime in the month of October Mr. Simolin, the New Minister Plenipotentiary from the Court of Petersbourg to the Court of London, passed through France in his Way to England and resided about three Weeks in Paris. From this Circumstance a Report has been spread in Europe, that the Court of Russia is about to undertake the Office of Mediator between the belligerent Powers. But from conversation with several Persons of distinction since my Arrival in Spain, particularly with Monsieur Le Comte De Sade the Chef D'Escadre commanding the French Men of War now in Ferrol, I am persuaded, that, if Russia has any thoughts of a Mediation, the Independence of the United States, will be insisted on by her as a Preliminary and Great Britain will feel much more reluctance to agree to this, than to the Cession of Gibraltar, which it is said Spain absolutely insists upon.

I have the honor to be with the greatest respect, Sir, your most obedient and most humble Servant   John Adams
His Excellency Samuel Huntington Esqr. President of Congress.

1779 December 17. Fryday. The Consul conducted me to the Souvereign Court of Justice where We visited three Halls, One of civil Jurisdiction, another of criminal, and a third of both. The Three Youngest Judges sit in the criminal Trybunals. I was introduced to the President and the other Judges, and to the Procureur du Roi, i.e. to the Kings Attorney who treated me with great Ceremony, conducted me into the Place in the Prison into which the Prisoners are brought who have any thing to say to the Judges, waited on me into each of the Three Halls, shewed me the three folio Volumes of the Laws of the Country, which are the ancient Laws of the Goths, Visigoths and Ripuarians incorporated on the Corpus Juris. There are no Seats in the Halls for any Body but the Judges and the Lawyers who are speaking. Every Body stands. The President told me, that on Monday next there would be argued an interesting Cause, invited me to come and hear it, said he would receive me in Character and place me by the Side of himself on the Bench, and when I said I should wish to avoid this parade, he said he would order an Officer to shew me a convenient Place to see and hear. Soon after this a Part of an Irish Battalion of Troops was drawn up, before the Court House and made a fine Appearance, but suggested melancholly Reflections that Justice could not be administered without a military force, and that too composed of Forreigners, to protect the Judges.

Dined with Don Pedro Martin Sermenio, The Governor of the Province of Gallicia or rather The Vice Roy of the Kingdom of Gallicia. Mr. Dana, Mr. Thaxter, Mr. Allen were with me. By the Assistance of two Irish Officers, I had much Conversation with the Governor who speaks only Spanish. We sent for our Books of Maps, at their desire and shewed them the Position of New York and Rhode Island and the Possessions of the English there. The Governor was very gay, and Don Patricio O Heir the Governor of the Town, with several other Irish Officers were present. They all advised Us to go by Land, and the Governor offered to procure Us a Guide who spoke French, was perfectly acquainted with the Country, Roads, Inn's and Inhabitants and was the best Man in the Kingdom for the purpose, and one who could the most readily procure Us the Carriages, Horses, Mules and Drivers and best know how to make provision for Us, for We must carry all our Necessaries as well as conveniences with Us. Nothing was to be had upon the road except at a few principal Towns, excepting the Wine of the Country, Bino de Pais, which might be had any where and it was very good and very wholesome, for it was an admirable Diuretic.

After Dinner We went with The Consull to see a Convent of Franciscan Friars. Walked into the Church and all round the Yards and Cells. As We passed by the Cells, "here," said the Consul, "are the habitations of Jealousy, Envy, Hatred, Revenge, Malice and Intrigue. There is more Intrigue in a Chapter of Monks for the Choice of a Prior, than was employed to bring about the entire revolution in America. A Monk has no Connections nor Affections to soften him, but is wholly delivered up to his Ambition." I was somewhat surprized at this and asked some questions. The Consull persisted and affirmed that there was no End to the Factions and intrigues among the Monks in Spain.

There were Inscriptions in Latin Verse over all the Cells and generally ingenious and pure in their Morals. I found this universal in all the Monastries, and had a strong Inclination to copy many of them: but generally I had not time. Upon this Occasion having a little Leisure I copied this Inscription over the Cell of a Monk at

Corunna which by no means breaths the Spirit imputed to them by the Consul.

Si tibi pulchra domus, si splendida mensa, quid inde?
Si Species Auri, atque argenti massa, quid inde?
Si tibi sponsa decens, si sit generosa, quid inde?
Si tibi sint nati; si prædia magna, quid inde?
Si fueris pulcher, fortis, divesve, quid inde?
Longus servorum, si serviat ordo, quid inde?
Si doceas alios in qualibet arte; quid inde?
Si rideat mundus; si prospera cuncta; quid inde?
Si Prior, aut Abbas, si Rex, si Papa; quid inde?
Si rota fortunæ, te tollat ad astra; quid inde?
Annis si fælix regnes mille; quid inde?
Tam cito præteriunt hæc omnia, quæ nihil inde.
Sola manet Virtus, qua glorificabimur inde.
Ergo Deo servi; quia sat tibi provenit inde;
Quod fecisses volens in tempore quo morieris
Hoc facies juvenis, dum corpore sanus haberis.
Quod nobis concedas Deus noster, Amen.[2]

We went and drank Tea with the Consul, The Attorney General of the Province was there, and Mr. Lagoanere, the American Agent, and the Captain of the French Frigate La Belle Poulle.

1779 December 18. Saturday. Walked all round the Town, the Wharves, Slips &c. on the Water and round the Walls towards the Country. Went to see the Artillery. A number of Stands of Arms, Cannon, Bombs, Balls, Mortars &c. had been packed up for some time. By the last Post, orders arrived to put up five thousands more in the same manner, ready to embark, but nobody knew where, nor for what purpose. We saw the Magazines, Arsenals, Shops &c. of Carpenters, Wheelwrights, Blacksmiths &c. shewn Us by the Commandant of Artillery. But after having seen Brest and Ferrol, I saw nothing worth describing. The Spanish Ships however both here and at Ferrol appeared equal at least both in Materials and Workmanship to any of American, French or English Construction that I had ever seen. If their Prudence in Navigation and the Activity and Intrepidity of their Seamen were proportionally equal to the English they would be a dangerous Enemy.

Went into the Church or Chapel of a Convent, found the Monks

[2] JA made a few small copying errors in transcribing this inscription from his Diary entry of this date.

in great numbers all upon their Knees, chanting their Pray[er]s to the Virgin Mary. It was the Eve of the holy Virgin. The lighted Wax Candles, by their glimmerings upon the Paintings and Gildings made a pretty Appearance and the Musick was good.

1779 December 19. Sunday. Dined with Monsieur De Tournelle, with all my Family. The Regent, or President of the Souvereign Court of the Kingdom of Gallicia, The Attorney General, the Administrator of the Kings Revenue of Tobacco, the Commandant of the Artillery, Mr. Lagoanere and others were there.

The Entertainment was very sumptuous in all respects, but there was the greatest Profusion and Variety of Wines I ever saw brought to any Table. In Addition to the Wines of France, Bourdeaux, Champaigne, Burgundy, We had Constantin and all the best Wines of Spain red and white. The names and qualities of all of them were given Us, but I remember only the Sherry, Alicanté and Navarre. The Spanish and Irish Gentlemen were very liberal in their Compliments to the Consul on the Excellence of his Wines which they pronounced the oldest and best they had ever seen. The Chief Justice and Attorney General were very gay and very jocular with the Consul and Mr. Lagoanere on his rich and rare Selection of Spanish Wines and archly insinuated that it was a studied Exhibition before the American Minister and a mercantile Speculation. I afterwards was informed that Mr. Detournelle and Mr. Lagoanere had some secret Connection in Trade, which could not be avowed, as an Ordinance of the King of France prohibits Commerce to his Consuls. Mr. Lagoanere avowed that he had procured the Wines.

The Chief Justice and Attorney General were very inquisitive with me about my Birth and Name. They asked very gravely whether I had not been born in Spain? or whether my Father was not a Spaniard? or whether I was not in some Way of Spanish descent? I thought these questions very whimsical and ridiculous, but I determined to keep my Spanish gravity and answered them civilly and candidly that I was born in America, and so was my Father and Grandfather, but my Great Grandfather and Great Great Grandfather came from England, where their Ancestors had lived for any Thing I knew, from the Days of the first Adam. Whether this was a peculiar Kind of Spanish Compliment, like that which was afterwards made me by the Secretary of the Tripoline Ambassador in England when he saw me smoke as gravely and profusely as his Master, who cryed out in rapture "Monsieur vous etes un Turque," I know not.[3] And whether there was any

---

[3] The incident alluded to is told in a justly famous letter JA wrote to Jefferson

foundation for what they said I know not: but they affirmed that there was a very numerous family of that Name in Spain and that in several Provinces there were very ancient, rich and noble Families of the Name of Adams and that they were all remarkable for their Attachment to the Letter S. at the End of Adam. They were so punctillious in this that they took it as an Affront to write their Name without this final Letter and would fight any Man that did it.

These Gentlemen however discovered on other Occasions more Sense and Solidity. They were very solicitous to know our American Forms of Government, and I sent to my Lodgings and presented each of them with a printed Copy of the Report of the Committee of Convention of Massachusetts Bay, made in this Year 1779, as a Specimen of what would probably be nearly the Constitution of that State. They said they would have them translated into Spanish and should be highly entertained by them.

We found the Pork and Bacon, this day, as We had often found them before, most excellent and delicious, which surprized me the more, as I had always thought the Pork in France very indifferent, and occasioned my Inquiry into the manner of raising it. The Chief Justice informed me, that much of it was fatted upon Chesnutts, and much more upon Indian Corn which was much better. That in some Provinces of Spain they had a peculiar kind of Acorns growing upon old pasture Oaks, which were very sweet and produced better Pork than either Chesnuts or Indian Corn. That there were parts of Spain, where they fatted hogs upon Vipers. They commonly cutt off their heads and gave the Bodies to their Swine and they produced better Pork, than Chesnuts, Indian Corn or Acorns. That the Swine were so fond of these Vipers that they would attack them when they would find them alive, put one of their fore feet upon the head and hold it down while they eat the Body, but would not eat the head. That they were so expert at this Art, that they very rarely got stung by them.

These Gentlemen told Us that all kinds of Grain would come from America to a good Market in this Country; even Indian Corn, for they never raised more than their Bread and very rarely enough of that. Pitch, Tar, Turpentine, Timber, Masts &c. would answer. Salt Fish, Sperm Cœti Candles, Rice &c.... Indigo and Tobacco came in sufficient quantities from their own Colonies. The Administrator of the Kings Tobacco, said that ten millions Weight was annually consumed in Spain, in smoking.

---

from London, 17 Feb. 1786 (Jefferson, *Papers*, ed. Boyd, 9:285–288); see also note 2 on JA's Diary entry of 29 March 1786, above.

We enquired concerning the manner of raising the Kings Revennue and were told that there were then no Farmers General. That having been tried they were found prejudicial and abolished. That all Taxes were now collected for the King, who appointed Collectors for particular Cities, Towns or other Districts. That Duties were laid both on Exports and Imports, and Taxes upon Land. Upon Inquiry into the manner of raising the Army We were informed, that some were enlisted for a number of Years, others were draughted by Lot for a number of Years, and that a certain number of Years Service intitled the Soldier to several valuable Priviledges and Exemptions but that their pay was small.

The Consul made me a Present of the Droit publique of France, a posthumous Work of the Abby Fleury, composed for the Education of the Princes, and published with Notes by Daragon Professor in the University of Paris.

1779 December 20. Monday. We went to the Audiencia, where We found the four Judges sitting in their Robes, the Advocates in theirs a little below them, and the Attornies lower down still. We heard a Cause discussed. The Advocates argued sitting, used a great deal of Action with their hands and Arms and spoke with Eagerness. The Language was not wanting in Harmony to the Ear, but the Accent, the Cadence, the Emphasis, in one Word the Power of Oratory seemed to be wanting. The deficiency was however most probably in Us, who were totally ignorant of the Language, understood none of the Arguments and felt none of the Sentiments. I dare say the Arguments at our Bars would appear more insipid and disgusting to them as our Language is less sonorous, and infested with very dissagreable Sibillations.

1779 December 22. Wednesday. Drank Tea at Senior Lagoaneres. Saw the Ladies drink Chocolate in the Spanish Fashion. A Servant brought in a Salver, with a number of Tumblers of clean clear Glass full of cold Water, and a Plate of Cakes, which were light Pieces of Sugar. Each Lady took a Tumbler of Water and a piece of Sugar, dipped the Sugar in the Tumbler of Water, eat the one and drank the other. The Servant then brought in another Salver of Cups of hot Chocolate. Each Lady took a Cup and drank it, and then Cakes and Bread and Butter were served. At last Each Lady took another Cup of cold Water and here ended the repast. The Ladies were Seniora Lagoanere, the Lady of the Commandant of Artillery, and another. The Administrator of the Kings Tobacco, The French Consul, and another Gentleman, with Mr. Dana, Mr. Thaxter and myself made the Company.

Three Spanish Ships of the Line, and two French Frigates came into the harbour this Afternoon; and a Packett from Havannah.

The Administrator gave me a Map of Gibraltar, representing the Lines around it by Land and the Spanish Ships about it by Sea.

The Orders of Ecclesiasticks at Corunna are only Three, The Dominicans, the Franciscans, and the Augustins,[4] but the numbers who compose the Fraternities of these religious Houses are a burthen beyond all proportion to the Wealth, Industry and population of this Town. They are Drones enough to devour all the honey of the Hive. There are in addition to these, two Convents of Nuns, those of St. Barbe and the Capuchins. These are a large Addition to the Number of Consumers without producing any Thing. Lord Bacons Virgines Deo dicatæ quæ nihil parturiunt. They are very industrious however at their Prayrs and devotions that is to say in repeating their Pater Nosters, in counting their Beads, in kissing their Crucifixes, and taking off their hair Shifts to whip and lacerate themselves every day for their Sins, to discipline themselves to greater Spirituality in the Christian Life. Strange! that any reasonable Creatures, any thinking Beings should ever believe that they could recommend themselves to Heaven by making themselves miserable on Earth. Christianity put an End to the Sacrifice of Iphigenias and other Grecian Beauties and it probably will discontinue the Incineration of Widows in Malabar: but it may be made a question whether the Catholick Religion has not retained to this day Cruelties as inhuman and antichristian as those of Antiquity.

I ventured to ask the Attorney General a few Questions concerning the Inquisition. His answers were guarded and cautious as I expected. Nevertheless he answered me civilly and candidly. That the Inquisition in Spain was grown much milder, and had lost much of its Influence. Europe in general was much inlightened and grown more moderate, and the public Opinion in Spain participated of the general Information, and revolted against the Cruelties of the Inquisition.

1779 December 24. Fryday. Dined on board the Bellepoule with the Officers [of] that Ship and those of the Galatea.[5]

We had now been about sixteen days in Spain at Ferrol and Corunna and had received Every Politeness We could desire from all the Officers civil and military both of the Army and Navy, and from the French Officers as well as the Spanish; the Climate was warm and salubrious, and the Provisions were plentifull, wholesome and agre-

---

[4] The following reflections are not in JA's Diary.
[5] JA's Diary entry for this day ends at this point.

able. But the Circumstance which destroyed all my Comfort and materially injured my health was the Want of rest. For the first Eight nights I know not that I slept at all and for the other eight very little. The Universal Sloth and Lazyness of the Inhabitants suffered not only all their Beds but all their Appartments to be infested with innumerable Swarms of Ennemies of all repose. And this torment did not cease at Corunna but persecuted me through the whole Kingdom of Spain to such a degree that I sometimes apprehended I should never live to see France.

We were now provided with a Guide and Horses and Mules and Mulateers and such miserable Carriages as the Country afforded, but at an Expence that in any other Country would have procured Us the best accommodations of every kind.

1779 December 25. Saturday. Christmas. At Eleven O Clock I went to the Palace to take Leave of the Vice Roy and General. Mr. O Heir the Governor of the Town went with me, because he spoke English. His Excellency repeated the thousand obliging things he had said to me when I made my first Visit to him, and afterwards again when I dined with him.

1779 December 26. Sunday. The General, the Governor, the French Consul and Mr. Lagoanere, had influence enough to procure Us the best Guides, accommodations and Attendants, which the Country afforded, upon Terms very hard for the miserable Things We had, according to a Contract made for Us by Mr. Lagoanere.

Senior Raymon San, the Owner of all the Post Chaises, or Chaises or Calashes or whatever other name they bore and the Horses and Mules that drew them, and the Man with whom Mr. Lagoanere made the Contract.

Senior Eusebio Seberino, the Postillion who drove my Chaise or rather who led my Horses.

Joseph Diaz the Postillion, who drove Mr. Dana and Mr. Thaxter. This was the Writer, and had been educated at St. Iago de Compostella.

Diego Antonio, the Postillion who drove Mr. Allen and Mr. Samuel Cooper Johonnot.

To these were Added two Men on foot Juan Blanco and Bernardo Bria.

At half after two We mounted our Carriages and Mules and rode four Leagues to Betanzos, the ancient Capital of the Kingdom of Gallicia, and the place where the Archives are still kept. The Building in which the records are deposited is a long Square, of Stone without any roof and stands over against one of the Churches. There are, in this little place, two Churches and two Convents. The last League of our road to it, was mountainous and rocky, to such a degree as to be very dangerous to Cattle and Carriages as well as Men. Mr. Lagoanere made Us the Compliment to attend Us to this place. The House, the Beds and the People appeared to me too romantick for description, but a tolerable Idea of them may be formed from something which will be said of the next House in which We lodged. I found that our Guide and all our Spanish Attendants thought this and all the other Houses where We dined and lodged were very good Inns.

1779 December 27. Monday.[6] We travelled from Betanzos to Castillano. The roads still mountainous and rocky. Neither the Horses nor the Mules could be trusted, in ascending or descending the rocky Steeps of the Mountains in the Carriges without two Men on foot to hold them by their bridles and their heads, and with all our precautions, We broke one of our Axle Trees, early in the day which prevented Us from going more than four Leagues in the whole. The House in Castillano where We lodged was of Stone, two Stories in height. We entered into the Kitchen, where was no floor but the Ground and no Carpet but Straw trodden into mire by Men, Hogs, horses and Mules. In the middle of the Kitchen was a Mound raised a little above the Level of the Ground with Stones and Earth, on which was a fire, with Potts, Kettles, Skillets &c. of the fashion of the Country, over it, and round about it. There was no Chimney filled the room [7] and if any of it ascended, it found no other passage to the open Air, but through two holes drilled through the Tyles of the roof, not perpendicularly over the fire, but at Angles of about forty five degrees. On one Side was a flew Oven, very large, black, smoaky and sooty. On the opposite Side of the fire was a Cabbin filled with Straw where I suppose the Patron del Casa, that is, the Master of the House, his Wife and four Chilldren, all lodged and slept together. On the same floor or rather on the same level of Ground, with the Kitchen was the Stable. There was indeed a Door which might have parted the Kitchen from the Stable: but this was always open, and indeed it would have been impossible to see or breath with it shut: and the floor or ground of the Stable, was covered with miry Straw like the Kitchen. I went

---

[6] A close comparison between the present entry and that of the same date in JA's Diary on which it is directly based, provides an excellent illustration of JA's habit of "writing up," that is to say, paraphrasing, expanding, and embellishing, passages from his Diary when composing his Autobiography.

[7] Thus in MS. JA doubtless meant to write: "There was no Chimney. Smoke filled the room," &c.

into the Stable and saw it filled on all Sides with Mules belonging to Us and several other Travellers who were obliged to put up, by the Rain. The Smoke filled every part of the Kitchen, Stable, and all other parts of the House, and was so thick that it was very difficult to see or breath. There was a flight of Steps of Stone covered with Mud and Straw, from the Kitchen floor up into a Chamber. On the left hand as you ascended the Stairs, was a Stage, built up about half Way from the Kitchen floor to the Chamber floor. On this Stage was a bed of Straw and on the Straw lay, a fatting hog. Around the Kitchen fire were arranged the Man and Woman of the House, four Children, all the Travellers, Servants, Mulateers &c. Over the Fire was a very large Kettle, like a Pot Ash Kettle, full of Turnips and Onions, very large and very fine boiling for the Food of all the Family of Men and Beasts inhabiting both the Kitchen and the Stable, and the Stage.

The Chamber in which We lodged, had a large quantity, perhaps an hundred Bushells of Indian Corn in Ears, very small however, not half so large as our Corn in America. These Ears were hanging over head upon Poles and pieces of Joist. In one Corner was a large Binn, full of Rape Seed, on the other Side, another full of Oats. In another part of the Chamber lay a few Bushells of Chesnuts. There were two frames for Beds with Straw beds upon them, and a Table in the middle. The Floor I believe had never been washed or swept for an hundred Years. Smoke, Soot and dirt, every where, and in every Thing. There were in the Chamber two Windows or rather Port holes without any glass. There were wooden dors to open and shut before the Windows. If these were shut there was no light and no Ventilator to draw off the unwholesome Air of the Chamber or let in any pure Air from abroad; if they were open We were exposed to all the cold and Vapours, from the external Air. My Inclination and Advice was to keep the Ports open, choosing to encounter the worst Air from abroad rather than be suffocated or poisoned with the Smoke and contaminated Air within.[8] In addition to all these Comforts in such a Tavern it was not to be expected that We should escape the Bosom Companions and nocturnal Ennemies, which We had found every where else. Nevertheless, amidst all these horrors I slept better, than I had done before since my Arrival in Spain.

1779 December 28. Tuesday. We went from Castilliana to Baamonde, and found the first part of the Road very bad, but the latter

---

[8] On this subject compare JA's account of his dispute with Franklin on the way to Staten Island, in the Autobiography under 9 Sept. 1776; and his observations on fresh air, in his Diary under 21 May 1783.

part tolerable. The whole Country We had passed hitherto had been very mountainous and rocky. There was here and there a Valley, and now and then a farm that appeared handsomely cultivated. But in general the Mountains were covered with Furze, and not much cultivated. We were astonished to see so few Trees. There was scarce an Oak, Elm, or any other Tree to be seen, except a very few Madeira Nuts and a very few fruit Trees. At Baamonde we were obliged to rest for the day, to procure a new Axle Tree to one of our Calashes. The House where We were, was better than our last nights lodgings. We had a Chamber for seven of Us to lodge in. We laid our beds upon all the Tables and Chairs in the room and the rest on the floor as last night. We had no Smoke and less dirt than last night, though the floor had never been washed I believe since it was laid. The Kitchen and Stable were below as usual but in better order. The Fire was in the middle of the Kitchen: but the Air-holes pierced thro the Tiles of the Roof, drew up the Smoke, so that one might sit at the Fire, without much inconvenience. The Mules, Hogs, fowls and human Inhabitants, however, all lived together below and Cleanliness seemed never to be regarded.

We had three Calashes, in Company. In one of them I rode with my two Children John and Charles: In another went Mr. Dana and Mr. Thaxter: In a third Mr. Allen and Samuel Cooper Johonnot. Our three Servants rode on Mules. Sometimes the three Gentlemen mounted the Mules of the Servants, who took our Places in the Calashes, and were as much worse for the Exchange as We were the better. Sometimes the Children rode upon the Mules. And very frequently We were all obliged to walk as much more safe and agreable than Carriages or Saddles. The Calashes were very clumsy and inconvenient, somewhat resembling those in Use in Boston an hundred years ago. There was some finery about them in brass nails and paint. But the Leather was very old, and had never felt Oil since it was made. The Harness was broken in many places and tied together with twine and cords. The Appearance and the Furniture of the Mules were equally curious. Their Ears, Necks, Backs, Rumps and Tails, were shorn close to the Skinn. They were lean, but very strong and sure footed and seemed to be well shod. The Saddles had large Ears and high Rims or Ridges, all round behind the Rider. They had a breast plate before and a Breech band behind. They had large Wooden Stirrips, made like Boxes in a semicircular form bound round with Iron. In these Wooden Boxes, close at one End and open at the other, you inserted your Foot, which is well defended by them from rain and Sloughs. We had magnificent Curb Bridles to two or three of the Mules; the rest were guided by Haltars, and there was an Halter as well as a Curb Bridle to each of the others. There were Wallets or Saddle bags made with Canvas on each mule in which We carried Bread and Cheese, Meat, Knives and Forks, Spoons, Apples and Nutts. Indeed We were obliged to carry on our Mules, in a Waggon that attended Us, or in the Calashes, through the whole of this Journey, our own Beds, Blanketts, Sheets, Pillows; our own provisions of Chocolat, Tea, Sugar, Meat, Wine, Spirits, and every Thing that We wanted. We carried our own Butter, Cheese, and indeed Salt and Pepper too. We got nothing at the Taverns but Fire, Water, and sometimes Salt and Pepper, and sometimes Wine of the Country at a reasonable rate.

I have always regretted that We could not find time to make a Pilgrimage to Saint Iago de Compostella. We were informed, particularly by Mr. Lagoanere, that the Original of this Shrine and Temple of St. Iago was this. A certain Shepherd saw a bright Light there in the night. Afterwards it was revealed to an Archbishop that St. James was buried there. This laid the Foundation of a Church, and they have built an Altar on the Spot where the Shepherd saw the Light. In the time of the Moors, the People made a Vow, that if the Moors should be driven from this Country, they would give a certain portion of the Income of their Lands to Saint James. The Moors were defeated and expelled and it was reported and believed, that Saint James was in the Battle and fought with a drawn Sword at the head of the Spanis[h] Troops, on Horseback. The People, believing that they owed the Victory to the Saint, very chearfully fulfilled their Vows by paying the Tribute. But within a few Years, a Duke of Alva, a desendant of the famous Duke of that name, but probably grown more Philosophical at least less catholick than his Ancestor, has refused to pay for his Estate. This Refusal has given rise to a Lawsuit, which has been carried by appeal to Rome. The Duke attempted to prove that Saint James was never in Spain. The Pope has suspended the Cause, and it is suspected because His Holiness doubts whether it is safe to trust the Dukes Evidence before the Public.

Upon the Supposition that this is the place of the Sepulture of Saint James, there are great numbers of Pilgrims, who visit it, every Year, from France, Spain, Italy and other parts of Europe, many of them on foot.

Saint Iago is called the Capital of Gallicia, because it is the Seat of the Archbishop and because Saint James is its Patron: but Corunna is in Fact the Capital as it is the Residence of the Governor, the Audiencia &c. &c.

We travelled this day from Baamonde to Lugo, and passed the River Minho which originates in the Mountains of Asturia, and flows down through Portugal.

1779 December 30 Thursday. We went to see the Cathedral Church at Lugo which is very rich.—A Youth came to me in the Street, and said he was a Bostonian, a Son of Mr. Thomas Hickling. He went a Privateering in an English Vessell, he said, and was unfortunately taken. Unfortunately inlisted, said I.... He wanted to make his fortune he said. Out of your Countrymen and by fighting against your Country? said I.

Two Irish Gentlemen came to pay their respects to me, Michael Meagher Oreilly, and Louis O Brien. These were Irish Officers in the Spanish Service. They invited me with great Earnestness to go to their house and spend the Evening and sup with them: but the Weather was now so cold and we were so fatigued with our uncomfortable Journey that I could not think of going out. We excused ourselves as well as We could, and when Obrien found that We could not go to his house, he sent Us a Meat Pie and a minced Pie and two Bottles of Frontinac Wine, which gave Us a fine Supper.

We went from Lugo to Galliego and arrived in good Season, having made six Leagues and an half from Lugo. The Road was mountainous but not rocky as it had been almost all the Way heretofore. We passed over a large Bridge over a River called Carasedo, which empties itself into the Minho not far from Lugo. I saw nothing but Signs of Poverty and misery among the People: a fertile Country not half cultivated: People ragged and dirty: the Houses universally nothing but mire, Smoke, Soot, fleas and Lice: nothing appeared rich but the Churches, nobody fat but the Clergy. Many of the Villages We passed, were built with Mud filled in between Joists, Nine tenths of them uninhabited and mouldering to dust. Yet in every one of these Scenes of desolation, you would see a splendid Church, and here and there a rosy faced Priest in his proud Canonicals rambling among the rubbish of the Village. The Roads the worst, without exception the worst that were ever travelled, in a Country where it would be easy to make them very good: No Simptoms of Commerce, or even of internal Trafick: No Appearance of Manufactures or Industry.

1779 December 31. Fryday. We rode from Galliego to Sebrero, seven Leagues. Our Journey was more agreable this day, than usual:

the Weather was remarkably fair and dry, and the roads not so bad as We had expected. There was the grandest profusion of wild irregular Mountains I ever saw: yet laboured and cultivated to their Summits. The Fields of Grain were all green. We passed a Range of Mountains that were white with Snow, and there were here and there Banks of Snow on the Mountain We passed over: but no Frost at all in the Ground.

We were now on the highest ground of all, and within Musquet Shot of the Line between Gallicia and Leon. The Houses all along our Journey were small and of Stone, except those of mud. Some of them were covered with Tiles of Brick, and some with Tiles [of] Slate, but by far the greater part of them, with Thatch. They interweave a Shrub of which they make brooms, among the Straw, and bind both together with Wyths. These thatched Roofs are very numerous, but universally dirty and smoaky. The People wore broad brimmed hats, or Caps made of Woolen Cloth, like their Coats, Jacketts and small Cloaths, which are made of black Sheeps Wool, without dyeing, and consequently are all of a colour. We were shewn some of the Marragatoes, a peculiar kind of wild wandering People, who were particularly dressed in a greasy leathern Jackett.

1780. January 1. Saturday. We arrived, from Sebrero, at Villa Franca, seven Leagues. The Road at first was very bad, in many places very steep, Hills with sharp Pitches, and encumbered with ragged rocks. We then came into the Road of Leon, which is made seemingly out of a Rock. It was an excellent road for a League and an half. We then came to a River, and travelled along the Banks of it for some Leagues. This Way was as bad as the other was good; miry, rocky, up and down, untill We came into a new road, about two Legues from Villa Franca. Here again We found a road made entirely by Art, at a great Expence, but it seemed to be made, forever. They ⟨are⟩ were going on with this Work, which is an honor to the Nation, as it shews that Improvements are beginning, and that some Attention is paid to the Ease, Convenience, Utility and Commerce of the People. We were told that the King had lately employed the Officers and Soldiers of his Army upon these Works and intended to pursue them. The Country We travelled over this day was the greatest Curiosity I had ever beheld. The River Barcarel[9] flows between two Rows, an uninterrupted succession of Mountains, rising on each hand to a vast hight, which appear the more sublime and awfull Objects, for the strange irregular Shapes of them. Yet they are cultivated up to their highest Summits.

[9] Diary: "Barcarcel." Presumably the Valcarce.

There were flourishing fields of Grain, on such steep declivities, near the Peaks of these Mountains, that I could not conceive it possible for Horses, Cattle or even Mules to stand upon them to plough them. I know not indeed how Men could stand to dig the Ground with Spades. The Houses had been uniformly the same, through the whole Country hitherto. Common habitations for Men and Beasts. The same smoaky, filthy Dens. Not one decent house had I seen, since I left Corunna.

We passed this day, the Ruins of an ancient Castle of the Moors, on the Summit of one of the steepest, highest, and most rugged of the Mountains.

There are in Villa Franca, three Parish Churches, one Convent of Men and one of Women. There is an old Brick Castle built in Feudal Times when Baron was at War with Baron; a defence against Lances, and Bows and Arrows and no more. Possibly it might ward off musquet Balls.

Here I bought a Mule, Saddle and Bridle for sixty two dollars and an half.

1780. January 2. Sunday. We rode from Villa Franca, da el Bierzo Rio P[uen]te, passed through several Villages, and over Rivers and Bridges; We passed also Campo de Narraya, Cacabelos Rio P[uente] and arrived at Ponferrada where We dined. The Country grew smoother.

1780. January 3. Monday. We rode to Astorga. We passed through the Town and Country of the Marragattoes. The Town is small and stands on a brook in a great Plain. As We went into Astorga, We met Coaches and genteel People.

1780. January 4. Tuesday. At Astorga, We found clean Beds and no fleas for the first time since We had been in Spain. Walked twice round the Walls of the City, which are very ancient. We saw the Road to Leon and Bayonne and the road to Madrid. There is a pleasant Prospect of the Country from the Walls. Saw the Market of Vegetables. The Onions and Turnips were the largest and finest I ever saw. The Cabbages, Carrots &c. appeared very good. Saw the Markett of Fuel, which consisted of Wood, Coal, Turf and Brush. Numbers of the Marragatto Women attended the Market with their Vendibles. These were as fine as any of our American Indian Squaws and a great deal more filthy. Their Ornaments consisted of Crucifixes, Beads, Chains, Earrings and Finger Rings, in Silver, brass or glass, about their Necks and Arms.

We went to see the Cathedral Church which is the most magnificent I had yet seen in Spain. Saw the Parliament House, or Casa del Cieudad, where the Corregidor and City Magistrates assemble, to deliberate, and to execute the orders of the King. Some of the Spaniards brought me the Gazette of Madrid of the 24th of December, in which was this Article.

Coruña 15 de Diciembre

Hoy mismo han llegado á esta Plaza el Cabellero Juan Adams Miembro del Congreso Americano, y su Ministro Plenipotentiario, á la Corte de Paris, y Mr. Deane [*i.e.* Dana] Secretario de Embaxada quienes salieron de Boston el 15 de Noviembre Ultimo á bordo de la Fregata Francesa de Guerra la Sensible que entro en el Ferrol el dia 8 del corriente. Trahe la Noticia de que habiendo los Ingleses evacuado a Rhode Island y retirado todas sus Tropes a Nueva York. Los Americanos tomaron Possession de todos los Puestos evacuados.

This Afternoon a genteel Spaniard came to my Lodgings to offer me, all Sorts of Services and good Offices, and to enquire if I wanted any kind of Assistance or if I wanted Cash. Said he had received a Letter from Mr. Lagoanere at Corunna desiring him to afford me every Aid in his Power, and to furnish me with Money if I wanted it. I thanked him and desired him to thank Mr. Lagoanere, but to assure him that I wanted nothing and that I had got so far on my Journey very well.

1780 January 5. Wednesday. We rode from Astorga to Leon, Eight Leagues. This was one great Plain, and the road through it was very fine. We saw large Herds of Cattle and immense flocks of Sheep. The Sheep were of an handsome Size, and their fleeces of Wool thick, long and extreamly fine. The Soil appeared to be rather thin and barren. We passed several small Villages, the vast range of Asturias Mountains all covered with Snow on our left hand. The Weather was cold, but otherwise very pleasant. We met with a good deal of Frost and Ice in the Road. Our Mules found more difficulty to keep their Steps firm upon the Ice over the Sloughs than they had among the roughest Rocks in the Mountains. We passed the Bridge over the River Orbigo, which in the Spring when swelled with the freshetts of melted Snow from the Mountains of Asturias, is a very great River. Leon, which We entered in the night, had the Appearance of a large City.

1780 January 6. Thursday. We went to see the Cathedral Church at Leon which though magnificent, is not equal to that at Astorga, if it is to that at Lugo. It was the day of the Feast of the King and We happened to be at the celebration of High Mass. We saw the Procession of the Bishop and of all the Canons, in rich habits of Silk, Velvet, Silver and gold. The Bishop as he turned the Corners of the Church spred out his hand to the People, in token of his Apostolical Benediction; and those, in token of their profound gratitude for the heavenly Blessing prostrated themselves on their Knees as he passed. Our Guide told Us We must do the same. But I contented myself with a Bow. The Eagle Eye of the Bishop did not fail to observe an Upright figure amidst the Crowd of prostrate Adorers: but no doubt perceiving in my Countenance and Air, but especially in my dress something that was not Spanish, he concluded I was some travelling Heretick and did not think it worth while to exert his Authority to bend my stiff Knees. His Eyes followed me so long that I thought I saw in his Countenance a reproof like this "You are not only a Heretick but you are not a Gentleman, for a Gentleman would have respected the Religion of the Country and its Usages so far as to have conformed externally to a Ceremony that cost so little."

We were conducted to see the Council Chamber of the Bishop and Chapter, hung round with Crimson Damask. The Seats all round the Chamber of crimson Velvet. This room and another, smaller one, where the Bishop sometimes took aside some of the Cannons, were very elegant.

We went to see the Casa del Cieudad: and the Castle of King Alphonsus which We were informed was Nineteen hundred and thirty six years old. It is of Stone and the Workmanship of it, very neat.

But there is in this City no Appearance of Commerce, Manufactures or Industry. The Houses are low, built of Brick and Mud and Pebble Stones from the neighbouring Fields. There was no Market worth notice. Nothing looked either rich or chearfull but the Churches and Churchmen. There was a Statue of Charles the fifth in the Cathedral Church, but very badly done, as were all the Statues and Paintings I had seen in all the Churches, for which reason among others I have taken no notice of them. Indeed it would be endless to describe all the Images of Angells and Statues of Saints who have been canonized not so much for their moral and social Virtues or their Christian Graces as for their Superstition and Enthusiasm, or what is worse for their pious frauds in the Service of the Sovereign Pontiffs. Besides I saw among them no Sculpture or Painting that was worthy of Observation or Remembrance.

There is here an Institution for the Education of noble Youths in

Mathematicks and Philosophy, which they call the School of Saint Mark.

We dined at Leon, and got into our Carriages and upon our Mules, about one O Clock, to proceed on our Journey. We passed the new Bridge of Leon, which is a beautifull Piece of Work, all of Stone. The River which comes down from the Mountains of Asturias, was not then very large, but in the Spring when the Snows melt upon the Mountains, it is swelled by the Freshets to a very great Size. This River also runs down into the Kingdom of Portugal. Not long afterwards We passed another Bridge over a River which the Peasants told me to call Rio y Puente de Biliarente. This River also comes from the Asturian Mountains and flows into Portugal. We passed through several little Villages, in every one of which We saw the Young People, Men and Women dancing the Fandango. One of the young Women beats an Instrument, somewhat like a Section of a Drum, covered with Parchment. She sings as well as beats on her drum, and the Company dance, with [a] Pair of Clackers in the hand of every Man and Woman. The Clackers are two Pieces of Wood, cutt handsomely enough, which they have the Art to rattle in their hands to the time of the Drum. They had all, Males and Females, wooden Shoes, in the Spanish fashion, that is mounted on Stilts. We stopped once, to take a view of one of these Companies. An old Man in the House before which the Festival was celebrating in the open Air, as he stood at the Door looking at the Dance, perceived Us and came out with a Bottle of Wine and a Tumbler, which he filled to the brim and held up to me, as I sat upon my Mule, with such an Air of Exultation and generous Hospitality, that I drank off the whole Glass in Complaisance to his good humour, though I had afterwards reason to repent it, for the Wine was very sour. I directed our Guide to give him something and be sure to pay him well for his Wine.

We stopped at night at a Village called Mansillas, through which runs another large River from the Asturias, stretching down to Portugal. A great Stone Bridge over it, appeared to have been half carried away by the Water in some Freshett. Mansillas was once a Walled City. The Towers were yet standing all round the Town; and the Ruins and Fragments of the Wall, and the Appearance of a Foss around it still remain. The Towers were all made of small round Stones, not larger than two hands, which is the only kind of Stone to be had here. They are bound together by the ancient Cement which is as hard and as durable as the Stones themselves. We went upon the Top of one of the Towers, from whence We had a full View of the

Town, which appeared to be gone to decay, though there were four or five Churches here still.

1780 January 7. Fryday. From Mansillas We rode to San Juan Segun.

1780 January 8 Saturday. We rode from San Juan Segun to Paredise de Nava. At the distance of every League, We had passed through a Village built altogether of Mud and Straw. They have no timber nor Wood nor brick nor Stone. These Villages all appear going to decay and crumbling to dust. Can this be the ancient Kingdom of Leon? Nevertheless every Village has Churches and Convents enough in it, to ruin it, and the whole Country round about it; even if they had nothing to pay to the King, or the Landlords. But all three together Church, State and Nobility exhaust the Labour and Spirits of the People to such a degree, that I had no Idea of the Possibility of deeper Wretchedness. Ignorance more than Wickedness has produced this deplorable State of Things, Ignorance of the true Policy which encourages Agriculture, Manufactures and Commerce. The Selfishness and Lazyness of Courtiers and Nobles, have no doubt been the Cause of this Ignorance: and the blind Superstition of the Church has co-operated with all the other causes and increased them. There were in this little Village four Parish Churches and two Convents one of Monks and one of Nuns, both of the order of St. Francis.

The Parish Churches and their Curates are supported here, by the Tythes paid by the People. They pay every tenth pound of Wool; every tenth part of Wine, Grain, Honey; in short, every tenth part of every thing. The good Curates sometimes aleviate the Severity of this, by Compositions or Modus's. The Convents are supported by the Incomes of their Estates and foundations. But one would think this would require the Produce of the whole Country.

Nothing seems to be considered as the good of the People but their Religion. The Archbishop is said to have power to do every Thing for the good of the People. But when you enquire what he does or what he has power to do for the happiness of the People? to alleviate their burdens? or increase their Enjoyments? You are told he does nothing of all this, nor has power to do any thing. All his Power, to do every thing for the good of the People, consists in that of making new Parishes, and altering old ones at his Pleasure. We were told there were but four Archbishopricks in Spain. The Splendor of these Establishments may be conceived from that of Saint Iago whose Archbishop has one hundred and Eighty thousand Ducats a Year, in Rent. The War which then prevailed between France and Spain on one

Side and England on the other, was said to be popular in Spain. The Clergy, the Religious Houses and other Communities had offered to grant large Sums of Money to the King for the Support of it. The English had become terrible to them, partly perhaps because English Sentiments of Liberty and Tolleration, had begun to creep in among the People and might threaten to become dangerous to the Wealth and Domination of the Clergy; and partly because their South American Dominions were too much in danger from the English and North America united.

From Astorga to this place Paredise de Nava, the Face of the Country was a great plain, and a striking Contrast to all the rest of the Country We had passed from Ferrol. But there was little Appearance [of] Improvement, Industry or Cultivation. Scarcely any Trees. No Forrest, Timber or fruit Trees. No Fences except a few Mud Walls for Sheep folds. This night We reached Sellada el Camino.

1780 January 11. Tuesday. We arrived at Burgos, from Sellada el Caminos, four Leagues. We had fog, rain, and Snow all the Way, very chilly and raw. When We arrived at the Tavern, We found no Chimney, though my Servant who went out to examine all the other public houses reported this to be the best. A Brazier, or Pan of Coals in a Chamber, without a Chimney and without Windows except Port holes, was all the heat We could procure. Uncomfortable however as We were, We went out to see the Cathedral which was ancient and very large. The whole Building was supported by four grand Pillars the largest I ever had seen. Round the great Altar were represented our Saviour, from the Scene of his Agony in the Garden, when an Angel presents to him the Cup, to his Crucifixion between two Thieves, his descent from the Cross, and his Ascension into Heaven. The Chappells round the great Altar were the largest I had ever seen. Round the Altar these several Stages were represented. 1. The Agony in the Garden. 2. Carrying the Cross. 3. The Crucifixion between two Thieves. 4. The Descent from the Cross. 5. The Ascension into Heaven.

There was no Archbishop at Burgos, there had been one, who made the fifth in the Kingdom: but the King had abolished this Archbishoprick and there remained but four. There was also a Chappell of Saint Iago.

We went into three Booksellers Shops to search for a Map or Chart of Spain, but could find none, except a very small and erroneous one in a Compendio of History of Spain.

For more than twenty Years I had been almost continually engaged in Journeys and Voyages and had often undergone severe Tryals, as I thought; great hardships, cold, rain, Snow, heat, fatigue, bad rest, indifferent nourishment, want of Sleep &c. &c. &c. But I had never experienced any Thing like this Journey. If it were now left to my Choice to perform my first Voyage to Europe with all its horrors, or this Journey through Spain, I should prefer the former. Every Individual Person in Company had a violent Cold, and were all of Us in danger of fevers. We went along the Road, sneezing and coughing, in all that uncomfortable Weather, and with our uncomfor[t]able Cavalry and Carriages, in very bad roads, and indeed were all of Us fitter for an Hospital than for Travellers with the best Accommodations on the most pleasant Roads. All the Servants in Company, were dull, discouraged and inactive, besides the total Ignorance of any Language in which they could converse with the People. The Children were sick. Mr. Thaxter was not much better, and as he understood neither Spanish nor French, he had enough to do to take care of himself.[1] In short I was in a deplorable Situation. I knew not what to do nor where to go. In my whole Life my Patience was never so near being totally exhausted.

With much difficulty We obtained Information of our future rout. From Burgos We were to go to Monasterio, four Leagues, from thence to Berebiesca, four more; from thence to Santa Maria del Courbo, two; from thence to Courbo, one; thence to Pancourbo, two; and here the Road Parts to Vitoria and to Bilbao. So that We had thirteen Leagues to go to the parting of the Roads.

This famous City of Burgos, the ancient Capital of the renouned Kingdom of Castile and once an Archbishoprick, dissappointed me very much. The Squares, public Buildings, Fountains and Walks are said to have been once very remarkable. But after I had taken some Walks about the Town, my Expectations were not answered. A River runs directly through the Town, the River Aranzon [Arlanzón], I believe they call it, and this in a City is always an agreable Circumstance. There is a great number of Bridges over the River. There is a Mountain too or rather a Hill upon which a part of the Town stands, and upon the Top of which are the Ruins of an Ancient Castle.

There were some few Trades and a little Appearance of Business here; but the principal Occupation was Religion. Upon my expressing some Curiosity to [know?][2] the Number of Religious Houses in Burgos, which appeared to me to be enough to devour a whole Country for

---

[1] JA's comment on Thaxter in his Diary entry of this date is considerably more pointed.
[2] Word omitted in MS.

an hundred miles round, our Guide went out and procured me the following Information.

Combentos de Fraires.		Parroquias.
Franciscos	1	Cathedral y St. Iago
La Trinidad	1	de la Capilla
Benitos	1	St. Nicolas
Augustinos	2	Sn. Roman
Dominicos	1	La Blanca
Mercenarios	1	Bejarua
Carmelitos	1	Sn. Martin
	8	Sn. Pedro
		Sn. Cosmes
Combentos de Monjas.		Sn. Lesmes
Sta. Dorothea		Sn. Esteban
Augustinas	1	Sn. Gil
Sta. Franciscas	2	
Carmelitas	1	Total
Augustinas	1	De Monjas — 10
Trinitarias	1	Fraires — 8
Bernardas	2	Parroquias — 15
Benitas	1	33
Calatrabas	1	
Sn. Il de fonso	1	

As the sum total is not conformable to the List I suppose the Monk who furnished our guide with it, omitted the names of two or three in the Enumeration. But what an Army of Ecclesiasticks is this for so small a Town as Burgos.

1780. January 12. Wednesday. We passed through several Villages, rode along the Side of a River; the Country more hilly than it had been for some time past, but it had a naked and poor appearance. We arrived at Bribiesca. Here there are two Convents one of Men, the other of Women, both Franciscans, and two Parish Churches. The Tavern was a large House and there were twelve good beds in it for Lodgers: Yet no Chimneys nor Windows, and the same indelicacy, the same Smoke and dirt as in all other Inns on the Journey. Yet they gave Us clean Sheets. The Kitchen was like all other Spanish Kitchens the greatest Curiosity and the most odious Object in the World. They are all very much alike.

1780. January 13. Thursday. We rode from Bribiesca to Pancourbo where We dined. We passed through Courbo, which is a little Village, with half a dozen other small Villages in Sight, in every one of which is a Church.

Pancourbo is at the beginning of the Rocks. There is the Appearance of an ancient Carriage Road up the steepest part of the Rocks. We passed between two Rows of Mountains consisting wholly of Rocks, the most lofty and craggy Precipices, I ever saw. These Rocky Mountains made the Boundary between the ancient Castile and Biscay. Pancourbo is the last Village in Old Castile. At Puente de la Rada, We were stopped by a Number of Officers and asked, if We had a Passport. When I produced my Passport from the Governor of Gallicia, they read it, with much respect, and let Us pass. We travelled four good Leagues this Afternoon and arrived at Ezpexo. Here We found the best public House, We had yet seen. The Neighbourhood of Biscay seemed to have had some Influence here; yet the Kitchen was Spanish like all others and their was neither Chimney nor Window in the House.

There was not a Tavern We had seen, but was filled with Religious Prints and Images, not indeed in the exquisite Style of Art of the ancient Greek and Roman Penates, but of very coarse and vulgar Workmanship. There were two beds in a Chamber, at the head of each of which was a Delph Vessell, for holy Water, Agua Santa, or Agua Benita. At the head of each also was a decent Cross about Nine Inches long, with an Image of Jesus Christ in some Metal, Tin, Bell-metal or Pewter, upon it. On the Wall was a Picture of the Virgin of Mount Carmel, or Virgo Maria de Monte Carmelo, and a great number of other Pictures, which I had not patience to enumerate.

1780 January 14. Fryday. We rode from Ezpexo to Orduña, four Leagues. The Road had been made by Art, all the Way, at a great expence: but the descent of the Mountains of Orduña was a great Curiosity. Those Mountains are chiefly Rocks of a vast height: but a Road has been blown out of the Rocks, from the Pinnacles of the Mountains, quite down into the Valley. After winding round and round the mountain, with the Road for a long distance, and observing the Marks of the Drills remaining in the Rocks all the Way, the Road came at last to a steep Pitch, where the only possible Method of making a passable Road for any Carriage, to go down or come up was by Serpentineing it thus

There is a fertile and well cultivated Valley at the Feet of these Mountains, in the Center of which is the Village of Orduña. In this narrow Space they have crouded two Convents one of Fraires and the other of Monjas. We saw the lazy Drones of Franciscans at the Windows of their Cells, as We passed. Att the bottom of the mountains We had a small Toll to pay, towards the Support of the Road. The Administrator sent to search our Trunks, but I sent him my Passport which produced a polite Message by his Clerk, that he had seen my Name in the Gazette; that he was very glad I was arrived; wished me Success and Prosperity; and desired to know if I wanted any thing, or if he could be any Way usefull to me? I returned in Answer to the Message that I was very much obliged by his Civility, and thanked him for his polite Attention; but that I wanted nothing.

In the Afternoon, We followed the Road, which pursues the Course of a little River, which originates in the Mountains of Orduña, and rode down between two Rows of Mountains to Lugiando, where We put up for the night four Leagues from Bilbao. In Lugiando, in the Lordship of Biscay, so near to Bilbao, where the King had no Officers, and the Grandees of Spain very little Land, where the Government was in a Biennial Parliament, I expected better fare, but We were disappointed and found the House as dirty and uncomfortable as almost any We had seen.

In the Course of this day and the day before We had seen great Numbers of Mules loaded with Merchandizes from Bilbao. The Mules and their Drivers looked well, in Comparison with those We had seen before. Their Burthens were Salt Fish, Sardines, Cod, and a sort of fish that We saw here, very plenty, called Besugo. The Mules carry also, Horse Shoes, ready made in Bilbao to be sold in various parts of the Kingdom. But what an Idea does this give of the State of Manufactures in a Country, when Horse Shoes must be carried many hundreds of miles upon the backs of Mules, to be sold for the Supply of the Farriers?

The Mountains of Biscay, of Bilbao, of Orduña, and Pancourbo, for by all these names are they called, are the most remarkable of any We had seen. Phillip the fifth made the first Carriage Road, through those of Pancourbo: The present King had done the most to those of Orduña.

The Mountains in Spain are the most irregular, misshapen Objects in Nature. They Resemble a tumbling Sea. Some are upright upon their Bases: others inclined to the North, the South, the East and the West in various Angles with the Horison. Some, under which We passed, projected over the Road and over our heads for hundreds of Yards, and will one day fall like that lately in Switzerland and bury all under them in an instant. It was a vexatious Sight to see the beautiful, fertile and well cultivated Valley, almost the only Spot We had yet seen in Biscay capable of cultivation, devoured by so many hives of Drones. We had hoped that there was enough of the Spirit of Liberty in Biscay, which they presumed to call a Republick, to have dissipated some of this tyrannical Superstition. But our hopes were all disappointed.

1780. January 15. Saturday. We followed the Road, by the Side of the River between two Rows of Mountains, untill We opened upon Bilbao. We saw the Sugar Loaf sometime before, i.e. a Mountain in the Shape of a Piramid which they call a Sugar Loaf.

The Town of Bilbao, which they call The Republick of Bilbao, is surrounded with Mountains. The Tavern at which We allighted was tolerable, for Spain, situated between a Church and Monastry. We were entertained with the Musick of the Convent from our first Arrival.

Soon after our Arrival Captain Babson and Captain Lovat made Us a Visit. Lovat was bound for America, by the first Wind, and Babson was soon to follow him; both in Letters of Mark. These opportunities to write to America were not to be neglected.

We took a walk down the River which We found pleasant enough; and while We were absent on our Walk, Mr. Gardoqui and Son came to visit me.

1780 January 16. Sunday. Reposed and wrote.

Sir   Bilbao January 16. 1780

I have the honour to inform Congress, that last night[3] I arrived in this place.

At Ferrol and Corunna, I was advised by all the Friends of America to undertake a Journey by Land. The Consul of France, and Mr. Lagoenere, a Gentleman who has acted for some time as an American Agent at Corunna, very obligingly offered me all the Assistance in their Power, and accordingly used their utmost dilligence to procure me the necessary Mules and Carriages, for the transportation of the small Number of Persons in company with me, and the small quantity of Baggage, which We found it indispensibly necessary to take with Us, having left more than two thirds of what We had with Us to take

---

[3] Here JA inadvertently omitted the phrase "and not before" in copying from his letterbook.

the chance of a Passage by Sea, to France. From the Eighth day of December, when We arrived at Ferrol, to the twenty sixth of the same month, when We sat off, from Corunna, We were detained by the violent Rains, and the impossibility of getting Accommodations for travelling.... All our Beds and Provisions We were obliged to carry with Us.—We travelled through the ancient Kingdoms of Gallicia, Leon, The Old Castile and Biscay, and although We made the best of our Way, without loss of time, We found it impossible to go more than eight Leagues a day, and sometimes not more than four. The Roads and Inns are inconvenient to a degree that I should blush to describe, and the Pains We suffered for want of Fire, in a cold Season of the Year, in a country where there are no Chimnies, gave Us all such violent Colds, that I was under great Apprehensions of our being seized with Fevers.

As We were so near Madrid, within about forty Leagues, I ballanced some time in my own mind, whether to go to that fine City. But considering that this would lengthen our Journey near an hundred Leagues; the severe Season of the Year, and above all the political Situation that I might be in, my Country not being yet acknowledged as a Sovereign State, by any formal Act of that court; and it being known that another Gentleman had a Commission to that Court, and expected soon to arrive, I thought it, upon the whole, the least hazardous to the Public Interest, to avoid that Route.

It may be of some Use to my Countrymen to transmit a few Observations upon the Country I have passed through, because it appears to me, that a Commerce extreamly advantageous to both Countries may be opened between Us and Spain as soon as our Independence shall be acknowledged by that Power, at least as soon as We shall obtain the great Object of all our Wishes, Peace.

The Province of Gallicia is one of the largest in Spain, and said to be one of the best peopled. Corunna is in effect the Principal City; although St. Iago, in respect to its Patron Saint, or more probably to the Archbishop, who resides there, is, in name, The Capital. This Province, one of those of which the antient Crown of Castile was formed, is washed by the Ocean for more than seventy Leagues, from Ribadeo on the Frontiers of Asturias, to the mouth of the River Minho, which seperates it from Portugal. This Coast, which is divided by Cape Finisterre, is provided on both Sides of the Cape, with Ports equally safe and convenient, which Nature seems to have prepared, around this Cape, an Object oftentimes so necessary to be made by Navigators, both at their departure from Europe and at their return, as so many Assylums both from the Apprehensions and the Consequences of Storms. The most known of these Ports are Ribadeo, Ferrol, Corunna and Camarinas, to the Eastward of Cape Finisterre: Corcubion, Muros, Pontevedra, Vigo, to the Westward, all proper to receive Vessels of the first rate, especially Ferrol and Vigo. The first, the most considerable Department of the Marine of Spain, is embellished with every Thing, that Art, and the Treasures profusely spent upon it for thirty Years past, could add to its happy Situation. Vigo, represented to be one of the most beautifull Ports in the World, is another Department of the Marine, more extensive and proper for such an Establishment than Ferrol itself. Besides these Ports, there is a Multitude of Harbours and Bays round Cape Finisterre, which afford a safe and convenient Shelter to Merchant Vessells.

With all these Advantages for foreign Commerce, this Province has but very little, but what is passive. It receives from abroad some Objects of daily Consumption, some of Luxury, some of convenience, and some even of the first necessity. At present it offers little for exportation to foreign Countries. The Sardine of its coast, the famous fish which it furnishes to all Spain; the Cattle which it fattens for the provision of Madrid; a few coarse linnens, which are its only Manufacture, and are well esteemed, are the Objects of its active Commerce, and form its ballance with the other Provinces. The Wine and the Grain, the chief productions of its Lands, seldom suffice for its consumption and never go beyond it.

The Liberty of Commerce with the Windward Islands, granted by the Court, within a few Years, and the particular Establishment of Couriers or Packet Boats to South America, in the Port of Corunna, have opened the Ports of that part of the new World to this Province, and although without Manufactures herself, or any of those Productions proper for America, she renders to foreign Hands the product of those which she receives from them and carries thither. In this Circulation of so many Treasures, she enriches herself with parts which she detaches from the whole.

The Civil Government of this Province is formed by a Superiour Tribunal called The Audience; to which an Appeal lies from all the subaltern Jurisdictions, public and private. This Court hears and determines as Souvereign and without Appeal all civil Affairs of a less Value than a Thousand Ducats or three thousand Livres. Appeals, in those which exceed that value are carried to the Chancery of Valladolid, or to the Council of Castile. Although Justice is gratis, on the Part of the Judges, who are paid by the Government, it is said to be not the less costly, tedious or vexatious. It may not be useless to observe that the Criminal Chamber, whose decrees extend to the punishment of Death and are executed without any Application to the King, or any other Authority, is composed only of three Judges, and these Three are the youngest of the whole Tribunal; and this order is generally followed in Spain, in the Composition of their Criminal Tribunals, altho' no one pretends to conjecture the Motive of so singular a Reverse of the natural order of Things. The Administration of the Royal Police, belongs also to the Audience, and forms the third Chamber into which this Tribunal is divided.

All the Military Authority, and the Government of the Troops in this Department, is in the Hands of the Captain General of the Province. There is not any one under him, who has even the Title of Commandant.... But in case of his Death or Absence, he is succeeded by the General Officer the most ancient in the Province. To this Title of Captain General, is added commonly that of President of the Audience, a Prerogative, which by uniting in his hands, the civil Authority to all that of his Place, gives him a Power the most absolute and unlimited.

The Inspection General and all the Œconomy of the Affairs of the King in the Province, belongs to the Intendant. The different Branches of the Public Revennue are all administered by Officers appointed by the King, as in the rest of the Kingdom, and there are no Farmers General as in France. Their Product is about twenty six Millions of Reals, or six millions five hundred thousand Livres, the Expence of Collection being deducted. The Expences of the Administration, including the Maintenance of three Regiments of Infantry, scattered about in different Places, do not exceed two Millions five hundred thousand Livres. The overplus goes into the Dry Docks, Arsenals, and Fortifications of Ferrol, to the Support of which, this Sum is far from being sufficient.

Such is in general The Government, Military, Political and Civil of this Province, and very nearly of all the others, except Biscay, Guipuscua and Alaba.

There is not in this Province any particular Jurisdiction for Commerce; but there is a Tribunal, under the Name of The Judge Conservator of Strangers, which takes Cognizance of all their Causes, civil and criminal, except the Case of Contraband. At this day the Judge Conservator of Strangers is the Governor of the Province himself, and the Appeals from his Judgment are carried directly to the Council of War, which is said to be a prescious Priviledge, by the form

233

and Brevity of Proceedure, compared with the expensive and insupportable delays of the ordinary Jurisdictions.

I cannot but think, that, if some measures could be taken, to convince the Court, that it is their Interest to take off the vast duties, with which Commerce is overloaded in this Part, fifteen per Cent being to be paid upon all Commodities exported and [4] upon all imported; and if the rigid Prohibition of Tobacco could be relaxed or repealed, several of the Productions of America would find a good Market here, and a Commerce opened, that would put a new Face upon this Province, and be profitable to America too. The Conveniency of such a Number of excellent Ports would be a vast Advantage, which Bilbao cannot have, as her Harbour is neither safe nor convenient, besides its being so much further down the stormy, turbulent Gulph of Biscay. Yet Biscay, which is now commonly used to comprehend Biscay proper, the principal City of which is Bilbao, though Orduña is the Capital, Guipuscoa the Capital of which is Saint Sebastian, and Alaba the Capital of which is Vitoria, three free Provinces whose Laws the Kings of Spain have hitherto been sworn to observe inviolate, have attracted almost the whole of the American Trade, because the King has no Custom House, nor Officers here, and there are no Duties to be paid.

It may seem surprising, to hear of free Provinces in Spain: But such is the Fact, that the High and independent Spirit of the People, so essentially different from the other Provinces, that a Traveller perceives it even in their Countenances, their Dress, their Air, and ordinary manner of Speech, has induced the Spanish Nation and their Kings to respect the Ancient Liberties of these People, so far that each Monarch, at his Accession to the Throne, has taken an Oath, to observe the Laws of Biscay.

The Government here, is therefore diametrically opposite to that of Gallicia, and the other Provinces. The King of Spain has never assumed any higher Title than that of Lord of Biscay. He has no Troops of any Sort in the Lordship, nor is there any standing Army; instead of which every Man is obliged to serve in the Militia. The King has no Custom House Officers, nor other Revenue Officers, nor other Officer whatsoever in the Lordship, except a Corregidor, and lately a Commissary of the Marine. This last is considered as an Encroachment and a Grievance; and the Authority of the Corregidor is very small as their lies an

---

[4] In LbC JA left a short blank space following this word, as if he meant to ascertain the duty levied on imports and supply it here. But no blank was left in RC (see the following note).

Appeal from his Judgment to another Tribunal, that of the Two Deputy Generals, who are biennially elected by the People. Few of the Grandees of Spain have any considerable Estates here. The Duke de Medina Cœli and the Duke of Berwick have some Lands here, of no great Value. The Lands generally belong to the Inhabitants and Possessors, who hold them of no Lord, but the King of Spain who is Lord of Biscay.

There is a Board of Trade here, which is annually constituted by the Merchants of the Place, partly by Lot and partly by Election, which decides all Controversies arising in Trade, and all the Affairs of Strangers. They have never admitted any foreign Consul to reside here, although it has been sollicited by Holland, England and France.

It is not at all surprizing that a Constitution, in its nature so favourable to commerce, should have succeeded.

In travelling through the Provinces of Leon and Castile, and observing the numerous Flocks of Sheep, with the most beautifull Fleeces of Wool in the World, I could not but wish, that some communication might be opened, by which the United States of America might be furnished with this necessary Article, from this Country. There are few of our Articles of Exportation, but might be sent to the Spanish Markett to Advantage. Rice, Pitch, Tar, Turpentine, Tobacco, Wheat, Flour, Ship timber, Masts, Yards, Bowsprits and Salt Fish, might be supplied to Spain at an Advantage, and in return she might furnish Us, with Wine, Oyl, Fruits, some Silks, some Linnens perhaps, and with any quantity of Wool, which is now exported to foreign Countries for Manufacture, and might as well be sent to Us, but above all, with Silver and Gold. It must be a work of time, of a freer intercourse between the two Nations, and of future Negotiations to ripen these Hints into a Plan, that may be beneficial to both. The System of Revenue, which it is dangerous and difficult to alter in Spain as well as in all other Countries of Europe, will be the principal Objection.

I have collected together with some difficulty a few Gazettes, which I have the honor to transmit to Congress, from which all the News may be collected, that I have been able to learn. Congress will easily perceive the Eagerness, with which the belligerent Powers are bent on War, without manifesting the least disposition for Peace, and most of all Great Britain, whose ostentatious display of trifling Successes, and weak Exultation in them, shews that nothing can divert her from her furious course.—But she is exhausting and sinking her Forces every day, without gaining any lasting or solid Advantage. And she has reason to fear, from the combined Fleets of France and Spain,

under such enterprizing, experienced and approved Officers as D'Estaing and Duchauffault, the entire ruin of her Commerce and Navy, in the course of a Campaign or two more.   John Adams
His Excellency Samuel Huntington Esq. President of Congress.[5]

1780 January 17. Monday. We dined with the two Messieurs Gardoqui, and a Nephew of theirs. The American Captains Babson, Lovat and Wickes dined with Us. I spoke to Mr. Gardoqui in behalf of Fifteen American Seamen, who had been Prisoners in Portugal, and he consented to furnish them Cloaths. I assured him that although I had no express and possitive Authority to interfere, I had no doubt that Congress would do all in their Power to repay him. This was afterwards done to his Satisfaction.

After Dinner the Gentlemen accompanied Us to the Parish Church over against Mr. Gardoqui's house, and then to the Old Parish Church of St. Iago, which is certainly known to have been standing in the Year 1300.... The High Altar appears to be very ancient, and wrought in wooden Figures, with very neat Work. The Choir and the Sacristie &c. like all others in the large Churches. We then went to the Chamber of the Board of Trade. This is a curious Institution. Annually on a certain day in the Beginning of January, all the Merchants of Bilbao meet, write their Names on a Ball or Ballot, which are put into a Box, from whence four are drawn by Lott. These four nominate a certain Number of Councillors or Senators.

This Board of Trade, in the first place, endeavours to persuade all Merchants between whom any Controversy has arisen, to agree, but if they cannot succeed Application must be made to the Board by Petition in Writing. It is then heard and determined, subject however to an Appeal, I know not where. This Board has successfully opposed the Reception of Consuls from all Nations. The Chamber is hung round with Pictures of the present King and Queen of Spain, the late King and Queen, the Royal Exchange of London, the Exchange of Amsterdam and the Exchange of Antwerp &c.

[5] LbC is a draft, written in detached parts, with the several parts marked by symbols to indicate their final order. RC (PCC, No. 84, I), in Thaxter's hand, with a formal leavetaking and signature added by JA, is endorsed by Thomson: "No. 3 Letter from John Adams Bilbao Jany. 16 1780 Read April 7." This is the first of the remarkable series of dispatches reporting on the political, diplomatic, commercial, military, and naval affairs of most of the nations of western Europe, often accompanied by newspapers and copies of innumerable documents, with which JA nearly overwhelmed Congress during the first months of his second mission to Europe.

There is an Academy, at Bergara, for the Education of the Youth of Biscay, Guipuscoa and Alava.

In the Spring Freshes, We were told, the Water is deep enough upon the Exchange and in the Streets for Vessells of an hundred Tons burthen, to float.

A Mr. Maroni, an Irish Gentleman, residing here as a Merchant, came to visit me. He told Us he had a Daughter in a Nunnery here: but it seemed by his conversation to be an incurable Grief to him: He appeared to have buried her in a more afflicting Sense than if she had been in her grave.

1780 January 18. Tuesday. We spent the Day in perambulating the Town. We visited the Wharves upon the River, went through the Marketts, which We found plentifully furnished with Fruits and Vegetables, Cabbages, Turnips, Onions, Beets and Carrots, Apples, Pairs, Raisins, Figgs and Nutts. We went as far as the Gate, where We had entered the Town, then turned up the Mountain by the Stone Stairs, where We saw some fine Gardens, with verdure and Vegetation. On our return We took a view of a Book Sellers Stall, but as this Country, though it gloried in its Liberty was not the Region of Litterature, We found nothing very curious or worth mentioning. We then walked in Succession, through every Street in the Town. After this, meeting The Messieurs Gardoquis, they went with Us to shew Us the trading part of the Citizens. They conducted Us to a Number of Shops, of Glass, China, Trinketts, Toys and Cutlary. We found nothing to give Us any great Idea of Bilboa or Biscay as a commercial Country, though there were several Shops and Stores, pretty large and full of Merchandizes.

1780 January 19. Wednesday. By particular invitation We went down the River on a Visit to the Rambler a Letter of Mark of Eighteen Guns, belonging to Mr. Andrew Cabot of Beverly, Captain Lovat Commander, and the Phœnix a Brigg of fourteen Guns belonging to Messieurs Traceys of Newbury Port, Captain Babson Commander. We were honoured with two Salutes of thirteen Guns each by Babson and one by Lovat. We dined at the Tavern on Shore and had an agreable Day. We were conducted to see a new Packett of the King on the Stocks, and his new Rope walks which were two hundred and ten Fathoms long.

1780 January 20th Thursday.[6] Although We endeavoured in Bil-

---

[6] This and the following four entries (through 30 Jan.) are wholly retro- spective, there being no entries in JA's Diary between 19 and 31 Jan. 1780.

bao to take as much Exercise as possible and to amuse ourselves as well as We could, and although the Attention and Hospitality of the House of Gardoqui had done every Thing in their Power to oblige Us, Our Residence in this place was nevertheless very far from being comfortable. We were all sick with violent Colds and Coughs, some of the Servants and Children were so ill that We lived under gloomy Apprehensions, of being detained a long time and perhaps loosing some of our Company. The Houses here as well as every where else were without Chimneys, fires or Windows, and We could find none of those Comforts and Conveniences to which We had been all accustomed from the Cradle, nor any of that sweet and quiet repose in Sleep upon which health and happiness so much depend. On the twentieth, however We summoned Resolution enough to take our departure from Bilbao, and passing over a mountainous Country and very bad roads arrived at the River or rather the Brook that divides Spain from France. The Houses in Biscay and Guipuscua appeared to be larger and more convenient than those in Gallicia, Castile or Leon, but the public Houses were much the same. In the last house in Spain We found one Chimney which was the only one We saw since We left that in the House of Mr. Detournelle the French Consul in Corunna.[7] In our Course We saw a few Villages and particularly Fontarabbia at a distance. We reached St. John De Luz, the first Village in France, and there We dined. And never was a Captive escaped from Prison more delighted than I was, for every Thing here was clean, sweet and comfortable in Comparison of any Thing We had found in any part of Spain.

1780 January 23. We arrived at Bayonne. Here We paid off our Spanish Guide with all his Train of Horses, Calashes, Waggon, Mules, and Servants. To do them Justice they had always shewn a disposition to assist and befriend Us to the Utmost of their Power, and We had no cause to complain of any improper Behaviour in any of them. I was obliged to sell my Mule, for which I was very sorry, as he was an excellent Animal and had served me very well. I sold him for what he cost me. We purchased a Post Chaise and hired some others for our Jour-

They are also the first entries in Part Three of the Autobiography included in CFA's edition, he having up to this point printed the original Diary entries for the voyage on the *Sensible* and the journey through Spain without drawing upon JA's occasional recollections and added comments in "Peace."

[7] Since JA made so much of the subject of chimneys, or rather the want of them, in Spain, it may be pointed out that on 24 Jan. he wrote from Bayonne to Joseph Gardoqui & Sons: "I assure you We discovered two or three fine Chimneys, besides that which you mentioned to us, which contributed not a little to our Health and Comfort" (LbC, Adams Papers).

ney. I made my Visit to the Governor and received his in return.

1780 January 25. We commenced our Journey to Bourdeaux. There is so much heath and uncultivated Land, and so many desolate Places, between Bayonne and Bourdeaux, that the Journey could not be very pleasant. It is a Region where one might expect to meet Robbers, but the Police of France was so vigilant and decisive that nothing of that kind was heard of at that time in any part of France. The Road in general was better because it was smoother than in any of the great paved Roads of the Kingdom. We found the Entertainment at all the Inns comfortable, the Horses and Carriages as alert and convenient as they are commonly in France, and I was too happy to be very anxious to make Observations on Minor Things.

1780 January 29. Saturday. We arrived at Bourdeaux. We had met Couriers and received Letters on the Road, inviting Us to alight at all the principal Inns in Bourdeaux. The Reputation of entertaining the American Ambassador, must have been the motive to all this Zeal, for our Number was so small, that the profit to be made of Us could not be great. As all the public Houses were alike unknown to me, I ordered our Postilion to drive Us to the best house in the City and left it to his Judgment to determine.

1780 January 30. We dined at the Hotel D'Angleterre, at the Invitation of Mr. Bondfield, in Company with Sir Robert Finlay, Mr. Le Texier and others. In the Evening We went to the Comedy where We saw Amphitrion and Cartouche.

1780 January 31. Monday. We dined at the Hotel D'Angleterre, again with Mr. Maccarty, Mr. Delap, Mr. Bondfield &c. at the Invitation of Sir Robert Finlay. Mr. Le Texier I found still entertained his Doubts and Scruples about the Success of the American Cause. Instead of entering into serious Argument with him, I treated his dismal forebodings with so much Levity, that he seemed to be hurt, as if he thought I was exposing him to ridicule. Perceiving this I desisted and only observed that I was perfectly satisfyed with our Prospects and [a] few Years if not months would shew that the American Cause stood upon firm Foundations. The Conversation at this as at all other such dinners, was upon commonplace Topicks and not worth Remembrance. Towards Evening Mr. Gabarus [Cabarrus] came in with the News of a Blow struck by Rodney upon the Spaniards off Gibraltar.

1780 Feb. 1. Tuesday. We spent the day in rambling about the Town viewing the principal Public Places, the Remains of Roman Antiquities, Vaubans Chateau Trompette &c. But as I had seen these before in April 1778 and as every Man who has been in Bourdeaux has seen them and every Man who shall travel to that City may see them, I shall not stay to give any Account of them. I heard a great deal concerning the manners and Morals of Bourdeaux which convinced me there was little difference from Paris.

1780 Feb. 2. Wednesday. We took Post [for] Paris and on

1780 Feb. 4. Fryday We arrived at Coué. We passed by Angouleme and encircled almost the whole Town. It stands on a high Hill and is walled all round. A fine healthy, Airy Situation, with several Streams of Water below it and fine interval Lands. The River Charente runs by it. The Lands from Bourdeaux to Angouleme, are chiefly cultivated with Vines, which afford but a poor Prospect in the Winter. In some Places Wheat was sown and Vines planted in alternate Ridges. Great Numbers of the Vineyards are in a Soil that has the greatest Appearance of Poverty. It is a red Loom intermixed with so many Pebbles and small Stones of a reddish Colour that it looks more like an heap of Stones or a dry gravel, than like a Soil where there is Earth enough for the Vines to take root. Other Vineyards are in a black Sand, intermixed with a few small Stones. Others are in fine, black, fat and mellow Mould. The numerous Groves, Parks and Forrests in this Country, form a striking Contrast with Spain, where the whole Country looks like a Bird deprived of its Feathers, every Tree, Bush and Shrub, being pared away.

We lodged at Coué, and in the Night it rained and froze at the same time, untill the Roads were become a glare Ice. The Postillions informed Us, it was impossible for their Horses, which in this Country are never frosted, to travel.

As this was the second time I travelled this road from Bourdeaux to Paris I shall pass over the remainder of the Journey.[8] On the fifteenth of Feb. I wrote to Congress

Sir   Paris 15. February 1780

I have the honor to inform Congress, that on the ninth of this Month, I had the good fortune to arrive in this City from Ferrol, where I arrived on the Eighth of December with Mr. Dana, Mr. Thaxter and the rest of the Company in tollerable health, after a Journey of near four hundred Leagues in the dead of Winter, through bad roads and worse Accommodations of every kind. We lost no time more than was indispensable to restore our health, which was several times much affected and in great danger: yet We were more than twice as long in

[8] For the arrival of the party in Paris and the events that immediately followed, see note on JA's Diary entry of 5 Feb. 1780.

making the Journey by Land, as We had been in crossing the Atlantic Ocean.

The next Morning after our Arrival in Paris, Mr. Dana and my self went out to Passy and spent the day with His Excellency Dr. Franklin, who did Us the honour the next day to accompany Us to Versailles, where We had the honour to wait on their Excellencies the Comte De Vergennes, Mr. De Sartine and the Comte De Maurepas, with each of whom We had the honour of a short Conference, upon the State of Public Affairs. It is sufficient for me at present to say in general, that I never heard the French Ministry so frank, explicit and decided, as each of these were, in the Course of this Conversation, in their declarations to pursue the War with vigour and afford effectual Aid to the United States. I learned with great Satisfaction, that they are sending under Convoy Cloathing and Arms for fifteen thousand Men to America: that seventeen Ships of the Line are already gone to the West Indies under Monsieur De Guichen, and that five or six more at least are to follow in Addition to ten or twelve they have already there.

I asked Permission of the Comte De Vergennes to write to him, on the Subject of my Mission, to which he chearfully and politely agreed. I have accordingly written to his Excellency and shall forward Copies of my Letter and of his Answer as soon as it may be safe to do so.[9]

The English are to borrow twelve Millions this Year, and it is said the Loan is filled up. They have thrown a Sop to Ireland, but have not appeased her Rage. They give out exactly such Threats, as they did last Year, and every other Year, of terrible Preparations: but Congress knows perfectly well how those Menaces have been accomplished. They will not be more fully executed next year than the last; and if France and Spain should throw more of their Force, expecially by Sea, into America the next Year, America will have no essential Injury to fear.

I have learned, since my Arrival at Paris, with the highest pleasure, the Arrival of Mr. Jay, Mr. Gerard and Mr. Carmichael at Cadiz, for whose Safety We had been under very great Apprehensions. I have now very sanguine hopes that a solid Treaty will soon be concluded with Spain; hopes which every Thing I saw and heard in that Country seemed to favour.

The Allyance Frigate, now under the Command of Captain Jones, with Captain Cunningham on board, is arrived at Corunna, where She is to be careened; after which She is to return to L'orient, and

---

[9] This exchange of letters is printed below.

from thence to go to America, as I am informed by Dr. Franklin.
Mr. Arthur Lee and Mr. Izzard are still in Paris, under many difficulties in procuring a Passage home. Mr. William Lee is at Brussells.
Mr. Izzard has been to Holland to obtain a Passage from thence, but
unfortunately missed his Opportunity and returned disappointed.

I have the Honor to be &c.   John Adams.
His Excellency Samuel Huntington Esqr. President of Congress.[1]

The first insinuation of the Propriety, Expediency, and necessity of
appointing a Minister Plenipotentiary to reside in Europe, ready to
negotiate a Peace whenever he might be invited to it, was made to
Congress, a year before this time by Mr. Gerard the French Minister
at Philadelphia by the Authority of the Count De Vergennes. But
Congress had neglected it, whether from a general Opinion that the
time had not yet arrived when there was a necessity for it, or whether
from the difficulty of agreeing on the Minister, I know not.[2] The Suggestion was renewed by the Chevalier De La Luzerne, upon his Arrival in Philadelphia. In both Cases it was the Expectation of the French
Ministry that Dr. Franklin would be elected.[3] In this respect Con-

[1] LbC is a draft. RC (PCC, No. 84, I), in Thaxter's hand, signed by JA, is endorsed in several hands: "No. 4 J. Adams Esqr. Paris Feby. 15th: 1780 Read May 15.—arrival in France—interesting News—" Several trifling variations in wording among the three texts have been disregarded here.

[2] This is somewhat disingenuous, or else JA's memory failed him badly. Gérard's proposal was in a communication to Congress dated 9 Feb. 1779 and sprang from the possibility that Spain's current efforts to mediate between Great Britain and France might succeed and thus bring on an early peace negotiation or at least a long truce (Wharton, ed., *Dipl. Corr. Amer. Rev.*, 3:39–40). The delay in appointing a peace commissioner was owing (1) to the inability of Congress over a period of seven months to agree on minimum American peace requirements (and hence on instructions to such a commissioner when he should be appointed), and (2) to the seesaw struggle between sectional factions in Congress over who should have this appointment and the coordinate appointment to Spain. Most of Gérard's activity in Philadelphia and most of his corre-

spondence with Vergennes in 1779 were concerned with these matters. See JA, Diary, 13 Nov. 1779, note 1, and references there.

[3] As early as 25 Dec. 1778 Vergennes reported to Gérard a conversation he had held with Franklin to ascertain "s'il avoit des pleins pouvoirs éventüels pour traiter avec la Cour de Londres." He had found Franklin did not have such powers. "Cependant M. franklin a pensé et je l'ai pensé comme lui, qu'il pourroit signé des traités et des conventions sub spe rati surtout y étant autorisé par nous." Since a negotiation might possibly begin very soon, not allowing time for the determinations of Congress, Vergennes went on, "je suis d'avis qu'il seroit d'autant plus utile que le Congrès lui envoyât à tout événément des pleins pouvoirs qui l'autoriseroient à prendre part aux négociations que pourrons entamer avec L'ang[leter]re" (Gérard, *Despatches and Instructions*, p. 451). In replying, 14 May, Gérard was obliged to tell Vergennes that such a proposal was hopeless. "Ce ministre [Franklin] vous a parlé en homme eclairé et dont les vües sont aussi justes qu'étendues; mais tous ses compatriotes ne lui ressemblent

gress disappointed them. In another point too, that is in the Commission to make a Treaty of Commerce with Great Britain Congress had gone farther than the French Ministry intended. Alone as I was in both Commissions, and feeling the whole Weight of the Trust reposed in me, I determined to proceed with the utmost Caution, deliberation and Prudence; to do nothing which should excite the smallest Jealousy in the French Court, or give our Ennemies the English the least Advantage of The United States or their Allies. But something appeared to be incumbent on me to do. Accordingly I began by writing to the Count De Vergennes the following Letter.

Paris, Hotel de Valois, Rue de Richlieu

Sir   Feb. 12. 1780

Having obtained Permission from your Excellency, Yesterday when I did myself the honour to wait on you at Versailles, to write on the Subject of my Mission, I have now the honour to acquaint you, that on the twenty ninth day of September last, The Congress of the United States of America did me the honour to elect me their Minister Plenipotentiary, to negotiate a Peace with Great Britain, and also to negotiate a Treaty of Commerce with that Kingdom, and the Honourable Francis Dana Esqr. a Member of Congress, and of the Council of Massachusetts Bay, Secretary to both Commissions.

As I was not at Congress, when this Transaction took place, I am not able to inform your Excellency, very particularly of the Rise and Progress of it. But from Conversation with Gentlemen at Boston, who

---

pas. . . . Son credit n'est plus tel qu'il puisse le sauver. On ne l'a confirmé dans son poste, que parce que cela faisoit planche pour M. [Arthur] Lée et si celui ci tombe, comme cela est probable, on pourra bien revenir à la premiere resolution de rappeller M. francklin" (same, p. 643). And again, 18 July: "Je ne dois pas vous dissimuler qu'aucun des deux partis n'a dans le Docteur Franklin la confiance que ses lumieres et sa probité meritent" (same, p. 794).

In the exceedingly complex maneuvers preceding and accompanying the elections in late September, though there was one proposal to join Franklin and JA together in the peace commission, in the end only a single ballot, that of John Dickinson, was cast for Franklin, and since Franklin had not been nominated, the vote of eleven states was considered unanimous for JA (Gérard to Vergennes, 25–27 Sept., same p. 895; Henry Laurens' Notes of Proceedings, Burnett, ed., *Letters of Members*, 4:438; Lovell to JA, 28 Sept., and Gerry to JA, 29 Sept., both in Adams Papers, Burnett, p. 450, 454; JCC, 15: 1103–1113).

It is not a little ironical that Gérard could observe to Vergennes immediately after JA's election: "Vos lettres, Mgr., à M. Adams ont produit des impressions très favorables sur lui" (letter of 25–27 Sept., *Despatches and Instructions*, p. 895). These letters were undoubtedly copies of JA's exchange with Vergennes, 11 and 13 Feb. 1779, introduced into the discussion of candidates by James Lovell; see Lovell to R. H. Lee, 27 Sept., Burnett, ed., *Letters of Members*, 4:443, and JA's Diary entry of 10–11 Feb. 1779.

were Members of Congress and from private Letters I learned in general, that it was not the Result of any sudden deliberation, or the Effect of any particular Event of War, prosperous or adverse: but a Measure that had been more than a Year under consideration, and finally adopted, upon this principle, that as it was uncertain at what time the belligerent Powers might be disposed to treat of Peace, which could not be concluded, without a Minister from the United States, it would save a great deal of time, for this Power to have a Minister in Europe, fully authorized to treat, and in concert with Ministers from the other Powers at War, to conclude a Peace with Great Britain, and a Treaty of Commerce consistent with that already made with his Most Christian Majesty, and such others as might be made with other Powers.

I am persuaded, it is the Intention of my Constituents and of all America, and I am sure it is my own determination, to take no Steps of Consequence in pursuance of my Commissions, without consulting his Majestys Ministers. And as various Conjectures have been and may be made concerning the nature of my Appointment and Powers, and as it may be expected by some that I should take some measures for announcing these to the Public, or at least to the Court of London, I beg the favour of your Excellencys Opinion and Advice upon these questions.

1. Whether, in the present Circumstances of Things, it is prudent, for me to acquaint the British Ministry, that I am arrived here, and have such Commissions, and that I shall be ready to treat, whenever the belligerent Powers shall be inclined to treat.

2. Whether it is prudent for me to publish, in any manner, more than the Journals of Congress may have already done, the Nature of my Mission?

3. Or whether, to remain, upon the Reserve, as I have hitherto done, since my Arrival in Europe?

If any Propositions should be made to me, directly or indirectly, from the British Ministry, I shall not fail to communicate them, without Loss of Time, to your Excellency: and I beg the favour of your Excellency, as I am the only Person in Europe, who has Authority to treat of Peace, that if any Propositions on the Part of Great Britain, should be made to his Majestys Ministers, that they may be communicated to me, at least as far as they may relate to the Interests of the United States.

Although I am not confined by my Commissions, nor Instructions, nor by any intimation from Congress, to reside in one place in Europe

rather than another; Yet my own Inclinations, as well as those of the Public, would be most gratified, and the public Service most promoted by my residing here. I must therefore request his Majestys Protection and permission to reside in this Kingdom for some time, either with or without assuming any Public Character, as your Excellency may think most adviseable. I have the Honour to be &c.   John Adams
His Excellency The Comte De Vergennes.[4]

I shall insert here the Answer of the Count de Vergennes, although it is not exactly in the order of Dates. It was in French, and the following is a litteral Translation of it.[5]

Versailles the 15 of February 1780
I have received, Sir, the Letter, which you did me, the honor to write me, on the twelfth of this month. I think, that before I resolve the different Points on which you consult me, it is convenient to wait for the Arrival of Mr. Gerard, because he is probably the Bearer of your *Instructions*[6] and he will certainly, have it in his Power to give me Explanations, concerning the Nature and Extent of your Commission; but in the mean time, I am of Opinion, that it is the part of Prudence, to conceal your eventual Character and above all to take the necessary Precautions, that the Object of your Commission remain unknown to the Court of London. Moreover, Sir, you may be assured, that The King sees you with Pleasure, in his Dominions, that you shall constantly enjoy his Protection, and the Prerogatives of the Law of Nations, and that I, in particular, will exert myself to give you Proofs of my Confidence, as well as of the Sentiments with which I have the honour to be, most perfectly, Sir, your most obedient and most humble Servant.   De Vergennes
M. Adams.

I request the Reader, to read attentively the foregoing Letter from the Count de Vergennes and make his own Observation upon it, before he reads mine, and then say whether I had reasons for the following Reflections which presented themselves irresistably to mind at that time, and which I have ever since thought and still think well founded.

[4] LbC is a draft with some corrections, none of them of consequence. RC (Archives Aff. Etr., Paris, Corr. pol., Etats-Unis, vol. 11) is in Thaxter's hand, signed by JA. Verbal differences among the several texts are negligible.

[5] RC (Adams Papers) is in a clerk's hand, signed by Vergennes, and en-dorsed by JA. But JA's translation was undoubtedly made from a copy of the French text that he had earlier recorded in a letterbook entitled "Peace. Correspondence with Vergennes & others" (Lb/JA/11).

[6] Emphasis added by JA.

1. The Instructions of a Sovereign to his Ambassador, are a Secret, and a confidential Communication between them: a sacred Deposit, committed by the Master to the Servant, which the latter is under the strongest tyes of honour, fidelity and Conscience to preserve inviolate, untill he has express Permission or Injunction to reveal it.[7]

2. The Count De Vergennes had been employed in several Embassies, and he had sent and in the Name of his Master instructed many Ambassadors. In short his Life had been spent in Diplomatic Courses. He could not therefore be ignorant of the sacred Nature of Instructions, or the Obligations of Ambassadors to keep them to themselves.

3. The Count de Vergennes had been so long in the habit of Intrigues to obtain the Instructions from foreign Courts to their Ambassadors, and probably paying for them very dear, that he had forgotten that the Practice was not lawfull.

4. The Count De Vergennes had probably instructed Mr. Gerard, by some means or other to penetrate into the Secrets of Congress and obtain from some of the Members or some of the Secretaries or Clerks, Copies of the most confidential Communications between Congress and their Ministers.

5. The Count De Vergennes expected that Mr. Gerard had succeeded, and would soon arrive with the Trophies of his Success. Of this Success, however, I have doubts. Mr. Jay with whom Mr. Gerard went to Europe in the same Ship can tell the World, if he will, as he has told me, the Arts and Importunities even to rudeness and ill manners, which he employed with Mr. Jay to obtain his Instructions. If he had been successfull in Pensilvania in obtaining Instructions he would not have been so zealous to procure a duplicate Copy from Mr. Jay.

6. The Count De Vergennes might imagine that I was so little read

[7] Actually the French minister in Philadelphia had not only instigated Congress' new measures relative to foreign affairs but had had the largest part in framing the instructions to the proposed peace commissioner. Gérard had constantly consulted with members of Congress while the debates on foreign affairs were in progress, furnished those who were favorably disposed toward France with arguments, and repeatedly memorialized Congress at Vergennes' express orders to explain just what the French government demanded. On the very day that they were adopted by Congress (14 Aug.), Gérard sent his principal a summary of the contents of both sets of the instructions that were eventually issued to JA, prefacing his summary with the remarkable statement that "Elles m'ont été communiquées avant d'etre portées au Congrès" (*Despatches and Instructions*, p. 847). His summary was perfectly accurate except for one item that is not to be found in the instructions for either peace or commerce. In respect to France, Gérard said, "le plénipotentiare lui communiquera ses instructions" (same, p. 848).

in the Law of Nations and the Negotiations of Ambassadors, and had so little Experience in the World, or to Use one of his own Expressions on another Occasion, so much Bonhommie, that upon the Intimation in his Letter, I would in all Simplicity and Naivete, send him a Copy of my Instructions.

7. Some allarming Ideas were excited by the Consideration that my Sovereign was an Assembly of more than fifty members, and fifty incorruptible Men all capable of containing a Secret, was not always to be expected. For the honor of that Congress however it is but Justice to say that I believe their Secrets were as well kept as Secrets ever were by any Government in the World.

8. The Nature of my Instructions, with which I was not at all satisfied and was consequently more determined to keep from the French as well as English and other Courts. The Articles of my Instructions relative to the Boundaries of the United States and to the Fisheries were by no means agreable to me, and I had already reasons enough to suspect and indeed to believe, that the French Court, at least that the Count De Vergence, would wish me to go to the utmost Extent of my Instructions in relinquishing the Fisheries and in contracting the Boundaries of the United States; whereas on the contrary it was my unalterable Determination to insist on the Fisheries and on an ample Extention of our Boundaries, as long as my Instructions would justify me: I foresaw that if these Instructions were communicated to the French, they would have it in their Power, in case of a negotiation to impart them to the British Ambassador and encourage him to insist on his part on terms that would greatly embarrass me and ultimately injure my Country in very essential Points.

The order of Dates would have required the Insertion of the following Letters, before.

A Versailles the 31. December 1779

I have received the Letter, which you did me, the honour to write me, on the sixth of October last.[8]

I was well persuaded that Mr. De Chavagne would endeavour, to procure for you, on board his Ship, every gratification in his Power. In this respect he has complied with the communications I made to him of the Intentions of the King.

It is with pleasure that I have learned, that having been charged by Congress with an important Mission, you have been able to take Advantage, a second time of the Frigate the Sensible, to return to France.

[8] LbC is in Adams Papers; printed in JA, *Works*, 7:117.

I have the Honour to be, with the most perfect Consideration, Sir, your most humble and most obedient Servant.   De Sartine
Mr. John Adams.[9]

Sir   Paris Feb. 13. 1780
    It was not, untill my Arrival at Passy, that I had the honor of your Excellencys Letter of the thirty first of December last.
    When his Majestys Intentions of granting me a Passage to America were communicated to me, I had little expectation of returning in the same Frigate: But The Congress having honoured me, with a fresh Mission to Europe, Their Excellencies the late and present Ministers from his Majesty to the United States, concurred in a Proposal to Congress and a requisition to the Commander of the Frigate to afford me a Passage, in her Voyage home, to which Captain Chavagne agreed, with particular marks of Politeness to me, Mr. Dana and the others who accompanied me.
    I have again the pleasure to express to your Excellency, the Obligations I am under to the Captain and all the Officers of the Sensible, for their goodness to me and mine. But it is more particularly my Duty to express again my Thanks to his Majesty for this fresh favour; to Mr. Gerard and the Chevalier De La Luzerne who procured it for me; and to your Excellency for your Approbation of it. I have the honour to be, with the greatest respect, your Excellencys most obedient and most humble Servant   John Adams
His Excellency Mr. De Sartine[1]

                                Paris, Hotel de Valois, Rue de Richlieu
Dear Sir   Feb. 15. 1780
    Since my Arrival at Paris, I had the pleasure of your Letter of the first of this month. I thank you, Sir, for your kind Congratulations on my Arrival, and am glad to learn that the Letters I forwarded to you went safe.
    When I left Boston, which was on the thirteenth of November, our public Affairs in the military Line[2] wore a very favourable Aspect. The News of General Lincoln's being in possession of Georgia, by the Aid of the Count D'Estaing, was expected every moment, and great preparations were making by General Washington to cooperate with

---

[9] RC (Adams Papers) is in a clerk's hand, signed by Sartine. JA doubtless made his translation from a copy he had recorded earlier in Lb/JA/11.
[1] LbC is a draft with corrections too minor to require indication here.
[2] Preceding four words are inserted from LbC; they were inadvertently omitted by JA in transcribing this letter.

that great Officer in the Reduction of New York. You are sufficiently informed of the Reverses, which have taken place, since. But by Letters I have since received from Boston, the Misfortune of Georgia, seems not to have made any great Sensation. The People of America are so habituated to disappointment in the Events of War, that they have learned Philosophy enough to bear them very steadily.

In the civil Way, the Settlement of foreign Affairs, which had given the People the greatest Anxiety, seemed to give general Satisfaction: how long it will last will depend upon Contingencies.

I was told by a Member of Congress from New Hampshire, that your Accounts had been received by Congress, but I did not learn that they had been decided on.

Mr. Johnson, to whom and Family please to present my respects, is appointed to examine and certify his Opinion, of all public Accounts in France.[3] The Award of your Arbitrators, I should be glad to see, and shall ask a Sight of it, the first leisure Opportunity.

Your Resolution to harbour no Enmity, and to be of no Party is amiable. Parties, in some degree or other, are common to all Countries, Nations and Governments: and although they may not be more real or more inveterate in free Governments than in others, yet they are more open, more public and make more noise. I fear it must be confessed that there has been a virulence of Party Spirit, in the foreign Affairs of the United States, which has injured worthy Characters on both Sides, and done Us much harm. I think therefore that it is the Duty of every good American to take up the same resolution with you, to be concerned in no personal disputes, or Party Animosities, at least any farther than they mix themselves unavoidably with the public Cause and Interest, from which they sometimes make themselves inseperable. I shall be pleased with the continuance of the same agreable Acquaintance, which has ever subsisted between Us, and wish you to believe me, with esteem your Friend and humble Servant   John Adams.

Jonathan Williams Esqr. at Nantes

Dear Sir   Paris Feb. 15. 1780

I have the pleasure to inclose to you, two Letters, from your Friends at Boston, who are all well except Mr. Gray your Brother, who is not probably now living, as he was supposed to be in the last Stage of a Consumption. I shall be glad of an Opportunity of sending Letters

---

[3] Johnson was appointed to this service on 29 Sept. 1779 (JCC, 15:1126), but he found it too thorny a task and soon resigned.

from you to your Family, or from them to you, and to hear of your Welfare.

Your humble Servant   John Adams
Revd. Isaac Smith[4]

Sir   Paris Feb. 15. 1780

I have the pleasure of inclosing two Letters from your Friends at Braintree to you, and one from Mr. Cranch to a Relation of his. It gave me pleasure to hear of your safe Arrival in Europe, And I shall be happy in an Opportunity of conveying any Letters to your Friends. I am, Sir, your most obedient Servant   John Adams
Mr. Joseph Palmer.[5]

Whether it was consistent with the Character of a great or an honourable Statesman or not, to give me, so early and so just cause of Jealousy of his Intentions, those of the Count De Vergennes were too manifest to be mistaken in his Letter of the 15th of February. His Aim was plainly to obtain from me Copies not only of my Commissions but of my most secret and confidential Instructions. I was determined to express however no Surprize, but to comply with his Wishes as far as I could with honour and Safety and no farther. I wrote him the following Letter.

Sir   Paris February 19. 1780

I have received the Letter which your Excellency did me the honour to write me, on the fifteenth of this month, and least I should not have explained sufficiently, in my Letter of the twelfth, the Nature and Extent of my Commissions, I have now the Honour to inclose, attested Copies of both, as well as of that to Mr. Dana.[6]

With regard to my Instructions, I presume your Excellency will not judge it proper, that I should communicate them, any further than to assure you as I do in the fullest manner, that they contain nothing,

---

[4] Isaac Smith Jr. (1749–1829), Harvard 1767, AA's first cousin; he left America for England on the eve of the Revolution but returned in 1784 and served, among other things, as librarian of Harvard College, 1787–1791 (JQA, *Life in a New England Town*, p. 20, note; Smith's correspondence with various members of the Adams family, in Adams Papers). "Mr. Gray your Brother" was Edward Gray, who had married Isaac's sister Mary. The enclosed letters have not been identified.

[5] Joseph Palmer, nephew of Gen. Joseph Palmer of Germantown in Braintree; he had just graduated from Harvard and was returning to his home near Plymouth, England (Gen. Joseph Palmer to Benjamin Franklin, 3 Aug., 12 Nov. 1779, summarized in *Cal. Franklin Papers*, A.P.S., 2:124, 168). The enclosed letters have not been identified.

[6] JA's commissions are printed at the beginning of Part Three of his Autobiography, p. 178–180, above.

inconsistent with the Letter or Spirit of the Treaties between his Majesty and The United States, or the most perfect friendship between France and America, but on the contrary the clearest orders to cultivate both.

I have hitherto conducted, according to your Advice, having never communicated to any Person, since my Arrival in Europe, the nature of my Mission, excepting to your Excellency and Dr. Franklin, to whom it was indeed communicated by a Resolution of Congress, and to him in confidence.

I shall continue to conceal, as far as may depend upon me, my actual Character: but I ought to observe to your Excellency, that my Appointment was as notorious in America as that of Mr. Jay or Dr. Franklin before my departure, so that it is probably already known to the Court of London, although they have not regular Evidence of it. I mention this least some Persons might charge me with publishing, what I certainly did not publish.

I thank your Excellency for the Assurances, of his Majestys Protection and of your Confidence, which it shall be my Study and Endeavour at all times to deserve. I have the honour to be, with the greatest respect, your Excellencys most obedient and most humble Servant

John Adams

His Excellency the Comte De Vergennes.[7]

To this Letter I received an Answer of which the following is a litteral Translation.[8]

Versailles the 24. of February 1780

I have received, Sir, the Letter which you did me the honor to write me on the nineteenth of this month. Your Full Powers, of which you have been so good as to send me a Copy, are perfectly conformable to the Account which Mr. Gerard had written me of them, and they leave Us nothing to desire, either in their form or Substance. I think there is no inconvenience, in informing the Public of the principal Object of your Mission, I mean to speak of the future Pacification. *It will be, indeed announced in the Gazette of France, when that shall make mention of your Presentation to the King and Royal Family:*

---

[7] LbC is a draft with minor revisions. RC (Archives Aff. Etr., Paris, Corr. pol., Etats-Unis, vol. 11) is in Thaxter's hand, signed by JA; above the text is the notation: "M. De Rayneval," to whom it was obviously referred.

[8] RC (Adams Papers) is in a clerk's hand, signed by Vergennes, and endorsed by JA. JA's translation is from a copy he had entered in Lb/JA/11. The passages in italics were underscored by JA when he wrote the translation into his Autobiography.

And it will depend upon you to give to your eventual Character, a greater Publicity, by causing it to be inserted in the public Papers of Holland. I should only desire, that you would be so good as to communicate to me the Article, before you send it. *As to the Full Power, which authorizes you to negotiate a Treaty of Commerce with the Court of London, I think it will be prudent, to make no communication of it to any Person whatsoever, and to take all possible Precautions, that the English Ministry may not have any Knowledge of it prematurely.* You will surely perceive, of yourself, the Motives which induce me, to advise you to this Precaution, and it would be superfluous in me to explain them.

As to what relates to your Instructions, Sir, I am certain, that they have for their essential and invariable Basis, the Treaties subsisting between the King and the United States; Mr. Gerard has assured the King of this in the most positive manner, and his Majesty renders too much Justice to the Rectitude of Congress, and to the Stability of Sentiments, which it has hitherto manifested, to have ever had, and for ever to have, the smallest doubt in this respect.[9] This manner of thinking, Sir, will convince you, that We have no Necessity to see your Instructions, to estimate their Principles and their disposition relative to Great Britain.

I have the Honour to be, most perfectly, Sir your most humble and most obedient Servant   De Vergennes
Mr. Adams.

I again request the particular Attention of the Reader to this Letter. The Count evades ingeniously enough his improper Attempt to draw out my Instructions, from their concealment. But his Anxiety to have my Commission to negotiate a Treaty of Commerce with Great Britain, concealed, excited some Surprize and some perplexity. I was not clear that I suspected his true Motives. The United States were clearly, at as full Liberty to negotiate concerning Commerce as concerning Peace. In both they must be governed by their Treaties with France. But not in one more than the other. However Time brought to light, what I but imperfectly suspected. The Count meditated at that time no doubt, what he soon carried into Execution with too much Success, his Intrigues with Congress at Philadelphia, to get my Commission to negotiate a Treaty of Commerce, annulled, without renewing it to the five Commissioners whom they afterwards appointed to negotiate

[9] RC: "... et sa Mté. rend trop de justice à la droiture du Congrès et à la stabilité des sentiments qu'il a manifestés jusqu'à présent, pour avoir jamais eû, et pour avoir jamais le moindre doute à cet egard."

Peace.[1] It was intended to keep Us embroiled with England as much and as long as possible, even after a Peace. It had that Effect for Eleven Years. The United States never had Spirit, decision and Independence, to remove this Obstacle to a friendly Understanding with England till 1794, when Mr. Jay sacrificed, and Mr. Washington diminished his Popularity by a Treaty which excited the insolent Rage of France without a Colour of Justice. The Members of Congress, who suffered themselves to become the Instruments of the Count, and His Minister the Chevalier De La Luzerne and his Secretary Mr. Marbois, in this humiliating and pernicious Measure of annihilating the Power of negotiating on Commerce, I am not able to enumerate very exactly. I have heard mentioned Mr. Livingston, Mr. Madison and Dr. Witherspoon. Those who are disposed to investigate this Subject are at Liberty to do it. If it would diminish the disposition which has long prevailed and still prevails in too many Individuals to sacrifice the honor and Interest of their country to their Complaisance to France, it would answer a good Purpose.

I thought it most prudent at present to conform to the Counts Advice, although it was not in this particular satisfactory to me, and wrote him accordingly. Although I could not perceive any candid, equitable or honourable Motives for concealing one of my Commissions more than the other, I did not think proper to tell him so.

Sir   Paris 25 February 1780.
I had last Evening the Honour of your Excellencys Letter of Yesterdays Date, and shall conform myself to your Advice.

I shall esteem myself highly honoured by a Presentation to the King and Royal Family, and shall wait your Excellencys Directions concerning the time of it. I shall not think myself at Liberty to make any publication of my Powers to treat of Peace, untill it shall have been announced in the Gazette; after which I shall transmit to your Excellency any Paragraph which may be thought proper to publish in the Gazettes of Holland, and take your Advice upon it, before it is sent. My other Powers shall be concealed, according to your Advice; and I shall have the honour, to pay my respects to your Excellency very

[1] On Congress' revocation, 12 July 1781, of JA's commission to negotiate a treaty of commerce with Great Britain, see Diary entry of 12 Jan. 1783 and note 1, with references there. The background and circumstances of this action remain even yet somewhat obscure. But it should be pointed out that it followed, rather than preceded, the joining of four other commissioners with JA in the negotiation for peace, under new instructions, 15 June 1781; see Diary entry of April 1782, note 1.

soon at Versailles. I have the honour to be with the greatest respect, Sir, your most obedient and most humble Servant   John Adams His Excellency the Comte De Vergennes.[2]

Having waited from the 25 of February to the 21. of March, without learning any Thing further on the Subject I wrote to the Count again.

Paris Hotel De Valois, Rue De Richlieu

March 21. 1780

In the Letter which you did me the honour to write me, on the twenty fourth of February, Your Excellency proposed that the principal Object of my Mission [*remainder missing*] [3]

[2] LbC is a draft. RC (Archives Aff. Etr., Paris, Corr. pol., Etats-Unis, vol. 11) is in Thaxter's hand, signed by JA. Textual variations among the several texts are negligible.

[3] LbC (of the complete letter) is a draft with several revisions and afterthoughts interlined and added; the text as revised is printed in JA, *Works*, 3: 266–267. RC (Archives Aff. Etr., Paris, Corr. pol., Etats-Unis, vol. 11) is in Thaxter's hand, signed by JA. JA went on to remind Vergennes that in his letter of 24 Feb. the Foreign Minister had stated that an announcement of JA's peace commission would appear in the *Gazette de France* after his formal presentation at court; this presentation had taken place on 7 March, "but no notice has been taken of it in the Gazette of France. Whether this omission is accidental, or whether it is owing to any alteration in your Excellency's sentiments, I am not able to determine." Vergennes waited nine days before replying, then calmly explained that a notice in the *Gazette de France* would be, he now realized, an irregularity, and attached a one-sentence draft of an announcement that would be inserted, instead, in the *Mercure de France* (an unofficial journal, the political news in which was controlled by the French government); see Vergennes to JA, 30 March, Adams Papers; translation in JA, *Works*, 7:139.

Chronology

Chronology

JOHN ADAMS' LIFE AND PUBLIC SERVICE, 1735–1826

1735
Oct. 30 (Oct. 19, O.S.): Born in the North Precinct of Braintree (which in 1792 was taken off and named Quincy), Mass.

1740's
Attends Mrs. Belcher's and Joseph Cleverly's schools in Braintree.

1750–1751
Attends Joseph Marsh's school in Braintree.

1751
Enrolls in Harvard College.

1755
July: Graduates A.B.
Aug.: Begins to keep school in Worcester, Mass.
Nov. 18: Begins his Diary.

1756
Aug.: Signs contract to read law with James Putnam for two years.

1758
July: Attends Harvard commencement and receives M.A.
Oct.: Returns from Worcester to live in Braintree.
Oct.–Dec.: Tries (and loses) first case as a practicing lawyer (Field v. Lambert) before Colonel and Justice Josiah Quincy in Braintree.
Nov.: Admitted to the Suffolk bar, Jeremiah Gridley serving as his sponsor, and begins to practice in the Inferior Court of Common Pleas.

1760

Drafts essays on appointment of new chief justice and on evils of licensed houses.

1761

Feb.: Records arguments in Superior Court of Judicature on writs of assistance.

May: Upon the death of his father, inherits Braintree property (later known as the John Quincy Adams Birthplace).

Nov.: Admitted to practice in the Superior Court of Judicature.

1762

Spring: Begins serving on town committees and traveling the Inferior and Superior Court circuits. His circuit riding continues for fourteen years.

Aug.: Admitted barrister in the Superior Court of Judicature.

Oct.: His surviving courtship correspondence with Abigail, daughter of Rev. William Smith of Weymouth, begins.

1763

June–July: His first known newspaper contributions, signed "Humphrey Ploughjogger," are published in the *Boston Evening Post* and *Boston Gazette.*

1764

April–May: Inoculated in Boston for the smallpox.

Oct. 25: Marries Abigail Smith (AA) and brings her to live in the house inherited from his father.

1765

Jan.: Joins a lawyers' "sodality" in Boston for the study of legal history and theory.

March: Elected surveyor of highways in Braintree.

June: Travels the eastern court circuit to Maine for the first time.

July 14: His 1st daughter, Abigail 2d (AA2), is born.

Aug.–Oct.: Publishes "A Dissertation of Canon and Feudal Law" in installments in the *Boston Gazette.*

Sept.: Composes the Braintree Instructions denouncing the Stamp Act.

Dec.: Named of counsel for Boston to plead for reopening of the courts.

1766

Jan.: Publishes three letters, signed "Clarendon," in the *Boston Gazette* on the British constitution and American rights.

March: Elected a Braintree selectman.

July: Becomes active in the improvement of professional practice of the law through the Suffolk bar association.

1767

July 11: His 1st son, John Quincy (JQA), is born.

1768

March: Declines to stand again for Braintree selectman.

April: Moves to the "White House" in Brattle Square, Boston.

June: Writes instructions for the Boston representatives to the General Court protesting the seizure of Hancock's sloop *Liberty*.

Dec. 28: His 2d daughter, Susanna (d. 4 Feb. 1770), is born.

Winter: Successfully defends John Hancock in admiralty court against charges of smuggling in connection with the sloop *Liberty*.

1769

Spring: Moves to Cold (or Cole) Lane, Boston.

May: Writes instructions for the Boston representatives to the General Court protesting the presence of British troops and the growing power of admiralty courts.

May–June: Successfully defends Michael Corbet and three other sailors in admiralty court for the killing of Lt. Panton of the British Navy.

Aug.: Takes two law clerks (Austin and Tudor) into his Boston office because of his expanding legal business.

Sept.: Engaged by James Otis as co-counsel following the Robinson affray; case concluded in Otis' favor, July 1771.

1770

Jan.: Begins serving as clerk of the Suffolk bar association.

March: Agrees to defend Capt. Thomas Preston, officer commanding the British soldiers in the "Boston Massacre."

May 29: His 2d son, Charles (CA), is born.

June: Elected a representative to the General Court from Boston; serves until April 1771.

Oct.–Nov.: Successfully defends Preston and the soldiers in the "Boston Massacre" trials.

Moves during this year to "another House in Brattle Square."

1771

April: Moves back to Braintree.

June: Travels to Connecticut for his health and takes the mineral waters at Stafford Springs.

1772

Spring: Writes and presumably delivers a patriotic oration at Braintree at the request of the town.

Sept. 15: His 3d son, Thomas Boylston (TBA), is born.

Nov.: Moves to Queen Street (later Court Street) in Boston and maintains his law office there until the outbreak of hostilities.

Dec.: Successfully defends Ansell Nickerson in admiralty court against charges of murder; case concluded in July–Aug. 1773.

1773

Jan.–Feb.: Publishes articles in the *Boston Gazette* answering William Brattle and opposing crown salaries to Superior Court judges.

May: Elected by the House a member of the Council but is negatived by Hutchinson.

1774

Feb.: Buys his father's homestead (later known as the John Adams Birthplace) from his brother Peter Boylston Adams.

March: Furnishes legal authorities for impeachment proceedings against Chief Justice Peter Oliver. About the same time drafts report for General Court on Massachusetts' northern and western territorial claims.

May: Elected by the House a member of the Council but is negatived by Gage.

June: Elected a Massachusetts delegate to the Continental Congress; moves his family to Braintree.

June–July: Travels "for the tenth and last time on the Eastern Circuit" in Maine, and parts with his loyalist friend Jonathan Sewall at Falmouth (Portland).

Aug.: Travels from Boston to Philadelphia with the Massachusetts delegation to the Continental Congress.

Sept.–Oct.: Attends first Continental Congress.

Oct.–Nov.: Returns from Philadelphia to Braintree.

Nov.–Dec.: Attends first Provincial Congress in Cambridge as a member from Braintree.

Dec.: Reelected to Continental Congress.

1775

Jan.–April: Publishes essays signed "Novanglus" in the *Boston Gazette* in answer to Daniel Leonard's "Massachusettensis" articles.

March: Elected a selectman of Braintree.

April–May: Travels from Braintree to Philadelphia.

May–July: Attends second Continental Congress; proposes George Washington as commander in chief.

July: Elected by the House a member of the Council; resigns in April 1776.

July: Writes letters to AA and James Warren ridiculing John Dickinson's conciliatory views; the letters are intercepted and published by the British in August and produce a great sensation.

Aug.: Returns from Philadelphia to Braintree, attends the Massachusetts Council in Watertown, and is reelected to Continental Congress.

Aug.–Sept.: Travels from Boston to Philadelphia.

Sept.–Dec.: Attends Continental Congress and plays a principal part in the measures leading to the establishment of an American navy, including the composition and publication of *Rules for the Regulation of the Navy of the United Colonies of North-America.*

Oct.: Appointed Chief Justice of Massachusetts; resigns in Feb. 1777 without ever serving.

Dec.: Obtains leave from Congress and returns from Philadelphia to Braintree, attends the Massachusetts Council in Watertown, visits the army headquarters in Cambridge, and is reelected to Continental Congress.

1776

Jan.: Drafts proclamation for the General Court to be read at the opening of courts of justice and town meetings.

Jan.–Feb.: Travels from Braintree to Philadelphia.

Feb.–Oct.: Attends Continental Congress.

March–April: Writes *Thoughts on Government*, which is "put ... under Types" by R. H. Lee and widely used in state constitution making.

May: Advocates establishment of new state governments and writes preamble to the resolution of 15 May recommending such action to the states.

June: Appointed president of the newly formed Continental Board of War and Ordnance.

June–July: Appointed to committee to draft a declaration of independence and makes the principal speech in favor of the resolution for independence.

June–Sept.: Drafts a "Plan of Treaties" and instructions to the first American Commissioners to France.

Sept.: Journeys to Staten Island with Benjamin Franklin and Edward Rutledge to confer with Admiral Lord Howe.

Oct.: Obtains leave from Congress and returns from Philadelphia to Braintree.

Nov.: Reelected to Continental Congress.

1777

Jan.: Travels from Braintree to attend Continental Congress sitting in Baltimore.

March: Travels to Philadelphia when Congress adjourns to that city.

March–Sept.: Attends Congress and continues to preside over the Board of War and Ordnance.

July 11: His 3d daughter, Elizabeth, is stillborn.

Sept.: Leaves Philadelphia upon the adjournment of Congress after the battle of Brandywine and travels to York via Trenton, Easton, Bethlehem, and Reading.

Nov.: Obtains leave from Congress, returns to Braintree, and resumes his law practice, traveling to Portsmouth in December to defend the owners of the *Lusanna*. Elected by Congress a joint commissioner (with Franklin and Arthur Lee) to France, replacing Silas Deane; commission dissolved Sept. 1778, with Franklin named sole minister.

1778

Feb.–March: Sails with JQA from Quincy Bay aboard the Continental frigate *Boston* to Bordeaux.

April: Joins Franklin's household at the Hôtel de Valentinois in Passy.

May: Received in first audience by Louis XVI of France.

1779

Feb.: Exchanges letters with Vergennes on the conduct of Silas Deane and in defense of Arthur Lee, and learns immediately thereafter he has been relieved of his joint commission.

March: Takes leave of the French court.

March–June: In Nantes, Brest, Lorient, Saint Nazaire, and on board the *Alliance* arranging for the exchange of prisoners of war and awaiting passage to America.

June–Aug.: Sails from Lorient to Boston with La Luzerne aboard the French frigate *La Sensible*.

Aug.: Proposes founding the American Academy of Arts and Sciences, incorporated May 1780.

Aug.–Nov.: Elected to represent Braintree in convention to frame a new state constitution; attends the convention and drafts *The Report of a Constitution ... for the Commonwealth of Massachusetts* which is adopted, after some amendments, by the voters of Massachusetts in 1780.

Sept.: Elected minister by Congress to negotiate treaties of peace and commerce with Great Britain; commissions revoked June–July 1781.

Nov.–Dec.: Sails with JQA and CA from Boston aboard *La Sensible* to Ferrol, Spain.

Dec.–Jan.: Travels across northern Spain.

1780

Jan.–Feb.: Travels from Bayonne to Paris and takes up residence at the Hôtel de Valois in Rue de Richelieu.

June: Commissioned an agent by Congress to negotiate a Dutch loan.

July–Aug.: Travels from Paris to Amsterdam, before learning of his commission, to explore the possibility of Dutch financial aid to the United States. Remains in the Netherlands until July 1781.

Dec.–Jan.: Elected minister by Congress to negotiate a treaty of amity and commerce with the Netherlands.

1781

March–May: Drafts, submits, and prints a memorial to the States General urging Dutch recognition of American sovereignty.

June: Elected by Congress first among five joint commissioners (JA, Franklin, Jay, Laurens, and Jefferson) to treat for peace with Great Britain.

July: Returns to Paris to discuss with Vergennes the proposed peace mediation of the Russian and Austrian courts; rejects Vergennes' proposals and returns to Amsterdam, where he remains until Oct. 1782.

July–Aug.: JQA leaves Amsterdam for St. Petersburg as private secretary to Francis Dana; CA begins his return voyage to America.

Aug.: JA awarded *in absentia* LL.D. by Harvard College.

1782

Jan.–March: Presses for recognition at The Hague.

April: Recognized by the States General as minister plenipotentiary to the Netherlands and granted an audience by the Stadholder, Willem V.

May: Takes up residence at the Hôtel des Etats-Unis at The Hague, purchased as the first American legation building in Europe.

June: Contracts with a syndicate of Amsterdam bankers for the first Dutch loan to the United States, 5,000,000 guilders.

Oct. 8: Signs at The Hague a treaty of amity and commerce with the Netherlands.

Oct.: Travels from The Hague to Paris.

Oct.–Nov.: Assists in negotiating and with his fellow commissioners signs at Versailles, 30 Nov., the Preliminary Treaty between the United States and Great Britain. Remains in Paris.

1783

April: JA, Franklin, and Jay begin conferences with David Hartley on terms of the Definitive Treaty.

July: Travels to The Hague to meet JQA, recently returned from St. Petersburg.

Aug.: Returns to Paris with JQA.

Sept. 3: Signs with his fellow commissioners the Definitive Treaty with Great Britain in Paris.

Sept.: Moves to Thomas Barclay's residence at Auteuil with a serious fever.

Oct.: Travels with JQA from Auteuil to London.

Nov.–Dec.: Visits Parliament and the sights of London, and journeys to Bath.

1784

Jan.: Crosses the North Sea to Amsterdam and executes a contract for a second Dutch loan as an emergency measure to save the credit of the United States.

May–June: Elected by Congress a joint commissioner, with Franklin and Jefferson, to negotiate treaties of amity and commerce with twenty-three European and African powers.

June–July: AA and AA2 sail from Boston to England aboard the *Active* and meet JQA in London.

Aug.: JA arrives in London from the Netherlands and joins his family; they travel to Paris and settle in Auteuil. The commissioners begin their deliberations, which continue until JA returns to London in May and Franklin leaves for America in July 1785.

1785

Feb.: Elected by Congress first American minister to the Court of St. James's; in March, Jefferson is named minister to Versailles in succession to Franklin.

May: JQA leaves France for America and Harvard College; JA, AA, and AA2 leave Auteuil for London.

June 1: JA is granted an audience with George III, and a dramatic conversation takes place.

June: Leases first United States legation in London, now No. 9 Grosvenor Square.

Aug.: Signs in London a treaty of amity and commerce with Prussia, Franklin having earlier signed at Passy and Jefferson at Paris.

1786

March–April: Visited by Jefferson in London to negotiate commercial treaties with Tripoli, Portugal, and Great Britain. JA and Jefferson tour English countryseats together.

June 11: AA2 marries William Stephens Smith (WSS) at the London legation.

July: JA takes an excursion to The Hyde and Braintree in Essex with AA, AA2, and WSS.

Aug.–Sept.: Visits the Netherlands with AA to exchange ratifications of the treaty with Prussia and to observe the constitutional reforms of the Dutch Patriots.

1787

Jan.: Publishes in London the first volume of *A Defence of the Constitutions of Government of the United States of America*; a second follows in September and a third in 1788.

May–June: Journeys to Amsterdam and executes a contract for a third Dutch loan to the United States.

July–Aug.: Takes excursion to the west of England with his family.

July–Sept.: Arranges for the purchase of the Vassall-Borland house in Braintree in preparation for his return from Europe.

Oct.: At his own request is recalled by Congress from London, his mission to the Netherlands, and his joint mission (with Jefferson) to the Barbary Powers; recall effective in Feb. 1788.

1788

Feb. 20: Granted final audience with George III.

Feb.–March: Travels from London to The Hague to take leave of the Stadholder and the States General. At Jefferson's request JA contracts for a fourth Dutch loan to the United States.

March–April: Returns to London and sets off with AA for the Isle of Wight.

April–June: Sails with AA from Portland Harbor aboard the *Lucretia* to Boston.

June: Elected a member of the Massachusetts delegation to the First Congress; did not serve.

June–Dec.: Stays in Braintree unpacking books, settling his new residence, and looking after his fields.

1789

March–April: Elected Vice President by 34 out of 69 votes.

April: Travels from Braintree to New York City, the seat of government, and establishes his residence at Richmond Hill.

April–Sept.: Presides over the Senate in 1st session of First Congress.

Oct.–Nov.: Returns from New York to Braintree between sessions of Congress.

Nov.–Dec.: Travels from Braintree to New York.

1790

Jan.–Aug.: Presides over the Senate in 2d session of First Congress.

April: Begins publication of his "Discourses on Davila" in Fenno's *Gazette of the United States*; continued until April 1791.

Sept.: Travels from New York to Philadelphia and back; leases Bush Hill for his new residence.

Nov.: Moves with AA to Philadelphia, the new seat of government.

Dec.–March: Presides over the Senate in 3d session of First Congress.

1791

May: Elected president of the American Academy of Arts and Sciences; serves until 1813.

May–Aug.: Becomes involved in a dispute with Jefferson growing out of the latter's endorsement of Paine's *Rights of Man* and subsequent attacks on Paine and Jefferson by JQA in his "Publicola" papers printed in the *Columbian Centinel.*

May–Oct.: Returns to Braintree with AA between sessions of Congress.

Oct.–April: Presides over the Senate in 1st session of Second Congress.

1792
April–May: Travels with AA from Philadelphia to Quincy.

Nov.–Dec.: Returns to Philadelphia alone.

Dec.–March: Presides over the Senate in 2d session of Second Congress.

1793
Feb.: Reelected Vice President by 77 out of 132 votes.

March: Travels from Philadelphia to Quincy.

Nov.: Returns to Philadelphia alone.

Dec.–May: Presides over the Senate in 1st session of Third Congress.

1794
May: JQA appointed by Washington minister resident to the Netherlands.

May–June: JA travels from Philadelphia to Quincy.

Nov.: Returns to Philadelphia.

Nov.–Feb.: Presides over the Senate in 2d session of Third Congress.

1795
Feb.: Travels from Philadelphia to Quincy.

May–June: Returns to Philadelphia, AA accompanying him as far as New York.

June: Presides over a special session of the Senate called to ratify Jay's Treaty.

June–July: Travels from Philadelphia to Quincy.

Aug. 29: CA marries Sarah Smith (sister of WSS) in New York.

Nov.–Dec.: JA returns to Philadelphia.

Dec.–May: Presides over the Senate in 1st session of Fourth Congress.

1796
May: Travels from Philadelphia to Quincy.

May–Nov.: Spends the summer at the Old House in Quincy making farm improvements recorded in a renewed diary.

Nov.–Dec.: Returns to Philadelphia.

Dec.: Elected President of the United States with 71 out of 139 votes, running against Thomas Jefferson, who became Vice President.

Dec.–Feb.: Presides over the Senate in 2d session of Fourth Congress.

1797

March 4: Delivers his Inaugural Address and takes office as President.

April 17: His mother, Susanna (Boylston) Adams Hall, dies.

April–May: AA travels from Quincy to Philadelphia to join JA; they occupy the executive mansion (the former house of Richard Penn).

May–July: Calls a special session of Congress to deal with the French crisis; appoints the 1st peace mission to France (Charles Cotesworth Pinckney, John Marshall, and Elbridge Gerry).

June: Appoints JQA minister plenipotentiary to Prussia.

July: Travels with AA from Philadelphia to Quincy.

July 26: JQA marries Louisa Catherine Johnson (LCA) in London.

Oct.–Nov.: JA returns with AA from Quincy to Philadelphia.

Nov.: Delivers his First Annual Message to Congress, which is largely devoted to the crisis in Franco-American relations.

1798

March: Delivers message to Congress on the dispatches from the American envoys to France; declares the existence of a state of quasi-war.

April: Releases and publishes the XYZ dispatches at the request of the House of Representatives.

Spring–Fall: Receives and answers scores of petitions and resolutions of loyalty; a number of them are published as *A Selection of the Patriotic Addresses, to the President of the United States.*

May–June: Recommends and oversees the adoption of measures for establishing the Navy Department and creating a "provisional army" of ten thousand men.

June: Appoints George Washington commander in chief.

June–July: Signs into law the Alien and Sedition Acts.

July–Aug.: Travels with AA from Philadelphia to Quincy; AA is taken seriously ill.

Nov.: Returns to Philadelphia alone.

Dec.: Delivers Second Annual Message to Congress revealing a more conciliatory disposition, and suggests the appointment of a new mission to France.

1799

Feb.: Appoints the 2d peace mission to France (William Vans Murray, Oliver Ellsworth, and Patrick Henry, the last being replaced by William Davie).

March: Travels from Philadelphia to Quincy.

Oct.: Travels to Trenton to meet his cabinet; precipitates a cabinet crisis by his order of 16 Oct. dispatching the commissioners to France.

Oct.–Nov.: AA travels from Quincy to Philadelphia and joins JA there.

Dec.: Delivers Third Annual Message to Congress urging peace and reconstruction and an end of civil disturbances. Federalist caucus supports JA for reelection.

1800

May: Dismisses James McHenry and Timothy Pickering from his cabinet. A second Federalist caucus reaffirms the choice of JA and C. C. Pinckney as the party's Presidential and Vice Presidential candidates. AA returns to Quincy.

May–June: Travels from Philadelphia to Washington to inspect the new seat of government.

June: Returns to Quincy, where, under AA's orders, the east wing has recently been added to the Old House.

Aug.–Sept.: Alexander Hamilton attacks JA's administration in his *Letter . . . concerning the Public Conduct and Character of John Adams, Esq.*

Sept.–Oct.: Convention with France concluded at Mortefontaine by JA's 2d mission to France, ending the quasi-war and the Franco-American alliance of 1778; news of this arrives too late to affect the national election.

Oct.–Nov.: Travels from Quincy to Washington; AA follows; and they are the first occupants of the still unfinished President's House.

Nov. 30: His son CA dies in New York City.

Dec.: Defeated for reelection to the Presidency, winning only 65 votes against 73 won by both Jefferson and Burr.

1801

Jan.: Extends the influence of the federal judiciary through the appointment of many new judges. Appoints John Marshall chief justice of the Supreme Court. Reports the successful conclusion of the Convention with France.

Feb.: Instructs John Marshall to prepare letters recalling JQA from Prussia.

March: Travels from Washington to Quincy, leaving early on the morning of Jefferson's inauguration.

Sept.–Nov.: JQA and LCA return from Berlin to Quincy.

1802

Oct.: JA begins writing his Autobiography, Part One, "John Adams"; completed in June 1805.

1803

JQA elected United States senator; serves until 1808.

1805

Feb.: JA resumes his correspondence with Benjamin Rush.

May 16: TBA marries Ann Harrod of Haverhill, Mass.

JA publishes collected edition of *Discourses on Davila.*

1806

Dec.: Begins Part Two of his Autobiography, "Travels, and Negotiations"; completed early in 1807.

1807

Writes Part Three of his Autobiography, "Peace"; breaks it off when he begins his controversy with Mercy Otis Warren about her *History* in July.

1809

April: Begins his documented letters of reminiscence in the *Boston Patriot* (his "second autobiography"), continued until May 1812.

April–May: Publishes four letters in the *Boston Patriot*, soon afterward issued in pamphlet form under the title *The Inadmissible Principles, of the King of England's Proclamation, of October 16, 1807 – Considered.*

June: JQA appointed by Madison minister plenipotentiary to Russia, and sails in August with LCA and their son Charles Francis (CFA).

1812

Jan.: JA resumes, through the intercession of Benjamin Rush, his correspondence with Thomas Jefferson.

1813

Aug. 14: His daughter AA2 dies at the Old House.

1814

April: JQA leaves St. Petersburg for Ghent to join other American commissioners in negotiations for peace with Great Britain, concluded in December.

1815

Feb.: JQA appointed by Madison minister plenipotentiary to Great Britain; serves in London from May 1815 to June 1817.

1817

March: JQA appointed by Monroe secretary of state.

Aug.: JQA and his family return to the Old House in Quincy before going into residence in Washington.

1818

Oct. 28: AA dies at the Old House.

1819

JA publishes collected edition of *Novanglus and Massachusettensis.*

1820

Nov.–Dec.: Attends sessions of the Massachusetts Constitutional Convention as Quincy delegate; proposes that the Bill of Rights be amended so as to remove all religious restrictions.

1822

June–Aug.: Gives to the town of Quincy various tracts of granite-bearing land, profits from which are to be used to build a church and an academy, and also his library, to be placed in the academy.

1824

Dec.: In the national election JQA receives 84 electoral votes, a minority, and in the House vote-off, 9 Feb. 1825, he is elected President of the United States.

1826

July 4: JA dies at the Old House during the jubilee celebration of national independence, a few hours after Thomas Jefferson's death at Monticello in Virginia.

Index

NOTE ON THE INDEX

The Index is designed to supplement the annotation by furnishing correct spellings of proper names, by supplying forenames for persons who appear only with surnames in the manuscripts, by identifying in very brief terms (such as occupation and place) persons whose forenames are either unknown or not known with certainty, and by distinguishing between persons with identical or nearly identical names. But the editors' efforts to carry out this design are admittedly imperfect, both because John Adams was so familiar with many of the persons he mentions (like the numerous Basses, Belchers, Boylstons, Bracketts, Fields, Greens and Greenes, Quincys, Smiths, Trumbulls, Webbs, and Whites) that he did not bother to distinguish among them, and because, at the opposite extreme, he was sometimes confused himself about persons with whom he was unfamiliar (like the several Lyndens prominent in Dutch public life in the 1780's). Adams' habit of spelling unfamiliar and especially foreign names phonetically complicates this problem.

Undoubtedly, therefore, the Index contains mistakes in both the gathering and the separation of references to names of persons with the same family names. The editors would warmly welcome corrections of mistakes of this kind, and indeed of every kind, from users who can put them straight.

References under any particular name or subject are arranged in the order in which they appear in the present four volumes, except that the reference to a "sketch of" a person (meaning either a brief or extended identifying note) always appears first, and all "mentions" appear at the end of the entry. Unassigned last names follow the entries for more fully identified persons bearing the same family names. Users should keep in mind that such references may in fact pertain to persons immediately preceding them. Personal names are given under what are believed to be their most nearly standard spellings, with John Adams' variants added after them in parentheses. When widely variant, his spellings are entered in their alphabetical places, with *see*-references to the standard spellings. Wives' names, with a few exceptions for special reasons, follow their husbands' names, with *see*-references under their maiden names.

Index

AA. *See* Adams, Mrs. John (Abigail Smith, 1744–1818)

AA2. *See* Smith, Mrs. William Stephens (Abigail Adams, 1765–1813)

ABA. *See* Adams, Mrs. Charles Francis (Abigail Brooks, 1808–1889)

Abbeville, France, 3:146

Abbots Langley, Parish of, England, 1:231

Abdrahaman, Tripolitan envoy in London, 3:182; 4:209

Aberdeen, Scotland, 3:162

Abigail (Indian squaw), 1:88

Abingdon, Earl of, 3:179–80

Abington, Mass., 1:134, 228, 305; 3:238–39, 241–42

Académie royale de chirurgie, 3:97

Académie royale de musique, 3:110–11

Académie royale des sciences, 2:307, 318, 370, 441; 4:67, 80–81

Acadian exiles (French neutrals), 1:16, 313

Active, ship, AA and AA2 sail to England aboard, 3:154–67

Adam, Robert, 3:149, 190

Adam (Biblical character), 2:47, 75

Adams, Rev. Amos, 1:313

Adams, Ann (1731–1794). *See* Savil, Mrs. Elisha

Adams, Ann ("Nancy," 1773–1818). *See* Bass, Mrs. Josiah

Adams, Bethiah. *See* Hunt, Mrs. Ebenezer

Adams, Betty, 2:88

Adams, Brooks (1848–1927, designated as BA in *The Adams Papers*): writing habits, 1:xxii, xxx; and Adams Papers, 1:xxxi, xxxiv; last occupant of Old House, 1:75; "The Convention of 1800 with France," 1:348

Adams, Charles (1770–1800, designated as CA in *The Adams Papers*): sketch of, 3:234–35; and JA's books, 1:57; tutored by John Thaxter, 1:280; 2:402; birth, 2:6–7; 3:291; accompanies JA on second mission to Europe, 2:400–04; 4:177, 191–93; journey across Spain, 2:406, 410–13,

417, 424; 4:203, 216, 226; in Pechigny's *pension* academy in Passy, 2:434, 439–40, 442; in JA's financial accounts, 2:438; and La Fontaine's *Fables choisies*, 2:442; in Brussels, 2:443; voyage on the *South Carolina*, 2:447; 3:3; in the Amsterdam Latin academy, 2:448; in Leyden University, 2:451–53; voyage on the *Cicero*, 3:54; residence in New York, 3:248

Adams, Mrs. Charles (Sarah Smith, 1769–1828, designated as Mrs. CA in *The Adams Papers*), 3:234

Adams, Charles Francis (1807–1886, designated as CFA in *The Adams Papers*): character and career, 1:xvii–xix; 4:7; as family archivist and editor, 1:xxvi–xxx, xxxiv–xxxv, xlii, xliii–xliv, xlvi–lii, lxiii; 2:270; 3:41; 4:63, 72

Adams, Mrs. Charles Francis (Abigail Brooks, 1808–1889, designated as ABA in *The Adams Papers*), character of, 1:xxi

Adams, Charles Francis (1835–1915, designated as CFA2 in *The Adams Papers*): on CFA's character, 1:xvii; papers of, 1:xxii, xxxiv; biography of CFA, 1:xxx; and stray Diary booklet, 1:226; Boston office of, 2:64; and Glades Club, 4:7

Adams, Charles Francis (1866–1954, designated as CFA3 in *The Adams Papers*), and Adams Papers, 1:xxx, xxxi–xxxii

Adams, Ebenezer (1704–1769): sketch of, 1:15–16; mentioned, 1:17, 95, 140, 340–41

Adams, Mrs. Ebenezer (Ann Boylston), 1:16

Adams, Ebenezer (1726–1764), sketch of, 2:40

Adams, Ebenezer (1737–1791), 2:88

Adams, Elihu (JA's brother, 1741–1775): sketch of, 2:53; seeks militia commission, 2:52–53; early death of, 3:255, 326; moves to South Parish of Braintree, 3:277; mentioned, 2:71; 3:316

125, 127, 131, 132, 134, 140, 142,
173, 177–79, 206, 211, 220, 225;
2:11
Adams, Capt., of Braintree, 1:304
Adams family: sketch of, 1:xiii–xxii;
custody and use of their papers,
1:xxiii–xxxiv; as book collectors, 1:
xxxvii; correspondence, 1:xxxix–xl;
early history in America, 3:253–57
Adams family library (Stone Library).
See Quincy, Mass., Adams Family
Library
Adams Manuscript Trust, 1:xxx–xxxiv
Adams Memorial Society, 1:75; 4:x
Adams National Historic Site (Old
House), various names of, 3:247–48.
See also JA, Residences
Adams Papers: history of, 1:xiii–xxxv;
history and plan of, 1:xxxii–xli; tex-
tual and annotation policy in, 1:lv–
lxii
Adams Papers, Microfilms, 1:xiv, xxxii–
xxxiii
Addison, Joseph, 1:200
Adélaïde, Mme. *See* Marie Adélaïde
Adhémar, Jean Balthazar d'Azémar de
Montfalcon, Comte d', 3:184
Admiralty courts: judges of, 1:55,
160; 2:66, 100; 3:289; severity of,
2:58; and declaration authorizing the
fitting out of privateers, 3:375;
Lusanna case, 4:2–3. *See also* Massa-
chusetts, Courts of law
Admiralty law, 1:52, 55
Admiralty Office in London, 2:174, 320
Affaires de l'Angleterre et de l'Amérique:
Court de Gébelin, an editor of,
2:323; prints French translation of
Common Sense, 2:351–52; edited by
Genet, 2:354–55, 434; 4:156; JA
contributes to, 2:354–55; Amer.
state papers and constitutions in,
2:442; Edward Bancroft writes for,
4:73; on Lafayette's action on the
Schuylkill, 4:156; extract of Heath's
letter on Franco-American alliance,
4:157
Africa, 2:210, 217; 3:84; 4:23
Agamentacus Mountain, Maine, 1:355
Agriculture. *See* JA, Agricultural and
Scientific Interests
Aguesseau, Henri François d', *Œuvres*,
2:437, 441
Aitken, Robert, 2:169, 173, 223; 3:334,
339
Aix-la-Chapelle, 2:444–45, 452
Alaska, 3:140
Alava, Spain, 2:432; 4:233–34, 237

Albany, N.Y., 2:21, 265; 3:234
Albany Congress, 2:141, 143
Alberda, of The Hague, 3:2
Alcibiades, 2:392–93
Alden, Briggs, 1:312
Alden, John, 3:255
Alden, Priscilla, 3:255
Alden family, 3:140
Alderney, Channel Islands, 2:321
Aldridge, of Uxbridge, Mass., 1:14
Alembert, Jean le Rond d': *Encyclo-*
pédie, 2:437, 441; and Académie
royale des sciences, 2:307; 4:67,
80–81
Alexander, Charles, 2:187, 221–22
Alexander, Mariamne. *See* Williams,
Mrs. Jonathan
Alexander, Robert, in Continental Con-
gress, 2:232–33, 237; 3:361
Alexander, William (Lord Stirling),
2:224; 3:48, 414, 416
Alexander, William Jr.: sketch of, 4:62;
relations with Franklin, 4:134; men-
tioned, 3:181–82
Alexander, from Scotland living in
France, 2:302, 317; 4:134
Alexander family, from Scotland living
in France, 4:62, 134
Alexander the Great, 1:9, 241, 306
Alexandria, Va., 2:225
Alfred the Great, 2:35
Alfred, ship, 3:350
Algemeen Rijksarchief, The Hague, Du-
mas collection in, 3:10
Algiers: at war with Spain, 2:192;
treaty of amity and commerce with,
3:168–69, 175; treaties with foreign
powers, 3:174; negotiations with, de-
puted to John Lamb, 3:182; Bancroft
proposed as agent to, 4:72
Alien Act, 3:189
Alison, Rev. Francis, 2:135, 144, 149
Alkmaar, Netherlands, 3:2–5
All, Isaac, 2:135
Allegheny Mountains, 2:156
Allen, Andrew, 2:127, 136–37
Allen, Ethan, 2:178
Allen, J., brother of Jeremiah Allen,
2:402
Allen, James, 2:177, 241
Allen, Jeremiah: passenger aboard *La*
Sensible, 2:402; 4:191–93; journey
across Spain, 2:411, 417, 422, 424;
4:207, 213, 216; in Paris, 3:38–39;
and Benjamin Vaughan, 3:58; and
fisheries question, 3:83
Allen, John, of Boston, 1:103

yers' fees in, 1:316; mentioned, 1:48, 216; 2:61, 324

Barbary States: negotiation of treaties of amity and commerce with, 3:168–69, 173–75, 201; joint commission of JA and Jefferson to, 3:211; mentioned, 2:320; 3:63. *See also* Algiers; Morocco; Tripoli; Tunis

Barbé-Marbois, François: sketch of, 2:380; personality and character, 2:382, 387; voyage to America with JA and JQA aboard *La Sensible*, 2:382–400; 4:72; and Benjamin Franklin, 2:384, 389–92; and JQA, 2:385; on Malesherbes, 2:386–87; and letter on Sam Adams, 3:55–56, 59; and North Atlantic fisheries question, 3:64; 4:187; negotiations with Congress, 3:105; on character of Boulainvilliers, 4:64; letter to JA on appointment as peace commissioner, 4:174, 176–77; influence in Continental Congress, 4:253; mentioned, 3:118; 4:173

Barbeu Dubourg. *See* Dubourg

Barbeyrac, Jean, 3:286

Barcarcel (Barcarel). *See* Valcarce

Barclay, Thomas: sketch of, 3:120; aids JA during serious illness in Paris, 3:143–44; rents Hôtel de Rouault in Auteuil, 3:143–44, 145, 171; committee report on letters from, 3:168; negotiations with Morocco, 3:182, 201; mentioned, 3:135

Baretti, Giuseppe Marc Antonio, *Dictionary of the English and Italian Languages*, 2:440, 442

Barfleur (*Balfleur*), ship, 2:322

Baring, Sir Francis, 3:152

Baring, Sir George, 3:152

Barker, Joshua, 1:279

Barker, Thomas, 1:279

Barlow, Joel, *Vision of Columbus*, 3:189

Barnard, Rev. Thomas, 1:320; 2:52

Barnes (Barns), Corbin, 2:334, 402; 4:171, 192

Barnes, of Worcester, Mass., 1:12

Barneveldt, Jan van Olden, 2:453

Barney, Joshua, 3:42, 54, 58, 96

Barns, ship, 2:321

Barnstable, Mass., 1:234, 319, 334–35, 336, 337; 2:46, 83; 3:229, 275, 281, 342; 4:5

Barozzi. *See* Vignola

Barrell, Colburn, 2:25–26, 33

Barrell, Mrs. Colburn, 2:25–26

Barrell, Joseph, 2:36–37; 3:244

Barrell, Mrs. Joseph (Anna Pierce), 2:36–37

Barrell, William, 2:121, 152, 157, 170, 178

Barrett, Nathaniel, 2:34, 176

Barrett, Mrs. Nathaniel, 2:34

Barrett, Samuel, 2:90–91

Barrington, William Wildman, 2d Viscount Barrington, 2:203, 225

Barrington, captured in Amer. Revolution, 2:225

Barristers, 1:300, 316; 3:276

Barron, Ann Mortimer, 2:287

Barron, William: sketch of, 2:284; death of, 2:286–87, 288; 4:25–26, 27; family of, 2:286–87; 4:25–26; character of, 4:23

Barrows, Daniel, 1:262

Barry. *See* Du Barry

Bartholomew, Robert, 2:322

Bartlett, Josiah, in Continental Congress, 2:172; 3:393

Barton St. David, England, 3:254

Basen. *See* Patten *v.* Basen

Basmarein, Pierre de, Bordeaux merchant and shipowner, 2:294; 4:36. *See also* Reculès de Basmarein et Raimbaux

Bass, David, 1:207

Bass, Hannah. *See* Adams, Mrs. Joseph

Bass, Henry, 1:294

Bass, Jed., 1:142, 301

Bass, Jo., 1:152, 225, 282, 303, 307

Bass, Rev. John: sketch of, 3:268; mentioned, 3:262

Bass, Jonathan, 1:301–02, 304; 3:280

Bass, Mrs. Jonathan, 1:304

Bass, Joseph: JA's accounts with, 2:163, 167, 170, 225–26; mentioned, 2:251

Bass, Josiah, 3:230, 248

Bass, Mrs. Josiah (Ann or Nancy Adams), 3:230

Bass, Samuel Jr., 1:130

Bass, Seth, 3:228, 230–41, 243–47

Bass, of Braintree, 1:95, 290; 2:16

Bass, Deacon, 1:145

Bass, militia officer of Braintree, 1:303; 2:53

Bassett, Cornelius, 3:285

Bassett *v.* Mayhew et al., 3:285

Bassinett, tavernkeeper at Bristol, Penna., 2:170

Batavia (ancient Netherlands), 2:403; 3:17

Batavia, Dutch East Indies, 2:366

Bath, England: description of, 3:151–52; mentioned, 3:144, 149

Clermont-Tonnerre, Stanislas Marie Adélaïde, Comte de, sketch of, 4:63–64

Cleverly, Benjamin, 1:302, 304

Cleverly, Joseph: sketch of, 1:64; political opinions of, 1:101, 280, 290, 301, 303; JA attends school of, 1:131; 3:257–59; conducts services in Christ Church, Braintree, 3:199–200; personality and character, 3:257; mentioned, 1:63, 302

Cleverly, Stephen, 1:77, 294

Cleverly family, of Quincy, 3:259

Clifford, Lord, 3:210

Clinton, Sir Henry, 2:319

Clinton, James, 3:405

Clopton, Dr., in Philadelphia, 2:146

Clossy, Dr. Samuel, 2:110

Clymer, George, 2:149, 157, 238; 3:400

Clymer, Mrs. George (Elizabeth Meredith), 2:104–05

Clyver, De, of The Hague, 3:1

Coats of arms, 1:228; 3:204

Cobb, Capt. Richard, 1:227, 319

Cobb, son of Capt. Richard Cobb, 1:319

Cobham, Viscount. *See* Temple, Sir Richard

Cobham, England, 3:191

Cocher supposé, stage play, 2:308; 4:85

Cochin, Henri: *Œuvres*, 2:437, 441; mentioned, 2:375

Cochleus, Jo., 2:51

Cochran, Charles B., 2:301

Cock, tavernkeeper of King's Bridge, N.Y., 2:102, 158

Cocker, Edward, *Decimal Arithmetick*, 3:xiii, 258, facing 289

Cockle, James: sketch of, 1:328–29; mentioned, 3:275–76

Cocks. *See* Cox

Coddington, William, 1:xiii; 3:199–200

Codman, merchant in France, 2:327

Coffin, Alexander, 3:74–75, 83

Coffin, Zebeda, 2:320

Coffin, Dr., of Portland, Maine, 2:44

Coffyn, Francis, letters from Amer. Commissioners on naval matters, 4:142–43, 159–60

Coffyn, Richard, 2:322

Cogswell, iron works in Conn., 2:268

Cohasset, Mass., 3:239

Cohasset Rocks, 4:7

Coinage, report on, in Continental Congress, 2:231–32

Coke, Sir Edward: *Institutes of the Lawes of England*, 1:55–56, 72, 90–91, 133, 158, 173, 174, 253, 255; 3:271; *Reports*, 1:231; on property titles, 1:240; commentary on Magna Charta, 1:273–75; Otis on, 1:286; *Book of Entries*, 3:271; mentioned, 1:170; 3:301

Colbert, Jean Baptiste, Marquis de Torcy, *Mémoires*, 4:146

Colburn, tavernkeeper of Stafford, Conn., 2:22

Colchester, Conn., 2:168

Colchester, England, 3:213

Colden, Cadwallader, 2:105, 110

Cole, of Providence, R.I., 1:300

Collas, Peter, sketch of, 2:321–22

Collé, Charles, *La partie de chasse de Henri IV*, 2:317; 4:145

Colleges. *See under names of individual colleges and universities*

Collier, tavernkeeper of Hartford, Conn., 2:99, 171

Collins, Peaslee, 3:264

Collins, Stephen, 2:116, 118, 137, 146, 155, 181–82

Collins, Englishman in Boston, 2:76

Collot d'Escury, Simeon Petrus, Baron, 3:2

Colman, George, and David Garrick, *Clandestine Marriage*, 2:62

Colman, Capt., master of the *Three Friends*, 2:381–82

Colonial Dames of America, 3:184

Colson, Thomas, 1:219–20

Colton, John, 2:255

Columbia, Penna., 3:222

Columbia University (formerly King's College), 1:122; 2:103, 109, 110, 112, 312

Columbus, ship, 3:350

Comets, 1:108, 356

COMMISSIONERS AT PARIS (*sometimes* American Commissioners, Peace Commissioners)

1st Amer. joint mission to France (Franklin, Lee, and JA [formerly Deane], 1777–1779): book purchases, 2:viii; antecedent discussion of and plan for, in Continental Congress, 2:229–32, 235–36; 3:315, 327–29, 335, 337–40, 393, 412, 413, 414, 432, 435; 4:70; JA succeeds Deane, 2:270; 4:3–6; JA joins Franklin's establishment at Passy, 2:297–98; 4:41–43, 108–09; JA received at Versailles, 2:298–301, 309–10, 316; 4:47–48, 56–57, 92–94, 130–33; "Disputes between the Americans, in this

20, 221–22; debates on fortifying the
Highlands, 2:197–98, 199–200; debates on and measures leading to establishment of U.S. Navy, 2:145–46,
198–99, 201–02, 205, 220; 3:328,
342–51; debate on stopping the "min-
isterial Post," 2:200–02; debate on
Conn.-Penna. land dispute, 2:200–
01; debate on mode of appointing
Continental officers, 2:202–04; and
Dumas as Amer. agent in Netherlands,
3:9–10; JA's recollections of his proposed measures, 3:315; "Olive
Branch" petition, 3:321, 324; appointment of Washington as commander, 3:321–25; JA's campaign for
independence rather than reconciliation, 3:327–30; secret committee of
correspondence and appointment of
Deane as its agent in Europe, 3:339–
41; instituting new state governments,
3:351–59

1776: Mass. delegates elected, 2:
227; 3:359–60; debates on Amer.
trade, 2:229–30; JA's memorandum
of measures to be pursued, 2:231–33;
"Declaration of Independency" first
mentioned, 2:231; plan and regula-
tions for cruising on British trade, 2:
231, 233; 3:371–72, 373–75; plan
of and Articles of Confederation, 2:
231–33, 241–50; 3:327, 335, 400–
04, 410–11; committee to go to Canada, 2:233–34; 3:372; JA's resolutions for encouraging agriculture and
manufactures, 2:234–35; 3:372–73;
relations with France, 2:235, 236;
3:337–38; JA's draft resolution concerning instructions to delegates, 2:
236–37; list of residences of delegates
in Philadelphia, 2:237–38; resolution and preamble on instituting state
governments, 2:238–41; 3:382–83,
385–86; conference of delegates with
Lord Howe at Staten Island, 2:250;
3:414–31; drafting and voting of
Declaration of Independence, 3:335–
37; plan of treaties, appointment of,
and instructions to 1st joint mission
to France, 3:337–38, 393, 400, 412,
413, 414, 432–33, 435; 4:70; appointment and work of Board of War,
3:342, 360, 394 ff.; controversy over
plural officeholding, 3:360–63; JA's
extracts from proceedings on various
subjects, 3:363–417, 420–22, 431–
37, 447; division in Va. delegation,

3:367–68; medal voted to Washington, 3:375–77; JA's defense of Esek
Hopkins, 3:382, 405–06, 408; JA's
defense of David Wooster, 3:382,
408–09; measures for a professional
army promoted by JA, 3:387–88,
431–32, 433–34, 437, 442–49; resolution of and voting of independence,
3:392–93, 395–98, 409–10

1777: Mass. delegates elected, 2:
256; Congress in Baltimore, 2:257–
61; work of the Board of War, 2:262;
flight from Philadelphia to Lancaster
and York, 2:262–67; Articles of Confederation printed and submitted to
the states, 2:267; recall of Deane and
election of JA as joint commissioner,
2:270; 4:3–4, 57–58; proposed appointment of minister to Netherlands,
4:44–46

1778: toasted in Bordeaux, 2:295;
4:36; dissolves joint mission to
France, 2:253–54, 390; 4:106–10;
dispute with Washington rumored in
France, 4:94; and commercial agents
in Europe, 4:52–53, 89–90, 99, 107–
08, 111, 113, 115–17, 170; and
Carlisle conciliatory commission, 3:
153–54, 157

1779: and Deane-Lee controversy,
2:345–46, 350, 352–53, 380–81; 4:
125, 145; Gérard and, 2:398; 3:63;
4:242; appoints and instructs JA as
minister to treat of peace and commerce with Great Britain, 2:401; 3:
81; 4:173–84, 242–44, 246; debates
on Atlantic fisheries, 3:64–65; instructs Franklin on Atlantic fisheries,
4:185–87

1780: appoints JA temporary agent
to Netherlands, 2:443, 451

1781: instructions to joint peace
commissioners, 3:38–39, 52, 59, 64–
65, 104–05, 116

1782: and Dutch loan, 3:9

1783: ratifies treaty with Netherlands, 3:17; and JA's "Peace Journal,"
3:41–43, 50; ratifies Preliminary
Treaty with Great Britain, 3:85; proposes joint commission to treat of
commerce with Great Britain, 3:141–
43, 156

1784: appoints joint commissioners
to negotiate treaties of amity and
commerce, 3:168–69

1785: appoints and instructs JA as
minister to Great Britain, 3:177–78

32; on water pumps and canals, 1:
128, 134, 143–44; on coal mines,
1:138–39; conducts glass manufactory in Braintree, 1:140; residence
and business in Salem, Mass., 1:318,
320; on dancing schools, 2:46–47;
and American Philosophical Society,
2:187; in JA's financial accounts, 2:
333; and AA2-Tyler engagement, 3:
192–93; birthplace and relatives in
England, 3:203, 206–10; and Quincy
genealogy, 3:204; mentioned, 1:46,
59, 71, 101, 115, 223, 232, 233,
235, 334; 2:11, 47, 50, 75; 3:249–
50, 316; 4:ix, 250
Cranch, Mrs. Richard (Mary Smith):
JA's first impression of, 1:108–09;
courtship and marriage, 1:122, 231–
32; on dancing schools, 2:46–47; AA
to, on voyage to England, 3:164–66;
and AA2-Tyler engagement, 3:192–
93; AA to, on Quincy genealogy, 3:
204; AA to, on excursion to west of
England, 3:206–10; mentioned, 1:
318, 320, 334; 3:155, 231
Cranch, Judge William (1769–1855):
sketch of, 2:46–47; mentioned, 2:442
Cranch, William (of Brook, England),
3:210
Cranch, Miss, daughter of Andrew
Cranch, 3:208
Cranch, son of Nathaniel Cranch, 3:208
Cranch family: of Germantown district,
Braintree, 1:233, 235; emigrate from
Devon, 3:203; in Kingsbridge, England, 3:209–10
Crane, Joseph, 2:34
Crane, of Braintree, 2:71
Crawford, B., 1:115
Crawford, William(?), of Worcester,
Mass., 1:10, 33, 37, 43
Créanci, at The Hague, 3:27
Creen, of Weymouth, Mass., 1:183
Cremou, at The Hague, 3:27
Creutz, Gustaf Philip, Count, 3:62–63
Crèvecoeur, Michel Guillaume Jean de
(Hector St. John), 3:187
Crimea, 3:14, 92
Crocker, of Portland, Maine, 1:358
Crommelin, Daniël, 2:444, 446–47,
449, 455
Crommelin, Gulian, 2:449
Cromwell, Oliver, 1:9, 187, 220, 287;
2:72, 386; 3:87, 185, 219, 448
Crosby, Joseph (Braintree justice): JA's
relations with, 1:100; holds court in
Braintree, Mass., 1:132–33, 140, 193,

224; 2:10; 3:277; and appointment
of Peter Boylston Adams as deputy
sheriff, 1:216–17; mentioned, 1:69,
109, 133, 189, 323
Crosby, Joseph (Harvard student), 2:52
Crosby, Mary. *See* Adams, Mrs. Peter
Boylston
Crossman, Henry, 1:227
Crown, British: JA's comments on jurisdiction of, 1:49, 289; 2:107, 249,
393–94; 3:70; and contract principle
in Ipswich Instructions, 1:283; petitioned by Ashfield Baptists, 2:153
Crown Point, N.Y., 2:21
Cruger, Henry, 3:234
Cruger, John, 3:234
Cuba, 4:85
Cudworth, Benjamin, 1:217, 343–44
Cullen, Capt., master of the *John*, 3:162
Culloden Moor, Scotland, 4:55
Cumberland, Duke of. *See* William
Augustus, Duke of Cumberland
Cumberland, Maine, 3:343
Cuming, John, sketch of, 2:13–14
Cumming, Rev. Alexander, 1:215
Cummings, James, 2:357, 370
Cummings, Boston printer, 1:48
Cunningham, James: sketch of, 1:239;
mentioned, 1:80, 235, 238, 252,
292, 294; 4:99
Cunningham, Mrs. James (Elizabeth
Boylston): sketch of, 1:80; mentioned, 1:79, 239
Cunningham, Nathaniel, 1:203
Cunningham, Ruth. *See* Otis, Mrs.
James Jr.
Cunningham, William, 1:88
Cunningham, Miss, of New London,
Conn., 1:171
Cunningham, of London, 3:179
Cunningham. *See also* Conyngham;
Forsey v. Cunningham
Curson, Samuel, 2:450; 3:90
Curtenius, Peter T., 2:108
Curtis, John, 1:100; 2:16
Curtis, Neddie, 3:247–48
Curtis, S., of Braintree, 2:16
Curtis, tavernkeeper of Stratford, Conn.,
2:102
Curwen, Samuel, 2:161
Cushing, Caleb, 1:218
Cushing, Charles, 1:19, 319, 358
Cushing, John: superior court judge,
1:305, 308, 310–11, 325, 337; 2:
36, 43; 3:299; personality and character, 1:335
Cushing, Mrs. John, 1:336

Index

Harrison, Hannah. *See* Thomson, Mrs. Charles

Harrison, John, 2:221-22

Harrison, Richard, 3:173

Harrison, Robert Hanson: commissioned in Continental Army, 3:392; letter to Continental Congress, 3:413; secretary to Washington, 3:431, 446

Harrison, of Boston, 2:5

Harrison, Miss, of Philadelphia, 2:133

Harrison, of Baltimore, Md., 2:257

Hart family, in litigation with Joseph Eaton in Salem, Mass., 1:321

Hartford, Conn., 2:27, 28, 29, 33, 98-99, 100, 104, 159, 161, 163, 171, 256, 271; 3:200, 296

Hartford Ferry, 2:28

Hartley, David: sketch of, 2:303; 3:112-13; unofficial mission to negotiate with Franklin, 2:303-04, 323; 4:65-66, 85; British commissioner to negotiate and sign the Definitive Treaty, 3:85, 112-13, 125-27, 139-41, 142, 156; against complete commercial reciprocity, 3:113-17, 123-25, 131-34, 138, 141; discussion with JA on aims of French court, 3:115-17; on British occupation of northwestern forts, 3:118-19, 178; full power under the Great Seal, 3:120-21, 130-31; on contending political factions in Netherlands, 3:121-22; delivers orders in council, 3:128-30, 133-34; *Letters on the American War*, 3:135; sister of, and peace negotiations, 3:135; on de Fonte's purported voyage, 3:139-41; residence in Hôtel d'York, 3:142; introduces JA to English ministers of state, 3:150; and Anglo-Amer. treaty of amity and commerce, 3:177; letter from Amer. Commissioners on exchange of prisoners of war, 4:138-39; mentioned, 3:149, 180

Hartley, Thomas, 2:267

Hartley, Winchcombe, 3:179-80

Hartman, tavernkeeper of Reading, Penna., 2:266

Hartsinck (Hartzinck), of Amsterdam, 2:445-46

Harvard College: JA's class of 1755, 1:ix, 78; 3:260-61; Waterhouse on use of tobacco at, 1:12-13; JA's master's degree from, 1:45; Winthrop's lecture on earthquakes at, 1:62; tutors of, 1:77-78; 3:259-60; Langdon, president of, 1:122; president

and fellows of, 1:231; commencements, 1:314, 316; 2:45; "Butter Rebellion," 1:322; meeting of overseers, 1:340; southern delegation visits, 1:364; gifts and benefactions to, 2:13-14, 441; 3:188, 271; public support of, 2:108; JQA's entrance to, 3:180; JA's entrance to, 3:258-60; mentioned, 1:19, 84, 176, 227, 237, 321, 358; 2:19, 20, 40, 46, 52, 64, 418; 3:299, 407

Harvard College Library, 1:xxxvi, 44-45; 4:250

Harvard University Press, 1:xxxiii

Harwich, England, 3:152, 170, 201

Harwinton, Conn., 2:269

Hasse, of Bethlehem, Penna., 2:266

Hasselt, Van, of Amsterdam, 2:449

Hastings, Selina, Countess of Huntingdon, 2:156

Hastings, Warren, 4:132

Hatch, Nathaniel, 1:311, 313; 2:1, 94

Hatfield, Mass., 2:17

Havana, Cuba, 2:209, 414; 3:151; 4:212

Haven, Rev. Jason, 1:14

Haverhill, Mass., 2:64, 152, 402

Haviland, tavernkeeper of Rye, N.Y., 2:102, 158

Havre, Le (Havre de Grace), France, 4:112

Hawkins, John, 3:xiii

Hawkins, William: *Pleas of the Crown*, 1:56-57, 173, 317; 3:271; *Abridgement*, 3:271

Hawkins family, of New England, 3:199

Hawley, Joseph: and Samuel Adams, 2:74; and Hutchinson, 2:81; on nonimportation agreements, 2:101; and JA's views on impeachment, 3:300-02; personality and character, 3:305; and plan for new state governments, 3:351; mentioned, 1:339; 2:95; 3:264, 289

Hayden, Benjamin, 1:130, 201

Hayden, Clement, 1:323

Hayden, Ebenezer, 1:135, 143, 146-50

Hayden, Nathaniel, 3:237

Hayden, Nehemiah, 1:189, 192-93

Hayes, England, 2:209

Hayley (Haley), George: partner of John Hancock, 2:135; mentioned, 2:122; 3:161

Hayley, Mrs. George (Mary Wilkes), sketch of, 3:160-61

Hays, of Salmon Brook, Conn., 2:269

Haytor Rock, Dartmoor, England, 3:210

Index

Howes, tavernkeeper of Barnstable, Mass., 1:334
Howland, tavernkeeper of Plymouth, Mass., 1:334–36; 2:158
Howland, Mrs., of Plymouth, Mass., 1:336; 2:15
Howorth, Col., in Boston, 2:85
Howorth, Miss, in Boston, 2:85
Hubbard, Caleb, 1:203
Hubbard, Mrs., of Braintree, 1:219
Hubbard, Col. and Mrs., of Weymouth, Mass., 3:238
Hudibras, Sign of (tavern), Princeton, N.J., 2:112, 158. See also Hyer, Jacob
Hudson Bay, 1:155; 3:109, 139–41
Hudson Bay Company, 3:138, 140
Hudson River (North River): and boundary disputes, 2:106; 3:304; fortifications on, 2:197–202; mentioned, 1:295; 2:103, 105, 108, 170, 179, 231, 256, 265, 268; 3:319, 441
Hudson's Strait, 3:141
Hughes, John, 1:285
Hughes (Hews), Capt., and Hannah Quincy's love letters, 1:114
Hughes (Hews), lawsuit against Gruchy, 1:90
Hughes, of New York City, 2:158
Huis ten Bosch. See Hague, The
Hull, tavernkeeper of New York City, 2:102–03, 158
Hull, England, 2:303
Hume, David, 2:391; 3:253
Humphrey, tavernkeeper of Simsbury, Conn., 2:269
"Humphrey Ploughjogger." See "Ploughjogger" letters, by JA
Humphreys, David, 3:169, 171, 173, 189
Hungary, 2:377
Hunt, Ebenezer ("Uncle Hunt"), 1:16, 201
Hunt, Mrs. Ebenezer (Bethiah Adams), 1:16
Hunt, Ephraim, 1:133, 193
Hunt, Isaac, Philadelphia loyalist, 2:177
Hunt, Rev. John, 2:79, 122
Hunt, Samuel, 1:179–81, 183
Hunt, Shrimpton, 2:63–64; 3:296–97
Hunt, Col. William(?), in Louisbourg expedition, 1:91
Hunt, tavernkeeper of Rowley, Mass., 1:259
Hunt, tavernkeeper of Spencer, Mass., 2:160

Hunt. See also Belcher v. Hunt
Hunt v. White, 1:179–81
Huntingdon, Countess of. See Hastings, Selina
Huntington, Samuel: in Continental Congress, 2:237, 249; president of Continental Congress, 2:401, 410, 431; 4:177–78, 179–80, 183–84, 185–87, 195–96, 204–06, 230–36, 240–42; JA's dispatches to, 2:434, 452–53; JA proposes national library and academy of languages to, 2:447; and JA's commission to the Netherlands, 2:456
Huntington Library, 3:303–04
Hurd, Nathaniel, 1:95; 2:13
Hurd, Richard, Moral and Political Dialogues, 1:251–52, 362
Hutcheson, Francis: Short Introduction to Moral Philosophy, 1:2; mentioned, 1:106; 3:198–99
Hutchinson, Eliakim, 1:101, 130, 230–31
Hutchinson, Elisha, 1:299, 300; 2:86
Hutchinson, Foster: sketch of, 2:39; mentioned, 1:230–31, 236, 292; 2:42, 51
Hutchinson, Thomas: and plural officeholding, 1:168, 260; 2:39; 3:275–76; role in Gray v. Paxton, 1:212; lieutenant governor and governor of Mass., 1:218, 232–33; 2:21, 96; 3:48; and Otis, 1:226, 237; 3:275; disputes with General Court, 1:240, 301, 313–14, 350–51; 2:77–78, 93; 3:295, 304–05; residence in Milton, Mass., 1:240; popular discontent with, 1:261, 323; 2:52; relations with judiciary of Mass., 1:281–82, 332; 2:41–42, 54–56, 90–91; 3:276; History of the Colony of Massachusetts-Bay, 1:283, 300–01, 305, 306–07, 348; 3:289; 4:42; Boston house of, damaged in rioting, 1:300; 3:285; adjourns superior court, 1:305, 308, 310–11; JA's relations with, 1:306–07, 309–11, 324; 2:11, 34–35, 55, 71, 81, 84–85, 90, 119; 3:287, 289, 298–300; and Panton admiralty case, 1:348; and Bernard, 2:34; entertains military and revenue officials, 2:35; on the "Centinel" articles, 2:48; on Nickerson murder case, 2:70; controversial letters to England, 2:79–81, 91, 119; 3:57; negatives JA's election to Council, 2:82–83; 3:325; and Tea Act dis-

335

JQA2. *See* Adams, John Quincy (1833–1894)

Judah (servant girl), 1:65–66

Judges: JA's comments on, 1:49, 268–70, 277, 326, 335; 2:36, 51; JA on appointment of chief justice, 1:167–68; JA's dispute with Brattle over independence of judiciary, 1:188; 2:65–67, 69, 77–79; 3:297–302; dispute over right of, to sit in Mass. House, 1:225–27; dispute over right of, to judge his own cause, 1:230–31; in Stamp Act disturbances, 1:286, 291–92, 305; of probate, powers of, 1:332; 2:41–42; and rights of juries, 2:3–5; JA on Hutchinson's appointment of, 2:39; Bulloch on role of, in Ga., 2:173–74; in Spain, 2:410–11, 414; 4:206–07, 211, 232–33; independence of, discussed in Continental Congress, 3:354; debates in U.S. Senate over power of removal of, 3:217–21. *See also* Massachusetts, Courts of law

Julian the Apostate, 3:198

Julie, ship, 2:292; 4:33

"Junius Americanus" (pseudonym of Arthur Lee), 4:70

Jupiter, 3:198

Juries: charges to grand juries, 1:281, 320; JA's comments on rights and duties of, 1:298, 347–48; 2:3–5; and Boston Massacre trial, 2:14–15; 3:292, 295–96; and attempt by House to impeach Oliver, 3:302; in local prize courts, 4:2

Jurieu, M., of the French Academy of Sciences, 4:81

Justices of the peace, 1:48–50, 215, 273, 277; 2:100

Justinian: *Institutes*, 2:375, 406; 3:11, 271; 4:200; *Codex Justinianus*, 2:406; 4:200; mentioned, 1:92. *See also* Vinnius, Arnoldus, *Institutionum*

Kalicheff, Russian minister at The Hague, 3:168–69

Kames, Lord. *See* Home, Henry

Kamtschatka, Siberia, 3:140; 4:39

Katherine, Queen of England, 1:275

Kearsley, John, 2:177

Keen, Francis, in case of Rex *v.* Keen, 1:317

Keen, Josiah, 1:312, 325; 2:39

Keith, in Plymouth, Mass., 2:158

Kemp, François Adriaan van der. *See* Van der Kemp, François Adriaan

Kempar (i.e. Kempenaer?), professor at Franeker, Netherlands, 3:167

Kennebec Company, 2:5. *See also* Plymouth Company

Kennebec River, Maine, 1:259; 3:281

Kensington, England, 3:190

Kent, Abigail. *See* Welsh, Mrs. Thomas

Kent, Benjamin: sketch of, 1:54; a leading lawyer, 1:58, 83, 161, 316, 321–22, 345–47; personality and character, 1:110; contempt for Otis, 1:236; on Boston committee to present memorial to governor, 1:266, 268; on death, 2:38; on religion, 2:50; and More's *Utopia*, 2:51; mentioned, 1:320, 350, 351; 2:87

Kent, in Nickerson murder case, 2:69

Kent, tavernkeeper of Suffield, Conn., 2:269

Kentucky, 2:218

Keppel, Augustus, 1st Viscount Keppel: admiral of British fleet, 2:394; 4:148, 154, 156–57, 168; and Fox-North coalition, 3:61, 66, 70

Kettle, deputy sheriff in Malden, Mass., 2:36

Kew, England, 3:187

Kibby, tavernkeeper of Somers, Conn., 2:27, 33

Killingworth, Conn., 1:140

King, Rufus, 3:221, 303

King, William, archbishop of Dublin, 1:257

King, of Braintree, 1:224

King, deputy sheriff in Salem, Mass., 2:36

King's Bridge, N.Y., 2:102, 158, 228; 3:209–10, 314

King's College. *See* Columbia University

King's Roads. *See* President Roads

Kingston, Mass. *See* Palmer, Mass.

Kingston-upon-Hull, Duchess of. *See* Chudleigh, Elizabeth

Kingweston, England, 3:254

King William co., Va., 3:194

Kippis, Rev. Andrew, 3:188, 193

Kitchin, Thomas, 4:ix

Kitts, George, 3:401

Knap, tavernkeeper of Horse Neck, Conn., 2:158, 169, 170

Kneeland, Mrs., of Boston, 1:322

Knollenberg, Bernhard, on JA-Washington relationship, 3:371

Knolton, Thomas, 3:405

Knox, Henry: transportation of artillery from Ticonderoga to Boston, 2:227;

172; attends the theater, 3:68; Beaumarchais and treasurer of, 4:54; and "Fête des longs Champs," 4:63; and Bancroft, 4:74; conduct in Court ceremonies, 4:131–33; mentioned, 2:316, 328; 3:101, 137; 4:71, 93, 165

Marie Catherine Sophie Félicité, Queen of France, 4:121–22

Mariee, Charles, 3:147

Marines, U.S.: in Continental Navy under John Paul Jones, 2:370–71; initiated by Continental Congress, 3:346; aboard the frigate *Boston*, 4:8

Marius, Caius, 3:219

Markow (Markoff), Arcadius, Russian minister at The Hague, 3:3, 29, 136, 137

Marlborough, Duke of. *See* Churchill, John

Marlborough, Mass., 2:18, 34

Marly, France: description of, 2:316, 318; 4:121; mentioned, 4:129

Marmontel, Jean François, *Poétique françoise*, 2:316; 4:120

Maroni, Irishman in Bilbao, Spain, 2:432; 4:237

Marriage: JA's discussion with Hannah Quincy of, 1:66–69; JA's comments on, 1:74, 87–88, 100, 114, 118–19, 193–96; 4:123; anecdotes of, 1:231–32; 2:1; discussions of, in France, 4:61

Mars, 3:198

Mars, ship, 2:322

Marsdam, Gen., governor of Breda, Netherlands, 3:30

Marseilles, France, 1:253; 2:286, 309; 3:90, 175; 4:25, 41, 91, 134

Marsh, Ann. *See* Quincy, Mrs. Josiah (3d wife)

Marsh, Elisha, of Braintree, 1:232

Marsh, Rev. Elisha, of Westminster, Mass., 3:268

Marsh, Rev. Joseph (1685–1726), 3:256, 258

Marsh, Mrs. Joseph (Ann Fiske), 1:225, 341; 3:256

Marsh, Joseph (1710–1761?): Braintree schoolmaster, 1:x, 187; 3:258–59; opinions on literature, 1:68; prepares JA for Harvard College, 1:77, 131; 3:260; mentioned, 1:82; 3:256

Marsh, Thomas, Harvard tutor, 3:259

Marsh, Dr., testifies in case of Edwards' will, 1:241; mentioned, 1:17, 53

Marshall, Christopher, 2:176–77

Marshall, John, *Life of George Washington*, 3:383

Marshall, Messrs., Philadelphia apothecaries, 2:163, 170

Martens, minister from Hanseatic League at The Hague, 3:3

Martha, ship, captured by the *Boston*, 2:285–86; 4:24–25, 31, 44, 171

Martha's Vineyard, Mass.: complex of cases dividing the Mayhew clan of, 1:263; 3:284–85, 290; mentioned, 1:336, 337; 2:29; 3:155, 343

Martin, Benjamin, British mathematician and instrument maker, 1:177

Martin, Henry, London tobacco importer, 3:179

Martin, Josiah (tavernkeeper of Lynn, Mass.), 1:318, 320, 322, 354; 2:36

Martin, Josiah (colonial governor of N.C.), 3:400

Martin, tavernkeeper of Northborough, Mass., 2:9, 18

Martin, Maj., British officer in Boston, 2:68, 71–72

Martinez (Martinus), Miguel, 2:422

Martinique, 2:209, 235, 293; 4:34

Mary, the Virgin: paintings of, 2:372; 3:31, 34; mentioned, 4:209

Mary I, Queen of England, 3:205

Mary II, Queen of England, 1:358

Maryland: delegates in Continental Congress, 2:118, 121, 132, 136, 176, 225; 3:375, 377; 4:76; Rush on laws of, 2:134; threatened by Dunmore, 2:194–95; convention of, 2:242; 3:360–62; and western land claims, 2:249–50; distilling in, 2:257; new constitution (1776), 2:258; social and economic conditions in, 2:261; in Amer. Revolution, 2:263; Jenings family of, 2:355; agent commissioned to borrow money for, 3:38–39; and improved navigation of Susquehanna, 3:223; militia of, 3:330; instructions to delegates on independence, 3:360–62, 395; Council of Safety ordered to seize Gov. Eden, 3:378; mentioned, 1:354; 2:247–48, 294, 304–05, 312, 357; 4:67, 98

Mary Magdalen, 3:31, 434

Mason, George, 2:391

Mason, Jonathan, 2:105

Mason, Mr., guides committee inspecting Boston Light, 1:363

Mason, of Princeton, N.J., 2:113

Mason, in Paris, 3:58, 91

⁌ The *Diary and Autobiography of John Adams* was composed on the Linotype and printed directly from type by the Harvard University Printing Office. Rudolph Ruzicka's *Fairfield Medium*, with several variant characters designed expressly for these volumes, is used throughout. The text is set in the eleven-point size and the lines are spaced one and one-half points. The photolithographic illustrations are the work of The Meriden Gravure Company. The cover fabric is a product of the Holliston Mills, Inc., and the books were bound by the Stanhope Bindery. The paper, made by the S. D. Warren Company, is a new grade named *University Text*. It was developed by Harvard University Press, for first use in *The Adams Papers*, and bears its mark. The books were designed by P. J. Conkwright and Burton L. Stratton.